T0329404

# Paying for the Liberal State

## *The Rise of Public Finance in Nineteenth-Century Europe*

Public finance is a major feature of the development of modern European societies, and it is at the heart of the definition of the nature of political regimes. Public finance is also a most relevant issue in the understanding of the constraints and possibilities of economic development. This book is about the rise and development of taxation systems, expenditure programs, and debt regimes in Europe from the early nineteenth century to the beginning of the First World War. Its main purpose is to describe and explain the process by which states raised and managed financial resources. The book presents studies of nine countries or empires that are considered highly representative of the widest European experience on the matter and discusses whether there are any common patterns in the way the different European states responded to the need for raising additional resources to pay for the new tasks they were performing.

José Luís Cardoso is Research Professor at the Institute of Social Sciences of the University of Lisbon and Visiting Professor at the Department of Economic History of the University of Barcelona. He was full Professor of economics and history of economics at the Technical University of Lisbon, Portugal, and visiting professor at several Portuguese and foreign universities. He is coauthor of *A History of Portuguese Economic Thought* (1998) and author of several books on the Portuguese history of economics from a comparative perspective. He has published in *History of Political Economy, The European Journal of the History of Economic Thought, Journal of the History of Economic Thought, History of Economic Ideas, Journal of Socio-Economics, History of European Ideas, Studies in the History and Philosophy of Science, Financial History Review*, and *Economies et Societés*. His research interests also include the economic history and methodology of economics. He is the General Editor of the series *Classics of Portuguese Economic Thought* and cofounder and coeditor of *The European Journal of the History of Economic Thought*.

Pedro Lains is Research Professor at the Institute of Social Sciences of the University of Lisbon. He is Editor of *Análise Social*, Secretary-General of the European Historical Economics Society, and member of the Instituto Laureano Figuerola at the Universidad Carlos III, Madrid. He was Director of Imprensa de Ciências Sociais (2004–2007) and President of the Portuguese Economic and Social History Association (2003–2007). He has published in *Análise Social, European Review of Economic History, Explorations in Economic History, Historical Research, Open Economies Review, Research in Economic History, Revista de Historia Economica*, and *Scandinavian Economic History Review*. His most recent books are *História Económica de Portugal, 1700–2000* (2005, with A. Ferreira da Silva); *Classical Trade Protectionism, 1815–1914* (2006, with J.-P. Dormois); *Em Nome da Europa, 1986–2006* (2007, with M. Costa Lobo); *História da Caixa Geral de Depósitos, 1910–1974* (vol. 2, 2008); *Agriculture and Economic Development in Europe since 1870* (2009, with V. Pinilla); and *Portugal sem Fronteiras: Os novos horizontes da economia portuguesa* (2009).

# Paying for the Liberal State

*The Rise of Public Finance in
Nineteenth-Century Europe*

Edited by

JOSÉ LUÍS CARDOSO
*University of Lisbon*

PEDRO LAINS
*University of Lisbon*

CAMBRIDGE UNIVERSITY PRESS
Cambridge, New York, Melbourne, Madrid, Cape Town,
Singapore, São Paulo, Delhi, Mexico City

Cambridge University Press
The Edinburgh Building, Cambridge CB2 8RU, UK

Published in the United States of America by Cambridge University Press, New York

www.cambridge.org
Information on this title: www.cambridge.org/9781107686489

First published 2010
First paperback edition 2013

*A catalogue record for this publication is available from the British Library*

*Library of Congress Cataloguing in Publication Data*
Paying for the liberal state : the rise of public finance in nineteenth-century Europe /
edited by José Luís Cardoso, Pedro Lains.
p.   cm.
Includes bibliographical references and index.
ISBN 978-0-521-51852-9 (hbk.)
1. Finance, Public – Europe – History – 19th century.   I. Cardoso, José Luís.
II. Lains, Pedro.   III. Title.
HJ1000.P39   2010
336.9409′034 – dc22      2009026770

ISBN 978-1-107-68648-9 Paperback

# Contents

# Contributors

*Richard Bonney* is Emeritus Professor at the University of Leicester and Professorial Research Fellow (South Asian Security) at the Royal United Services Institute for Defence and Security Studies (RUSI), Whitehall. He has published widely on French and European fiscal history and initiated the European State Finance Database (ESFDB): europeanstate.financedatabase@googlemail.com. His two most recent books are *False Prophets: The 'Clash of Civilizations' and the Global War on Terror* (2008) and *Confronting the Nazi War on Christianity: The Kulturkampf Newsletters, 1936–1939* (2009).

*José Luís Cardoso* is Research Professor at the Institute of Social Sciences of the University of Lisbon and Visiting Professor at the Department of Economic History of the University of Barcelona. He has been coeditor of *The European Journal of the History of Economic Thought* since 1993. His recent publications include "F. Solano Constâncio on political economy: A 'science of proportions,'" *History of European Ideas* (2009); and "Free trade, political economy and the birth of a new economic nation: Brazil 1808–1810," *Revista de Historia Económica – Journal of Iberian and Latin American Economic History* (2009).

*Francisco Comín* is Professor of Economic History at the Universidad de Alcalá, Madrid. He was the recipient of the National Award of History in 1990. His recent publications include the books: *Tabacalera y el Estanco del Tabaco; 150 años de Historia de los Ferrocarriles en España; La Empresa Pública en Europa; Historia de la Hacienda Pública; Privatisation in the European Union: Public Enterprises and Integration; Transforming Public Enterprise in Europe and North America; Historia de la*

*Cooperación entre las Cajas de Ahorros*; and *Economía y Economistas Españoles en la Guerra Civil.*

*Martin Daunton* is Professor of Economic History at the University of Cambridge and Master of Trinity Hall. His most recent publications include *Trusting Leviathan: The Politics of Taxation in Britain, 1799–1914* (Cambridge University Press, 2001) and *Just Taxes: The Politics of Taxation in Britain, 1914–1979* (Cambridge University Press, 2002); as well as *Wealth and Welfare: An Economic and Social History of Britain, 1851–1951* (Oxford University Press, 2007).

*Giovanni Federico* is Professor of Economic History at the European University Institute, Florence, and at the University of Pisa. His most recent publications include *The Economic Development of Italy* (Cambridge University Press, 2001, with J. Cohen) and *Feeding the World: An Economic History of World Agriculture 1800–2000* (Princeton University Press, 2005).

*Pedro Lains* is Research Professor in Economic History at the Institute of Social Sciences, University of Lisbon. His recent publications include "The power of peripheral governments: Coping with the 1891 financial crisis in Portugal," *Historical Research*, vol. 81 (2008); and *Agriculture and Economic Development in Europe since 1870* (Routledge, 2009, with V. Pinilla).

*Larry Neal* is Professor Emeritus of Economics at the University of Illinois at Urbana-Champaign and a Research Associate of the National Bureau of Economic Research. Currently, he is Visiting Professor at the London School of Economics. He is past president of the Economic History Association and the Business History Conference. From 1981 through 1998, he was editor of *Explorations in Economic History*. His recent publications include *A Concise Economic History of the World*, 4th ed. (Oxford University Press, 2002); *The European Union and the European Economies* (Cambridge University Press, 2008); and *The Origins and Development of Financial Markets and Institutions* (Cambridge University Press, 2009, coeditor, with J. Atack).

*Michael Pammer* is Associate Professor of Economic History at Johannes Kepler University, Linz. His recent publications include *Entwicklung und Ungleichheit. Österreich im 19. Jahrhundert* (Stuttgart, 2002); and "Risiko Unehelichkeit. Cisleithanien 1880–1913," in H. Alexander et al. (eds.), *Menschen, Regionen, Unternehmen* (Innsbruck University Press, 2006).

*Arthur van Riel* works as a senior economist and policy advisor at the Dutch Ministry of Finance. Trained as an economic historian, his previous publications include analyses of the German interwar economy and of Dutch industrialization, the latter resulting in *The Strictures of Inheritance: The Dutch Economy in the 19th Century* (Princeton University Press, 2004, with J. Luiten van Zanden).

*Lennart Schön* is Professor of Economic History at Lund University. His recent publications include "Swedish industrialisation and the Heckscher-Ohlin theorem," in R. Finlay et al. (eds.), *Eli Heckscher, International Trade and Economic History* (MIT Press, 2006); *Swedish Historical National Accounts, 1800–2007* (Lund, 2007, with O. Krantz); and "Electrification and energy productivity," *Ecological Economics*, vol. 68 (2009, with K. Enflo and A. Kander).

*Mark Spoerer* is Invited Fellow at the German Historical Institute in Paris. Recent publications include "The imposed gift of Versailles: The fiscal effects of restricting the size of Germany's armed forces, 1924–1929," *Economic History Review* (forthcoming, with M. Hantke) and "The Laspeyres-paradox: Tax overshifting in nineteenth century Prussia," *Cliometrica* (2008).

*Jan Luiten van Zanden* is Professor of Economic History at Utrecht University and President of the International Economic History Association. He has published widely on the economic history of the Low Countries and Indonesia and is now working in the field of global economic history. His recent publications include *The Road to the Industrial Revolution: The European Economy in Global Perspective, 1000–1800* (Brill Publishers, 2009) and "Girlpower: The European marriage pattern (EMP) and labour markets in the North Sea region in the late medieval and early modern period," *Economic History Review* (forthcoming, with T. de Moor).

# Acknowledgments

The idea for this book occurred in the Azores in November 2006, at the annual conference of the Portuguese Association of Economic and Social History. We organized for that conference a session on the formation of public finance systems in nineteenth-century Europe. This session included papers contributed by some of the authors of the chapters in this book. Our initial aim was to explain the functioning of public finance institutions using parliamentary debates as a main source of historical analysis. This was conceived as a partial outcome of a research project at the Research Centre on Portuguese Economy (CISEP), Technical University of Lisbon, and Instituto de Ciências Sociais, University of Lisbon, funded by the Fundação para a Ciência e a Tecnologia (project reference POCTI/HAR/44207/2002) and the Banco de Portugal. However, we realized that the scope of the project could be considerably enlarged, given the relevance and opportunity of launching comparative research on different European experiences concerning the formation and consolidation of contemporary fiscal states. This idea of a broader comparative analysis was discussed and enriched in a seminar organized at the European University Institute, Florence, in March 2008, where the final structure and outline of the book were established. We are most grateful to the authors of chapters in this book for their active participation in the discussions during the preparatory meetings in Azores and Florence, as well as for their comments and responses during the subsequent phases of preparation of the book. We wish to especially thank Giovanni Federico for his collaboration in the organization of the Florence meeting.

Larry Neal joined the group at a later stage with suggestions and recommendations that proved essential for the final writing of the

Introduction. We are most grateful for his contribution, which resulted in the concluding chapter of this book.

We owe a personal debt of gratitude to Patrick O'Brien, who attended the Azores and Florence meetings and was closely involved in the entire design of the book. His continued support to this project and his invaluable recommendations that improved our Introduction to this book are gratefuly acknowledged.

We wish to acknowledge the financial support given to this project by Fundação para a Ciência e a Tecnologia, Banco de Portugal, and Instituto de Ciências Sociais. With this support we were able to organize the Azores and Florence meetings. We are also grateful to the anonymous readers of the manuscript for their encouraging recommendations and to Scott Parris of Cambridge University Press, who supported the project with enthusiasm. Finally, we would like to thank António Castro Henriques, who provided essential editorial assistance, and João Fialho for his help with the index.

José Luís Cardoso and Pedro Lains
July 2009

Paying for the Liberal State

*The Rise of Public Finance in Nineteenth-Century Europe*

# Paying for the Liberal State

## José Luís Cardoso and Pedro Lains

## Introduction

In recent decades, economists and economic historians alike have turned their attention to the study of the relations between institutional development and the comparative economic performance of nations. One major conclusion of that discussion is that the success of national institutions depends to a large extent on the existence of consolidated national political systems. The vitality of institutions that provide services for the management of particular fields of economic activity, such as transport networks, banks, or schools, is crucially dependent on a nation's overall national institutional background. Yet at present, the new institutional economics is bereft of a foundational theory for state formation. One way to overcome that deficit is to study the financing of liberal states in nineteenth-century Europe. As economic historians, the contributors to this volume recognize that the reform of fiscal and financial systems at the end of the ancien régime and in the aftermath of nearly a quarter century of revolutionary warfare (1792–1815) was crucial for both the establishment of liberal regimes and the development of European economies in the century to 1914. The aims of this book are, first, to outline the history of the reconstruction of fiscal and financial regimes and, second, to look for patterns in the processes by which the European states obtained funds as they responded to the new and evolving tasks of government throughout the period under analysis.

Nineteenth-century Europe was marked by sustained institutional and economic progress at national levels, as well as increasing exchanges of people, goods, capital, and ideas at international levels. It was globally a century of peace. Between 1815 and 1914, the only wars that occurred in Europe were short and confined regionally. It was also a century in which nation-states were consolidated or, in some cases, formed. Because it was a century of peace and prosperity, the strengthening of states was compatible with increasing levels of institutional and economic integration across borders. Stronger liberal governments and the consolidation of nation-states opened the way to a stronger international economy, which, however, promoted the transmission of ideas related to the political economy of states.[1] The institutional developments observed in this book had both a national and an international character. Nevertheless, the success of the modern European state was dependent on how it financed itself. This book studies that process, by looking at the institutional arrangements for the financing of the modern nineteenth-century state.

By 1815, most European states were not new, and the states that formed thereafter were solidly grounded in experiences of political integration (e.g., Italy, Germany) (Crouzet 2003). The nineteenth century was clearly a period in which states increased their role in everyday social, political, and economic life, as populations were converted from subjects to citizens. This transition had important roots in the past but gained momentum in the century of peace and economic progress, and the problems facing nineteenth-century liberal states in Europe were different in many ways from the problems that those states had faced in previous centuries.[2] After 1815, central states became more liberal and connected with their populations. Governments imposed taxes and regulations, such as standard weights and measures or compulsory education, and provided domestic and international security (see Teichova and Matis 2000: intro.). The public had to accept taxation and regulations. That acceptance became a crucial factor that determined the success of the states and the speed with which they managed to implement policies. Levels of acceptance varied across time and across states and depended on the capacities of states to supply services to their citizens. Political, and occasionally military, confrontation occurred more frequently in the poor countries of Europe, where states had more difficulties providing their citizens with services because lower levels of

---

[1] This is not unlike what happened during the process of European integration after the Second World War. See Milward (1992). See also Daunton and Trentmann (2004).

[2] For previous centuries, see, among others, Bonney (1995a, 1995b), Neal (2004), and O'Brien (2008). See also Dincecco (2009a, 2009b).

institutional and economic development resulted in fewer resources for managing and funding government. Because of the reduction in war expenditures, and despite the increase of state activity, tax burdens declined in several of the more developed economies after 1815, whereas in the poorer economies, they became proportionally greater. The relative weight of taxation was linked both to levels of economic development and to the history of debt accumulated before Waterloo. In many instances, such as in the United Kingdom, that history weighed heavily, and the management of public debt became a major institutional challenge – particularly in states that raised considerable shares of their debts on international capital markets, where the ability to borrow, as well as the price paid for loans, depended on the states' credibility.

The use of national case studies is the best way to construct a framework to analyze these problems in Europe, because historical problems tend to be national in character and their sources are fundamentally national. In this book, we have attempted to arrive at a taxonomy based on a number of case studies, each of which illustrates a broader European pattern. Historical processes can be best understood by systematically comparing experiences across time, regions, and countries, and it is necessary to generate a broader and deeper perspective on institutional developments that emerged everywhere in nineteenth-century Europe.

Such meta-questions derive directly from Gerschenkron's seminal work on European banking and have also been addressed with respect to other institutional developments, such as international finance, the building of railway networks, and education.[3] We address the rise of public finance systems in nineteenth-century Europe and emphasize the following questions: How were tax regimes established? In what ways were they extended and deepened over time? What other forms of revenue continued or became available? How did governments secure compliance for their fiscal and financial policies? How was public debt raised, and how did it evolve? With what degree of efficiency did governments manage their needs for credit and loans? How were public revenues spent? How did citizens evaluate government activity? How did the reputation of national governments evolve in the international markets? and, finally, What were the main theoretical and political debates around taxation and public finance?

---

[3] See Gerschenkron (1962). See O'Brien (1983) and Milward (2005) on transport. See Cameron (1972) and Kindleberger (1993) on banking and financial markets. See Tortella (1990) on education.

We engage in comparative analysis to generate insights and to expose a pattern for the evolution of taxation and public finance in nineteenth-century Europe. Questions posed about Europe closely follow those raised in the individual country studies but go beyond national levels of inquiry. We provide hypotheses about taxation and public finance that we hope will contribute to a better understanding of the problems involved, and we offer generalizations that transcend nineteenth-century Europe. The fiscal and financial institutions of states are connected to policy-making processes. They contribute to the shaping and design of economic policies and to the assessment of their outcomes, at political, social, and economic levels. A general overview of institutional settings with respect to the implementation of public policies helps to explain cross-country variations in economic performance. This book 'looks from one country to another for general explanations' (see Kindleberger 1993: 3–4; see also Hatton, O'Rourke and Taylor 2007). It presents studies on nine nation-states that are representative of the European experience, including early developers in which sets of rules governing taxation and public finance had already reached some stability by the beginning of the century (i.e., Great Britain, the Netherlands, and Sweden), countries for which the creation of such systems was crucial for the construction of the new nation-states (i.e., Germany, Italy, and the Austro-Hungarian Empire), and countries that entered the modern age for taxation and public finance after major political revolutions (i.e., France, Spain, and Portugal). The sample includes national economies of various levels of economic development; of different levels of foreign and imperial connections; and of disparate size in terms of population, area, and geography.

## The Legacy of the Ancien Régime

According to Schumpeter (1954), fiscal systems evolved from domain states in antiquity to the tax state in the early modern period, which arose from the need of governments to raise money to pay for war.[4] Bonney (1995) and Bonney and Ormrod (1999) expanded the model to four stages and considered a tribute state, a domain state, a tax state, and a fiscal state. Their approach updates Schumpeter's taxonomy and offers a concept of gradual transition that accommodates fiscal reforms in successive phases. This is not a teleological process, which would imply the

---

[4] Schumpeter first formulated these ideas in 1918 in Germany.

completion of each stage of evolution in sequence. Rather, it is an open-ended model that allows for the possibility that a given country skip one of the stages of evolution and admits the coexistence of diverse national states at different fiscal stages in the same historical period. According to Bonney and Ormrod (1999), by 1815, fiscal states ruled in most of Europe, which means that taxation was overwhelmingly controlled by central governments and geared toward financing their goals. The centralization of public finances was largely the outcome of the need to finance the almost-permanent state of warfare in which the European states engaged throughout the eighteenth century, and particularly the extensive warfare that followed the French Revolution (1789–1815). Warfare accounted for more than half of total expenditures in a number of European states throughout the century (Körner 1995a: 416). Wars were also financed by raising public debt, which accounted for an increasing share of total financial resources within the reach of the central state.[5]

The rise of fiscal states was associated with an increase in the ability of centralized states to manage the administrative apparatus for raising taxes, as well as with the ability of the sophisticated financial institutions to manage public debt. The latter led to important financial innovations, such as the creation of central banks and the development of financial markets where bonds and other assets were traded (Körner 1995b: 532–5). Such developments meant that states depended increasingly on their ability to service debt and concomitantly on their financial reputation. By increasing taxation on credits and loans, states became more dependent on well-functioning financial and commodity markets. Disruptions to the economy meant lower revenues from taxation, and disruption in the financial markets meant that less public debt could be raised or that more taxes had to be allocated to pay for existing debts. This greater dependency on the markets emerged by the end of the Napoleonic Wars as a major problem for most European states. The creation of public debt as a means to cover public expenditures was linked to the ability to increase the collection of tax revenues on a regular basis. The main issue faced by the ancien régime was the management of the trade-off between the need to borrow and the capacity to tax.

Yet national tax systems were loosely integrated and suffered from many inconsistencies. The finances of the ancien régime in European states reveal different degrees of fiscal centralization. The structure and rates of taxation in the same political national unit varied considerably,

---

[5] For further discussion of the model, see O'Brien (2008) and Spoerer (2008).

either between urban and rural areas or between different provinces. Taxes were imposed on domestic trade across regions and between rural and urban areas. Taxes were also mainly indirect, that is, based on the taxation of economic and in some cases financial activity. In England, for example, indirect taxes accounted for 70 percent of total taxes in the second half of the eighteenth century (Bonney 1995b: 502). Such ratios were, however, disparate across Europe and they did not necessarily converge. Tariffs on international trade were also an important aspect of indirect taxation. In many circumstances, tariffs were imposed to raise revenue, not to protect manufacturers or agriculture (see Dormois and Lains 2006). Direct taxes were overwhelmingly fixed and thus not related to changes in the values of outputs, which implies that levels of direct taxation did not closely follow the economic cycle. Historically, the states' fiscal institutions were geared toward collecting taxes to pay for the administration of the state; the judiciary; the consumption of the aristocracy; and most of all, war, the military, and the navy.

The coercive functions of the state were not abandoned in the liberal age, but their relevance declined substantially as new functions related to universal law enforcement; the management of economic and monetary issues; and investment in social overhead capital, health services, and education emerged. The structure of state revenues also transformed and adapted to the new state functions.

When dealing with the development of public finance in nineteenth-century Europe, we need to understand how modern tax regimes were constructed at national levels and how they were made acceptable to the public. Modernity in the organization of public finance is used here to refer to the enhancement and consolidation of the functions that are generally ascribed to fiscal states. These functions are usually associated with the management of new types of state revenues, based on both direct and indirect taxes, as well as with the administration of an expansionary state committed to increasing control over its territory and to fostering public education, welfare, justice, investment in economic infrastructures, and defense. This agenda called for a continuous increase in public spending and, above all, an efficient process of public debt creation, management, and servicing. The ability to extract taxes, a coherent program of public expenditure, and a sound system of public debt management – these were the main changes that contributed to the development of modern fiscal state in nineteenth-century Europe. It should be noted that this is not the only available model for analyzing the evolution of fiscal systems. As Larry Neal discusses in the conclusion to this book, a different framework is offered by Hinrichs (1966), who explains the transition from traditional society to modernity through changes in taxation systems. Traditional economies were characterized by restricted use of direct taxation, whereas in modern economies, a regular system of taxation is an indispensable condition for the financing of increased public expenditures.

The state's power to tax implies the coercive means of government, as well as the tacit acknowledgement of the fiscal rules that direct the process of tax collecting (Bonney 1999: 6). The alternative to the predatory role of states, associated mainly with periods of crisis or warfare, was the creation of economic opportunities in the marketplace, through cooperation between the state and the private sphere. The rent-seeking processes associated with negotiating privileges and the concession of special monopoly conditions exemplify the mastering of peaceful means of fiscal enforcement that are the origins of the strengthening of modern fiscal states. The study of the evolution of public finance regimes in different European countries is a first step of inquiry that points to promising research directions. National differences were undoubtedly important and explain specific features of fiscal doctrines and taxation regimes in each of the countries considered herein (see Kayaalp 2004). However, we are concerned not only with explaining how national regimes of taxation, expenditure, and debt management were implemented during the nineteenth century but also with elucidating the underlying economic and political interests that such regimes were serving or challenging, and how they were made acceptable to society.

The conventional wisdom about the allegedly autonomous roles of states derives from the claim that the state performs a variety of functions that are not subject to dispute, namely those related to the pursuit of general objectives of well-being that serve society as a whole. The engagement with the common good is certainly a strong caveat for justifying the provision of public goods and services. However, it does not prevent us from recognizing the existence of vigorous interactions between governmental institutions and organized interest groups in civil society. It is precisely such interactions that explain both the prevalence of redistributive tax policies in a certain historical context and why in different settings preferences may emerge in support of policies for investment and economic growth.

Public finance is about taxing, spending, and balancing budgets. These activities are assigned to governments, and it is therefore their mission to make the appropriate choices while bearing in mind the effects of such activities on the welfare of their citizens. One may concede that governments have goals and an agenda, which implies costs. The objectives of governments are made possible through a set of fiscal policy decisions designed to extract sufficient resources from the population under the state's control. Limits to the growth of fiscal states depend not only on the ability to develop the tax bases without endangering social and political support but also on the ability of governments to service and redeem the debt. To raise the amount of funds required to finance the government's activities, supposedly devoted to the common good, politicians and bureaucrats may be impelled by personal interests and are therefore subject to the rules of utility-maximizing behavior. The agenda for public expenditure can also be appointed in ways that reveal the tendency of governments toward excess spending in order to maximize future political results. These issues inform the public choice approach to the discussion of the functioning of different fiscal and financial regimes.[6]

As to the functioning of political process, public choice theorists consider that governments are not organic or institutional entities that make decisions with an abstract public interest in mind. By extending the methods of economics to the analysis of political decision-making processes, public choice theorists emphasize the role of self-interest and incentives as a main motivation for political action. For this reason, the study of the political decision structure and the conditions within which taxing and spending choices are made is of paramount relevance. The peculiarities of the political process elucidate the outcomes that arise from changes in fiscal institutions (Wagner 2007). One may dispute whether a certain fiscal reform is an attempt to limit the role of the government or to control its tendency to increase spending when revenues raise. Nevertheless, taxing and spending decisions should not be left to the arbitrariness of central and local governments acting in contexts of political constraint. According to the arguments put forward by public choice theorists, constitutional rules (i.e., common law, general legislation passed in parliament, and institutionalized values and traditions) form indispensable conditions for the creation of a reliable system of public finance. Furthermore, governments in modern societies are obliged to deal with increasingly complex sets of issues with respect to the formation and use

---

[6] See Buchanan (1979). On the continuity between certain types of continental European public finance theory and the public choice approach, see Backhaus and Wagner (2005). The methodological and conceptual differences concerning the interpretation of the economic functions of the government should not be dismissed, as is clearly shown in the debate between Buchanan and Musgrave (1999). The appeal to the public choice approach in the analysis of the functioning of state finance regimes has also been summarized in Bonney (1995a) and Daunton (2001: 8–9).

of proper economic knowledge, which supports the process of legitimization or the rejection of policy decisions.[7] Governments need to justify their actions on the basis of sound constitutional rules and credible economic reasoning.

When applying this type of approach to the nineteenth-century realities, we may find worthy attempts to create fiscal constitution procedures designed to restrain expenditures and to make feasible the abolition of certain unpopular taxes and duties. Such was the case in Britain of Gladstone's 1853 proposal to phase out the income tax as a strategy to create constitutional limitations to public spending.[8] However, the classic nineteenth-century contributors to the theory of public finance were more concerned with the ability-to-pay approach, viewing the problem of taxation as more or less independent of the process of determining both the amount and the allocation of public expenditures. Although this approach did not reduce public finance to taxation, it has nevertheless imposed a separate account on both sides of the balance.[9] The success of the implementation and development of tax regimes across Europe had much to do with different levels of legitimacy, the credibility of governments and their budgetary policies, and the outcome of those policies. To take those issues into account, this book looks at the evolution of political stability at the national level and at the credibility of governments. Moreover, several chapters take into account the efficiency of public expenditure in terms of the provision of public goods, including infrastructures, schools, police, and defense. A further aspect that can be better understood through a public choice approach, which is implicitly addressed in the chapters, is the relationship between economic interests and their support by politicians in the government or parliament (see Nehring and Schui 2007; Schonardt-Bailey 2006).

## Nineteenth-Century Transformations

This book deals with nine countries that represent about 90 percent of the total population and gross domestic product of Europe to the east

---

[7] On the role and contribution of economic knowledge to strengthen government decisions, see Furner and Supple (1990), introduction.

[8] See Baysinger and Tollison (1980), who argue in favor of the coherence of that constitutional strategy, and Leathers (1986), who claims that the project was condemned to fail.

[9] On the theoretical principles explaining this tradition, see the authors' introduction to Musgrave and Peacock (1958). See also Dome (2004) for a survey of the fiscal problems by Enlightenment and Victorian British political economists.

of Germany and Austria-Hungary in 1900, as well as a wide variety of experiences in the field of public finances (Maddison 1992). As we shall see, financial distress was common in both the poor southern countries and in the wealthier cases of Britain and the Netherlands. The speed with which governments solved the problems of debt inherited from wars varied significantly, but again the divide was not between more or less developed countries; it depended on other factors of a political or social nature. France, for example, did not have as great a debt inheritance as Britain, but the French governments throughout the century faced more difficulties in balancing the budget. The same was the case for Portugal and Spain.

The major source of differentiation came from the degree of institutional development, which depended on the ability of governments to reach some kind of consensus involving both the taxpayer and the purchaser of public bonds and other debts. The main task was to reach that consensus before creating the necessary institutions. In fact, as the century evolved, the economies integrated, and the public became more educated, the creation of the institutions became within reach of every country in western and southern Europe. When that consensus was reached, it was possible to find balanced solutions that satisfied the concerns of taxpayers and borrowers as well as those of the state at the central or local levels.

The case of Great Britain is highly revealing of the role of political coordination in the governing of public finances. Britain was in a difficult position in terms of state finances by the end of the Napoleonic Wars. In 1815, government expenditures were a staggering 23 percent of national income. In that same year, debt charges accounted for 26.6 percent of gross public expenditures and climbed to 54.4 percent in 1825. In the eighteenth century, public expenditures and the national debt were considered by the public as the 'bulwarks of liberty and Protestantism against the French,' as, to a large extent, they were raised to pay for past wars. Yet having reached such large sums, the state could easily become the major threat to those liberties. Trust in the eighteenth century was higher in the United Kingdom than in France because the British state was more responsible in dealing with its financial affairs. But if trust were to be regained, the tax system had to change, and it did so in the following decades.

The recovery of trust was dependent on the reduction of the fiscal pressure on the economy. That was made possible because Britain was no longer fighting the expensive wars of the previous century. Yet the reversal was achieved only gradually. By 1840, public expenditure was still high in contemporary terms (at 12.4 percent of GDP). Further reforms implied political initiatives and agreements across parties in parliament, which was achieved first with the reintroduction of the income tax by Robert Peel, in 1842, and carried further by Gladstone in the early 1850s. Those men and their successors also recognized that taxes, which were interlinked with votes, could introduce risks into the financial system. Thus, they took care to implement sets of rules that would limit the ability of governments and parliaments to overspend. By 1905, the cost of debt service was 16.6 percent of gross expenditures, and total debt in relation to British gross national product had fallen by 90 percent. There were other major changes, including the increase in the share of direct taxes to total revenues and changes of the structure of indirect taxes, which meant that the level of taxation became more connected with the growth of the economy. The fact that the economy was growing, though not as fast as in other places on the continent, provided a basis on which trust could be recovered. Yet the major factor in that recovery was not the ability to tax in itself, but the ability to tax in an acceptable way, linking the state with those who had to finance it. Such levels of trust were reached in some parts of Europe but not others, and the reason that was so becomes a major question for understanding the evolution of the modern European fiscal state.

In the Netherlands, the evolution of public finances reflected more clearly the balance of power among different social groups with access to the state and other institutions. Thus, the broader political setting necessarily has a large impact on the evolution of state finances. There were three different phases: the first started with a strong monarchy with limited parliamentary interference, from 1815 to about 1840; that phase was followed by two decades of liberal offensive, to the 1860s; and a third period followed to the end of the century, which was marked by mass movements and the democratization of society with the gradual extension of the franchise and the move to welfare. This last period coincided with the adoption of the gold standard by the Netherlands, which partially determined how the state was financed. As in Britain, the status quo before 1815 had to be changed, and it was changed. Yet the set of problems that emerged in the following century was considerably different, mainly because levels of political pressure were higher, as the franchise expanded and the welfare state came into existence. The differences between the types of pressure imposed on both countries derive from specific national characteristics, and we need to understand how the state managed the demands imposed on it by those who paid taxes and loaned the money.

In the Netherlands, the departing point was rather bleak, as the debt had amounted to an astonishing level of 147 percent of GDP by 1814. However, the fiscal system inherited from the eighteenth century was already efficient in the sense that it was centralized and well connected to a sophisticated commercial economy. The annexation of the southern Netherlands was another positive factor, as it enlarged the tax base for the central state. Moreover, another source of revenue developed quickly, namely revenues from the colonies. State finances remained highly problematic at the beginning of the century because parliament (States-General) was weak and state finances were made a major political battlefield by King Willem I. In the following liberal period, the needed reforms were effectively implemented because of two factors that were paradoxically linked. The first is that the liberal governments ceased to act as though the Netherlands was a great power and military expenditure was substantially reduced. The second is that the colonies supplied revenues. It was also a great help that the economy continued to expand at a reasonable rate. But in the end, throughout the century, the Netherlands carried a heavy debt and heavy interest payments – in 1900, the debt amounted to about 80 percent of GDP, and interests amounted to 35 percent of total government expenditures. One may speculate that trust must have been high, as those high levels of indebtedness did not lead to public default. That is even more relevant if we take into account that the Netherlands was part of the gold standard and did not experience major macroeconomic problems after 1875. Large state debts thus could coexist with political stability.

In France, the health of public finances was intimately linked with levels of political stability. But the main determinants of how the state expanded its capacity to tax and was financed were slow population growth and the longevity of an oligarchic social order, which was over-represented in parliament. Slow population growth meant that the fiscal basis of the state expanded only gradually. The existence of powerful oligarchies meant that they were able to slow the rise of the state expenditure by opposing the development of direct taxation that affected their interests. By 1913, in terms of GDP, the size of the French state was half that of the German state. However, the financial problems of the state were particularly acute up to the war with Prussia. Ultimately, the growth of public expenditure was halted from the beginning of the 1880s onward, and that was a crucial element for the stabilization of the system.

The central government was unable tax the whole territory of France and did not resort to local sources of taxation.

Because tax revenues were harder to collect in France, increased public debt paid for a large part of state expenditure. Financial problems were rendered less serious because the economy grew rather quickly throughout the century, both in terms of total GDP and in terms of foreign trade. Also the banking system expanded and made an important contribution to funding the state mobilizing domestic savings, guaranteeing monetary stability and low interest rates. Monetary stability was crucial and was strongly supported by the political elites, namely members of parliament who held rentes. The main basis of the rise of the state, however small that rise was, was not the increase in taxation but the increase of public debt. Excessive debt creation was avoided because total government expenditure remained low in comparison to other large countries, such as Britain and Germany. France is a case that illustrates how reforming the fiscal constitution was not a priority of governments in the nineteenth century. The increase of state expenditures was particularly restrained and paid for by an expanding economy (though population did not increase significantly) or by debt creation, which was well managed given the favorable monetary conditions. France, thus, was a wealthy country in which the elites opted for a financially constrained state.

Countries that integrated with new political units in the nineteenth century had a different set of problems. The growth and consolidation of central states was intimately linked to the process of political unification – and on some occasions was the single most important element of that process. A wide range of financial practices appeared in the territories that would ultimately form the German empire in 1871. In some of the smaller German territories, the tax system was based on indirect taxes. In other German territories, taxes were predominantly impersonal and applied to property, as in Prussia. Changes occurred during the Napoleonic period and its aftermath, with the introduction of constitutions in some states, in the years from 1818 to 1849, which included norms for the administration of public finances. Meanwhile, the creation of the Zollverein in 1833 also led to greater integration and unification of tariffs on foreign trade.

When the German Empire was created, in 1871, some degree of institutional convergence had already been achieved, but the tax regimes and economic and financial conditions remained different. The empire did not manage to unify them. The central government became responsible for defense and international relations, and it needed a smaller tax base than elsewhere in Europe, where central governments exercised a wider range of functions. The central government collected customs revenues and managed state monopolies such as the post office. Member states could be called on to help finance the central government in case of need, and that effort was distributed on a per capita basis. The share of military expenditure declined throughout the nineteenth century but increased again in the decade preceding the First World War, whereas expenditures on education, administration, utilities, transport, and welfare expanded considerably and were mostly covered by the budgets of member states or municipalities.

In the Austro-Hungarian Empire, the devolution of power under the 1867 compromise had an impact on the administration and evolution of public finances in the two halves of the empire. This compromise led to the creation of two states with independent political and fiscal institutions. As in Germany, after 1867, the Austro-Hungarian central government managed defense and international relations. However, different from Germany, revenues were collected by the two governments of Austria and Hungary, and they were then reallocated to a central military and diplomatic budget according to quotas that were renegotiated every ten years. The contribution of the Austrian government was never less than 73 percent, which implies a small albeit politically relevant redistribution effect.

The transition from the precompromise to the postcompromise fiscal arrangements implied important institutional developments, particularly in the case of Hungary, which had to converge institutionally to the more developed Austrian fiscal system. Thus, for example, the share of direct taxes in Hungarian public revenues increased steeply even before 1867. Clearly there was an objective of political harmonization that was absent in the other large European countries studied herein, namely Germany and, as we will see here, Italy. The distribution of expenditures was linked to the relative size of the population. The empire's common budget was dominated by military expenditures. In addition to the common budget, both states had to pay for the debt incurred before 1867. Overall, public finance contributed to the integration of the two halves of the empire. The initial steps of integration were taken during the neo-absolutist period, from 1848 to the 1867 compromise, but fiscal integration proceeded despite that there was an increase in political autonomy in the separate kingdoms. Fiscal policy, by way of investments in education and infrastructure, also contributed to integration of the dual monarchy. Whether this was an express purpose or a means of gaining political support for the central government remains an open question.

Of all the states that would form Italy after 1861, only Piedmont had significant levels of taxation and expenditure. Its ambitions materialized in the growth of public administration and investments in public infrastructures, namely railways, paid for by taxes and by the issue of sovereign debt. Increased taxation in Piedmont was made possible by institutional reforms, including the introduction of yearly budgets controlled by the parliament, and increases in the levels of taxation on consumption, land, and interest from capital and wages. Yet the increase in taxation did not match the increase in public expenditure, and as a result, debt surged. Piedmont was responsible for more than half of the total debt of Italian states in the 1850s, and that share increased even more after the wars against Austria from 1859 to 1861.

After unification, Piedmont extended to the rest of Italy its ambitious development policies, which led to an increase in public debt and then to difficulties in servicing it. A decade of reducing expenditures unfolded, and from the mid-1870s, Italy's state budget was relatively balanced. The Italian government was, however, able to increase taxation throughout the rest of the period to the First World War. First, that implied an increase of revenues as a share of GDP, but after 1890, Italy entered a period of economic boom and the ratio of taxation to GDP declined. Despite such achievements, Italian financial history is marked by the promises of successive governments to reduce the deficit and the debt, and by attacks from the opposition parties accusing governments of not being able to achieve that goal. Yet the deficit-GDP ratio averaged just 0.64 percent in the period, peaking at higher levels of about 3 percent only after the 1861 war. The deficit became a problem again only in the 1880s. Although the state budget was never on firm ground, it also never fell into the abyss, as fiscal policy was successively adapted and revised so that revenues could rise to meet expenditures. There was a major reason behind such a consistent position of Italian governments: the fact that sound financial policies were the basis for financing the military and achieving great-power status. Public expenditures were, however, not a unifying factor. On the contrary, unification meant that the tax load of the poorer South increased. During the early 1910s, changes were introduced, namely through the centralization of education expenditures, which had some slight redistributive effects.

The northern European periphery is, in many ways, different from the southern peripheries, as it had high levels of political stability and a more developed economic and institutional setting. In Sweden, the institutions ruling public finances were thoroughly transformed, but that was achieved without major disturbances and negotiated by different political forces. Sweden started the century with a fiscal regime with many ancien régime characteristics, which included some taxes of medieval origin, based above all on indirect taxation, and with a large share of expenditure devoted to the army. But then it evolved into a modern fiscal regime based on the taxation of income and monetary transactions. Such transformations meant that the structure of the fiscal regime adapted to the broader transformations in the structure of the economy. The starting point was bleak if taken out of context, given that Sweden emerged from the Napoleonic Wars with a large public debt and relatively high shares of expenditures and revenue in the national income, though still much smaller than elsewhere in Europe. Yet in the years to about 1850, that would change considerably. The share of revenues and expenditures was reduced from about 10 percent to about 5 percent of GDP between the early and mid-nineteenth century, and public debt was reduced even further. The reduction of military expenditures was the key factor in the overall reduction of public expenditures.

From the 1850s, the size of government started to increase again but was geared toward other kinds of modernizing expenditures. Increases in wealth and political consensus led Sweden through a smooth transition to become a development state. The rise of expenditures was, however, not immediately followed by substantial institutional reforms, which gained momentum only from the 1870s. By 1900, 90 percent of the state revenue was still based on indirect taxation, including a large share of revenues from customs duties. The speed of reforms was not conditioned by political conflict, which was relatively low, and the increasing role of the parliament in the design of fiscal policies contributed largely to that outcome. As the economy expanded and went through considerable structural transformations, the gap between the fiscal structure and the economy became more evident but did not cause institutional problems. True change in the fiscal structure came only in the early twentieth century, and in that decade, the share of the income tax in total revenues increased to 25 percent. Again, the change was led by parties in the parliament with high political representation. The tax reforms, however, took decades of public investigations engaging economists and political scientists, as taxes and political voting rights were intricately interwoven.

In Spain, the transition from the ancien régime fiscal structure to one in tune with the needs of an expanding economy was far from smooth and was achieved with much political tension. The period of political instability lasted to the 1870s, which made fiscal reforms particularly hard to implement. Liberal tax reforms were linked to successive plans for constitutional reform and were attempted in 1813, 1821, and 1845. The 1845 reform introduced a rather complex tax system, based on quotas, set by the parliament, for the central government, the provinces, and the municipalities, which reflected the complex administrative system of the Spanish kingdom. The reform was mildly successful, as budgets were approved annually in the parliament, the fiscal system as envisaged became more centralized, the privileges of the nobility were abolished, and some proportionality was introduced. But the new system was composed of a large array of indirect taxes, which made it difficult to estimate revenues and deficits. Slightly increased fiscal pressure, from 7.8 percent to 8.5 percent of GDP between 1850 and 1865, followed. The structure of public spending also changed, as military expenditures were somehow reduced, whereas expenditures on education and public infrastructure increased.

The success of the reform was soon to be checked by political instability, which affected the collection of revenues, led to increased expenditures, and reduced the role of the parliament in controlling the budget. Instability became common for most of the second half of the nineteenth century, on a somehow reduced scale after the end of the short republican experience, in 1874. A period of other reforms followed. The Bank of Spain, founded in 1874, was granted the monopoly on note issue in return for lending to the government. Printing money became a source of revenue for the public budget, which ultimately led to the abandonment of the gold standard by Spain in 1883. In the following years, state revenues increased, as did expenditures, deficit, and debt. The debt was financed domestically, which may have had a negative impact on the private capital markets, and about 25 percent was financed abroad. A new tax reform was implemented in 1900, this time slightly more successful, leading to a substantial modification of the tax structure and ultimately to government surpluses from 1903 to 1908 on the eve of the war in Morocco, which was followed by another period of political instability. The debt service accounted for 8.1 percent of total expenditure in 1849, peaked at 52.6 percent in 1870 and then declined to 31 percent in 1913.

The fiscal history of nineteenth-century Portugal was also largely marked by severe political instability. Military confrontations ended in 1834, but some level of political stability was achieved only after 1851 and only then could serious attempts to reform the fiscal state inherited by the ancien régime be made. By midcentury, the government in Lisbon did not have full control over its territory in terms of military security and abilities to tax income or trade and to enforce legislation. The task of state building was more difficult because, in many instances, the presence of the central government had to be built anew, not by reforming existing local institutions. To engage in the tremendous efforts of state building, the government in Lisbon had to raise financial resources, which meant that it was of paramount importance to build an efficient fiscal system. This was a task that was never fully accomplished, and the history of nineteenth-century Portugal is partially the history of that process. Many would argue that an efficient and just fiscal system was not fully accomplished because people in government were too busy with their own private interests and less concerned with the public good. Yet to understand this problem, we also need to take into account the vast dimension of the tasks involved.

Figures I.1–I.3 quantify the extent of converging and diverging features of the European states that have just been reviewed. They show a general increase in the shares of revenues to total GDP and a convergence of the shares of expenditure in GDP to levels between 7 percent and 15 percent. The most important divergence in terms of how state finances were managed is share of debt as a percentage of GDP. Such differences appear not only as we compare countries but also across time. Austria-Hungary had more debt than France did before the compromise

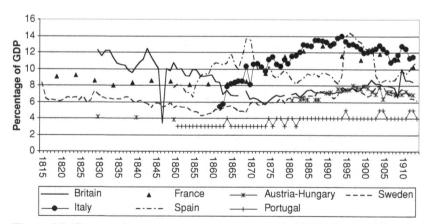

Figure I.1. Government revenue as percentage of GDP. *Sources:* Britain: Mitchell (1992: 808, 815, 825, 889, 891, 897). See Valério et al. (2006) for France (Figure 3.2), Austria-Hungary (Figure 5.2); Sweden (Figure 6.1); Italy (Figure 7.3); Spain (Figure 8.3); and Portugal, Valério et al. (2006: 240–2).

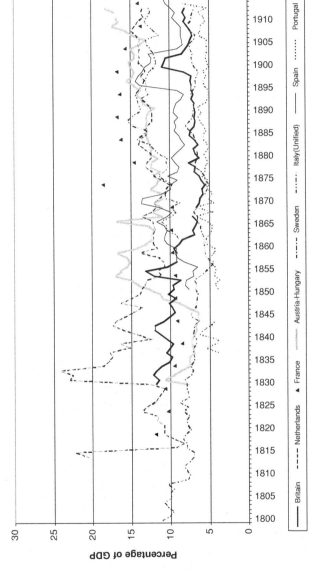

Figure I.2. Government expenditure as percentage of GDP. *Sources:* For Britain, Mitchell (1992: 796, 798, 801, 889, 891, 897); Netherlands, Figure 6.1; Italy, Figure 7.3; and Spain, Figure 8.3.

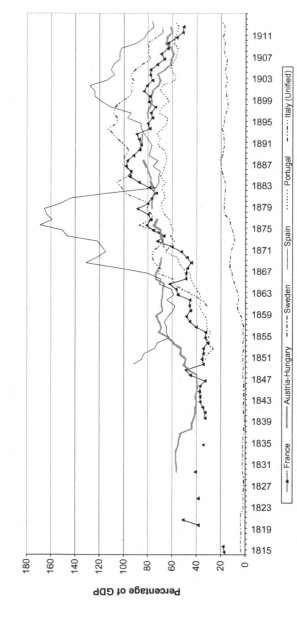

Figure I.3. Public debt as percentage of GDP. *Sources:* For France, Figure 3.2 and Mitchell (1992: 889–90, 893); Austria-Hungary, Figure 5.4; Sweden, Figure 6.2; Spain, Figure 8.7; and Portugal, Table 9.6.

(1867), but then the two countries evolved in a similar way. Two countries appear as quite different from the rest, namely Spain, which registered two spurts of public debt, and Sweden, which managed to have very low debt ratios throughout the period.

### Patterns of European Convergence and Differentiation

Nineteenth-century European history was clearly marked by the rise of the state as a political and economic actor. This book explains how that rise was financed and provides a European answer to the question in the form of a complex set of different responses. We conclude that there is not a European model and no ideal model. National models were, however, gradually defined, as the functions of states were largely centralized, even when there was some sort of regional distribution of the administrative functions. No national model dominated or was exported from one nation to another. Moreover, there was also no national model that proved ideal or dominant in terms of efficiency or geopolitical outcomes. Thus, the European answer to the question of how the liberal state came to be financed is the sum of different national outcomes.

But there was a European pattern defined by the execution of forms of financing government activity by taxing the economy efficiently and by servicing political and social consensus. The concern with efficiency is reflected in the search for policies that relate levels of taxation to the rhythm of economic activity. Because of their negative impact on the economy, tariffs might be perceived as a worse source of revenue than taxes on domestic activity. The concern for consensus is reflected in the option for systems based on the backing of parliaments, that were not regressive, and that possibly generated some social and regional redistribution effects. There is also a pattern in which most governments and political forces considered that the public deficit and the public debt should be held at the minimum levels, as large debts could undermine political systems. And there were other less-generalized sources of convergence in fiscal matters, namely the idea that the state could raise money to fund certain types of investment in social overhead capital and education. There was also convergence in the reduction of levels of expenditures on defense, although that occurred more rapidly in some countries than in others.

But differences were more important, particularly concerning the institutional forms of how tax policies were conducted (see Steinmo 1993: 12–13). Domestic political institutions developed according to different political and institutional experiences, as institutions were intimately connected with the past practices in the realm of public finances. The nineteenth century was markedly different from previous centuries in the field of public finances. Yet inheritance had a relevant role in shaping nineteenth-century tax policy and tax institutions. Different financial systems had been developed in the Netherlands, Great Britain, and France between Westphalia and Waterloo (Neal 2004). Great Britain may have been a good model for an eighteenth-century state, but it certainly was not for the nineteenth-century state, simply because the increasing role of the state meant that it had to be more in tune with national institutional and other characteristics.[10] Moreover, the institutional format of taxation also responded to differences in how states were formed. Looking at the widest range of cases, from Britain to Austria-Hungary and from Sweden to Portugal, we can conclude that each state had concerns and purposes of its own. Thus, taxation reflected the strong divergence in terms of institutional responses to the same type of problems at the European level. Different regimes were the outcome of different stages of state building and different levels of economic development. The case studies in this volume show that no modern liberal state, including the British one, which was widely appraised by contemporaries, could be replicated elsewhere, because historical legacies narrow the range of political options, as shown in Chapter 10 in this volume.

Public finances were an instrument with which to construct public policies. The degree of failure or success of governments in dealing with deficits and debts was not an outcome of levels of institutional development but an outcome of policy options. Britain balanced its budget because that represented the equilibrium of power between parties and between parliament and the government. France was not too concerned with reducing its increasing deficits and debt because doing so would imply a change in the relative strength of political force. A sound monetary system, facilitated by the growing economy and the development of the banking sector, helped fulfill its goal and implied that the burden

---

[10] Grossman (qtd. in Bordo 2001: 461–2) tellingly asks: 'Why have the British institutions of Commons, Lords and constitutional monarchy, or the American variant of Congress, Supreme Court, and president, not been readily transferable to other nations? The answer, I think, is that the British legacy of a state that protects property rights and that is accountable to its citizens is not attributable to institutional design. Rather, the key to the British legacy, starting with the success of the Glorious Revolution of 1689, is its foundation on a consensus of the citizenry.'

of the debt remained manageable. Germany developed a three-tier system of central, state, and municipal levels of government, the latter being remarkably autonomous. The central government was more preoccupied with defense and the state and municipal governments with economic and social issues. The system provided the needed funds for the three levels. When comparing Spain and Portugal with Sweden, we have to conclude that the main issue was not the ability to reform in itself but the ability of the state to tax the economy even with the old institutional framework. In Sweden, the low levels of political dispute and high levels of political stability enabled the state to increase the levels of taxation of the economy until the end of the century within the institutions inherited from the ancien régime. This is important because it helps clarify the counterfactual scenario with which many contemporaries and historians have worked. The absence of reforms was just another aspect of the incapacity of the state to tax. The analysis of the sources of that incapacity to tax is what we should concentrate on. It is important to note that reformation of the old tax regime in Sweden was not paramount in the political debate, as we will find in other parts of the European periphery or, for that matter, in France.

The history of nineteenth-century public finance was interrupted by the First World War, which caused many distresses in the domestic and the international order at all levels. During the interwar period, a period of economic, institutional, and political divergence ensued, notwithstanding the development of some points of ideological convergence. Thus, the development of the efficient state was interrupted. Such developments were resumed after the Second World War, but then Europe became clearly divided by the iron curtain. But in the West, developments proceeded again with generally common purposes in terms of the role of the states and generally different institutional solutions. It may be that institutional integration is greater now than it was in the nineteenth century. However, fiscal and financial institutions are still far from integrated. That is probably why, after having achieved economic and monetary integration, the European Union has still not made any serious attempts to introduce a common fiscal policy.

### References

Backhaus, J. and Wagner, R. (2005) "From Continental public finance to public choice: Mapping continuity," in S. Medema and P. Boettke, *The Role of Government in the History of Economic Thought* (annual suppl. to vol. 37 of *History of Political Economy*). Durham, NC: Duke University Press, 314–32.

Baysinger, B. and Tollison, R. (1980) "'Chaining Leviathan': The case of Glad-stonian finance," *History of Political Economy*, 12(2), 206–13.

Bonney, R. (1995) "Revenues," in R. Bonney (ed.) *Economic Systems and State Finance*. Oxford: Oxford University Press, 423–505.

Bonney, R. (ed.) (1995) *Economic Systems and State Finance*. Oxford: Oxford University Press.

Bonney, R. (ed.) (1999) *The Rise of the Fiscal State in Europe, c. 1200–1815*. Oxford: Oxford University Press.

Bonney, R. and Ormrod, W. (1999) "Introduction: Crises, revolutions and self-sustained growth – towards a conceptual model of change in fiscal history," in W. M. Ormrod, M. Bonney, and R. Bonney (eds.) *Crises, Revolutions and Self-Sustained Growth: Essays in European Fiscal History, c. 1130–1830*. Stamford, CT: Shaun Tyas, 1–21.

Bordo, M. D. and Cortés-Conde, R. (eds.) (2001) *Transferring Wealth and Power from the Old to the New World*. Cambridge: Cambridge University Press.

Buchanan, J. (1979) "Public choice and public finance," in *What Should Economists Do?* Indianapolis: Liberty Press, 182–97.

Buchanan, J. and Musgrave, R. (1999) *Public Finance and Public Choice: Two Contrasting Visions of the State*. Cambridge: Massachusetts Institute of Technology Press.

Cameron, R. (1972) *Banking and Economic Development: Some Lessons of History*. Oxford: Oxford University Press.

Crouzet, F. (2003) "Economic factors and the building of the French nation-state," in A. Teichova and H. Matis (eds.) *Nation, State and the Economy in History*. Cambridge: Cambridge University Press, 34–55.

Daunton, M. (2001) *Trusting Leviathan: The Politics of Taxation in Britain, 1799–1914*. Cambridge: Cambridge University Press.

Daunton, M. and Trentmann, F. (eds.) (2004) *Worlds of Political Economy: Knowledge and Power in the Nineteenth and Twentieth Centuries*. Basingstoke, UK: Palgrave Macmillan.

Dincecco, M. (2009a) "Fiscal centralization, limited government, and public revenues in Europe, 1650–1913," *Journal of Economic History*, 69(1), 48–103.

Dincecco, M. (2009b) "Political regimes and sovereign credit risk in Europe, 1750–1913," *European Review of Economic History*, 13(1), 31–63.

Dome, T. (2004) *The Political Economy of Public Finance in Britain, 1767–1873*. London: Routledge.

Dormois, J.-P. and Lains, P. (eds.) (2006) *Classical Trade Protectionism*. London: Routledge.

Furner, M. O. and Supple, B. (eds.) (1990) *The State and Economic Knowledge: The American and British Experiences*. Cambridge: Cambridge University Press.

Gerschenkron, A. (1962) *Economic Backwardness in Historical Perspective: A Book of Essays*. Cambridge, MA: Harvard University Press.

Grossman, H. I. (2001) "The state in economic history," in M. D. Bordo and R. Cortés-Conde (eds.) *Transferring Wealth and Power from the Old to the New World*. Cambridge: Cambridge University Press, 453–63.

Hatton, T. J., O'Rourke, K. and Taylor, A. (eds.) (2007) *The New Comparative Economic History: Essays in Honor of Jeffrey G. Williamson*. Cambridge: Massachusetts Institute of Technology Press.

Hinrichs, H. (1966) *A General Theory of Tax Structure Change during Economic Development*. Cambridge, MA: Law School of Harvard University.

Kayaalp, O. (2004) *The National Element in the Development of Fiscal Theory*. Basingstoke, UK: Palgrave Macmillan.

Kindleberger, C. P. (1993) *A Financial History of Western Europe*. Oxford: Oxford University Press.

Körner, M. (1995a) "Expenditure," in R. Bonney (ed.) *Economic Systems and State Finance*. Oxford: Oxford University Press, 393–422.

Körner, M. (1995b) "Public credit," in R. Bonney (ed.) *Economic Systems and State Finance*. Oxford: Oxford University Press, 506–38.

Krüger, K. (1987) "Public finance and modernisation: The change from the domain state to tax state in Hesse in the sixteenth and seventeenth centuries," in P.-C. Witt (ed.) *Wealth and Taxation in Central Europe: The History and Sociology of Public Finance*. New York Berg, 49–62.

Leathers, C. G. (1986) "Gladstonian finance and the Virginia School of public finance: Comment," *History of Political Economy*, 18(3), 515–21.

Maddison, A. (2001) *The World Economy: A Millennial Perspective*. Paris: Organisation for Economic Development and Co-operation.

Milward, A. (1992) *The European Rescue of the Nation State*. London: Routledge.

Milward, R. (2005) *Private and Public Enterprise in Europe: Energy, Telecommunications and Transport, 1830–1990*. Cambridge: Cambridge University Press.

Musgrave, R. and Peacock, A. (eds.) (1958) *Classics in the Theory of Public Finance*. London: Macmillan.

Neal, L. (2004) "The monetary, financial and political architecture of Europe, 1648–1815," in L. Prados de la Escosura (ed.) *Exceptionalism and Industrialization: Britain and Its European Rivals, 1688–1815*. Cambridge: Cambridge University Press, 173–90.

Nehring, H. and Schui, F. (eds.) (2007) *Global Debates about Taxation*. Basingstoke, UK: Palgrave Macmillan.

O'Brien, P. (1983) *Railways and the Economic Development of Western Europe, 1830–1914*. London: Macmillan.

O'Brien, P. (2008) "Historical conditions for the evolution of successful fiscal states: Great Britain and its European rivals from the Treaty of Munster to the Treaty of Vienna," in S. Cavaciochi (ed.) *Fiscal Systems in the European Economy from the 13th to the 18th Centuries*. Florence: Firenze University Press, 131–51.

Ormrod, W. M., Bonney, M. and Bonney, R. (eds.) (1999). *Crises, Revolutions and Self-Sustained Growth: Essays in European Fiscal History, c. 1130–1830*. Stamford, CT: Shaun Tyas, 1–21.

Petersen, E. L. (1975) "From domain state to tax state: Synthesis and interpretation." *Scandinavian Economic History Review*, 23, 116–48.

Scales, L. and Zimmer, O. (eds.) (2005) *Power and the Nation in European History*. Cambridge: Cambridge University Press.

Schonhardt-Bailey, C. (2006) *From the Corn Laws to Free Trade: Interests, Ideas, and Institutions in Historical Perspective*. Cambridge: Massachusetts Institute of Technology Press.

Schumpeter, J. A. (1954) "The crisis of the tax state," *International Economic Papers*, 4, 5–38. (Original German edition: 1918.)

Spoerer, M. (2008) "The revenue structures of Bradenburg-Prussia, Saxony and Bavaria (fifteenth to nineteenth centuries): Are they compatible with the Bonney-Osmond model?" in S. Cavaciochi (ed.) *Fiscal Systems in the European Economy from the 13th to the 18th Centuries*. Florence: Firenze University Press, 781–91.

Steinmo, S. H. (1993) *Taxation and Democracy: Swedish, British and American Approaches to Financing the Modern State*. New Haven, CT: Yale University Press.

Teichova, A. and Matis, H. (eds.) (2003) *Nation, State and the Economy in History*. Cambridge: Cambridge University Press.

Teichova, A., Matis, H. and Pátek, J. (eds.) (2000) *Economic Change and the National Question in Twentieth-Century Europe*. Cambridge: Cambridge University Press.

Tilly, C. (1992) *Coercion, Capital, and European States, AD 990–1992*. Cambridge, UK: Blackwell.

Tortella, G. (ed.) (1990) *Education and Economic Development since the Industrial Revolution*. Valencia: Generalitat Valenciana.

Wagner, R. E. (2007) *Fiscal Sociology and the Theory of Public Finance*. Cheltenham, UK: Edward Elgar.

Wallis, J. J. (2000) "American government finance in the long run: 1790 to 1990," *Journal of Economic Perspectives*, 14(1), 61–82.

Webber, C. and Wildavsky, A. (1986) *A History of Taxation and Expenditure in the Western World*. New York: Simon and Schuster.

Winch, D. and O'Brien, P. (eds.) (2002) *The Political Economy of British Historical Experience, 1688–1914*. Oxford: Oxford University Press.

# Creating Legitimacy

## *Administering Taxation in Britain, 1815–1914*

### Martin Daunton

## 1.1 Introduction

The notion of the state as a tax eater formed a central tenet in radical rhetoric in Britain after the Napoleonic Wars, when the British fiscal state was deeply resented and criticized, to a much greater extent than it had been in the eighteenth century. Trust was lost and needed to be rebuilt by the British political elite. During the eighteenth century, a powerful fiscal-military state emerged in Britain, without serious political problems and with a remarkable level of compliance from the public. The fiscal regime of eighteenth-century Britain can be understood in terms of the construction of two forms of trust. First, the supply of loans to the state at modest rates of interest depended on the ability of the state to make a credible commitment to lenders that they would not suffer from default and that their interest would be paid on time and in full. This form of trust in the credibility of the state is measured by an assessment of risk reflected in the interest rates on loans, which dropped as confidence grew in the ability of the state to commit (Epstein 2000). The second form of trust is more difficult to achieve: a high level of convergence between the purposes of the state and the interests of the political and economic elites. There were, it is true, complaints that a new, parasitic, monied interest was subverting republican virtue – the belief that the state should be ruled by a landed elite with the ability

This chapter is a revised version of 'Trusting Leviathan: The politics of taxation, 1815–1914,' which appeared in D. Winch and P. K. O'Brien (eds.) *The Political Economy of British Historical Experience, 1688–1914.* Oxford: Oxford University Press, 2002: 319–50.

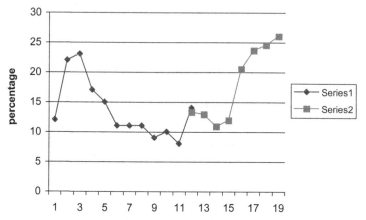

Figure 1.1. Total government expenditure as a percentage of gross national and domestic product, Britain, 1790–1937. *Source:* Middleton 1966: 90–1.

to bear arms in defense of the state or to spend time on its governance, free from immediate economic interests. However, the national debt and taxation were widely considered bulwarks of liberty and Protestantism against the French. The elites did largely identify with the purposes of the state (Pocock 1985; Dickson 1967; Hoppit 1990, 2002; O'Brien 2002; Peden 2002). Underlying both forms of trust were administrative and political processes: the small scale of tax farming and the sale of offices; the weakness or absence of provincial estates and exemptions, with the consequent ability to impose universal taxes; and the development of accounting methods to monitor the state. Although Parliament rarely opposed finance bills, it did have a vitally important role in securing trust and consent through the annual votes on funds and through monitoring spending. Parliament met annually after the Glorious Revolution of 1688 and provided a forum for bargaining and for the construction of consent. The contrast with ancien régime France is clear: the British state was able to extract a higher level of taxation, with less resistance and tension, and to use the revenue to fund loans for warfare and imperial expansion (Brewer 1989; Mathias and O'Brien 1976; Daunton 2006).

Trust in the tax system and the state started to weaken during the wars with Revolutionary and Napoleonic France between 1793 and 1815 – and most seriously during the return to peace. During the war, government expenditure increased to about 23 percent of national income (see Figure 1.1), which caused alarm and contributed to a debate over the incidence of taxation that was central to the emergence of a middle-class identity (Wahrman 1995). But so long as hostilities continued, taxes and the heavy burden of debt had an obvious justification: the external threat from French absolutism and Catholicism, succeeded by the dangers of Revolutionary ideology and Napoleonic ambition, justified a fiscal-military state as a means of sustaining the social hierarchy, preserving liberty, and securing commercial hegemony (Dickson 1967; Hoppit 1990; Pocock 1985). After 1815, the justification was no longer present, and the burden of the postwar debt meant that criticism of the state and the tax system did not disappear, despite the peace dividend of reduced defense expenditure. In 1815, debt charges amounted to 26.6 percent of gross public expenditure in the United Kingdom; by 1825, they accounted for 54.4 percent. The threat to liberties was perceived as coming from within the country rather than from France: the costs of servicing the debt and the rentiers it sustained; the menace of militarism and a luxurious court; the subversion of the social order by a class of rich financiers and mighty landowners benefiting from pensions and sinecures. Such a view could potentially bring together working-class and middle-class radicals in hostility to the tax-eater state, and it might have appealed to many others with little sympathy for radicalism, such as country gentlemen who feared that high taxes sustained rentiers and subverted the social hierarchy (Hilton 1977).

Although similar debates were apparent after the Seven Years' War and the American War of Independence, which inspired the attempts of Edmund Burke and William Pitt to introduce 'economic reform' (Torrance 1978), there was a new radical edge to the debates after 1815. The government failed in its attempt to renew the wartime income tax in 1816, which resulted in much greater dependence on customs and excise duties, which fell on domestic producers and working-class consumers. Meanwhile, the land tax had not been readjusted since 1694, despite the increase in land values and rents from the later eighteenth century (see Table 1.1). The payment of large sums of interest to rentiers at a time of falling prices meant that the real income of lenders rose – and the burden of taxes on producers became more onerous (Hope-Jones 1939: chap. 7; O'Brien 1988). The outcome was clear: the fiscal system lacked legitimacy, and trust (in the form of a widely shared consensus on the uses of tax revenue) was much weaker than it had been in the eighteenth century. There was a lack of trust that fellow taxpayers were making a reasonable contribution to the expenses of the state, and that the state was spending its revenues in a way that was equitable among classes and interests.

In the 1820s, many considered the British state undemocratic, bloated, and inefficient. The government responded in the same way that it had

Table 1.1. *Structure of Tax Revenue of the Central Government, Britain and the United Kingdom, 1696–1700 to 1910–14 (percentage)*

| | Direct Taxes on Wealth and Income | | | | | Indirect Taxes on Goods | | |
|---|---|---|---|---|---|---|---|---|
| | Land/Assessed | Stamps | Death | Income | *Total* | Customs | Excise | *Total* |
| 1696–1700 | 40.1 | 1.8 | – | – | *41.9* | 29.2 | 28.9 | *58.1* |
| 1711–15 | 32.4 | 2.5 | – | – | *34.9* | 27.6 | 37.5 | *65.1* |
| 1731–5 | 17.6 | 2.6 | – | – | *20.1* | 28.2 | 51.7 | *79.9* |
| 1751–5 | 22.3 | 1.9 | – | – | *24.3* | 24.2 | 51.5 | *75.7* |
| 1771–5 | 19.0 | 3.5 | – | – | *22.4* | 26.8 | 50.7 | *77.6* |
| 1791–5 | 17.4 | 8.4 | – | – | *25.8* | 22.7 | 51.5 | *74.2* |
| 1811–15 | 11.1 | 8.9 | – | 19.8 | *39.8* | 20.4 | 39.8 | *60.2* |
| 1831–5 | 10.5 | 14.7 | – | – | *25.2* | 38.3 | 36.4 | *74.8* |
| 1851–5 | 6.5 | 12.5 | – | 12.4 | *31.4* | 40.1 | 28.5 | *68.6* |
| 1871–5 | 3.8 | 6.3 | 8.2 | 10.3 | *28.6* | 31.7 | 39.7 | *71.4* |
| 1891–5 | 3.0 | 6.7 | 12.7 | 17.2 | *39.7* | 24.1 | 36.2 | *60.3* |
| 1910–14 | 1.8 | 6.5 | 17.0 | 27.1 | *52.3* | 22.3 | 25.4 | *47.7* |

*Notes:* Net income to 1791–5, thereafter gross. The figures exclude income from nontax revenue, such as the Post Office, telegraphs, and crown lands. Death duties are included with stamps before 1870. The land and assessed taxes include the land tax, inhabited house duty and taxes on servants, carriages, and so on. From 1871, the last category was replaced with excise licenses and the revenue was therefore transferred to 'excise.'
*Source:* Mitchell and Deane 1962: 386–8, 392–4.

in the late eighteenth century, through a strategy of auditing spending by using commissions and investigations to defuse opposition (Harling 1996: 137–9, 144–50). The issue facing politicians after the Napoleonic Wars was how to reestablish trust in the state and the tax system, and how to restore legitimacy. As this chapter aims to show, the process was remarkably successful, such that in the second half of the nineteenth century, the British state and the taxes that supported it were widely considered to be neutral among classes and interests. (McKibbin 1990). Trust was re-created, in part, by using some of the auditing techniques of the eighteenth century but also by developing new languages, political cultures, and administrative techniques appropriate to the changed circumstances of the nineteenth century. How was the British state able to achieve a high level of trustworthiness?

When the British fiscal regime is placed in a wider European context, a number of divergences are apparent that point to the most significant factors. First, there were different trends in the level of taxation in relation to gross national product. The claims of the British state on gross domestic product were among the highest in Europe by 1815, but the reduction in expenditure was subsequently longer and deeper than it was in other European countries. Second, the relative importance of direct and indirect taxes moved in opposite directions, with a marked fall in the share of indirect taxes in Britain and a marked rise in many European countries. Third, there were divergences in the nature of fiscal administration. The interactions of these three variables led to the creation and maintenance of an unusually high level of trust in the British state, and thus to consent to taxation, which stands in striking contrast with the early nineteenth-century criticism of the tax-eater state. The achievement of a high level of trust in the central state, and in fellow taxpayers, reduced the costs of collective action and created the opportunity for the British state to take on new functions in the early twentieth century. The greater success of the British state in creating trust in taxation is clear at the end of the period, when the burdens of the First World War exposed the flaws in the fiscal systems of many other European countries. At the outbreak of the war, the British government was able to secure loans more easily and on cheaper terms than were other European countries, which indicates that the market accepted the credibility of the state's commitment to paying interest and honoring loans. At the end of the war, France, Germany, and Italy all experienced serious political crises, in part triggered by the lack of consent to taxation. By contrast, the British state emerged from the First World War with a high degree of legitimacy and trustworthiness, and without the crises experienced after 1815 (Forsyth 1993; Ferguson 1995, 2001; Maier 1975; Daunton 1996c).

## 1.2 Reducing Taxation and Creating Consent

The first point to consider is the difference in trends of taxation in relation to national income between Britain and other European states in the nineteenth century. In the eighteenth century, Britain was at the top end of European fiscal extraction and was able to escape some of the constraints on early modern state finance. In the nineteenth century, the story is different: the British state was more effectively contained. In Britain, taxation fell from the level of 1815, initially by about the same amount in proportion to national income as it had after the Seven Years' War and the American War of Independence. But from about 1830, the fall continued and the level of spending remained low relative to other European countries to the end of the century, when there was a modest increase (see Figure 1.1). In Continental Europe, the reduction in taxes at the end of the Napoleonic Wars was more modest and was soon reversed (Schremmer 1989: 362; Harling and Mandler 1993). The British state was more effectively constrained than its Continental neighbors until the outbreak of the First World War – in other words, the state was actually rolled back as well as monitored. This raises the issue that Baysinger and Tollison (1980; see also Leathers 1986) posed in their study of the fiscal policies of Gladstone: how was Leviathan chained and how was the British state able to reduce its claims on GNP to a greater extent than its European counterparts? The process of containment was a precondition for taxpayers and lenders accepting the trustworthiness of the state.

At the end of the Napoleonic Wars, politicians came under criticism from radicals who complained about the subversion of the constitution by a corrupt court and sinecurists; from disaffected farmers and gentry concerned about their position relative to the greater landowners and the monied class; and from Evangelical critics of dissipation and luxury. The demand for 'economical reform' of the 1780s had new force. The campaign was self-reinforcing, for the appointment of parliamentary inquiries to rectify one abuse placed more information in the public sphere on related issues, and so led to renewed demands for reform. Historians have devoted much attention to these criticisms of 'old corruption,' the system of sinecures, and pensions created by Tory ministers and their hangers-on (Rubinstein 1983; Thompson 1963: 676). However, the emphasis on the language deployed by the critics of 'old corruption' may obscure two other points.

The first point is that the actual scale of 'old corruption' was not as massive as was implied by radical language and rhetoric, which has misled some recent historians. As Harling (1996) has remarked, there was a dramatic widening of the gap between radical perception and administrative reality from around 1806, which further increased after the war. Of course, the attack on pensions and sinecures was a symbol of the existence of privilege in an unreformed political and fiscal system that was skewed against producers to the benefit of parasites. Second, more attention should be paid to the response of politicians to radical language, for at least some members of the ruling elite countered the rhetoric of their critics by articulating an image of probity, stressing office as a public trust and learning a new code of political manners. Between the end of the war and 1830, Tory ministers introduced precisely the measures of economic and administrative reform that radicals believed their greed made impossible (Langford 1997: 118–23; Harling 1986: 138–9 and 150–96; Collini 1991: 104–12).

The retrenchment of the Tory ministries between 1815 and 1830 and the export of some of the costs of the fiscal-military state to the empire did mark a turning point in the fiscal-military state, which reduced its claims on the economy to below the levels of the eighteenth century (Bayly 1994a, 1994b). But the shrinking state did not achieve legitimacy and trust as the Tory ministers had hoped, in part because the strategy was designed to prevent a wider definition of citizenship and in part because the taxes levied to pay for the reduced level of public expenditure were widely perceived as inequitable. Politicians in Hanoverian Britain usually calibrated indirect taxes to avoid, or to fall lightly, on the necessities of the poor, and such considerations meant that the ministry wished to retain the income tax at the end of the war to avoid overburdening those who were least able to pay taxes. But the government was forced to abandon the proposal in 1816 by an alliance of radicals and Whigs, so that it was obliged to rely on customs and excise duties, which fell on working-class consumers and on domestic production (see Table 1.1) (O'Brien 1988; Hilton 1977). By acceding to pressure for retrenchment through the abolition of the income tax, the ministry was contributing to criticism of the unfair incidence of taxation, to which the radical response was further cuts in expenditure. The attempt to create a sense of trust in a patrician elite and state failed, and the constitutional reform so assiduously opposed by the Tories was introduced by the Whigs in the early 1830s.

In 1832, the parliamentary franchise was extended and rotten and pocket boroughs removed; in 1835, self-electing municipal corporations were replaced by elected councils; the judiciary was reformed; and the privileges of the Church of England reduced. Such constitutional reform was portrayed as an onslaught on the structure of 'old corruption' and was linked with a further onslaught on expenditure. However, the legitimacy of the state was not reasserted, and public agitation mounted in the 1830s, with pressure to remove the agricultural protection of the Corn Laws, which imposed import duties on grain, and demands from the Chartist movement for universal manhood suffrage and annual elections. The problem faced by the Whig government was that retrenchment left it susceptible to charges of financial mismanagement when a serious depression resulted in budget deficits. Although indirect taxes were reduced, the tax system was not reformed by introducing new taxes – particularly the income tax, which was anathema to radicals as the engine of warfare and a bloated state (Harling 1986: 197–227; Taylor 1995; Hilton 1977). Despite the considerable reduction in the scale of public expenditure by 1840 (to 12.4 percent of GNP), state finance was still far from achieving legitimacy and trust. Contemporaries had little appreciation of taxation as a proportion of national income, and they focused instead on absolute levels of spending and on the size of any budgetary surplus or deficit (Peden 2002: 354–5). Protection of landed interests through the Corn Laws suggested that policy was still biased; and regardless of the overall level of extraction, the tax system was heavily dependent on indirect taxes, which fell on working-class consumers and middle-class producers.

The successful creation of legitimacy and trust in the state rested on the measures of the Tory ministry of Sir Robert Peel, whose policies were continued in the Liberal Party by William Gladstone. Liberals were the heirs to the notion of public duty developed by Tory politicians after the Napoleonic Wars, with the difference that it was now integral to their character as public men rather than a (possibly cynical) response to outside pressure. The rhetorical strategy was helped by the fact that many leading politicians were drawn from a group of landowners that straddled interests, coming, like Peel, from a background in the cotton industry of Lancashire or, like Gladstone, from Liverpool merchants and slave traders (Harling and Mandler 1983: 70). Above all, their devotion to public duty was linked to a claim that they – and the state – were disinterested. Their ambition was conservative, but in a different sense from that of the postwar Tory ministries that aimed to preserve the rule of a narrow political elite in an unreformed constitution. Rather, Peel concluded that the best strategy for preserving the rule of the political elite and protecting property was to adopt policies that were even handed among all types of property and between the propertied and the nonpropertied. By constraining state expenditure and, as far as possible, excluding the state from involvement with economic interests, it was hoped to protect the political elite from challenge and to define the state as a neutral arbitrator between interests. Politicians must rise above personal greed and self-interest; they must also rise above any temptation to use the state to favor one interest against another, whether a trade group in search of protection or a social group seeking tax breaks.

In 1842, Peel reintroduced the income tax in an attempt to balance the budget, in two senses: first, by removing the deficit left by the Whigs and restoring order to government finances; second, by establishing a sense of equity between different types of wealth and income. In 1846, he took a further step by abolishing agricultural protection, a measure that split the Tory Party. On the one side, there were the supporters of protectionism, such as Benjamin Disraeli, who finally realized in the 1850s that the policy was no longer tenable. On the other side were the supporters of the reforming and modernizing thrust of Peel – such as William Gladstone. The result was a new political alignment and nomenclature. The Tories became the Conservative Party, with a commitment to imperialism and patriotism, as well as support for some measures of social reform. Meanwhile, Gladstone moved to the Liberal Party, which brought together former radicals who now accepted that the state had been able to reform itself, free traders who supported the repeal of the Corn Laws, religious Dissenters who wished to have greater civil liberties, and old Whigs.

Peel's policies were continued by Gladstone, most notably in his budget of 1853. Peel and Gladstone established the principles that the state should not appear to favor any particular economic interest and that taxes should be a carefully devised system of checks and balances. This issue arose most clearly in the debate over differentiation of the income tax. Critics of the income tax argued that it was biased against industrial or earned income (which was liable to loss during ill health or trade depression) compared with spontaneous or unearned income (which was supported by capital assets that produced income regardless of health or economic depression). In his abortive budget of 1852, Disraeli, as the Conservative Chancellor of the Exchequer, proposed to differentiate between the two forms of income by reducing the taxation of earned income to take account of the need to save for old age, retirement, and dependents. Gladstone was strongly opposed to such an approach, which would use the tax system to define one economic interest or class against another. He argued that the fiscal system should instead be balanced among different forms of income through taxation of property at death and should allow a tax break on life insurance premiums, available to people of all forms of income, which would encourage everyone to be more prudent (Harling 1986: 228–54; Hilton 1977; Matthew 1979, 1986; Biagini 1991, 1992; McKibbin 1996).

Peel and Gladstone therefore articulated a language of public trust, and the creation of at least the appearance of neutrality was achieved more successfully in Britain than it was in other European countries. The willingness of the elite to shoulder the burdens of the income tax and to abandon the Corn Laws marked a triumph of disinterestedness. The success of the policy was clear in 1848, when revolutions in the rest of Europe contrasted with the demise of Chartism as a movement. The radicals of mid-Victorian Britain were willing to trust elite politicians, such as Peel and Gladstone, and to accept the legitimacy of the state rather than castigate them as selfish and corrupt (Read 1987; Biagini 1992).

The ability to restrict the state and to create widespread acceptance of the trustworthiness of the state and of the political elite did not depend only on the assiduous cultivation of a sense of public duty and the creation of a class-neutral state. Both Gladstone and the officials at the Treasury were very conscious that, with the extension of the franchise and the ambitions of spending departments, there were new dangers arising from the pursuit of votes by competing politicians. They feared that the result would be a replacement of retrenchment by expenditure, unless there were clearly established, rigid conventions; it was easier to bring down spending from the heights of the Napoleonic Wars than to keep it at the new, lower level. The first convention was a rejection of hypothecation of tax revenue or the pledging of particular revenues to particular purposes. Hypothecation threatened an increase in the role of the state by treating it as a collection of services and functions, each of which was individually desirable with a protected source of revenue. Revenue therefore was to be unified, treated as a single pool of money that was separate from the purposes for which it was raised. A dread of hypothecation was high on the list of the Treasury's constitutional principles for the financial system. The second convention was a ban on *virement* of funds. Although revenue was treated as a single sum without any ties to a specific purpose, expenditure was minutely subdivided by annual votes of the Commons, which could not be vired or shifted between different budget heads. The danger of *virement* was that spending would always rise to the available revenue. By removing freedom to reallocate funds, spending on any new venture had to be carefully argued, and annual votes and the ban on *virement* helped to chain the state. At the same time, the need for approval for every item of spending led to transparency and trust, for each item of spending had been specifically sanctioned.

There was a very strong emphasis on the need for constant vigilance by Parliament as a protection for the public against the spending plans of the executive. Reformers argued for a change in the franchise prior to 1832, less for its own sake in creating a more democratic political system than as a means of changing the composition of members of Parliament to purge the Commons of interest and to make parliamentary control more effective in eliminating militarism and waste. Indeed, between 1832 and 1867, parties had limited cohesion and the Commons was considered an autonomous arena from which the executive could be chosen and prevented from becoming overmighty. Although the emphasis shifted in the 1870s to greater stress on the role of strong and stable parties based on their platforms and electoral supremacy, it was still assumed that the Commons would scrutinize spending plans (Taylor 1995: 30–2, 45, 135; Hawkins 1989).

The ban on hypothecation and *virement*, and the insistence on annual votes, meant that there was the possibility of surplus at the end of the year as a result of buoyant tax revenues or underspending on any vote. A further financial convention was that this surplus would not carry forward to the next year. Here again was a temptation that self-interested, ambitious politicians might not resist: a Chancellor would be able to carry over surpluses to make a dramatic reduction in taxation prior to an election, which would turn the tax system into a gigantic system of jobbery. Since 1829, the convention was that any surplus should be transferred to the sinking fund to reduce the national debt, so releasing funds that could be more efficiently used elsewhere. Repayment of the national debt would also create confidence that the state was trustworthy, so maintaining British credit and ensuring that the public would lend to the state in times of war, when the revenue from annual tax revenues would need to be supplemented (*Select Committee on Public Monies* 1857: app. 1; *Select Committee on Public Income and Expenditure* 1828: 4–6; Daunton 2001). The cost of servicing the national debt did fall. By 1905, the cost of debt service was down to 16.6 percent of gross expenditure. Between 1822 and 1914, the British national debt fell by 90 percent relative to GNP. The explanation cannot be found in inflation over the period, which had a minimal impact; rather, there was a combination of debt-repayment and economic growth (Ferguson 2001: 174–5).

In the nineteenth century, unlike in the eighteenth century, the spending of the central government expanded less than the national income did. Of course, a major reason for this change in the relationship between taxes and economic growth was the shift from an aggressive to a pacific foreign policy – or perhaps more accurately, a shift from expensive conflicts with major European powers to cheaper imperial wars against less effective military forces. Despite technical change and speedier obsolescence over the course of the nineteenth century, military spending did not push government spending ahead of economic growth, at least until the Boer War – neither, still, had central government spending on civilian welfare (Middleton 1996; Mann 1993). But even if the technical accounting procedures were not themselves the major reason for the shrinking claims of the state on the national income, they were significant in establishing trust and legitimacy in the state and taxation to meet the new claims in the twentieth century. These technical accounting procedures and the annual votes of the Commons were erected into matters of high constitutional principle that were integral to English liberty and national identity. In the hands of Gladstone, the annual budget became a matter of high theatricality and 'fiscal probity became the new morality' (Matthew 1986: 76). The budget and the amalgamation of all sources of revenue into a single entity made government finances transparent to a much greater extent than they had been in the eighteenth or early nineteenth centuries, when budgets were opaque or incomprehensible (Binney 1958). It was clear to the public and taxpayers where money came from and where it was going. Above all, spending was open to parliamentary scrutiny on an annual basis. The state was, as a result, trusted or tamed – and hence liberated for action. This high level of trust in the British state meant that it was able to secure taxes and loans for warfare on easier terms than its rivals, with less threat of social and political upheaval. It also meant that public expenditure on welfare came to be viewed as efficient and equitable, so allowing a much higher reliance on central tax-funded welfare than in other European countries.

## 1.3 Direct versus Indirect Taxes

At the same time that public expenditure fell as a proportion of GNP, there was a second major transformation in the structure of taxation, away from indirect taxes (in particular customs and excise) to direct taxes. The trend was especially marked from the 1870s, but the composition of indirect taxes changed from the 1830s, with a marked reduction in the number of goods affected and a shift away from necessities. British experience ran counter to the pattern in France. Between 1842 and 1914, the share of direct taxes rose in Britain and fell in France, where indirect taxes at the end of the period reached the level from which Britain had started. The British tax system in 1842 was extremely limited, for the failure to renew the income tax in 1816 left the government heavily dependent on customs duties and a few excise duties, a fiscal regime attacked both by working-class groups and by industrialists and traders. The reintroduction of the income tax in 1842 marked the start of a new trend, for direct taxes on wealth and income rose from 25.2 percent of central government revenue in 1831–5 to 52.3 percent in 1910–14 (see Table 1.1) (Daunton 2001: 175–7). In France, the trend was almost exactly the opposite, and the comparative position of the two tax regimes was therefore reversed over the nineteenth century.

How can the change in the structure of taxation be related to the constraints imposed on the growth of the British state in the nineteenth century? At first sight, the two features might appear to be working in opposite directions, for it could reasonably be assumed that the introduction of the income tax was intended to raise more revenue for the state so that containment of public expenditure occurred despite the existence of the income tax. However, it would be more accurate to argue that the reintroduction of income tax in 1842 became a crucial link in the chains binding the British state, helping to remove political tensions and so improve governability and trust, rather than – as feared at the time of its repeal in 1816 and by radical opponents in the 1830s – as a means of increasing the revenue of the state.

Peel's decision to reintroduce the income tax was part of a process of political and social stabilization by creating a tax system that was neutral among interests and that protected property in general. However, care had to be taken that it was not interpreted as a means of fueling the expansion of the state. Free traders who attacked the protection of the landed interest and demanded the liberalization of the economy feared that the income tax offered an alternative to retrenchment and would be used to finance war; they were initially suspicious of the motives of Peel (Hilton 1977: 138). Acceptance of the income tax therefore rested on creating a belief that it would help to constrain the state rather than provide it with additional resources. Peel and Gladstone argued, and their claims were not without foundation, that the tax was temporary and would be abolished as soon as retrenchment had done its work: it was simply a socially equitable means of covering expenditure in the interim, before economic growth in a free market led to higher tax revenues (Peel 1842: cols. 431, 437–9, 444; Biagini 1991: 156). It was also argued that the tax would create a sense of political responsibility. The principle was no representation without taxation: there was a close correlation between paying income tax and possessing a vote in parliamentary elections under the terms of the Reform Act of 1832. Consequently, electors would have an incentive in voting for cheap government because their public choices would have immediate private consequences in their tax bills (Matthew 1986: 125–8; Daunton 1996a: 149–50). The income tax was, therefore, linked to the process of dismantling the fiscal-military state rather than to the provision of revenue for new functions. Richard Cobden was convinced and came to accept the virtues of the income tax.

Intention was one thing; outcome in the longer term was another, for the income tax became permanent and formed a rising proportion of revenue, though innocent of any redistributive intent for many years. Although the link between payment of the income tax and the franchise was broken in 1867, when Disraeli extended the vote to a larger number of electors, and further sundered in the third reform act of 1884, it took some time for the redistributive potential of the wider franchise to be realized. Most working-class voters still viewed the state as a source of spending on war and waste rather than on socially desirable expenditure, which was largely left to local government. It was only in the 1890s that attitudes started to change. The expansion of trade unions to unskilled workers meant that the Trades Union Congress was no longer dominated by skilled men who provided their own welfare benefits through trade unions (for unemployment pay) and friendly societies (for sick pay and treatment). Unskilled workers could not afford the high level of contributions and looked instead to tax-funded finance. Pressures started to mount in the Liberal Party as working men demanded more progressive and expensive policies that threatened to alienate middle-class taxpayers. This trend went a step further in 1900, for legal attacks on the position of trade unions led them to form their separate political party. The new Labour Party pressed not only for legal protection for trade unions but also for tax-funded welfare. The Liberals were in a dilemma as they tried to retain working-class support in the party or to secure the support of the Labour MPs who were increasingly important for the survival of the government after 1910. If the Liberals went too far in meeting their demands, many middle-class voters would move to the Conservative Party (Duffy 1961–2; Harris 1983; Hennock 1987).

Up to 1914, the Liberal government managed to reconcile these competing pressures. One response was to form an alliance against a third grouping: landowners who received 'unearned' income from increases in rents and values as a result of the energies of productive labor and capital. Hence the emphasis of the Liberal Chancellor William Harcourt in 1894 on the taxation of estates left at death and of the Liberal government elected in 1906 on the taxation of land values in the so-called 'people's budget' of 1909. Members of the House of Lords – dominated by the great landowners – saw these measures as a direct attack on their position and attempted to block the budget of 1909, which led to a major constitutional crisis, for the House of Lords was not meant to challenge the authority of the Commons in financial measures. A second response was to proffer an alternative to tax-funded welfare (e.g., old age pensions in 1908) by introducing insurance-funded welfare for unemployment and health in 1911, which limited the contribution of the state and placed the burden on employers and employees. Labour MPs realized that the government was adopting insurance to block their own demands for more progressive, tax-funded schemes, but they could scarcely oppose the measures. Above all, the Liberals were able to create support for a modest degree of progressive taxation as an alternative to a much less desirable approach: the Conservatives' advocacy of tariff reform or imperial preference, which threatened free trade. The Liberals insisted that tariff reform would lead to higher food prices, threaten the standard of living of workers, and transfer resources to the great landowners. At the same time, the Liberals were careful to ensure that the new progressive income tax did not hit crucial groups of electors, by offering tax breaks to married men with children, for whom the tax rate actually dropped (Daunton 1996b; Murray 1980; Hennock 1987: 206–9; Harris 1983).

By 1910–14, the income tax accounted for 27.1 percent of central government tax revenues (Table 1.1). At the same time, death duties rose in importance, and the two taxes together accounted for 44.1 percent of revenue by 1910–14. An important point about these taxes is not just the revenue they produced but also the way they were linked to the rhetoric of balance, ensuring that each form of income or property paid its due proportion to the state (Daunton 1996a). A further element of this search for balance was a restructuring of indirect taxes. Although customs and excise duties remained a major part of the government's revenue, they were increasingly confined to a few commodities whose consumption was in some sense voluntary – above all, the excise on beer and spirits, and import duties on tobacco, spirits, wine, and tea. In the 1830s, writers on public finance argued that the yield of duties would rise as the rate was reduced, so as to encourage consumption. Peel accepted this proposition and argued that modest duties would allow workers to share in the material success of the British economy and so win them to supporting the social order. By the 1870s, the continued growth of the economy meant that the Chancellor had a surplus, which resulted in large concessions to customs duties retained for revenue purposes and to a fall in the overall share of indirect taxes (Daunton 2001: 79–80, 173–4).

The constraints imposed on the state in the mid-Victorian period and the stress on class neutrality created a high degree of legitimacy and trust, which removed the virulent attacks on the 'tax-eater' state of the early Victorian period. The success of Gladstonian financial reform created a high degree of acceptance of the tax system in general, in contrast with other countries where the role of indirect taxes had increased. The tax system in France in the early nineteenth century had a wider base than in Britain, for it was much less dependent on consumption taxes and had a variety of direct taxes. These took the form of the *contribution foncière* on real estate; the *droits de patente* on the presumed profits of trade, industry, and professions according to three criteria of the category of trade, scale of the business, and its location; and the *contribution personnelle*, based on presumed income measured by conspicuous expenditure, above all on residences. The reintroduction of the income tax in Britain in 1842 should be seen as bringing the British fiscal system into line with France by seeking to extract revenue from the same range of activities through the different schedules of the income tax (Koepke 1979–80). The main difference between the direct tax systems in the two countries was that the French taxes were less flexible and buoyant than in Britain, and less capable of extracting increases in the national income. The point may be made by a comparison between the *droits de patente* in France and income tax on profits from trade and business (schedule D) in Britain. The three criteria that determined the *droits de patente* created a mass of categories, between locales, trades, and scale of the business. Any adjustment of the tax was exceedingly difficult, for doing so would affect a plethora of trade and regional interests. By contrast, the British income tax involved a single rate and was likely to produce more revenue in line with economic growth and increased profits, without the political ramifications found in France and without creating serious tensions between classes and interests. The French state became more dependent on indirect taxes as a result of the lack of buoyancy in direct taxes and the difficulty of reform. Moreover, it was possible to manipulate the income tax in Britain to produce a different incidence between classes than in France. The British income tax had a relatively high threshold, and its rate was modified to offer degression for the lowest levels of taxable income. In the Edwardian period, income tax was raised on large incomes, especially those with a large socially created element; and taxation was reduced on modest middle-class incomes, especially those of family men with dependent children. Modest middle-class incomes therefore paid a lower effective rate of tax than did the well-to-do (Daunton 1996a: 157–65; Murray 1980). In France, the package of direct taxes was less flexible, less buoyant, and fell more heavily on the middle class than the rich, which reduced consent to taxation and eroded trust in the state; and the case for an income tax was deeply divisive as a socialist menace to property (Gross 1993: 121,123–5). In Britain, the appeal of reforming the income tax was precisely that it prevented greater threats. The income tax could contain the growth of a separate

Labour Party by funding increased social expenditure while retaining middle-class support by ensuring that the costs fell on the recipients of large 'unearned' incomes who could be separated from productive, morally superior 'earned' incomes.

A combination of political factors and the nature of the tax system therefore led to a reversal of the proportions of direct and indirect taxes in the two countries at the end of the nineteenth century. The income tax was introduced into Britain as a part of the strategy designed to dismantle the fiscal-military state and to constrain expenditure, but it also contained within itself the possibility of providing a buoyant source of revenue that was widely accepted as legitimate and fair. Although the various taxes in Britain and France were designed to extract revenue from the same sources of income, they were connected with the underlying economic base in very different ways, which made them more or less responsive to changes in the level of activity and more or less easily modified as a result of political contingencies. The result in France was rigidity in direct taxes, which pushed the government toward indirect taxes. In Britain, direct taxes were more flexible and responsive to economic growth, allowing a remission of indirect taxes and allowing the rate of income tax to be kept at a modest rate. However, the high reliance on income tax for central government revenue, a widening of the franchise to non–income tax payers, and the deliberate attempt to reduce the burden of direct taxation on modest middle-class family incomes created the circumstances for a separation between public choices and private costs that might potentially slacken the constraints on expenditure.

## 1.4 Fiscal Administration

It is sometimes suggested that Britain had a strong civil society and a weak state, whereas France and Germany had strong states and weak civil societies. This interpretation is misleading for two reasons. First, recent work on France and Germany shows that they had strong civil societies as well; second, the British state might have been small, but it was effective. The British state was more effective and stronger than is often assumed, in a way not captured by the notion of a laissez-faire state. The state and tax system in nineteenth-century Britain operated on the basis of a high level of delegation, characterized by two features. First, functions were delegated to voluntary associations (education, voluntary hospitals, care for orphans, or trade unions and friendly societies in the provision of unemployment and health insurance) and to local bodies (the poor law and, subsequently, education). Until about 1860, these voluntary societies were largely distinct from public bodies and formed part of civil society; for the rest of the nineteenth century, they drew together with the municipalities in a strong, localized associational and municipal culture. The result was to limit the growth of the central state (Morris 2000).

Tax reform was a significant component in the creation of a cheap, neutral state and in the legitimization of aristocratic governance. The creation of a sense of equity in taxation and the removal of the fear of placemen and sinecurists made it possible to establish new government agencies without alarm at creating new opportunities for privilege and patronage; it was necessary for the state to be cleansed and curtailed before a more positive role was feasible. Tax reform and economy alone were not enough, for Innes (1994: 839) has remarked that 'the experience of penny-pinching Prussian kings...suggests that economy – and bureaucratic impartiality – could only do so much to legitimate systems of government.' A willingness to provide a large measure of self-rule was a further requirement. The legitimization of aristocratic governance at the center rested not only on its cheapness and apparent impartiality but also on its ability to shed large areas of responsibility. It was a process with antecedents in the eighteenth century and was not only the product of reappraisals of the British state after the Napoleonic Wars. During the eighteenth century, the central government became more concerned with issues of war and empire, and less involved with local initiatives and administration, which had been devolved to local authorities. Such a trend was less obvious in other European countries in the eighteenth century; in France and Prussia, for example, the central government increased its control over the localities to mobilize troops and obtain revenues (Innes 1994: 96, 101–2, 118–19).

The reforms of the second quarter of the nineteenth century did not mark a shift in this process of devolution or subsidiarity; what the reforms did achieve was the imposition of greater constraints on spending at the local level. In the early nineteenth century, the largest element of local expenditure was the poor law, where costs seemed to be mounting inexorably as a result of supplements to wages of the 'able-bodied' poor. These grants in aid of wages were denounced by many economists and politicians as counterproductive, as weakening the need for 'preventive' checks on population growth, and therefore as leading to a further reduction in wages and an ever-larger burden of poor relief. Further, it seemed in the early 1830s that the poor law was no longer preserving social order at a time of agrarian riots and discontent. In 1834, the solution was to remove control of the poor law from individual parishes, where the vestries and overseers were largely coterminous with the beneficiaries of relief, and to group parishes into unions with Boards of Guardians elected on a franchise that gave more votes to large owners and occupiers of property. The right of appeal from the parish to any Justice of the Peace in the county was abolished, a procedure that had made sense when social order rested on the ability of the local governing elite to exercise discretion and therefore to command deference and respect. An alternative pattern of order emerged after 1834, based on a professional police force, prisons, and workhouses. The elected Guardians would bring the Justices into line, and the new bodies would – at least in theory – obey codes laid down from the center. As a result, spending would be brought under control (Mandler 1987; Crowther 1981).

Similarly, municipal spending fell. The reform of municipal corporations in 1835 removed elite, oligarchic corporations and gave control to modest middle-class ratepayers drawn from small traders and shopkeepers, who were particularly sensitive to the burden of the local property tax or rate. They were likely to remove spendthrift councils at elections, with the danger that concern for their own purses could lead to deterioration in the health and efficiency of towns. Furthermore, spending on many new services rested on support from a local referendum that gave power to ratepayers to block expenditure. Public meetings of owners and ratepayers were called to approve private bills needed for major ventures: the result could be to delay spending but equally to create consent to particular, desirable forms of expenditure when a majority was obtained (Daunton 2008: 102–7). When conflicts did occur over the level of local expenditure, they were confined to the council chamber without threatening the central state. As one politician put it in 1850, 'It is evidently wise to put as little on the Government whose overthrow causes a revolution as you can and to have as much as you can on the local bodies, which may be overthrown a dozen times and nobody be the worse' (qtd. in Waller 1983 244–5). The result was that, at least until the last quarter of the nineteenth century, it was safe to delegate responsibilities to the localities without a fear of spending running out of control and without disrupting the central state.

Although the central government became more coordinated and hypothecation was rejected, there was a different pattern at the local level, where government became more polyarchic, with specific property taxes imposed for various purposes. The Guardians levied a poor rate;

school boards were created in 1870 to provide for elementary schools supported by a separate rate; in addition, the town council levied its own rate. By the third quarter of the nineteenth century, the earlier constraints were weakening. The municipal franchise was widened in 1867 and 1869 and again in 1878 and 1882, and spending levels increased with a new cross-class alliance between large property owners, industrialists, and professionals who wished to invest in the infrastructure of towns and working-class voters who saw benefits from clean water and sanitation (Aidt, Daunton, and Dutta 2007). The provision of public education after 1870 led to rising costs, and from 1894, plural voting was abolished for the poor law so that beneficiaries of relief again had the prospect of a voice in its operation. The various referenda on adopting different services meant that spending not only was delayed by 'economists' but also legitimated by popular support. Specific taxes for specific purposes acted as a ratchet increasing spending (Daunton 2008: 106–7). Not surprisingly, local taxation and expenditure increased more rapidly than central taxation. In 1840, local expenditure amounted to 21.9 percent of total government expenditure; in 1890, 38.4 percent; and in 1910, 47.9 percent. The annual growth rate of central government expenditure was 1.5 percent between 1850 and 1900, and it was 2.9 percent for local government expenditure; the elasticity of government expenditure in respect of GNP was low for the central state and higher for local government (Flora, Kraus and Pfenning 1983: 441; Peacock and Wiseman 1967: 202; Prest 1990; Szreter 1997; Bellamy 1988; Hennock 1963, 1973). As a result, the local tax base – the rates or tax on real property – came under pressure around 1900 and led to a shift in funding toward more buoyant central taxes.

Not only did the central state delegate responsibilities to voluntary associations and the localities; there was also a second form of delegation in tax administration. The potential for conflict in collecting the income tax was minimized by avoiding the need to assess total income. When the income tax was first introduced in 1799, it was levied on global income from all sources, with the result that there was a low level of compliance and considerable tension. In 1803, the tax was transformed and was collected on each schedule – for example, A on real estate or D on trade, industry, and the professions – without seeking to establish the individual's entire income. The result was a significant increase in compliance and in the yield of revenue. The new system rested on the collection of as much tax as possible by deduction at the source, so that a tenant farmer paid his rent to the landowner net of tax and handed the balance to the tax collector; similarly, tax was deducted from interest payments. The main difficulty came in schedule D, where it was impossible to collect at source on a flow of earnings; it was not clear until the end of the year how much profit had been earned and whether it was above the tax threshold. The way around this difficulty was to follow the same pattern as in the land and assessed taxes in the eighteenth century – to delegate tax collection and assessment to lay commissioners, assessors, and collectors. The lay commissioners were drawn from the local business and professional community and had general oversight of the administration of the income tax in the area; lay assessors determined the liability of individual taxpayers; and the money was handed to collectors who were paid a commission. The role of official bureaucrats – the Surveyors – was relatively modest; they were mainly concerned with providing oversight and supplying information to the lay commissioners and assessors. Further, it was left to the commissioners in each district to come to an agreement with organized trade associations on how to treat depreciation allowances in particular trades, a matter of interpretation of the legislation, which was delegated to the localities (*Commissioners of Inland Revenue* 1870: 101–7, 121; *Royal Commission on Income Tax* 1920: pt. 4; *Departmental Committee on Income Tax* 1905: apps. 3–4).

Such an approach seemed curious to commentators from other countries, which had preferred a more centralized and bureaucratic approach (Ingenbleek 1908: 309–10), but it contributed to creating trust in the state. Lay commissioners and assessors entrenched the income tax within civil society, so creating a high level of compliance, trust in the fairness of the tax, and widespread acceptance of the legitimacy of the state. In practice, the power of officials – the Surveyors or inspectors of taxes – increased over time as the system became more complicated with the addition of various allowances to personal income tax and a more sophisticated system of degression and progression. These modifications to the personal income tax meant that there was a trade-off between, on the one hand, equity and balance, which were necessary to maintain consent to taxation, and, on the other hand, higher costs of compliance and administration, with an increase in the power of state bureaucrats (*Royal Commission on Income Tax* 1920: pt. IV). Despite these strains in the system and the change in the balance of power, the principle of lay control continued to sustain widespread trust in the income tax – and the need to work with the taxpaying public to ensure that consent became a leading feature of the rhetoric of the Inland Revenue into the twentieth century.

The administration of the tax system and the construction of compliance started to change at the end of the nineteenth century, away from the use of commissioners to mediate between taxpayers and the state to a growing reliance on the relationship between the Inland Revenue and the taxpayers' professional advisers. The process of reaching agreements and precedents in the interpretation of tax codes was more a matter of negotiation between autonomous professional bodies and tax officials than of formal administrative law. The relationship between these professional advisers and the tax authorities rested on mutual support and respect, for the advisers needed a degree of confidence in the competence of the authorities in interpreting rules, and the authorities needed a degree of confidence in the integrity of the professionals. The nature of the relationship between professions and the state was another area of divergence between Britain and continental Europe.

Tax advice was provided by solicitors and accountants, whose professional status and integrity rested on the Law Society and the Institute of Chartered Accountants. The emergence of these bodies should be considered in the context of two features of the formation of the British state that date from the seventeenth century. The first feature was the notion that the ideal form of law was precedent and immemorial custom, which guaranteed freedom and liberty. As David Sugarman (1996) has suggested, the emphasis on freedom under the law linked Englishness with law and liberty, and legitimated the state. Second, there was the emergence of a public sphere in the eighteenth century in the form of clubs or voluntary hospitals or paving commissioners, which reconstituted civil society and often utilized private legislation to provide services (Brewer 1982; Langford 1991). The large measure of autonomy granted to professional bodies reinforced the wide discretion of the law. The combination of the two elements meant that the state was careful not to interfere with the professions, which had a high degree of autonomy at a time when self-governing professions in France and Germany were being subjected to state control (Burage 1989). The result was important not only for the professions but also for constituting the British state.

The counterpart of the delegation of administration and interpretation was the exclusion of interest groups from any bargaining over tax rates and exemptions to be included in the legislation. The legislation was, as far as possible, general rather than particular, unlike in the United States, where the tax system was written by Congress and was open to lobbying, which resulted in thousands of exemptions, deductions, and credits for various activities, often in particular locations (Steinmo 1989). Such a pattern applied in eighteenth-century Britain, when the fiscal regime was so heavily dependent on indirect taxes and there was a complex process of negotiation among trade interests through a pattern of power-broking, which contributed to the formation of the British state (Brewer 1989: 231–49). In the nineteenth and twentieth centuries, consent was created by different methods such as the exclusion of interest-group negotiation and the propagation of an aura of independence. Unlike in the United States, tax measures emanated from the executive, and in circumstances of some secrecy. The annual budget was written by the Chancellor with the advice of a small group of Treasury officials who had a strong commitment to general measures. The proposals were often not discussed in detail even by the Cabinet, and from the 1870s, the passage of the Finance Bill through the Commons was normally guaranteed as a result of party discipline (Steinmo 1989). Defeat of the budget in the Commons amounted to a vote of no confidence in the government, and the opportunity to bargain in detail over measures was strictly limited. The outcome of this legislative process was that the British tax code gave very few concessions to particular trades or districts. Tax breaks might be offered to certain activities – for example, the purchase of life insurance – or might grant allowances for children. However, these concessions were of general application. The authorities did not wish to become involved in the use of the tax system to encourage particular types of activity: if the government wished to offer encouragement, it should be in the form of explicit grants that were open to parliamentary scrutiny rather than through the gerrymandering of taxes. As the Inland Revenue argued during the First World War, 'The object of taxation, as known in this country, is solely to provide money; taxes are of general application and, as equality of treatment between taxpayer and taxpayer is a cardinal principle, the scope and conditions of liability are closely defined by statute and discretionary powers are taboo' (Daunton 1996c: 899).

The same sentiment contributed to the weakening of the associational voluntarism that was so strong in the nineteenth century. The desire for general rules on the disbursement of public money meant that the Treasury was uneasy about allowing charities to have tax breaks. Equality of treatment among taxpayers required everyone to pay tax on their income rather than to set donations against tax; any grants for education or hospitals would be made by the government from its revenue rather than by taxpayers diverting their taxes from the state to objects of their own choosing (Daunton 1996b: 191–3). Even when the state did delegate some authority for the disbursement of money to friendly societies and trade unions with the status of approved societies under the National Insurance Acts of 1911, their autonomy was curtailed and their authority to decide whether to spend their surpluses on, say, dental care was removed (Whiteside 1983). There was, therefore, a tension between the Treasury's concern for control of expenditure and the use of delegated bodies, which tended to be resolved in favor of centralization. The local auxiliaries might no longer be so dependable, for Guardians and town councils could fall into the hands of Labour with the extension of the franchise and the end of plural voting, which favored larger property owners. Spending was more easily controlled by relocating authority to the center and removing the danger that national finances be subverted by irresponsible localities. Consequently, 'the municipal culture of the local state with its associated agencies slowly disintegrated' (Morris 2002: 415–8, 425–6). In the nineteenth century, the central state shrank in the face of voluntarism and the local state; in the twentieth century, the process was reversed.

The fiscal system should therefore be located in the context of voluntarism and the strength of civil society, the role of municipal culture, and the relative autonomy of professional bodies. The British fiscal system combined a diffuse pattern of delegation or subsidiarity in the collection and administration of the tax, with an attempt to preserve generalized legislation that removed discretionary power from the authorities. A comparison with other countries suggests that Britain was unusual in this combination of features, which helped to create a high degree of acceptance of taxation – and hence an effective state. The strategies of balance and consent, of equity and fairness, prepared the ground for a shift to central government responsibility for an increasing range of functions in response to the mounting crisis of financing both voluntary and local bodies in the early twentieth century. By about 1900, the voluntary hospitals were facing problems in securing sufficient donations and subscriptions to meet their rising costs; friendly societies, which supplied sick pay and medical treatment to their members, were facing mounting financial pressure as a result of actuarial miscalculations and competition for new members; and the local property tax proved inflexible and regressive in the face of the increased costs of urban government. As delegation to voluntary and local bodies faltered, it proved possible to turn to the central state – and above all the income tax – for a solution (Daunton 1996b).

## 1.5 Conclusion

The shackles on the state were loosened by the First World War, which marked a displacement in the share of government revenue in GNP, without the subsequent reduction experienced after the Napoleonic Wars. The use of the income tax as a shackle on the state and the process of delegation in administration, combined with hostility to specific exemptions, created very broad acceptance at an earlier date than in most other European countries. By creating the appearance of neutrality as part of the defense of property and the state, there was a greater willingness than in other countries to use central, direct taxation to fund new welfare services.

The process of establishing trust in the fiscal system is therefore complicated and contingent. It cannot be read from the level of extraction, for there was a mounting criticism of taxation in the early nineteenth century as expenditure fell as a proportion of the GNP. Equally, there was a successful negotiation of a massive increase in the level of extraction between the two world wars without a serious loss of trust and consent (Daunton 2002). Of course, the way money was spent – or perceived to be spent – was an important consideration but is not as simple as it might first appear. Expenditure on warfare might be tolerated in one period when linked with patriotism and hostility to an external other; it might be rejected in another period when militarism was seen as in some sense un-British. The same point applies to expenditure on welfare, which might have been seen at one time as a socially desirable pooling of risks and at another time as the source of national decay. Clearly, there were other factors at work, not least the ability of politicians, as a conscious act of policy, to foster a sense of disinterestedness and an image of the state as class neutral. This process was linked with carefully devised procedures to ensure that government finances were transparent and accountable, so that taxpayers were assured that the money was spent in the way that had been agreed on. Transparency in expenditure was complemented by opacity in the procedures by which the structure of taxes was adjusted. Alterations in taxes were excluded as far as possible from the interplay of interest groups, to prevent any suggestion that the fiscal system was open to special pleading. Further, the administration of taxes in Britain did not create the rigidities found in France, where the system was more inflexible and adjustments created problems. The method of assessing and collecting taxes in Britain worked with civil society and limited hostility to bureaucratic intervention. By these means, the British state in the mid-nineteenth century was able, with a remarkable degree of success, to move from deep suspicion to widespread acceptance of taxation. Collective action and taxation were given new legitimacy: the state was constrained and, perhaps more important, trusted and so released for effective action.

## References

Aidt, T. S., Daunton, M. and Dutta, J. (2007) "The retrenchment hypothesis: An example from the extension of the franchise in England and Wales." Cambridge Working Papers in Economics 0818. www.econ.cam.ac.uk/faculty/aidt/papers/web/Retrenchment.pdf (accessed August 16, 2007).

Bayly, C. A. (1994a) "Returning the British to South Asian history: The limits of colonial hegemony," *South Asia* 17, 1–25.

Bayly, C. A. (1994b) "The British military-fiscal state and indigenous resistance: India, 1750–1820," in L. Stone (ed.) *An Imperial State at War*. London: Routledge, 322–54.

Baysinger, B. and Tollison, R. (1980) "Chaining Leviathan: The case of Gladstonian finance," *History of Political Economy*, 12, 206–13.

Bellamy, C. (1988) *Administering Central-Local Relations, 1871–1919: The Local Government Board in Its Fiscal and Political Context*. Manchester: Manchester University Press.

Biagini, E. F. (1991) "'Popular Liberals,' Gladstonian finance and the debate on taxation, 1860–1874," in E. F. Biagini and A. J. Reid (eds.) *Currents of Radicalism: Popular Radicalism, Organized Labour and Party Politics in Britain, 1850–1914*. Cambridge: Cambridge University Press, 134–62.

Biagini, E. F. (1992) *Liberty, Retrenchment and Reform: Popular Liberalism in the Age of Gladstone, 1860–1880*. Cambridge: Cambridge University Press.

Binney, J. E. D. (1958) *British Public Finance and Administration, 1774–1792*. Oxford: Oxford University Press.

Brewer, J. (1982) "Commercialisation and politics," in N. McKendrick, J. Brewer, and J. Plumb (eds.) *The Birth of a Consumer Society: The Commercialisation of Eighteenth-Century England*. London: Hutchinson, 197–262.

Brewer, J. (1989) *The Sinews of Power: War, Money and the English State, 1688–1783*. London: Unwin Hyman.

Burage, M. (1989) "Revolution as a starting point for the comparative analysis of the French, American and English legal profession," in R. L. Abel and P. S. C. Lewis (eds.) *Lawyers in Society*, vol. 3. Berkeley: University of California Press, 322–74.

Clarke, P. F. (1978) *Liberals and Social Democrats*. Cambridge: Cambridge University Press.

Collini, S. (1991) *Public Moralists: Political Thought and Intellectual Life in Britain, 1850–1930*. Oxford: Oxford University Press.

Crowther, M. (1981) *The Workhouse System, 1834–1929: The History of an English Social Institution*. London: Methuen.

Daunton, M. J. (1996a) "The political economy of death duties: Harcourt's budget of 1894," in N. Harte and R. Quinault (eds.) *Land and Society in Britain,*

*1700–1914: Essays in Honour of F. M. L. Thompson*. Manchester: Manchester University Press, 137–71.

Daunton, M. (1996b) "Payment and participation: Welfare and state-formation in Britain, 1900–51," *Past and Present*, 150, 169–216.

Daunton, M. (1996c) "How to pay for the war: State, society and taxation in Britain, 1917–24," *English Historical Review*, 111, 882–919.

Daunton, M. J. (2001) *Trusting Leviathan: The Politics of British Taxation, 1799–1914*. Cambridge: Cambridge University Press.

Daunton, M. (2002) *Just Taxes: The Politics of Taxation in Britain, 1914–1979*. Cambridge: Cambridge University Press.

Daunton, M. J. (2006) "The fiscal-military state and the Napoleonic Wars: Britain and France compared," in D. Cannadine (ed.) *Trafalgar in History: A Battle and Its Afterlife*. London: Palgrave, 18–43.

Daunton, M. (2008) *State and Market in Victorian Britain: War, Welfare and Capitalism*. Woodbridge, UK: Boydell.

Dickson, P. G. M. (1967) *The Financial Revolution in England: A Study in the Development of Public Credit*. London: Macmillan.

Duffy, A. E. P. (1961–2) "New unionism in Britain, 1889–90: A reappraisal," *Economic History Review*, 2, 306–19.

Epstein, S. R. (2000) *Freedom and Growth: Markets and State in Pre-Modern Europe*. London: Routledge.

Ferguson, N. (1995) *Paper and Iron: Hamburg Business and German Politics in the Era of Inflation, 1897–1927*. Cambridge: Cambridge University Press.

Ferguson, N. (2001) *The Cash Nexus: Money and Power in the Modern World, 1700–2000*. London: Penguin.

Flora, P., F. Kraus and W. Pfenning (1983) *State, Economy and Society in Western Europe, 1815–1975, Vol. 1, The Growth of Mass Democracies and Welfare States*. London: Macmillan.

Forsyth, D. J. (1993) *The Crisis of Liberal Italy: Monetary and Financial Policy, 1914–22*. Cambridge: Cambridge University Press.

Gross, J.-P. (1993) "Progressive taxation and social justice in eighteenth-century France," *Past and Present*, 140, 79–126.

Harling, P. (1996) *The Waning of "Old Corruption": The Politics of Economical Reform in Britain, 1779–1846*. Oxford: Oxford University Press.

Harling, P. and Mandler, P. (1993) "From 'fiscal-military' state to laissez-faire state, 1769–1850," *Journal of British Studies*, 32, 44–70.

Harris, J. (1983) "The transition to high politics in English social policy, 1880–1914," in M. Bentley and J. Stevenson (eds.) *High and Low Politics in Modern Britain*. Oxford: Oxford University Press, 58–79.

Hawkins, A. (1989) "'Parliamentary government' and Victorian political parties, c. 1830–1880," *English Historical Review*, 104, 638–69.

Hennock, E. P. (1963) "Finance and politics in urban local government in England, 1835–1900," *Historical Journal*, 6, 212–25.

Hennock, E. P. (1973) *Fit and Proper Persons: Ideal and Reality in Nineteenth-Century Urban Government*. London: Edward Arnold.

Hennock, E. P. (1987) *British Social Reform and German Precedents: The Case of Social Insurance, 1880–1914*. Oxford: Oxford University Press.

Hilton, B. (1977) *Corn, Cash and Commerce: The Economic Policies of the Tory Government, 1815–1830*. Oxford: Oxford University Press.

Hope-Jones, A. (1939) *Income Tax in the Napoleonic Wars*. Cambridge: Cambridge University Press.

Hoppit, J. (1990) "Attitudes to credit in Britain, 1680–1790," *Historical Journal*, 33, 305–22.

Hoppit, J. (2002) "Checking the Leviathan, 1688–1832," in D. Winch and P. K. O'Brien (eds.) *The Political Economy of British Historical Experience, 1688–1914*. Oxford: Oxford University Press, 267–94.

Ingenbleek, J. (1908) *Impots directs et indirects sur le revenue: la contribution personnel en Belgique, l'Einkommensteuer en Prusse, l'income tax en Angleterre.* Brussels: Misch et Thron.

Innes, J. (1994) "The domestic face of the military-fiscal state: government and society in eighteenth-century Britain," in L. Stone (ed.) *An Imperial State at War*. London: Routledge, 96–127.

Koepke, R. L. (1979–80) "La Loi des patentes of 1844," *French Historical Studies*, 11, 398–440.

Langford, P. (1991) *Public Life and the Propertied Englishman, 1689–1798*. Oxford: Oxford University Press.

Langford, P. (1997) "Politics and manners from Sir Robert Walpole to Sir Robert Peel," in *Proceedings of the British Academy, 94, 1996 Lectures and Memoirs*. Oxford: Oxford University Press, 103–25.

Leathers, C. G. (1986) "Gladstonian finance and the Virginia school of public finance," *History of Political Economy*, 18, 515–21.

Maier, C. (1975) *Recasting Bourgeois Europe: Stabilization in France, Germany and Italy in the Decade after World War I*. Princeton, NJ: Princeton University Press.

Mandler, P. (1987) "Making of the new poor law *redivivus*," *Past and Present*, 117, 131–57.

Mann, M. (1993) *The Sources of Social Power, II: The Rise of Classes and National-States, 1760–1914*. Cambridge: Cambridge University Press.

Mathias, P. and O'Brien, P. K. (1976) "Taxation in Britain and France, 1715–1810: A comparison of the social and economic incidence of taxes collected for the central government," *Journal of European Economic History*, 5, 601–50.

Matthew, H. C. G. (1979) "Disraeli, Gladstone and the politics of mid-Victorian budgets," *Historical Journal*, 22, 615–43.

Matthew, H. C. G. (1986) *Gladstone, 1809–1874*. Oxford: Oxford University Press.

McKibbin, R. (1990) *Ideologies of Class: Social Relations in Britain, 1880–1950*. Oxford: Oxford University Press.

Middleton, R. (1996) *Government versus the Market: The Growth of the Public Sector. Economic Management and British Economic Performance, c. 1890–1979*. Cheltenham: Edward Elgar.

Mitchell, B. R. and Deane, P. (1962) *Abstract of British Historical Statistics*. Cambridge: Cambridge University Press.

Morris, R. J. (2000) "Structure, culture and society in British towns," in M. Daunton (ed.) *Cambridge Urban History of Britain*, vol. 3. Cambridge: Cambridge University Press, 395–426.

Murray, B. K. (1980) *The People's Budget, 1909/10 Lloyd George and Liberal Politics*. Oxford: Oxford University Press.

O'Brien, P. K. (1988) "The political economy of British taxation, 1660–1815," *Economic History Review*, 2nd ser., 41, 1–32.

O'Brien, P. K. (2002) "Fiscal exceptionalism: Great Britain and its European rivals from Civil War to the triumph at Trafalgar and Waterloo," in D. Winch and P. K. O'Brien (eds.) *The Political Economy of British Historical Experience, 1688–1914*. Oxford: Oxford University Press, 245–65.

Offer, A. (1981) *Property and Politics, 1870–1914: Landownership, Law, Ideology and Urban Development in England*. Cambridge: Cambridge University Press.

Peacock, A. and Wiseman, J. (1967) *The Growth of Public Expenditure in the United Kingdom*. London: Allen and Unwin.

Peden, G. C. (2002) "From cheap government to efficient government: The political economy of public expenditure in the United Kingdom, 1832–1914," in D. Winch and P. K. O'Brien (eds.) *The Political Economy of British Historical Experience, 1688–1914*. Oxford: Oxford University Press, 351–80.

Pocock, J. G. A. (1985) *Virtue, Commerce and History: Essays on Political Thought and History, Chiefly in the Eighteenth Century*. Cambridge: Cambridge University Press.

Prest, J. (1990) *Liberty and Locality: Parliament, Permissive Legislation and Ratepayers Democracies in the Nineteenth Century*. Oxford: Oxford University Press.

Read, D. (1987) *Peel and the Victorians*. Oxford: Oxford University Press.

Rubinstein, W. D. (1983) "The end of 'old corruption' in Britain, 1780–1860," *Past and Present*, 101, 55–86.

Schremmer, D. E. (1989) "Taxation and public finance: Britain, France and Germany," in P. Mathias and S. Pollard (eds.) *Cambridge Economic History of Europe, Vol. 8, The Industrial Economies: The Development of Economic and Social Policies*. Cambridge: Cambridge University Press, 315–94.

Steinmo, S. (1989) "Political institutions and tax policy in the United States, Sweden and Britain," *World Politics*, 41, 500–35.

Sugarman, D. (1996) "Bourgeois collectivism, professional power and the boundaries of the state: The private and public life of the Law Society, 1825–1914," *International Journal of the Legal Profession*, 3, 81–135.

Szreter, S. (1997) "Economic growth, disruption, deprivation, disease and death: Or the importance of the politics of public health for development," *Population and Development Review*, 23, 693–728.

Taylor, M. (1995) *The Decline of British Radicalism, 1847–1860*. Oxford: Oxford University Press.

Thompson, E. P. (1963) *The Making of the English Working Class*. London: Gollancz.

Torrance, J. (1978) "Social class and bureaucratic intervention: The commissioners for examining the public accounts, 1780–87," *Past and Present*, 78, 56–81.

Wahrman, D. (1995) *Imagining the Middle Class: The Political Representation of Class in Britain, c. 1780–1840*. Cambridge: Cambridge University Press.

Waller, P. (1983) *Town, City and Nation: England, 1850–1914*. Oxford: Oxford University Press.

Whiteside, N. (1983) "Private agencies for public purposes," *Journal of Social Policy*, 12, 165–93.


## Sources

Peel, Robert, *Parliamentary Debates 3rd series 61*, 11 March, 1842.

PP 1828 V. *Second Report from Select Committee on Public Income and Expenditure of the UK, Ordnance Estimates.*

PP 1857 (2nd sess.) IX. *Report from the Select Committee on Public Monies*, appendix 1, "Memorandum on financial control put in by the Chancellor of the Exchequer, April 1857."

PP 1870 XX. *Report of the Commissioners of the Inland Revenue on the Duties under Their Management for the Years 1856 to 1869*, vol. 1.

PP 1905 XLIV. *Report of the Departmental Committee on Income Tax 1905*, appendices 3–4.

PP 1920 XVIII. *Report of the Royal Commission in the Income Tax*, part 4.

# The Development of Public Finance in the Netherlands, 1815–1914

## Jan Luiten van Zanden and Arthur van Riel

### 2.1 Introduction

Public finance, to a large extent, reflects the balance of power between the social classes controlling the state and the basic institutions underlying its society and economy. The nineteenth century was a period of dramatic changes in political relationships, which resulted, after an initial retreat into conservative monarchism during the years after the 1815 restoration, in a pan-European process of democratization during the second half of the period. These processes – restoration after 1815, followed by a move toward liberalism in the 1840s, again followed by the gradual extension of the franchise in the post-1870 period – to a large extent shaped the development of public finance, as this chapter demonstrates. This interaction between the political developments, the way in which the state was governed, and the dynamics of public finance – patterns of taxation, spending and debt management – are the focus of this chapter on the Netherlands. The period has been divided into three parts, thus making it possible to analyze the three major experiments that were carried out: first, a strong monarchy with limited parliamentary influence (in combination with a union of the Northern Netherlands with Belgium); second, the liberal offensive that came gained momentum during the 1840s and dictated the political agenda until the mid-1860s; and third, the rise of modern mass movements (trade unions, political parties) that began in earnest in the 1870s and led to a gradual extension of the franchise and a renewed restructuring of the political map of the

This contribution is to a large extent based on the work of van Zanden and van Riel (2004).

country, slowly resulting in a move toward the welfare functions that the twentieth-century state developed on a much larger scale.

These changes and developments built on pre-1800 foundations. Public finance in the nineteenth-century Netherlands was based on a long tradition of relatively well-functioning capital markets, and close cooperation between urban bourgeoisie and the state had produced sophisticated ways of financing government expenditure – among others, relatively modern taxes on income and wealth. The taxation levels in the sixteenth- and seventeenth-century Netherlands, and Holland in particular, were much higher than elsewhere (van Zanden and Prak 2006). However, the decentralized structure of the Dutch Republic had created free-rider problems, which were surmountable in times of crisis and extreme pressure from external aggression (e.g., during the war with Spain between 1572 and 1648) but became more difficult to manage during the course of the eighteenth century. This led to a very unbalanced structure of taxation, in which Holland paid a much higher share of total taxation than its population and/or wealth justified (van Zanden and van Riel 2004: chap. 1). In the long term, more precisely after a lost war against Great Britain, this factor led to near bankruptcy of the state, and after the liberation by the French in 1795, to the creation of a unitary state to cope with these problems. The French, however, also considered the Netherlands rich bounty that had to be squeezed to finance its military ambitions on the Continent. This further contributed to the growth of public debt after 1795, until Napoléon in 1811, after the full integration of the Netherlands into the French Empire, decided to reduce public debt by two-thirds. Another inheritance from earlier times, one that would play a big role in financial developments during the nineteenth century, was the large colonial empire created by the Dutch East Indies Company, whose debts and possessions were taken over by the state when the company went bankrupt in 1799.

## 2.2 The Autocratic Experiment of Willem I, 1815–40

The financial development of the new kingdom of the Netherlands created in 1814–15 was, to a large extent, dominated by the complex inheritance of the Dutch Republic (1579–1795) and the revolutionary period that had followed after the French conquest of the country in 1795. The huge government debt, the result of the attempt to be a major player in the European arena during the seventeenth and eighteenth centuries, as well as exploitation by the French after 1795, was the most durable and pressing part of this inheritance. After the reform of the public debt in 1814, its total amount was 1.726 million guilders, of which one-third was actual debt, on which interest was paid, and two-thirds deferred (to be transformed again into actual debt according to a schedule covering the following three hundred years!), a sum of 440 percent of total gross domestic product. The actual debt was, by implication, 147 percent of GDP, and interest payments amounted to 3.7 percent of GDP! The Dutch, and especially the dominant Holland urban elite, had invested a sizable part of their wealth in government debt (and this share increased the more closely linked one was to the political establishment), and its redemption had been and continued to be a dominant theme in government policy.

On the asset side of the equation, things looked brighter: the public debt pressed on a highly commercial economy, in which high incomes were being earned (although times had been better before the 1790s), with a wealthy population used to paying considerable direct and indirect taxes. Moreover, the revolutionary reforms of the 1790s and 1800s had brought the introduction of a centralized system of public finance, which solved the free-rider problems inherent to the decentralized state structure of the pre-1795 republic and improved capabilities of taxing the peripheral provinces of the state, which had largely escaped heavy taxation before 1795. On top of this, the Congress of Vienna enlarged the kingdom by incorporating the Southern Netherlands, thus more than doubling the population that could be taxed to sustain the debt. In return, however, the new kingdom was supposed to invest heavily in defense, especially along its southern border with France, the country that had to be kept under control.

What was also new was the role played by the king, Willem I, who managed to get a constitution (in 1814–15) that gave him enormous powers in the field of government policy, and in particular in financial matters, which he would use to gradually sidetrack the parliament and to increasingly dominate the political playing field. The 1815–40 period is therefore the only experiment in near-autocratic rule that the Netherlands has on offer, an experiment that, to make a long story short, ended in a series of disasters, beginning with the secession of Belgium in 1830 (terminating the kingdom as Willem had conceived of it in 1814–15) and resulting in the near bankruptcy of the state in the early 1840s (when the national debt increased to more than 200 percent of GDP). This led to the early retirement of Willem I and was followed by a switch toward liberal democracy in the rest of the decade.

What went wrong? Was it the personal failure of the king? In fact, Willem I was a highly competent politician and administrator, extremely hard-working, open to new ideas (in particular during his early years), and arguably a financial genius who was able to design numerous ingenious plans to further the economic and financial development of the nation. He founded the Nederlandsche Bank (the new central bank, in 1814) almost single-handedly, pioneered investment banking in the south (by setting up the Société Générale), established a major trading body in the north (the Nederlandsche Handel-Maatschappij, or NHM), introduced a highly successful system of colonial exploitation in Indonesia (which is discussed herein), and initiated many other plans and policies, some of which were successful and others failures. Willem I planned and financed the construction of canals, subsidized newly emerging industries, in particular in the south (e.g., the initiatives by John Cockerill), and tried to reform education; in short, at first sight, he did everything one could hope for from an enlightened ruler. Yet his grand scheme failed. Why?

One of the main challenges of the new kingdom created in 1815 was to merge the tax systems of the North and the South, to sustain the high public debt and to pay for the expensive plans of the king. The Belgians were used to low taxes, dominated by high import or export levies, to protect their growing industry. The Dutch were used to very high taxes, in the form of direct taxes on wealth, which were very unpopular with the Belgian aristocracy, and indirect taxes on consumption (e.g., beer, bread, meat, gin). Moreover, Dutch merchants strongly disliked the import and export taxes introduced during the French period, because they interfered too much with international trade. Initially, the king attempted to find compromise solutions, but these generally brought in insufficient funds and, therefore, led to increasing deficits. In the early 1820s, he was more or less forced to introduce a system that was largely based on the Dutch model, which led to much resentment in the South. The way taxes were raised not only was inconsistent with southern preferences (e.g., in terms of protection of industry) but also resulted in the South paying much more than it received in terms of government expenditure: between 40 percent and 50 percent of taxes originated in the South, whereas the South's share of expenditure was between 20 percent and 25 percent. The main reason for this low share in expenditure was that interest payment on public debt increasingly dominated the budget, its share

Table 2.1. *Income and Expenditure of the Central Government during the Reign of Willem I, 1814–40 (in million guilders)*

|  | 1814–20 | 1821–5 | 1826–30 | 1831–5 | 1836–40 |
|---|---|---|---|---|---|
| *Income* | | | | | |
| Direct taxation | 16.1 | 15.5 | 14.3 | 17.4 | 16.0 |
| Indirect taxation | 7.0 | 6.0 | 6.7 | 7.1 | 7.5 |
| Excises | 8.3 | 11.2 | 12.0 | 13.2 | 16.0 |
| Tariffs | 3.7 | 3.5 | 4.0 | 3.3 | 4.0 |
| Other | 6.6 | 6.9 | 8.0 | 5.6 | 6.5 |
| TOTAL | 41.7 | 43.2 | 45.0 | 46.5 | 49.9 |
| *Expenditure* | | | | | |
| Finance | 21.3 | 35.0 | 43.6 | 43.6 | 57.4 |
| Defense | 28.0 | 20.9 | 21.9 | 38.4 | 22.8 |
| Other | 12.5 | 14.1 | 16.4 | 8.3 | 4.8 |
| TOTAL | 61.8 | 70.0 | 81.8 | 90.3 | 85.0 |
| Percentage of GDP | 14.3 | 18.9 | 19.8 | 20.9 | 16.3 |
| *Net transfers* | | | | | |
| Belgium | 11.8 | 25.3 | 28.8 | – | – |
| Indonesia (*batig slot*) | – | – | – | 10.5 | 28.4 |
| Percentage of expenditure | 19.1 | 36.1 | 35.2 | 11.6 | 33.4 |
| Deficit | 8.3 | 1.5 | 8.0 | 33.2 | 6.7 |
| Percentage of expenditure | 13.4 | 2.1 | 9.8 | 36.8 | 7.8 |

*Source:* van Zanden 1996.

increasing from about 21 percent in 1816–20 to 44 percent in 1825–9 (Table 2.1). The estimated transfer of funds from the South to the North increased from about 12 million guilders annually between 1816–20 to almost 30 million guilders in 1825–9 (Table 2.1), amounting to about 5 percent of Belgian GDP in the latter years. This created a deep resentment and was one of the factors behind the breakdown of the kingdom in 1830; it is no coincidence that the Belgian secession occurred after these facts had again been discussed in the parliament, where the powerlessness of Belgian representatives to change things had become evident.[1]

The underlying problem of the 1820s had been that, despite the heavy taxation introduced in the new kingdom, the state continued to run considerable deficits (see Figure 2.2). These resulted from the king's many ambitious projects, which the parliament was unable to check because

---

[1] The story is, as always, much more complex: religious policies and educational policies also contributed much to the divide between the North and the South.

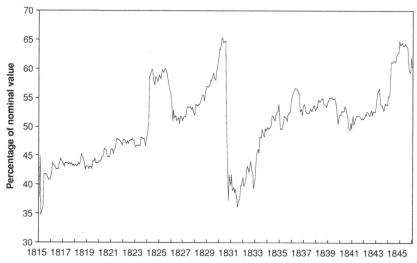

Figure 2.1. The price of NWS bonds (2.5%), monthly figures, 1815–45 (percentage of nominal value). *Source:* Compiled from *Prijscourant der Effecten*, 1815–45. The figures relate to end-of-month quotations.

of the overwhelming position of the king in combination with the large deficits on the colonial budget (partly a result of the expensive Java War of 1825–9). The Belgian secession came as a sudden blow to the ambitions of the king and caused an enormous loss of both national and international prestige. The stock market's confidence in the national debt and in government in general had increased during the 1820s, as is evident from the prices of government bonds (Figure 2.1). Yet the market collapsed in August 1830, when the success of Belgian revolt became clear. Suddenly, the net transfer of almost 30 million guilders disappeared from the budget, but the crisis of confidence was suppressed to some extent because of the special wartime circumstances. These gave the king the power to be even more secretive about the state of the public finances and to increase taxes, in particular excises on foodstuffs and peat. Nevertheless, despite the higher taxation, the phony war with Belgium (which continued until 1839) contributed to significantly increased expenditure and deficits (Figure 2.2).

On a more positive note, at least from the Dutch perspective, there was the success of the new colonial policy in Indonesia. In 1830, Willem I appointed another governor-general, Johannes van den Bosch, with the explicit aim to abandon the liberal economic policies of the 1820s and to introduce a new system of forced cultivation of cash crops, which

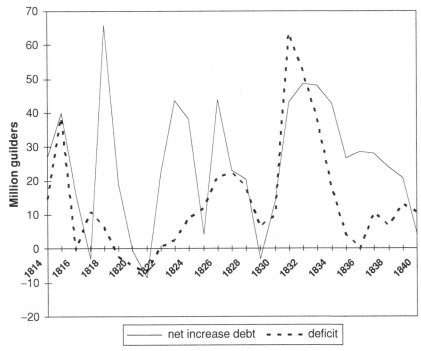

Figure 2.2. Estimates of the budget deficit and of the net-increase of public debt, 1814–40 (in million guilders). *Source:* van Zanden (1996).

later became known as the cultivation system. In this system, local farmers were compelled to set aside part of their land for cultivating export crops such as coffee, sugar and indigo, and to supply these to the government in exchange for wages, which were used to pay their land taxes. The indigenous elite and Dutch civil servants were given a share in the profits of the system and therefore had a vested interest in ensuring that the local population met the responsibilities forced on them. Finally, Chinese and later Dutch entrepreneurs were awarded contracts by the government to process the produce (especially sugar); contracts contained agreements on the supply of processed sugar from particular regions against certain conditions. Forced labor was also used in the transport and processing of goods for export. The NHM was given a monopoly over the purchase, transport and sale of these products in the Netherlands. Although the colonial treasury was the recipient of the net profits from sales, the NHM was generously compensated for the costs, including, for example, extra costs due to the higher freight charges of Dutch shipping companies (Elson 1994; Fasseur 1975).

The instant success of the system was due to its peculiar mix of forced labor and monetary incentives. Export production expanded strongly during the 1830s, and the deficit on the colonial budget turned into a large surplus, which was transferred to the Netherlands. Already in the second half of the 1830s, it matched the surplus that had been acquired from Belgium before 1830 (see Table 2.1); however, the king considered colonial administration a royal privilege, and part of the money flowing from Java was used for his personal projects and ambitions, something that was largely concealed to the public until 1839–40. Despite the important colonial surplus (*batig slot*), deficits in the 1830s were huge, and the public debt continued to grow rapidly. When, after peace with Belgium, the poor condition of public finances became widely known and the state was almost unable to honor its obligations, a crisis of confidence ensued. Finally, after having been suppressed and ignored for quite some time, the parliament came into action and made it clear that it had lost confidence in the king and in his servant, the minister of finance, which started a chain reaction to force the resignation of Willem I and induce a change of regime toward a more balanced distribution of power between those in office and the parliament.

The ultimate cause of the failure of Willem I's fiscal policy must be sought in the institutional infrastructure, particularly in the Constitution of 1815. The system of government finance and the distribution of executive and legislative powers it introduced were highly ambivalent. The parliament's influence was limited and stripped even further, whereas that of the king was unrestricted to the point of turning a financial conflict into a constitutional one. A similar financial policy would, for instance, not have been possible during the republic, given the fact that, for most of its existence, the group that decided on government outlays and taxation was the same that had invested its wealth in government paper: by and large, the financial elite of Holland. This situation, however, in turn had led to inflexibility, given that a lack of alternative investment opportunities of adequate size deprived investors of the incentive to institute redemption and reduce the tax burden. For this reason, the eighteenth-century attempt to repay the debt was resisted, which in the long term led to a rise in the national debt and a commensurate increase in the tax burden. The British system of separate government and crown, in which the monarch and his or ministers annually seek parliamentary approval for their proposed budgets, which set the allocation of expenditure and taxes, had been explicitly created with the purpose of curbing the monarch's prerogative and expanding the influence of taxpayers. However, in the version introduced in the Netherlands in 1815, equal balance of power between monarch and the parliament was absent. This allowed Willem I ample opportunity to develop the tangled financial policies mentioned here. The weakness of the opposition combined with the ambitions and personality of Willem I complete the explanation of the events.

The 1839 financial and political crisis sealed the fate of Willem I's autocratic experiment. He had been unable to command sufficient loyalty from the citizens of Holland in decisive moments, despite several attempts. An example of this was the debt reform of 1814, which planted the seed for the financial problems Willem I would struggle with throughout his reign. In the 1830s, Willem I became entangled in the contradictions created by his own policies: to uphold his position, he found it increasingly necessary to hold back information on the true extent of the problems. When these became apparent, he lost almost all his authority. The 1840 reform of the constitution and the abdication of Willem I partly solved the problems. The king's failure meant that his direct successors, Willem II and Willem III, were no longer able to adopt similar policies. Thus, the period after 1840 would witness a search for a better way of formalizing political relations between the monarch and the parliament.

## 2.3 The Liberal Offensive: 1840–70

In the thirty years after the abdication of Willem I, Dutch society saw the evolution and execution of a consistent liberal program of political and economic reforms. The former increased the power of the parliament and the influence of its underlying constituency, while the latter contributed to limiting the influence of the state, reducing the size of the public debt, and curbing taxation. Together, the reforms had long-term positive consequences for the national economy. For the purposes of this chapter, it is sufficient to say that the most important political changes were the constitutional reform of 1840 and the introduction of a new constitution in 1848. With the introduction of the 1848 constitution, the Netherlands unwittingly adopted a modern constitution, mainly because of the brilliant liberal politician Johan Rudolf Thorbecke, who redressed the major flaws in the previous drafts. One of the reasons the rather diffuse political and economic ideas that had traditionally dominated political thinking of the Dutch bourgeoisie converged into a consistent program in a relatively short time was probably the fact that Willem I had personified the antithesis of these traditions: as already argued here, he demonstrated his indifference to the interests of the urban, middle-class taxpayer; he opted for interventionist policies; and he mismanaged government finances to such an extent that bankruptcy of the state seemed imminent.

Together with the rising international tide of liberal economic ideas, the new constitutional settings helped articulate the reforms that were deemed necessary for the rejuvenation of the economic structure of the Netherlands. There was another new element: the 1840s were years of depression that struck the Dutch economy quite hard. The downturn of the economy was also linked to the country's gradual loss of international economic leadership; the liberal plans seemed to offer solutions for this crisis.

Liberal reforms began with restructuring the public debt. Under pressure from the minister of finance, Floris van Hall, high-yielding debt titles were swapped against low-yielding ones, to ensure the long-term security of the debt. This reorganization was also followed by a long period of conservative financial policies aimed to balance the budget and, if possible, lower taxation levels to create more room for private enterprise. An important factor that made large reductions in spending possible was that the Netherlands finally came to terms with the fact that it was a second-rank power, one that no longer had an important role to play in international politics and that, in case of war, would rather remain neutral. These policies led to a strong decline in government spending as a share of national income, dropping from about 12 percent to 14 percent in the early 1840s to 8 percent to 9 percent in the late 1850s, and even to less than 8 percent in the 1870s (see Figure 2.3). The relative decline of government spending was made possible by a fall in the share of interest payments in the budget. In the 1840s, the ratio between interest payments and total expenditure had been as high as 60 percent to 65 percent, reflecting the urgency of the financial crisis; after 1850, this started to fall to slightly more than 50 percent in 1860 and further to about 40 percent in 1880.

Moreover, in the early 1850s, when the financial crisis seemed to be a thing of the past, the liberals began to institute a long series of tax reforms, the most important of which were the abolition of excises on pork and lamb (1852), milling (1855), and peat and coal (1863), as well as the special stamp duty on newspapers (1871). In 1865, the extremely inefficient system of local excises was abolished (van der Voort 1994: 116). Another important element of the liberal program, which was realized after the first reforms in the tax system had been implemented, was

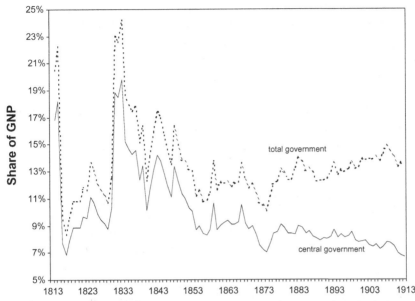

Figure 2.3. Expenditure by the central government (lower line) and total government as share of GDP, 1813–1913. *Source:* Database national accounts; see Smits, Horlings and van Zanden (2000).

the increase of investment in infrastructure. This had been crowded out by financial considerations during the 1830s and 1840s, a factor that had led, for example, to the lagging behind of railway construction in the Netherlands.

Together with the international economic boom of the 1850s and 1860s, the liberal reform package resulted in renewed growth of the Dutch economy. This was largely made possible by the continuation of the cultivation system, a set of policies ultimately based on coercion and the monopoly of power in Indonesia. What politicians such as Thorbecke did during the 1840s and 1850s was streamline the system to increase the share of surplus going to the state at the expense of the share going to other partners, such as indigenous elites and the NHM, the trading body that organized the system. The streamlining and increase of export prices of coffee and sugar during the 1850s and 1860s led to an enormous growth of the *batig slot*, which truly became the cork on which Dutch state and society floated. When compared with total internal taxation in the Netherlands, the colonial surplus was indeed high: it ranged from more than 30 percent in the 1830s to more than 50 percent in the 1850s. In other words, if this surplus suddenly disappeared, a balanced budget would require internal taxation to increase by 50 percent. The direct contribution of the surplus to GDP was on average between 2.8 percent and 3.8 percent, which is a quite substantial net addition to income. In terms of the GDP of Java, the colonial drain was even bigger: between 1835 and 1865, it amounted to an average of 6 percent of GDP! So, the success of the liberal reform program was, to a large extent, grafted onto the continued exploitation of the colony; its strategy was liberal in the Netherlands, conservative in the colonies.

Only during the 1860s did the direction of colonial policy really change. The abolition of the cultivation system and its replacement by a system in which private enterprise would play a pivotal role in the exploitation of the colony became the goals of colonial policy. In slightly more than a decade, the complete liberalization of trade with the colony (and abolition of the NHM's monopoly), the termination of forced cultivation of sugar for the colonial government, and the opening up of the colony to private enterprise was realized (Oud 1987: 87). These changes resulted in a sharp decline of the colonial surplus, which was replaced by net subsidies to the colonial treasury in the second half of the 1870s. Three explanations of the abolition of the cultivation system have been suggested in the literature. The first stresses ideological reasons: a system of forced cultivation based on the coercion of Javanese peasants for labor and the monopolization of colonial trade by the NHM was inconsistent with the liberalism that had become dominant after 1848. Second, Fasseur (1975: 57 ff.) has put forward a different interpretation, stressing the gradual reforms in the system that had already been introduced there in the 1840s and 1850s to lay preparations for the more radical changes in its operation in the next decade. A third view stresses the economic interests behind the changes in the 1860s. A side effect of the growth of exports from Java after 1830 was the rise of a group of merchants who were involved with, for example, the processing of the crude cane into sugar or the trade in tobacco and coffee. They became increasingly confident that they could organize the export agriculture in a more efficient way themselves and that free wage labor could be used much more efficiently than forced labor. These entrepreneurs began to argue, therefore, in favor for the ending of the system (Reinsma 1955). The overcoming of the crisis in public finance in the 1860s contributed to the abolition of the cultivation system. Moreover, in contrast to the situation in the 1840s, the good performance of the Dutch economy in the 1860s contributed to the increase in government income.

Table 2.2. *The Yield of Tariffs on Imports and Exports as a Percentage of the Value of Imports, the Netherlands, Belgium, United Kingdom and France, 1816–20 to 1911–13*

| Period | Netherlands | Belgium | United Kingdom | France |
|---|---|---|---|---|
| 1816–20 | 3.2 | | | |
| 1821–5 | 3.7 | | 53.1 | 20.3 |
| 1826–30 | 3.9 | | 47.2 | 22.6 |
| 1831–5 | 2.9 | | 40.5 | 21.5 |
| 1836–40 | 2.5 | 4.8 | 30.9 | 18.0 |
| 1841–5 | 2.4 | 5.1 | 32.2 | 17.9 |
| 1846–50 | 2.2 | 5.2 | 25.3 | 17.2 |
| 1851–5 | 2.2 | 4.4 | 19.5 | 13.2 |
| 1856–60 | 1.5 | 3.2 | 15.0 | 10.0 |
| 1861–5 | 1.1 | 2.5 | 11.5 | 5.9 |
| 1866–70 | 1.1 | 2.3 | 8.9 | 3.8 |
| 1871–5 | 1.0 | 1.7 | 6.7 | 5.3 |
| 1876–80 | 1.1 | 1.5 | 6.1 | 6.6 |
| 1881–5 | 1.2 | 1.8 | 5.9 | 7.5 |
| 1886–90 | 1.2 | 2.0 | 6.1 | 8.3 |
| 1891–5 | 1.3 | 2.1 | 5.5 | 10.6 |
| 1896–1900 | 1.7 | 2.4 | 5.3 | 10.2 |
| 1901–5 | 1.7 | 2.0 | 7.0 | 8.8 |
| 1906–10 | 1.6 | 1.6 | 5.9 | 8.0 |
| 1911–13 | 1.5 | 1.5 | 5.4 | 8.8 |

*Source:* Horlings (1995: 136).

Liberalization of trade policy was another important part of the liberal agenda. Since 1815, trade policy had been dominated by the divergent interests of the different parts of the kingdom: Holland's merchants called for low tariffs, and the southern provinces wanted the adequate protection of new industries. The Tariff Act of 1821 implied that northern interests gained the upper hand in this issue. By international standards, the degree of protectionism had been relatively low, and so it remained during the 1820s and 1830s (Table 2.2). Ironically, when independent, Belgium would adopt relatively liberal tariffs as well. Other Western European countries, like France and the United Kingdom, for example, protected their markets with far heavier tariffs.

It would be incorrect to characterize Dutch commercial policy before 1840 as an early manifestation of laissez-faire. Low tariffs clearly were a pragmatic means aimed to restore the international trade of Holland. Colonial policies resulting in the establishment of the decidedly nonliberal cultivation system are a case in point. Another area in which liberal attitudes did not predominate was the shipping and trade along the Rhine, a vital link between the major Dutch harbors and the German hinterland that the government eagerly sought to control. Traditionally, this meant that a rather diffuse system of differentiated import and export levies was applied, geared toward channeling trade from the hinterland to the staple markets of Rotterdam and Amsterdam. Tariffs on transit trade, for example, were extremely high so as to discourage trade that would bypass either Rotterdam or Amsterdam. Moreover, a large number of tolls – some based on feudal privileges dating from the Middle Ages – were levied on river trade, thus restricting the free movement of goods. During the Napoleonic period, the French attempted to liberate the Rhine trade as much as possible from these constraints, implementing reforms that would eventually also be accepted by the Vienna Congress; the Rhine was formally declared an open river. The Netherlands continued to resist, however, as it feared that the reforms would harm the privileged position of its ports. In 1829, international pressure led to the formal acceptance of free transport on the Rhine (Nusteling 1974: 1–10). However, Dutch resistance against the liberalization of Rhine traffic did not end with the ratification of the Treaty of Mainz (1831), which was intended to settle the issue. The government continued to obstruct implementation of the treaty. For the following three decades, relationships among the Netherlands, Prussia and the Zollverein continued to be tense. By obstructing transit trade and manipulating import and export tariffs, a distinctly protectionist attempt to retain as much of German trade flows in Dutch hands took place. The Dutch government underestimated the growing economic and political importance of its eastern neighbor, acting as if the Netherlands were still able to dictate the terms by which the Rhine trade was to be pursued. In response, Prussia began to develop a close relationship with Belgium, undermining the position of the Dutch ports. The construction of the Iron Rhine, a railway connection between Antwerp and Cologne in 1843, was a decisive move, as it provided the latter with a strong competitive position in transit trade (Nusteling 1974: 23).

The Iron Rhine and the withdrawal of Willem I – a staunch defender of Dutch privileges in this matter – from the political arena in due course resulted in a policy change. Given the more complaisant Dutch stance, new negotiations resulted in a treaty that granted equal rights to Dutch and German ships and skippers in 1851 (Horlings 1995: 195–6). In the meantime, however, the diplomatic frictions with Prussia had also resulted in a substantial delay in the railway construction connecting the Dutch network with that of the Zollverein; it would take until 1856 for the line linking Arnhem to Oberhausen to open and for Amsterdam and Rotterdam to become directly connected to Cologne, thirteen years after Antwerp (Jonckers Nieboer 1938: 62). Other important steps toward the liberalization of international trade in the 1840s were also closely linked to the changing relationship with Prussia. The Tariff Act drafted by van Hall in 1845 and Peter van den Bosse's 1850 Shipping Act, which ended discrimination in transit trade and against foreign ships, cannot be considered in isolation from the change in the Dutch policy position with respect to the economically unfolding German hinterland. At the same, increasing Belgian competition forced the Dutch government to step up its efforts to improve the infrastructure of both major ports, Amsterdam and Rotterdam. This led to the construction of the Noordzeekanaal – the first direct shipping route between Amsterdam and the North Sea, cutting through the western dunes – and the Nieuwe Waterweg, which improved access to Rotterdam for a larger number of seagoing vessels (van der Voort 1994: 158–60).

The turn toward economic liberalism in the 1840s, symbolized by the repeal of both the Corn Laws in 1845 and the much-resented Navigation Acts in 1848, had important consequences for the Dutch economy. Thus, halfway through the nineteenth century, an era of about two centuries of international mercantilism was momentarily drawn to an end. Protectionism had formed a persistent barrier to the expansion of the open Dutch economy. Oliver Cromwell's first Act of Navigation (1651) and the protectionism of Colbert and Louis XIV (1667) had served the explicit purpose of undermining the economic supremacy of Holland, and that goal had been reached. Nearly every politician or economist that has engaged this issue has viewed international protectionism as a principal cause for the relative decline of the Dutch economy; even Adam Smith, as the arch advocate of liberalism in foreign trade, had acknowledged the advantages to the British economy of Cromwell's economic policy. After 1840, however, this long-term cause of relative stagnation was removed at a moment when surrounding nations had surpassed or caught up with the Dutch income level. Ironically, it was mainly the Dutch agricultural sector that profited initially from the new opportunities offered: exports of livestock products to the United Kingdom increased enormously between 1842 and the mid-1860s, and the Netherlands increasingly specialized in supplying foodstuffs and international services to its industrial neighbor. The industrial sector, in contrast, faced increased competition and, in fact, stagnated until the mid-1860s (van Zanden and van Riel 2004: chap. 6).

## 2.4 The Gold Standard and Public Finance

In 1875, the Netherlands adopted de facto the gold standard, but only after some public discussion, as it involved the abandonment of the silver standard that had previously been in force (De Jong 1967: 2:224). The immediate reason for doing so was the newly formed German Reich's adoption of the gold standard in 1873, a step made possible by the imposition of a large war indemnity on France after the Franco-German War of 1870–1 and a major transfer of gold to the new Reich in 1871–3 (Flandreau 1996: 884). The adoption of the gold standard by Germany meant that, in the immediate future, one could expect a demonetization of a comparable amount of (German) silver into gold, which would have a strong impact on the monies' relative prices (De Jong 1967: 2:240). As a result, a number of European countries, fearing a relative decline in the price of silver, which would entail the inflation of silver-tied currencies, switched to gold. Dutch authorities followed their example in 1875.

Before 1871, the debate on the currency standard had focused on two issues. On the one hand, the introduction of the gold standard would entail greater stability in the exchange rate vis-à-vis the dominant trading partner, Great Britain, which had already moved to the gold standard. On the other hand, there would be disadvantages in dropping the silver standard when all neighboring countries were sticking to it (De Jong 1967: 2:241 ff.). Moreover, French monetary policy had guaranteed a stable relationship between silver and gold, despite the radical changes in the supply of both metals, in particular after large finds of gold in California and Australia. The developments of the early 1870s wholly changed the outcome of this balance, and the cabinet De Vries–Geertsema appointed a commission in 1872 to formulate proposals to change monetary policy (De Jong 1967: 2:240–1). After an initial rejection of their proposals by the parliament in 1874, amid fears of weakening the monetary union with the East Indies, a redrafted version in 1875 passed. The new proposal boiled down to the introduction of a ten-guilder gold coin to the circulating silver guilders. In combination with changes in the policies of the central bank, which were to focus on the sale and purchase of gold, this meant a transition to the gold standard, which would be the central concern of monetary policies until September 1936 (De Jong 1967: 2:241–311).

The de facto introduction of the gold standard had important consequences for financial and monetary policies. First of all, it led to strong
growth in demand for gold, which, in combination with a highly inelastic
supply, resulted in more than two decades of almost continuous deflation in all countries that had adopted the gold standard. This happened
in the Netherlands, too, albeit deflation began relatively late there: in
about 1878 instead of directly after 1873. On world markets, the prices
of agricultural commodities became severely depressed during the 1880s
and 1890s – although the agricultural depression of the period had other
causes as well – and the general level of prices continued to decline until
the mid-1890s. Another unintended consequence of the deflation caused
by the gold standard was that the burden of public debt grew once more
during these years. The ratio of public debt to GDP had declined dramatically from the 1850s and 1860s, but it was still about 80 percent. Deflation and some net borrowing brought it back to 100 percent in the late
1880s, when a new decline set in that lowered it to the 80 percent level by
about 1900. Interest payments on the public debt continued to be about
40 percent of total public expenditure during the final decades of the century, limiting the possibility of new expenditures, such as those intended
to respond to the social question.

The advantages of the gold standard were mainly associated with the
lowering of transaction costs, in particular those related to capital movements (Williamson 1996). If a country abode by its rules, the risk of
changes in the exchange rate was minimal, and interest rates could fall
to the low levels of the international (British) market (Bordo and Rockoff 1996). This indeed occurred in the Netherlands between 1870 and
1913: the difference between the interest rate on the public debt and
British consols fell to 10 percent around 1895, after having leaped to
40 percent during the years of political and monetary instability in the
early 1870s (see Figure 2.4). This not only had consequences for public
finance, which profited from the decline, but was of some importance for
the economy as a whole, as it stimulated investment.

One of the rules of the game was that monetary policy had to make
sure that gold reserves were kept above a certain threshold (40 percent of
the money supply). At the end of the 1870s, when the economy was still
booming and, as a consequence, deflation on world markets had been
much more severe than domestically, a large deficit in the trade balance
occurred, resulting in a strong decline of gold reserves. This necessitated
a number of increases in the base rate in 1880–1, showing that the central
bank was observing the rules of the game (De Jong 1967: 2:418–22). The

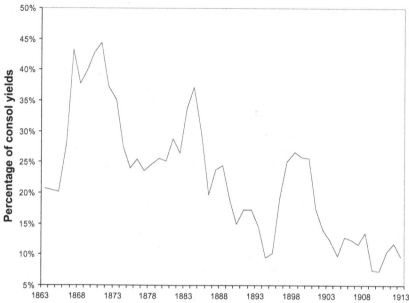

Figure 2.4. The spread between NWS 2.5-percent bonds and British 3-percent consols, 1863–1913 (in percentage of the interest on consols). *Sources:* NWS: Jonker (1996); Homer and Sylla (1991); Klovland (1994).

economic crisis that set in after 1882 and the sharp decline in domestic price levels that followed restored the balance. This in turn resulted in a strong increase in gold reserves. A similar external crisis did not occur again before the First World War, but then the Dutch central bank was able to manipulate gold flows rather easily.

The gold standard also dictated the margins of financial policy. Large deficits and a sharply growing public debt were to undermine confidence in the guilder and show that the Dutch were not able to manage their economy properly. Because of the small margins of financial policy and because colonial surplus turned into net subsidies to the colonial empire after 1875, the state did not really respond during the 1880s and 1890s to the challenge posed by the growing social question. However, pressure to do so increased after the constitutional changes of 1887.

The rather conservative management of public finance is evident from the fact that the share in the GDP of public expenditure by the central government fell slightly during the period between 1870 and 1913, although this was, to some extent, compensated for by the grow-ing importance of municipalities (see Figure 2.3) (van der Voort 1994:

Table 2.3. *The Structure of Income and Expenditure of the Central Government, 1850–1913 (in percent)*

|  | 1850 | 1860 | 1870 | 1880 | 1890 | 1900 | 1913 |
|---|---|---|---|---|---|---|---|
| *Structure of income (%)* | | | | | | | |
| Income tax | 0.0 | 0.0 | 0.0 | 0.0 | 0.0 | 11.3 | 14.6 |
| Other direct taxes | 35.3 | 36.4 | 30.8 | 26.3 | 27.4 | 18.2 | 16.7 |
| Excises sugar and drink | 10.5 | 14.1 | 27.6 | 30.5 | 31.4 | 34.6 | 32.9 |
| Other excises | 27.2 | 18.4 | 12.5 | 11.5 | 11.5 | 7.2 | 6.4 |
| Other indirect taxes (including tariffs) | 27.0 | 31.1 | 29.1 | 31.8 | 29.7 | 28.6 | 29.4 |
| Total income | 100.0 | 100.0 | 100.0 | 100.0 | 100.0 | 100.0 | 100.0 |
| Total tax income ($10^6$ guilders) | 54.0 | 55.6 | 69.7 | 94.1 | 102.5 | 121.5 | 169.6 |
| Total income ($10^6$ guilders) | 59.2 | 61.9 | 79.7 | 109.5 | 123.1 | 146.7 | 225.2 |
| *Structure of expenditure (%)* | | | | | | | |
| Core tasks[a] | 10.7 | 15.4 | 25.3 | 11.7 | 12.0 | 14.9 | 22.1 |
| Debt and finance | 58.9 | 51.3 | 45.0 | 39.1 | 37.2 | 39.8 | 31.0 |
| Defense | 19.5 | 22.2 | 25.5 | 27.6 | 24.5 | 25.8 | 22.2 |
| Other | 10.9 | 11.1 | 4.2 | 21.5 | 26.2 | 19.5 | 24.8 |
| Total expenditure | 100.0 | 100.0 | 100.0 | 100.0 | 100.0 | 100.0 | 100.0 |
| Of which, infrastructure | 4.2 | 4.3 | 16.9 | 16.8 | 10.9 | 9.2 | 6.6 |
| Education | 0.7 | 0.7 | 1.8 | 4.4 | 5.5 | 7.2 | 12.2 |
| Total expenditure ($10^6$ guilders) | 69.3 | 74.4 | 88.5 | 106.8 | 111.2 | 127.4 | 194.2 |
| Budget surplus ($10^6$ guilders) | −10.1 | −7.4 | −8.8 | 2.8 | 11.9 | 19.3 | 31.0 |
| Expenditure/GDP (%) | 12.2 | 10.5 | 9.4 | 9.7 | 8.9 | 8.8 | 8.0 |
| Budget surplus/GDP (%) | −1.8 | −1.0 | −0.9 | 0.3 | 1.0 | 1.3 | 1.3 |

[a] King, justice and internal affairs. All figures are three-year averages.

*Sources:* van der Voort (1994; 208–76); GDP: Smits, Horlings and van Zanden (2000).

209–12). After the sharp decline in public spending between 1850 and 1870, on balance, the role of the state in the economy stabilized, but the structure of expenditure changed. The share of debt fell in the long run, which created some room for education (rising from 1 percent to 12 percent of expenditure); infrastructure (peaking at 29 percent of expenditure in the mid-1860s); and economic affairs, including agriculture (see Table 2.3). Spending on poor relief and health care also rose in the long run, but the municipalities funded most of this. On the income side of the budget, the introduction of income taxation by Minister of Finance Pierson in 1893 was the most important change (Vrankrijker 1967). The importance of excises on staple foods decreased slowly, with the exception of those on alcohol and sugar.

Other evidence points into the same direction: laissez-faire remained the dominant ideology during those years, despite growing pressures for more interventionist policies. The estimates of the level of protectionism presented in Section 2.5 also point to the fact that free trade remained the dominant ideology in the Netherlands, despite the fact that the tide was changing from the mid-1870s onward in neighboring countries (Germany, France). Peter Lindert's (1994) estimates on the scale of income transfers to the poor in Western Europe show that the Netherlands was lagging behind in this respect: between 1850 and 1875, income transfers may even have declined from 0.5 percent of GDP in 1850 to 0.45 percent in 1875, followed by a very moderate increase (again to 0.5 percent) until 1890. The most important factor singled out by Lindert to explain the patterns found is the process of democratization. The very slow and gradual extension of the franchise seems, indeed, to confirm this connection (Flora, Alber, Eichenberg, Kohl, Kraus, Pfenning, Seebohm 1983: 99–105). As a result, the Netherlands remained one of the most liberal countries in Europe, in which the state continued to lean strongly toward laissez-faire.

The role of the central government in the economy therefore changed only very slowly in the decades following 1870, in spite of increasing demands from voters for the state to do more. Some of the pressure for more active policies to serve the interests of large parts of the population resulted in changes in policy at the local level. Relations between the central government and municipalities had been clearly regulated in the new Gemeentewet (Law on Municipalities) of 1851, a direct consequence of the Constitution of 1848. The central issue was that, on the one hand, the (former) autonomy of the cities in matters of taxation was severely curtailed; on the other hand, certain responsibilities and tasks were allocated to this lowest level of the state. The authority to levy excises, for example, was restricted, and in return for it, the municipalities received a share of central taxation. However, for example, responsibility for health care and public utilities were delegated to the municipalities, which were expected to play a large role in education and economic policies. A certain balance between municipalities and the central state developed, in which the central state was naturally the source of legislation in the fields, whereas major tasks were delegated to the local level.

The growing pressure to change the role of the state resulted first, therefore, in changes at the local administration. Whereas the limitations of public finance made it almost impossible to introduce new taxes at the national level before the 1890s, local direct taxes increased sharply after about 1870, both to replace the old excises and to cater to the growing needs at the local level. In particular, direct taxes on income proved a highly elastic source of tax income, greatly facilitating the expansion of expenditure that local politicians deemed necessary (De Meere 1979).

In the late 1880s, city politics were strongly affected by the constitutional changes of 1887, which broadened the electorate at the local level. Left-wing liberals (known as radicals), for example, dominated city politics in Amsterdam for quite some time, urging more dynamic city politics. The nationalization of public utilities was at the top of their agenda, as were initiatives in the field of public housing and the first attempts to regulate the labor market (Maas 1985: 22–4). To recapitulate, whereas the central state relatively stagnated in this period, local governments began to experiment with a new, more active role in society, in response to the social question that was, of course, more urgently felt at the local level. No city government could, for example, continue to ignore massive unemployment in times of economic depression, and the first systematic plans for unemployment relief were experimented with in the 1880s (Knotter 1991: 115–17). These experiments were important and were often interlinked with the development of unions or other interest groups, with the local schemes to subsidize the unemployment insurances of the trade unions being a good example. But in the end, progress at the local level was constrained by the legal and budgetary framework that the central state defined.

At the central level, progress in the field of social policy was slow. After initiation of the law against child labor in 1874, it took another fifteen years for new initiatives to materialize. The *Inquiry into the Situation at Factories and Workplaces*, induced by growing complaints about the exploitation of women and child labor, resulted in a new law in 1889 that established more detailed rules and an organization (Inspection of Labour) that was to monitor the law's implementation.

The next stage in the development of social legislation consisted of plans to introduce legislation to insure workers for loss of income from workplace accidents. It was typical for the situation before the rise of corporatism that neither employers nor laborers (nor their organizations) were involved with the preparation of the new law, which was submitted to the parliament in 1898 (Roebroek and Hertogh 1998: 132–5. Although there was a consensus that something should be done about the issue and that all employers had to be covered by the new law, the centralist approach of the proposed Ongevallenwet (Industrial Accidents Act) was strongly criticized because it would be managed through a central fund (van Zanden 1998: 4–5). The opposition leader Abraham Kuyper argued in favor of a decentralized administration in which employers in each branch of industry would themselves manage the implementation of the law. This approach was supported by the organization set up in 1899 to argue the employers' case for a more privatized and decentralized administration of the law, the Association of Dutch Employers (Vereniging van Nederlandsche Werkgever), which would become the foremost organization of employers in the Netherlands during the twentieth century. They could argue, too, that in important industries social entrepreneurs had already developed comparable, often more generous, plans for their workers, and that the new law would interfere with those – often more efficient – experiments at the local level. The question of whether the neutral state or the employers themselves would control the new organization was closely linked to the issue of its efficiency. Left-wing liberals expected a centralized bureaucracy to be more efficient, whereas their critics praised the advantages of decentralized management and control. The initial proposal was approved by the Second Chamber of Parliament, but that did not convince a majority of the often-more-conservative First Chamber, and the proposal was rewritten to meet their criticisms (Roebroek and Hertogh 1998: 134–5. The final result, which passed the parliament in 1901, created a few possibilities for private management of the implementation of insurance against accidents.

This debate was more or less representative of the discussion on social policies in the years before the First World War. There was consensus that something had to be done and that laws had to be introduced to improve the lot of the workers, who were dependent on unstable sources of income (i.e., wage labor). The way forward was to induce them (and/or their employers) to insure themselves against accidents, unemployment, illness and old age. The social security that people had in mind consisted of a postponed wage, paid for by premiums on the wage income of the laborers (which could be considered part of this wage income). An alternative approach, advocated by only a small minority, consisted of schemes of national social insurances for everyone (e.g., farmers, shopkeepers) that was to be paid for by the government (Roebroek and Hertogh 1998: 161). This approach was considered etatist and as ignoring the responsibilities of those involved, as well as being too costly, for that matter.

It is striking that so little progress was made before 1913 in view of the fact that there was consensus among the left-wing liberals, the Christian parties and the socialists that an extension of social legislation was necessary. As in the debate on the Industrial Accidents Act of 1901, disagreement focused on the precise role of the state and how much should be delegated to the trade unions and employers and their organizations. The left-wing liberal party and the Christian parties were unable to reach a compromise on the issue, which meant that both boycotted the proposals of the other, and legislation stagnated as a result. The political elites of both groups were not yet able to work together closely: they were still involved in a learning process, in developing the rules of the politics of pacification of the interwar period (Lijphart 1968). The pressure from below – from organized labor and from employers' organizations – to make more progress in this field was also still relatively weak (compared with the post-1914 period). Therefore, also in this respect, the 1870–1914 period saw only the initial development of the new rules of the game that would regulate sociopolitical and economic matters during the twentieth century (van Zanden 1998: passim).

## References

Bordo, M. and H. Rockoff (1996) "The gold standard as a 'Good-Housekeeping Seal of Approval,'" *Journal of Economic History*, 56, 389–428.

Elson, R. E. (1994) *Village Java under the Cultivation System*. Sydney: Allen and Urwin.

Fasseur, C. (1975) *Kultuurstelsel en koloniale baten: de Nederlandse exploitatie van Java 1840–1860*. Leiden: Universitaire Pers.

Flandreau, M. (1996) "The French crime of 1873: An essay on the emergence of the international gold standard," *Journal of Economic History*, 56, 862–97.

Flora, P. et al. (1983) *State, Economy, and Society in Western Europe 1815–1975*, vol. 1. Frankfurt: Campus Verlag.

Homer, S. and R. Sylla (1991) *A History of Interest Rates*. New Brunswick, N.J.: Rutgers University Press.

Horlings, E. (1995) *The Economic Development of the Dutch Service Sector 1800–1850*. Amsterdam: Netherlands Economic History Archives.

Jonckers Nieboer, J. H. (1938) *Geschiedenis der Nederlandsche Spoorwegen 1832–1938*. Rotterdam: Nijgh & van Ditmar.

Jong, A. M. de (1967) *Geschiedenis van de Nederlandsche Bank*, 4 vols. Haarlem: Enschedé.

Jonker, J. (1996) *Merchants, Bankers, Middlemen: The Amsterdam Money Market during the First Half of the Nineteenth Century*. Amsterdam: Netherlands Economic History Archives.

Klovland, J. T. (1994) "Pitfalls in the estimation of the yield on British consols, 1850–1914," *Journal of Economic History*, 54, 164–87.

Knotter, A. (1991) *Economische transformatie en stedelijke arbeidsmarkt.* Amsterdam: Waanders.

Lijphart, A. (1968) *The Politics of Accommodation: Pluralism and Democracy in the Netherlands.* Berkeley: University of California Press.

Lindert, P. H. (1994) "The Rise of Social Spending, 1880–1930," *Explorations in Economic History*, 31, 1–37.

Maas, P. F. (1985) *Sociaal-democratische gemeentepolitiek 1894–1929.* The Hague: Staatsuitgeverij.

Meere, J. M. M. de (1979) "Inkomensgroei en-ongelijkheid in Amsterdam 1877–1940," *Tijdschrift voor sociale geschiedenis*, 13, 3–46.

Nusteling, H. P. H. (1974) *De Rijnvaart in het tijdperk van stoom en steenkool 1831–1914.* Amsterdam: Holland Universiteits Pers.

Oud, P. J. (1987) *Honderd Jaren: een eeuw staatkundige vormgeving in Nederland, 1840–1940.* Assen: van Gorcum.

Reinsma, R. (1955) *Het verval van het cultuurstelsel.* The Hague: van Keulen.

Roebroek, J. M. and M. Hertogh (1998) *"De beschavende invloed des tijds." Twee eeuwen sociale politiek, verzorgingsstaat en sociale zekerheid in Nederland.* The Hague: Vuga.

Smits, J.-P., Horlings, E. and Zanden, J. L. van (2000) Dutch GNP and its components, 1800–1913. Groningen: Growth and Development Centre. nationalaccounts.niwi.knaw.nl/.

Voort, R. H. van Der (1994) *Overheidsbeleid en overheidsfinanciën in Nederland, 1850–1913.* Amsterdam: Netherlands Economic History Archives.

Vrankrijker, A. C. J. de (1967) *Belastingen in Nederland 1848–1893.* Haarlem: F. Bohn.

Williamson, J. G. (1996) "Globalization, convergence, and history," *Journal of Economic History*, 56, 277–306.

Zanden, J. L. van (1996) "The development of government finances in a chaotic period, 1807–1850," *Economic and Social History in the Netherlands*, 7, 57–72.

Zanden, J. L. van (1998) *The Economic History of the Netherlands 1914–1995.* London: Routledge.

Zanden, J. L. van and Riel, A. van (2004) *The Strictures of Inheritance: The Dutch Economy in the Nineteenth Century.* Princeton, NJ: Princeton University Press.

Zanden, J. L. van and Prak, M. (2006) "Towards an economic interpretation of citizenship: The Dutch Republic between medieval communes and modern nation states," *European Review of Economic History*, 10, 121–47.

# 3

# The Apogee and Fall of the French Rentier Regime, 1801–1914

## Richard Bonney

## 3.1 Introduction

Any analysis of the long nineteenth century (1801–1914) in terms of state finance has to consider first the issue of political instability and regime change. Three revolutions, two coups d'état, and three types of regime (monarchical, imperial, and republican) made for critical disjunctures in fiscal policy. To facilitate discussion, the data have been presented in separate tables according to regime. Bruno Théret (1995) argues for a different categorization of disjunctures, between the constitutional monarchies (1815–30, 1831–47, and 1851–70) and the Third Republic (1878–1939), with a significant transitional phase (1871–7) in between. These periods, he argues, can be further subdivided, notably into an opportunist Third Republic (1878–93) and a moderate (1894–1913) and then radical Third Republic (1914–39) (Théret 1995: 58–9). There is no doubt that political instability and regime change were important factors in limiting the possibilities for government innovation in state finance; but in this analysis, two long-term realities are emphasized as of primary importance – first, the failure of population growth in France, in comparison with its economic rivals; and second, the longevity of an oligarchic rentier social order, in spite of the various constitutional crises and regime changes. Thus in France, again in comparison with its two main European economic rivals, Germany and the United Kingdom, the growth of the state was regarded as a serious threat to the economic interests of the ruling social class. By 1913, government expenditure as a percentage of gross domestic product in France was significantly less than that of its two main European economic rivals, and particularly so in comparison with Germany (8.9 percent of GDP in comparison with 17.7 percent), against which it was about to embark on a life-and-death struggle. Moreover, France was about to enter the Great War against Germany with a population that was a third less numerous (nearly 23.6 million citizens fewer – 41.5 million in comparison with 65.1 million).

### 3.2 Accounting Methods and the Reliability of the Resulting Fiscal Data

Bruno Théret's (1995: figures 1–3) graphs, which draw on the research of Louis Fontvieille (1976, 1981), are the most sophisticated representation of the growth of expenditure and revenues in France in real terms, that is, deflated by the price index calculated by J.-C. Toutain (1987). Théret (1988: 9) considers Fontvieille as having constructed a statistical source of high quality for a long-term study of public finance, but he questions some of the assumptions on which Fontvieille's data is presented.[1] Fontvieille's figures are grouped together in Table 3.1 for the purposes of comparing the general trend of French finances between 1815 and 1914. From the point of the fiscal historian, one might have wished for a clearer presentation of the sources by Fontvieille in addition to his thorough discussion of accounting practice (Fontvieille 1976: 2019–41). It is clear that his figures differ from those presented in the *Annuaire Statistique Rétrospectif* of 1929, published by the Statistique Générale de la France, which are presented here in quinquennial totals as the nominal figures (i.e., not deflated by the rise or fall in prices) in Figure 3.1 These figures were also used by François Bouvier (1969: 299, 301) in his analysis of the growth of French expenditure between 1815 and 1950.

The implementation of double-entry bookkeeping, a significant change in accounting practice brought about by Count Nicolas-François Mollien and Charles-Louis Gaston, Marquis d'Audiffret in 1815 – fourteen years before the change in England in 1829 – is attributable to the need for proper accountability before the Parlement that was re-established in 1814. Article 14 of the Constitution of 1791 had conferred on 'all citizens ... the right to see – for themselves or through their representatives – the necessity of the public contribution, the right to consent to freely and to check on the uses made of it' (Nikitin 2001: n15). The parliamentary deputies had to wait until 1814 before the principle

---

[1] The criticism rests on the arbitrary division of categories of expenditure into those that were, or were not, linked to the regulation of the economy.

Table 3.1. *Average Expenditure, Taxation, and GNP in France by Quinquennium, 1815–1914 (Fontvieille) in Millions of Francs (nominal), Except for Column 3 (percent)*

| | GNP (Toutain) | Expenditure | Expenditure in Terms of GNP | Taxes (central government) | Taxes (total including communes and departments) | Debt-Servicing Costs | National Defense |
|---|---|---|---|---|---|---|---|
| 1815–19 | 8,071 | 961.6 | 11.92 | 724.8 | 831.8 | 142 | 258 |
| 1820–4 | 7,646 | 792.6 | 10.37 | 751 | 872.6 | 196.4 | 301.2 |
| 1825–9 | 8,840 | 955.8 | 10.81 | 776 | 913.8 | 186.6 | 298.6 |
| 1830–4 | 9,653 | 923.2 | 9.56 | 777.4 | 923.3 | 201.2 | 374.4 |
| 1835–9 | 10,012 | 859.2 | 8.58 | 842.8 | 1,033.4 | 195.6 | 293 |
| 1840–4 | 12,033 | 1,106.2 | 9.19 | 953.8 | 1,183.9 | 199.6 | 411.2 |
| 1845–9 | 13,039 | 1,231.2 | 9.44 | 1,003.0 | 1,261.5 | 235.8 | 404.2 |
| 1850–4 | 12,799 | 1,210.6 | 9.46 | 997.8 | 1,287.2 | 259.2 | 391.2 |
| 1855–9 | 16,690 | 1,640.4 | 9.82 | 1,226.2 | 1,566.8 | 326.8 | 686.2 |
| 1860–4 | 17,339 | 1,723.2 | 9.94 | 1,346.4 | 1,779.2 | 354.6 | 601.4 |
| 1865–9 | 17,757 | 1,729.4 | 9.74 | 1,489.8 | 1,991.5 | 371.4 | 586.8 |
| 1870–4 | 19,288 | 3,595.2 | 18.64 | 1,782.8 | 2,330.0 | 681.6 | 980.6 |
| 1875–9 | 18,367 | 2,679.0 | 14.58 | 2,938.2 | 3,062.4 | 877.2 | 918.2 |
| 1880–4 | 19,068 | 3,112.6 | 16.32 | 2,535.0 | 3,250.2 | 914.0 | 958.8 |
| 1885–9 | 17,824 | 2,984.8 | 16.75 | 2,559.8 | 3,311.2 | 962.4 | 963.0 |
| 1890–4 | 18,677 | 3,056.2 | 16.36 | 2,771.4 | 3,549.0 | 967.6 | 955.8 |
| 1895–9 | 18,439 | 3,091.6 | 16.77 | 2,875.5 | 3,713.1 | 895.2 | 988.8 |
| 1900–4 | 20,783 | 3,251.0 | 15.64 | 2,947.6 | 3,835.0 | 871.2 | 1,079.0 |
| 1905–9 | 24,377 | 3,362.4 | 13.79 | 3,174.0 | 4,146.2 | 844.0 | 1,140.6 |
| 1910–13/14 | 28,453 | 4,703.2 | 14.15 | 3,666.6 | 4,759.8 | 814.0 | 2,057.4 |

*Sources:* For columns 1 and 3: Fontvieille (1976: 1673, 1743 [the figure in column 2 is reduced by three decimal places and then divided by the figure in column 1]). For column 2: Fontvieille (1981: 38). For columns 4 and 5: Fontvieille (1981: 39). For columns 6 and 7: Fontvieille (1981: 2042–80).

*Richard Bonney*

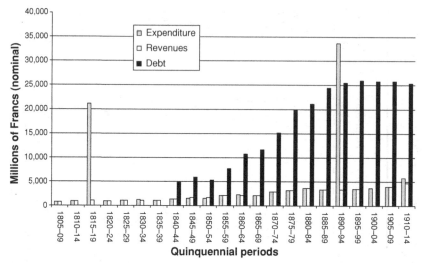

Figure 3.1. Quinquennial averages of expenditure, revenues, and public debt in France, 1805–1914 (nominal values). *Note:* For 1810–14, average of four years only.

of discussing revenues and expenditure openly on the basis of evidence was put into practice. Article 150 of the budget law of March 25, 1817, required ministers to reveal their accounts to the two chambers, while an order of September 14, 1822, insisted on double-entry bookkeeping in their ledgers (Nikitin 2001: nn19, 21). The introduction of double-entry bookkeeping by Britain in 1829 was modeled on French practice: 'the system of accounts as adopted in France has afforded perfect security against default and dilapidation...and has again and again been eulogized, after elaborate and detailed examination, by statesmen of all parties in both Houses of the French Legislature' (Nikitin 2001: n44). For a country frequently said to be a generation or more behind Britain in its institutional practices and economic development, this practical influence is often overlooked. Because Mollien had visited Britain in 1797–8 to study the banking and financial system there, it may be regarded as a reciprocal influence (Nikitin 2001: 92).

## 3.3 The Growing Reliance on Borrowing

The era of Napoléon, until his final costly wars, might well be termed 'After Hyperinflation: The Return to Fiscal and Monetary Rectitude' (Crouzet 1993; Sargent and Velde 1995). In 1803, six years after the end of the notorious assignat system, France returned to a bimetallic system,

Table 3.2. *Expenditure, Revenues, and Deficit under Napoléon, 1801–14 (in millions of old francs)*

|      | Total Revenues | Total Expenditure | Actual Deficit |
|------|----------------|-------------------|----------------|
| 1801 |                | 549.6             |                |
| 1802 |                | 499.9             |                |
| 1803 |                | 632.3             |                |
| 1804 |                | 804.4             |                |
| 1805 | 698            | 700               |                |
| 1806 | 880            | 902.1             |                |
| 1807 | 724            | 731.7             |                |
| 1808 | 758            | 772.7             |                |
| 1809 | 783            | 786.7             |                |
| 1810 | 782            | 785.1             |                |
| 1811 | 942            | 1000              | 6.3            |
| 1812 | 915            | 1006              | 178.1          |
| 1813 | 908            | 975.4             | 104.1          |
| 1814 |                | 609.4             | 75.8           |

*Sources:* Expenditure data from 'Tableau comparatif des budgets ordinaires de l'État, depuis 1801, époque où le gouvernment a présenté le premier budget en règle, jusqu'en 1844,' in Tapiès (1845: 191). Deficit data from Bruguière (1969: 175–7). Income data from Branda (2004, 2005).

with a legal ratio of 15.5 of gold to silver. The commercial rate, unlike the legal ratio set in 1803, fluctuated somewhat over the course of the century. It went through long periods in which it hovered slightly above (1821–50 and 1867–73) or slightly below (1851–66) the legal ratio.

Expenditure doubled between the Peace of Amiens in 1802 and the intervention in Portugal and Spain in 1808–14 (Table 3.2). At the same time, though more efficient collection in the French departments improved revenue yields by 1810, the overall revenue available to the Bonapartist regime declined as a number of the departments formerly subject to French taxation fell under the control of the allies. As the research of Pierre Branda (2004, 2005) has demonstrated, revenues were divided into two categories, those levied under the Consulate and new revenues levied under the empire. Yet the new revenues were difficult to levy. By 1811, 77 million francs were still *à trouver*, to be found or levied, with this figure rising to 150 million in 1812 and 579 million in 1814. Under the Bourbon restoration, the actual deficit recorded was found to be considerably less than the earlier estimates.

For 1820, expenditure has been estimated at 8.6 percent of GDP, and this percentage scarcely changed in the period of the restored

Table 3.3. *French Revenues, Expenditure, and
Public Debt under the Restored Bourbon
Monarchy, 1815–29 (in millions of old francs)*

| Date | Total Revenues | Total Expenditure | Public Debt |
|------|-----|-----|-----|
| 1815 | 876 | 931 | 1272 |
| 1816 | 1037 | 1056 | 1610 |
| 1817 | 1270 | 1189 | |
| 1818 | 1414 | 1434 | |
| 1819 | 937 | 896 | |
| 1820 | 939 | 907 | 3456 |
| 1821 | 935 | 908 | 4713 |
| 1822 | 950 | 949 | |
| 1823 | 1043 | 1118 | |
| 1824 | 990 | 986 | |
| 1825 | 978 | 982 | 3941 |
| 1826 | 982 | 977 | |
| 1827 | 948 | 987 | |
| 1828 | 1029 | 1024 | |
| 1829 | 1022 | 1015 | |

*Sources:* See Tables 3.1 and 3.2.

monarchy; in 1830, it was 8.8 percent. Revenues increased significantly between 1815 and 1818; but 1818 was a record year (Table 3.3). Overall, the increase of both revenues and expenditure was evident, though the figures recorded by Eugene N. White (2001) are lower in each case, with a growing deficit reaching 494 million by 1818.[2] Notwithstanding these increases, the most important development was the growth in the public debt: this rose from 1,272 million in 1815 to 4,627 million in 1830, virtually a quadrupling. The cost of war reparations to the allies (1,863.5 million actually paid, or between 18 percent and 21 percent of GDP), transformed into funded debt, had led to more than a trebling of the debt by 1821 to 4,173 million (White 2001: 341, 348). There seems much to commend the argument of White advanced in 2001 (355), that these were 'the largest reparations in terms of the burden on the economy that were [ever] actually paid, with a lasting negative impact upon growth' (also cited by Crouzet 2003: 235).

There was, nevertheless, a fourfold increase in the volume of foreign commerce between 1816 and 1850, while national income grew by

[2] Note that White's data differs from that of Fontvieille (1976: 2043).

50–60 percent in nominal terms between 1820 and 1848 or 1.5–2 percent per annum (increasing to 2–3 percent in real terms as the period was one of declining prices). The growth in national wealth was not spread evenly, however; the top strata of society – the landlords, the industrialists, the financiers, and the rentiers – were the chief beneficiaries: it was in their interest that the various regimes (imperial, monarchist, republican) operated before 1914 (Cameron 1958; Casson and Cameron 1961: 36, 65). A well-managed portfolio of investments might have grown by 1.8 percent per annum between 1815 and 1850 and by 2.4 percent per annum between 1851 and 1913. If the sums were reinvested, the growth rates of the portfolio would be, respectively, 7 percent and 6.2 percent, in an era when there was scarcely any taxation to pay on such investments.[3] The compounded annual growth rate in per capita GDP between 1870 and 1913 has been calculated by Angus Maddison (1995: 194–206) as 1.45 percent in France, second only to that of the United States (1.81 percent) and significantly higher than Germany, Italy, the United Kingdom, and Russia, at 1.63 percent, 1.25 percent, 1.01 percent, and 0.88 percent, respectively.[4] However, Maddison's figures suggest that the total GDP of France in 1913 was significantly less than that of three of its rivals – the United States, Germany, and the United Kingdom – whereas Italy and Japan lagged behind France (Maddison 2001: table B-18).[5]

The rentier classes in France were overrepresented in the parliament and were determined to replace direct taxes – which fell on them – by long-term loans, the only alternative source of immediate government finance. Indirect taxes fell heavily on the lower classes, which were vulnerable because they had not yet gained significant parliamentary representation. However, as *impôts de quotité*, the indirect taxes were less susceptible to a sudden rise except by means of an overall increase in tax

---

[3] 'Les cours des actions augmentent de manière régulière, malgré les quelques accidents conjoncturels de 1838, 1848, 1870, 1882 ou 1901. L'indice des cours des actions calculé par P. Arbulu augmente ainsi de 1,8% par an pendant la première moitié du siècle, et de près de 2,4% par an de 1851 à 1913. Si on suppose les dividendes réinvestis, on atteint respectivement 7 et 6,2% de croissance annuelle pour un portefeuille, à une époque ou presqu'aucun impôt ne grève le revenu des valeurs mobilières' (Hautcoeur et al. 2007: 12; see also Arbulu and Gallais-Hamonno 2002).

[4] The data are helpfully produced in tabular form in Chapra (2008: 90, table 6). The calculations are made in international dollars at the 1990 value.

[5] The figures, in millions of 1990 international dollars, were, respectively, 517,383 (United States), 237,332 (Germany), 224,618 (United Kingdom), 144,489 (France), 95,487 (Italy), and 71,653 (Japan) (www.theworldeconomy.org/publications/worldeconomy/statistics.htm; accessed November 18, 2008).

rates.[6] Monetary stability facilitated the credit of the state, though the long-term stability of the regime depended critically on confidence that the state would honor its debts (Théret 1995: 64–5).[7] Interest was paid on the loans at a rate of 3.5 percent between 1831 and 1877 and 2.5 percent after 1877 (Théret 1995: 72 n1).[8]

The stability of interest rates and the low level of interest payable on government borrowing reveal the stark contrast between the French fiscal structure of the nineteenth century and that of its ancien régime predecessor. Governments in eighteenth-century France found it very difficult to pay debt-servicing costs. Whereas Britain was able to pay for its (much larger) national debt by raising new and increased taxes, France was forced to contain its debt by partial default, such as that ordered by Joseph-Marie Terray in 1770. The rate of interest was also higher in France than in Britain because of this default risk. In 1789, another default was required, but though the Crown's creditors were less cohesive than before, it failed to happen: there was, by this time, a political consensus that default was to be branded an exercise in despotism (Bonney 1999: 148; Velde and Weir 1992: 36; Hoffman, Postel-Vinay, and Rosenthal 2000: 174–5). There were, nevertheless, two additional types of default in the 1790s – first, the inflation tax caused by the rapid depreciation of paper money (assignats), estimated by Hoffman, Postel-Vinay, and Rosenthal (2000) at 1.67 billion livres; second, the two-thirds bankruptcy (*banqueroute des deux tiers*) of September 30, 1797, estimated by the same authors (following Marion) as a loss of 2.6 billion livres to the government's creditors (Hoffman, Postel-Vinay, and Rosenthal 2000: 200). The same authors contend that 'it was not until the 1850s that the psychological connection between political stability and financial crisis was finally broken. In the first half of the nineteenth century, credit markets were thus clouded by the continuing threat of political instability and its dire financial consequences' (Hoffman, Postel-Vinay, and

[6] 'Dans le système de la quotité, le taux de l'impôt est fixé à l'avance par le législateur. Il est invariable, quelle que soit le volume total de la matière imposable détenue par l'ensemble des contribuables soumis à l'impôt.' *Encyclopédie Universalis*, s.v. 'Impôt de quotité' (www.universalis.fr/encyclopedie/T400982/QUOTITE_IMPOT_DE. htm; accessed November 18, 2008).

[7] 'Bref, l'impôt et la rente sont bien intrinsèquement liés par un régime des finances publiques qui est en même temps régime d'accumulation de capital rentier' (Théret 1995: 83).

[8] The point is made quite explicitly by Théret (1995). Yet Hoffman, Postel-Vinay, and Rosenthal (2000: 224) argue that 'the yield on government bonds' fell from more than 6 percent in 1815 to 4.3 percent in 1870.

Rosenthal 2000: 208). Only gradually was it evident that the political crises had ended and that bankers had became numerous. There were more than two hundred bankers by 1840 and more than three hundred by 1862. It was not until the Second Empire that joint-stock banks and corporate banks finally blossomed (Hoffman, Postel-Vinay, and Rosenthal 2000: 226; Hautcoeur et al. 2007).

Although France had lagged behind Britain as far as its financial system was concerned at the beginning of the nineteenth century, rapid progress was made by midcentury, and a powerful and solid banking system was achieved (Crouzet 2003: 235, and sources cited there). Guaranteeing the franc was said to be the principal aim of the Banque de France. From 1800 to 1914, the convertibility of the notes it issued was guaranteed at an invariable rate, except in two cases of political origin, from 1848 to 1852 and from 1870 to 1878. Despite the preoccupation with convertibility, exchange-rate crises rarely required a high interest rate. In 1836, the bank lost 55 percent of its reserves without raising its discount rate, thus preventing the international crisis from affecting France. In 1855, 1857, and 1864, the solvency of the bank was imperiled by high London rates, and its rate rose to 10 percent in 1857, the highest level of the century. But after 1866, high English interest rates did not attract enough gold to force the Banque de France to raise its rate. The reason for the relative insulation of France from world crises was the very high ratio of reserves to liabilities (often more than 80 percent) that the bank maintained.

## 3.4 French Fiscal Developments from the Revolution of 1848 to 1896

The July Monarchy witnessed a perceptible increase in expenditure: total expenses rose from 1,095 million francs in 1830 to 1,364 million in 1840, or 9.2 percent of gross national product. At the same, the public debt remained stable or even declined somewhat. By 1847, expenditure had risen still further, to 1,630 million francs, considerably outstripping revenues (Table 3.4). The 1848 revolution was anticipated by the financial markets, which were selling off rentes well before the decisive events of March. Louis Napoléon's coup d'état in 1851, by contrast, 'was a solution of doubts which had for some time affected the market unfavourably and its influence at first was to give the market firmness there' (Ferguson 2006: 82).

The short period from the Revolution of 1848 to the coup d'état of Louis Napoléon Bonaparte on December 2, 1851, saw a decline in all

*Richard Bonney*

Table 3.4. *French Revenues, Expenditure,*
*and Public Debt under the July Monarchy,*
*1830–47 (in millions of old francs)*

| Date | Total Revenues | Total Expenditure | Public Debt |
|------|------|------|------|
| 1830 | 1020 | 1095 | 4627 |
| 1831 | 1306 | 1219 | |
| 1832 | 1063 | 1174 | |
| 1833 | 1162 | 1134 | |
| 1834 | 1039 | 1064 | |
| 1835 | 1068 | 1047 | 4175 |
| 1836 | 1072 | 1066 | |
| 1837 | 1087 | 1079 | |
| 1838 | 1112 | 1136 | |
| 1839 | 1181 | 1179 | |
| 1840 | 1234 | 1364 | 4458 |
| 1841 | 1381 | 1425 | 4613 |
| 1842 | 1331 | 1441 | 4785 |
| 1843 | 1378 | 1445 | 5021 |
| 1844 | 1385 | 1428 | 5118 |
| 1845 | 1393 | 1489 | 5205 |
| 1846 | 1399 | 1567 | 5521 |
| 1847 | 1372 | 1630 | 5715 |

*Sources:* See Tables 3.1 and 3.2.

three indicators: revenues, expenditure, and the public debt (Table 3.5).
By 1850, total expenditure, at 1,473 million francs, was only 8.5 percent
of GDP, the lowest estimate since 1820. Although the figures for the public debt do not show a consistent trend toward decrease (the year 1849
actually saw an increase to 6,860 million francs), the figure in 1851 was
less than that for 1848.

Table 3.5. *French Revenues, Expenditure,*
*and Public Debt, 1848–51 (in millions of*
*old francs)*

| Date | Total Revenues | Total Expenditure | Public Debt |
|------|------|------|------|
| 1848 | 1768 | 1771 | 5838 |
| 1849 | 1432 | 1646 | 6860 |
| 1850 | 1432 | 1473 | 4886 |
| 1851 | 1361 | 1461 | 5012 |

*Sources:* See Tables 3.1 and 3.2.

Table 3.6. *French Revenues, Expenditure,
and Public Debt under the Second Empire,
1852–69 (in millions of old francs)*

| Date | Total Revenues | Total Expenditure | Public Debt |
|------|------|------|------|
| 1852 | 1487 | 1513 | 5516 |
| 1853 | 1524 | 1548 | 5577 |
| 1854 | 1802 | 1988 | 5670 |
| 1855 | 2793 | 2309 | 6083 |
| 1856 | 1914 | 2196 | 7558 |
| 1857 | 1799 | 1893 | 8032 |
| 1858 | 1871 | 1859 | 8422 |
| 1859 | 2179 | 2208 | 8593 |
| 1860 | 1962 | 2084 | 9334 |
| 1861 | 2006 | 2171 | 9717 |
| 1862 | 2178 | 2213 | 9925 |
| 1863 | 2265 | 2287 | 12020 |
| 1864 | 2205 | 2257 | 12316 |
| 1865 | 2169 | 2147 | 13026 |
| 1866 | 2193 | 2203 | 11029 |
| 1867 | 2168 | 2170 | 10932 |
| 1868 | 1935 | 1903 | 11925 |
| 1869 | 1962 | 1904 | 11178 |

*Sources:* See Tables 3.1 and 3.2.

Under the Second Empire, government expenditure continued to rise in proportion to the ambitions of French foreign policy, first with regard to the Crimean War (1853–6) and later with adventures in Italy, in the colonies, and in Mexico. Both revenues and expenditure peaked in 1855, but the public debt continued to grow every year until 1866 (Table 3.6). Expenditure reached 9.1 percent of GDP by 1860, an increase of 1.1 percent since 1850. The period between 1851 and 1873 was one of high prices, so increased levels of expenditure, revenues, and public debt were an inevitable reaction for the state to maintain its capacity in a period of inflation. In spite of these increases, France was found to be woefully unready to meet the Prussian threat in the war of 1870, the disaster of which swept aside the Second Empire.

The *Economist* detected the approaching nemesis of the Bonapartist regime when it noted on July 8, 1870: 'securities on the Paris Bourse fell on the news that a Prince of Hohenzollern had been offered and had accepted the Spanish Crown, and by the solemn declaration of the French Government that it would go to war to prevent him from taking it' (Ferguson 2006: 82). The 1871 war indemnity payable by France to Prussia amounted to 5,000 million francs, equivalent to one-quarter of one year's GDP and more than two years of government revenue, or 1.6 times France's annual exports. France was rescued only by a sudden trade surplus in the years 1872–7; about half the increased burden of public debt was purchased domestically (White 2001: 353, quoting Gavin 1992 and 1997). By 1875, the value of French government bonds quoted in London exceeded that of Britain (24.8 percent of the total of great-power government bonds against 23.3 percent for Britain), though the balance had been reversed by 1905 (Ferguson 2006: 75, table 1). By 1887–8, the burden of France's public debt as a proportion of revenue in nominal terms was greater than that of Britain by 0.3 percentage points but by 2.2 percentage points when adjusted; in terms of the value of its exports, the French debt was 6.1 percentage points higher and 5.5 percentage points higher when adjusted (Ferguson 2006: 92, table 5).

One consequence of defeat in the Franco-Prussian War was to force France off the bimetallic system, which had operated to a considerable extent in its interests in the period 1846–70 (Flandreau 1996), and onto the gold standard. During the 1840s, the stock of metallic currency grew at a rate of about 2.6 percent per year, though in 1848, the quantity of specie in France was still less than 3 billion francs. The first finds of gold in California accelerated the pace of specie accumulation. From 1848 to 1859, the metallic stock grew at an average annual rate of 9 percent. After 1865, the new mintings were channeled primarily into the Banque de France's reserves, which rose to a record level of 1 billion francs. This stock was later released in response to the events of 1870. After 1870, the war and its associated problems resulted in the first net reduction in France's specie holdings. Yet toward the end of the decade, specie stocks in France were back on an upward path. In 1874, the Banque de France began redeeming its notes in ten-franc gold coins, and the premium on gold disappeared. These were years of deficit in Germany and gold flowing into France, allowing the bank to replenish its reserves. In late 1878, the country's gold and silver stocks totaled nearly 8 billion francs (Flandreau 1995). Adherence to the gold standard by the main Western European powers was subsequently an important factor, though by no means the only one that facilitated the growth of their public debts. France was no exception to this European trend (Flandreau and Le Cacheux 1997: 532, graph 1). Whether or not adherence to the gold standard was a seal of approval for other states has been contested by Flandreau and Zumer

(2004), but there is little doubt that, in the French case, it was because of the very high ratio of reserves to liabilities (often more than 80 percent) maintained by the Banque de France (Hautcoeur 1997; Flandreau and Zumer 2004).

Following the bloody suppression of the Commune, the Third Republic continued Napoléon III's policy of allowing the growth of the public debt, damping down the increase in expenditure and revenues, at least until 1879 (Table 3.7). The growth of expenditure, which had been the norm for most years from 1815, was finally halted in 1883. As François Bouvier (1969) has observed, economic commentators were increasingly convinced that the state had 'grown too much.' Paul Leroy-Beaulieu in 1912 identified the causes for this growth in expenditure.[9] His contention was that the deputies elected to the parliament wanted to see investments in their localities, and that collectively this was an important pressure toward increased expenditure. It seems unlikely, however, that this was as significant an overall factor as the increased costs of government in an era of inflation. The psychological impact on the deputies of the Third Republic of arguments such as those of Léon Say in 1886 against the continued growth of expenditure was nevertheless considerable. In principle, although the deputies wanted more expenditure in their localities, they also wanted to see a state with a lighter rather than a more burdensome touch. For a relatively short period, between 1883 and 1891, this attitude prevailed, and expenditure declined from 3,715 million to 3,258 million francs.

---

[9] Quoted by Bouvier (1969: 312–13). Leroy-Beaulieu (1912: 169) wrote: 'Il arrive… parfois que ceux qui votent les dépenses dans les démocraties paient médiocrement d'impôts: c'est ce que l'on rencontre dans les pays où existe l'impôt sur le revenu, et dans les communes où il n'y a d'autres taxes que les taxes directes. La connivence, la collusion sont aussi plus fréquentes dans les démocraties. Bref, sans contester aucun des avantages des gouvernements démocratiques, il est impossible de nier qu'ils ont une tendance, si l'on n'y prend garde, à être le plus coûteux des gouvernements… une grande partie de ces crédits supplémentaires vient de l'initiative des députés… Les intérêts électoraux, représentés par les députés, livrent un terrible assaut au Trésor public.' Sharif Gemie (1992: 352, 360) notes that Leroy-Beaulieu was a regular critic of the size of the budget from the 1870s. His 'orthodox economic doctrines provided apparently sophisticated arguments against any social reform.' Gemie concludes that Leroy-Beaulieu's writings suggest that the bourgeoisie was an 'internally divided class, split into pro-State (or bureaucratic?) and anti-statist camps.' Certainly, Leroy-Beaulieu's arguments did not favor the bourgeois rentier groups that benefited from the Third Republic's fiscal policies. Interestingly, he provided a comparison of revenues and taxes in France, England and Germany on the eve of World War I, see Leroy-Beaulieu (1914).

Table 3.7. *French Revenues, Expenditure, and Public Debt, 1870–1914 (in millions of old francs)*

| Date | Total Revenues | Total Expenditure | Public Debt |
|------|------|------|------|
| 1870 | 3125 | 3173 | 11516 |
| 1871 | 3221 | 3047 | 12454 |
| 1872 | 3062 | 2723 | 14988 |
| 1873 | 2691 | 2874 | 17463 |
| 1874 | 2609 | 2782 | 18752 |
| 1875 | 2870 | 2936 | 19918 |
| 1876 | 3187 | 3031 | 19909 |
| 1877 | 2896 | 3027 | 19895 |
| 1878 | 3427 | 3348 | 19879 |
| 1879 | 3490 | 3323 | 20356 |
| 1880 | 3531 | 3365 | 20391 |
| 1881 | 3785 | 3616 | 20366 |
| 1882 | 3644 | 3687 | 20405 |
| 1883 | 3653 | 3715 | 21493 |
| 1884 | 3449 | 3539 | 22804 |
| 1885 | 3320 | 3466 | 23754 |
| 1886 | 3169 | 3294 | 23730 |
| 1887 | 3244 | 3261 | 24662 |
| 1888 | 3268 | 3221 | 24919 |
| 1889 | 3271 | 3247 | 25178 |
| 1890 | 3376 | 3288 | 25153 |
| 1891 | 3364 | 3258 | 25129 |
| 1892 | 3370 | 3380 | 25099 |
| 1893 | 3366 | 3451 | 26017 |
| 1894 | 3458 | 3480 | 25992 |
| 1895 | 3416 | 3434 | 25967 |
| 1896 | 3436 | 3445 | 25942 |
| 1897 | 3528 | 3524 | 25914 |
| 1898 | 3620 | 3528 | 25889 |
| 1899 | 3657 | 3589 | 25864 |
| 1900 | 3815 | 3747 | 25839 |
| 1901 | 3634 | 3756 | 25813 |
| 1902 | 3582 | 3699 | 25778 |
| 1903 | 3668 | 3597 | 25985 |
| 1904 | 3739 | 3639 | 25959 |
| 1905 | 3766 | 3707 | 25934 |
| 1906 | 3837 | 3852 | 25884 |
| 1907 | 3968 | 3880 | 25851 |
| 1908 | 3966 | 4021 | 25826 |
| 1909 | 4141 | 4186 | 25511 |
| 1910 | 4274 | 4322 | 25461 |
| 1911 | 4689 | 4548 | 25410 |
| 1912 | 4857 | 4743 | 25360 |
| 1913 | 5092 | 5067 | 25311 |
| 1914 | 4549 | 10065 | 25261 |

*Sources:* See Tables 3.1 and 3.2.

## 3.5  The French Fiscal Challenge on the Eve of World War I

The effort could not be sustained, not least with the increase in prices after 1896 and with the need for rearmament as the militarist intentions of Germany became evident on the eve of World War I. Yet as late as 1903, with expenditure at 3,597 million francs, it was still less than that for 1883. The exponential growth was between 1913 and 1914, with the outbreak of World War I. With expenditure at 10,065 million francs, it can be estimated that the first year of the war saw expenditure at 22.1 percent of GDP, whereas revenues amounted to only 10 percent of GDP. The public debt was more or less stable and had not returned to its level in 1893, which means that, given the inflation in the intervening period, it had declined in real terms.

The most striking fact about the French economy in the nineteenth century, and the strongest contrast with earlier periods of French history, is the very slow increase in population, which ended in zero population growth by the end of the century. It had been France's large population that had provided resources for direct taxes in the ancien régime and the large size of the French army in comparison with those of its European rivals. Both these trends, too, were reversed. As François Crouzet (2003) observes, 'If the population of France had grown at the same rate as that of Britain, it would have been 100 million or more in 1914 (instead of 41 million).' The decision of French couples to practice birth control secured for most of them 'a mediocre but acceptable standard of living'; however, 'they reduced their country from first to fourth or even fifth place among economic powers and they also reduced its military potential, with dire consequences in two world wars' (Crouzet 2003: 238). Maddison's (1995) figures for the total population increase in the three large European economies provides telling evidence of Crouzet's argument: in 1820, France had a population of 31.2 million, higher than that of its two main European economic rivals; by 1913, with a population of just less than 41.5 million, it had declined from first to third among its immediate rivals.[10]

---

[10] The population figures for France were 31.2 million (1820), 38.4 million (1870), and 41.5 million (1913). Those for Germany were 24.9 million (1820), 39.2 million (1870), and 65.1 million (1913), and those for the United Kingdom were 21.2 million (1820), 31.4 million (1870), and 45.6 million (1913). Of course, all three were dwarfed by the United States, the population of which rose from 9.9 million in 1820 to 40.2 million in 1870 and 97.6 million by 1913 as a result of mass immigration (Maddison 2001: table B-10, downloaded from www.theworldeconomy.org/publications/worldeconomy/statistics.htm; accessed November 18, 2008).

For those French politicians responsible for constructing realistic annual budgets, the 1890s posed a serious problem. It was a decade of economic recession, a soaring arms race, and declining tax revenues. Other countries faced similar problems and dealt with them by introducing graduated income taxes. Germany did this in 1891, as did the United States in 1894. Opposition to the introduction of income tax in France was particularly intense.[11] But the need was clear: the campaign that led up to the presentation of a reforming tax bill was led initially by Godefroy Cavaignac and later by Léon Bourgeois. Both men appreciated the rapid advances in military technology as they did the onerous burden of equipping France's army with modern weapons. They were also, like all their countrymen, extremely nervous about living in the shadow of the German Empire. These factors accounted for their sense of urgency about the income tax (*impôt sur le revenu*). The new French cannon, which was the most closely guarded secret in the country, could fire twenty-five rounds per minute, while the old cannon could fire only three or four. Cavaignac seems to have been the first politician to understand that the new firepower could revolutionize the battlefield.

How then to pay for it? The French fiscal system relied too heavily on consumption taxes, and the income tax was, its defenders argued, a democratic attempt to reform a socially regressive fiscal system. In November 1895, Bourgeois formed his ministry and the battle over the new tax began immediately, but the government fell the following year without having succeeded in introducing it. A general income tax was not enacted in France until 1914, just a few weeks before the declaration of war. It was applied for the first time in 1915 (i.e., the incomes of 1915 had to be declared by taxpayers at the beginning of 1916) and has been applied ever since.

In 1905, the French national debt stood at 25,934 million francs, representing 18.1 percent of the total of great-power government bonds quoted in London. This was less than that of Britain, it is true (20.7 percent of the total), but still considerably higher than other great powers such as Russia (9.3 percent of the total), Germany and Prussia (8.2 percent of the total), and Austria (3.3 percent of the total). France,

[11] Kaplan (1995) argues that this conflict was more intense even than the Dreyfus affair, which few specialists of the period have been prepared to accept. For the example of the German income tax of June 24, 1891, see Kaplan 1995: 38. Godefroy Cavaignac (1895), the reporter of the military budget for the Budget Committee, had written on the importance of the German tax and had argued the case for a French version.

at 22.8 percent of the foreign total holding, was still in some considerable way the largest Continental power quoted at London (Ferguson 2006: 75, table 1). By 1910, the French savings banks had more than 8 million depositors among them; by 1913, their total assets were close to 6 billion francs – equivalent to about 18 percent of the French national debt. There was also a sustained effort to sell government debt directly to small investors by issuing rentes in small denominations; the number of rentiers rose from 824,000 in 1850 to more than 1 million in 1872 and reached 4.6 million in 1909 (Ferguson 2006: 96–7).

A constant of French pre–World War I politics was that some day there would be another war with Germany, during which France would conquer and reannex the provinces of Alsace and Lorraine that Germany had annexed in 1870. French military strategy depended on a large, active, allied Russian army in Poland threatening Berlin and forcing Germany to divide its armies while the French marched to the Rhine. Hence boosting the power of the czar by buying Russian bonds became a test of French patriotism. France subsidized the pre–World War I industrialization of Russia, the luxury of its court, and the expansion of the Russian military by substantial investments in Russian government and railway bonds. Such transfers of capital were facilitated by the operation of the international gold standard. The repudiation of the Russian loans during World War I dealt a damaging blow to investor confidence. The French rentiers never quite recovered from this blow, and after World War I, French loans were less common than before. The massive expenditures associated with the war had also weakened the position of Paris as a financial center (Horn 2006).

Théret (1995: 86–7) has commented that the years 1894–1912 were ones of strict budgetary control, 'une politique de puissance nationale et non une politique favourable aux rentiers,' a policy that halted the accumulation of private capital and permitted a restructuring of public expenditure in favor of national defense. This argument is borne out by the fact that, after 1895, the costs of national defense consistently exceeded those of debt servicing: there was no repetition of the reverse process, as in the quinquennium 1890–4. Although it was expected that the cost of reequipping the French artillery with its new rapid-fire cannon in 1895 would amount to 300 million francs (Kaplan 1995: 77, 195), and that to find this sum the deeply controversial income tax was needed, in reality new loans financed the project (Kaplan 1995: 88). The really significant sums of money were still being spent on the cost of debt servicing.[12] Here, to the lament of conservatives (Kaplan 1995: 127), the French government was assisted by the long-term fall in interest rates in the late nineteenth century and shorter-term cycles of economic growth.

However, this short period between 1894 and 1912 is in contrast to the rest of the period. Théret (1995) argues that the originality of the fiscal structure of France during the long nineteenth century, in comparison with that of the ancien régime, arises from the consistent growth in the public debt. Above all, the nineteenth century witnessed a growth of rentiers' incomes, and the fiscal system that they controlled through the parliament was essentially geared toward a perpetuation of such wealth. Thus, first and foremost, there was no repeat of the successive defaults of the ancien régime monarchy or of the massive default of 1797 under the Revolution (Hoffman, Postel-Vinay, and Rosenthal 2000: 200, table 8.2).

Hoffman, Postel-Vinay, and Rosenthal (2000) contend that the experience of nineteenth-century France shows that de jure stable public financial practices 'do not guarantee the rapid diffusion of credit.' During this period, they write, 'even though the unit of account's value remained constant in terms of gold and silver, government debt was being repaid with exacting precision, and lenders' interests were carefully protected, individuals were not convinced that these favourable practices would endure from one political regime to the next.' Instead, 'the public associated political instability with the risk of financial chaos. The fear of inflation was felt far more severely by private borrowers than by the state,' as it was they who had suffered from it in the 1790s. 'Capital markets,' Hoffman, Postel-Vinay and Rosenthal (2000) conclude, 'therefore remained segmented, and bilateral transactions continued to predominate.'[13] Although monetary stability was the basis of the

---

[12] Alexandre Ribot, finance minister in 1895, claimed that 1,497 million francs out of a total budget of 3,400 million francs was for debt-servicing costs. This figure is much greater than that of Fontvieille for this year (Kaplan 1995: 29).

[13] Hoffman, Postel-Vinay, and Rosenthal (2000: 290, 294, chaps. 10–11) argue that 'the differences between the countryside and Paris can by and large be explained by the different demand structure for loans in these two areas. These different demand structures explain why 'modern' credit intermediaries arose first in Paris and diffused only slowly through the countryside.' Also, 'none of the national banks [was] eager to open provincial branches – except in the largest cities – at least until the 1880s. It required considerable government pressure, for example, to get the Bank of France to open a

regime and reinforced the creditworthiness of the state, there was no equivalent assumption about debt stabilization. The nature of the debt itself – mostly in the form of perpetual or life rentes – was 'a more or less direct incitement' to further reliance on borrowing rather than increasing taxation, though this still poses the question of how an excessive – that is, unmanageable – debt burden was avoided: 'le recours à la rente,' it has been suggested, 'règle le recours a l'impôt et non l'inverse' (Théret 1995: 88).[14]

It is, thus, perhaps no surprise that Angus Maddison's (1995) calculations suggest that, in France, total government expenditure as a percentage of GDP at current prices in 1913 was significantly less than that of its two main European economic rivals; and among the big-four economic powers, the French figure was greater than only that of the United States.[15] In contrast, the holdings of foreign debt were much higher in France than elsewhere. Since the 1890s, the French government had helped to float Russian bonds on the Paris Stock Exchange. On the eve of the World War I, French private investments in Russian shares and bonds amounted to between 15 billion and 18 billion francs. After the Soviet debt repudiation of February 8, 1918, it was found that 1.6 million French investors held Russian bonds. The money lost to this debt repudiation has been estimated at 4.5 percent of French private wealth in 1919 (Oosterlinck and Szafarz 2004; Oosterlinck and Landon-Lane 2006: 507 n1). It was the trauma of World War I, with its unprecedented levels of government expenditure and borrowing, the imposition of income taxes, and the final shock of the Soviet debt repudiation that the golden age of the French rentier regime came to an inglorious but decisive end (Horn and Imlay 2005).

---

branch in every prefecture after 1880' (Hoffman, Postel-Vinay, and Rosenthal 2000: 272).

[14] Théret adds: 'il doit y avoir complémentarité entre rente et impôt, et non pure substituabilité comme sous l'ancienne monarchie absolue. C'est cette complémentarité qui est au centre d'une autorégulation du déficit budgétaire organisant un régime d'accumulation du capital rentier compatible avec des croissances de la dépense publique plus ou moins vives.'

[15] In descending order, Maddison's (2001) figures suggest percentages of 17.7 (Germany), 13.3 (the United Kingdom), 8.9 (France), and 8.0 (the United States). The arithmetic average for four European powers (i.e., including the Netherlands, at 8.2) was 12.0 percent, considerably greater than France's figure (table 3-9, downloaded from www.theworldeconomy.org/publications/worldeconomy/statistics.htm (accessed November 18, 2008).

## References

Arbulu, P. and Gallais-Hamonno, G. (2002) "Valeurs extrêmes et changements d'appréciation du risque à la Bourse de Paris sur deux siècles, 1802–2000," *Finance*, 23(12), 145–76.

Bonney, R. (1999) "France, 1494–1815," in R. Bonney (ed.) *The Rise of the Fiscal State in Europe, c. 1200–1815*. Oxford: Oxford University Press, 123–76.

Bouvier, F. (1969) "La croissance quantitative des finances publiques françaises et l'attitude des économistes (XIXe-XXe siècles)," *Revue Internationale d'Histoire de la Banque*, 2, 299–314.

Branda, P. (2004–5) "Les finances et le budget de la France napoléonienne," *Revue du Souvenir Napoléonien*, (Dec. 2004–Jan. 2005 and Feb–March 2005). www.napoleon.org/fr/salle_lecture/articles/files/financesbudget_branda_ sn455_janvier2005.asp accessed September 9, 2009; www.napoleon.org/fr/ salle_lecture/articles/files/financesbudget2_branda_sn457mars2005.asp accessed September 9, 2009; www.napoleon.org/fr/salle_lecture/articles/files/ financesbudget_bilan1814_branda_sn458_2005.asp#informations accessed September 9, 2009.

Bruguière, M. (1969) *La première Restauration et son budget*. Geneva: Droz.

Cameron, R. E. (1958) "Economic growth and stagnation in France, 1815–1914," *Journal of Modern History*, 30(1), 1–15.

Cameron, R. E. and Casson, M. (1961) *France and the Economic Development of Europe, 1815–1914. Conquests of Peace and Seeds of War*. Princeton, NJ: Princeton University Press.

Cavaignac, G. (1895) *Pour l'impôt progressif*. Paris: A. Colin.

Chapra, M. U. (2008) *Muslim Civilization: The Causes of Decline and the Need for Reform*. Leicester: Islamic Foundation.

Crouzet, F. (1993) *La grande inflation. La Monnaie en France de Louis XVI à Napoléon*. Paris: Fayard.

Crouzet, F. (2003) "The historiography of French economic growth in the nineteenth century," *Economic History Review*, 56, 215–42.

Ferguson, N. (2006) "Political risk and the international bond market between the 1848 Revolution and the outbreak of the First World War," *Economic History Review*, 59, 70–112.

Flandreau, M. (1995) *L'or du monde. La France et la stabilité du système monétaire international, 1848–1873*. Paris: Harmattan.

Flandreau, M. (1996) "Adjusting to the gold rush: Endogenous bullion points and the French balance of payments, 1846–1870," *Explorations in Economic History*, 33, 417–39.

Flandreau, M. and Le Cacheux, J. (1997) "Dettes publiques et stabilité monétaire en Europe. Les leçons de l'étalon or," *Revue Économique*, 48, 529–38.

Flandreau, M., and Zumer, F. (2004) *The Making of Global Finance 1880–1913*. Paris: Organisation for Economic Co-operation and Development.

Fontvieille, L. (1976) *Évolution et croissance de l'Etat français, 1815–1969*. Paris: Institut des Sciences Mathématiques et Economiques Appliquées.

Fontvieille, L. (1981) *Évolution et croissance de l'Administration Départementale française, 1815–1974*. Paris: Institut des Sciences Mathématiques et Economiques Appliquées.

Gemie, S. (1992). "Morality and the Bourgeoisie: The Work of Paul Leroy-Beaulieu (1843–1916)," *Journal of Contemporary History*, 27, 345–362.

Hautcoeur, P.-C. (1997) "The Bank of France," in D. Glasner (ed.), *Business Cycles and Depressions: An Encyclopedia*. New York: Garland, 39–42.

Hautcoeur, P.-C., Kang, Z., Romey, C., Seck, T. and Straus, A. (2007) *Le marché financier français au xixe siècle. I. Récit*. Paris: Publications de la Sorbonne.

Hoffman, P. T., Postel-Vinay, G. and Rosenthal, J.-L. (2000) *Priceless Markets: The Political Economy of Credit in Paris, 1660–1870*. Chicago: University of Chicago Press.

Horn, M. (2006) Review of *London and Paris as International Financial Centres in the Twentieth Century*, by Youssef Cassis and Éric Bussière. *H-France Review*, 6(June).

Horn, M. and Imlay, T. (2005) "Money in Wartime: France's Financial Preparations for the Two World Wars," *International History Review*, 27, 709–753.

Kaplan, R. E. (1995) *Forgotten Crisis: The Fin-de-Siècle Crisis of Democracy in France*. Oxford: Berg.

Leroy-Beaulieu, P. (1912) *Traité de la Science des Finances*. Paris: F. Alcan [8th edn.] www.archive.org/details/traitdelascienc01lerogoog accessed September 10, 2009. [5th edn., 1891.]

Leroy-Beaulieu, P. (1914) *Les Impôts et les Revenus en France, en Angleterre et en Allemagne*. Paris.

Maddison, A. (1995) *Monitoring the World Economy, 1820–1992*. Paris: Organisation for Economic Co-operation and Development.

Maddison, A. (2001) *The World Economy: A Millennial Perspective*. Paris: Organisation for Economic Co-operation and Development.

Nikitin, M. (2001) "The birth of a modern public sector accounting system in France and Britain and the influence of Count Mollien," *Accounting History*, 6, 75–101.

Oosterlinck, K. and Landon-Lane, J. S. (2006) "Hope springs eternal: French bondholders and the Soviet repudiation, 1915–1919," *Review of Finance*, 10(4), 507–35. ideas.repec.org/p/sol/wpaper/05-013.html (accessed November 28, 2006).

Oosterlinck, K. and Szafarz, A. (2004) "One asset, two prices: The case of the tsarist repudiated bonds," Centre Bernheim ULB Working Paper 04–022 (August 24, 2004), ssrn.com/abstract-582041 (accessed November 18, 2008).

Sargent, T. J. and Velde, F. R. (1995) "Macroeconomic features of the French Revolution," *Journal of Political Economy*, 103(3), 473–518.

Tapiès, F. de (1845) *La France et l'Angleterre ou statistique morale et physique comparée à celle de l'Angleterre*. Paris: Guillaumin.

Théret, B. (1988) *La place de l'État dans les théories de la régulation: revue critique et repositionnement à la lumière de l'histoire*. Unpublished communication at the Colloque International Sur la Théorie de la Régulation. Barcelona, June 1988.

Théret, B. (1995) "Régulation du déficit budgétaire et croissance des dépenses de l'Etat en France de 1815 à 1939. Une modélisation économétrique simple des régimes fisco financiers libéraux," *Revue Économique*, 46 (1), 57–90.

Toutain, J.-C. (1987) *Le Produit Intérieur Brut de la France de 1789 à 1982*. Paris: Institut des Sciences Mathématiques et Economiques Appliquées.

Velde, F. R. and Weir, D. R. (1992) "The financial market and government debt policy in France, 1746–1793," *Journal of Economic History*, 52, 1–39.

White, E. N. (2001) "Making the French pay: The costs and consequences of the Napoleonic reparations," *European Review of Economic History*, 5, 337–65.

4

# The Evolution of Public Finances in Nineteenth-Century Germany

## Mark Spoerer

### 4.1 Introduction

In contrast to many other countries of nineteenth-century Europe, Germany was not a nation-state until the unification of 1871. In 1789, Germany consisted of more than three hundred territories that were formally subjected to the emperor in Vienna but were in practice independent. Under the pressure of Napoléon, Germany was mediatized, a policy that was continued by the Congress of Vienna. The central European political landscape that emerged in 1815 was dominated by the Habsburg Empire and Prussia, followed by a number of midsize states, which were, ranked by population, Bavaria, Hanover, Württemberg, Saxony, and Baden. What was later to become imperial Germany (excluding Alsace-Lorraine) consisted of altogether thirty-five states, Frankfurt am Main, and three Hanseatic cities. Figure 4.1 depicts Germany in the boundaries that emerged after the Congress of Vienna.

In terms of public finances, a formal and a material criterion each highlight the most important differences among these states. The first is whether the public finances were based on a constitution. Although the three southern German states adopted constitutions quite quickly after 1815, most northern German states were reluctant in this respect, with Prussia being the most prominent example. Whether a state was based on a constitution roughly coincided with a specific tax structure, which might serve as an alternative, material criterion. The tax systems of the southern states – Bavaria, Württemberg, and Baden – were primarily based on impersonal taxes on land, buildings, and business, as in France. The Prussian tax system, in contrast, followed more the English example

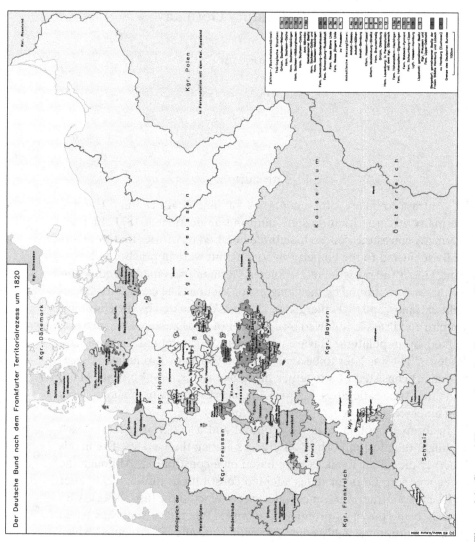

Figure 4.1. Central Europe after the Congress of Vienna, circa 1820. *Source:* IEG Maps (www.ieg-maps.de).

and relied partially on personal taxes. A third group of German states, for the most part small and poor states with little administrative control over the country counted primarily on indirect taxes.

Given the limited scope of this chapter, it may be useful to focus for the period before 1871 on Prussia, which accounted for 55 percent of the German population until the annexations of 1866 (more than 60 percent thereafter), and Württemberg in the Southwest, which has been characterized as the most consequent example of the south German impersonal tax systems (Gerloff 1929: 52). The other midsize German states appear only when their development contributes to the general understanding of how German public finance evolved over the long nineteenth century. The development in Austria-Hungary is described in a separate chapter in this volume by Michael Pammer.

Modern literature on the history of public finances in Germany is by no means abundant. A thoughtful narrative that intertwines public finances with political history is a more recent book of Hans-Peter Ullmann (2005). Whereas Ullmann's monograph has not a single table or graph, a solid account by Eckart Schremmer (1989) reliably summarizes many empirical facts. Andreas Thier (1999) has researched the politics behind Prussia's tax policies in depth. Mark Spoerer (2004, 2007) has focused on the distributional effects of taxation in Germany.

## 4.2 The Constitutional and Institutional Framework

One of the central propositions of finance sociology, a new discipline that emerged toward the end of the period covered in this book, is that the power relations of a given country are nowhere better reflected than in its fiscal structures, especially its budget. Rudolf Goldscheid (1926), the early pioneer of finance sociology, emphasized this view by remarking that the "budget is the skeleton of the state, recklessly stripped of misleading ideologies" (my translation).

The public budget, however, was a product of the nineteenth century. During the ancien régime, no German state ever published budget data. Moreover, no German territorial state would have been able to compile a complete and unified budget, as the princely finances were usually split into one or more exchequers that formed the *camerale*, and many more exchequers belonging to the *contributionale*. The *camerale* was the financial administration of all revenues that emerged from the property and the regal rights of the prince, such as revenues from domains, forests, mines, the salt monopoly, customs, and so on. The *contributionale* comprised revenues from taxes levied on the subjects of the princes, such as property taxes on land and excises. Whereas the prince was formally autonomous in managing the *camerale* revenues, he originally needed the consent of the estates if he wished to increase the revenues from direct taxes for the *contributionale*. During the period of absolutism, however, many princes were able to push back the estates, so that the princely control of the *contributionale* increased.

Early modern public finances did not end in the *camerale* and the *contributionale*, however. Gentry, church, and cities levied a multitude of taxes and duties for local purposes that were never recorded centrally. Even a state like Prussia, notorious for its rigid bureaucracy, was not able to draw up a complete overview of all expenditures and revenues at the levels below the central administration, that is, the provinces and the municipalities, before 1911. As other German states were even less successful, the German Empire was never able to fully record total public expenditure and revenues.[1]

### 4.2.1 The Legacy of the Napoleonic Wars

The complete shake-up of Germany during and after the Napoleonic Wars led to a far-reaching reorganization of public finances, part of which followed reforms introduced by the French occupation. A number of other factors contributed to this reorganization. The first and foremost is that most princes were forced by the "enlightened" ideas imported by the French to decree a constitution, the heart of which was a regular budget that had to be prepared, enforced, and controlled. The second is that, except for some very small territories and independent cities, no German state escaped territorial changes – in fact, most of those who survived the Napoleonic Wars and the mediatization added substantial territories to their existing ones. The incorporation of the new territories induced the princes and their governments to undertake administrative reforms on large scale, and reforms of the public finances were given highest priority. This was a consequence of, third, the large public debts accumulated by the German states in the course of the wars between 1792 and 1815. A financial review in Prussia, for example, resulted in an accumulated debt of 863 million marks in 1815. As the lenders, however, were mostly

---

[1] Apart from a heavily criticized government memorandum (Reichsschatzamt 1908), the first effort to record all public expenditure and revenues for Germany dates back to 1916, and another, more reliable one, to 1930; see Gerloff 1916; Statistisches Reichsamt 1930; for an assessment, see Spoerer (1997: 165–7).

to be found among Prussia's ruling elite, a debt default was not a viable option. Instead, new and higher taxes were introduced (Schissler 1982: 372, 380–382).[2]

The southern German states, strongly influenced by France, were the first in Germany to introduce constitutions, among them Bavaria and Baden in 1818 and Württemberg in 1819. The public revenues of these three southern German states relied heavily on impersonal taxes, which built on the example of the French *contributions*. The case of Württemberg is illustrative. Building on impersonal taxes inherited from the ancien régime, in 1821, the parliament created a system of property taxes on land, buildings, and businesses. The system followed the allocation principle, which meant, first, that the total revenues of the three taxes were capped by the parliament, and second, that the revenue shares of the three taxes were fixed. Originally, the land tax contributed 71 percent; the buildings tax, 17 percent; and the business tax, 12 percent. The allocation of the tax to the individual taxpayers followed detailed regional breakdowns that were partly based on the land register and partly on "local usage" (Spoerer 2004: 85).

### 4.2.2 The Impact of the Revolutions of 1848
In the aftermath of political unrests sparked by the July Revolution in France, Saxony, Hanover, and Hesse-Kassel introduced constitutions in 1830–1. The Prussian kings were able to resist the trend until 1848–9, when a conservative constitution and the notorious three-class suffrage were decreed after the violent turmoil of 1847–8.

The Prussian three-class suffrage is the most prominent example for the nexus between political participation and taxation in nineteenth-century Germany. An important element of the Prussian tax reforms around 1820 was the creation of the graduated capitation tax (*Klassensteuer*), a direct tax that was levied in the countryside and in a small part of the cities, and the milling and butchery tax, an indirect tax that was levied in all other cities. The graduated capitation tax stood halfway between a poll tax and a primitive income tax. The taxpayers were not taxed according to their actual income – whose assessment would have overstrained the local authorities – but according to their societal status: day laborer, baker, estate owner, and so on. Whereas the tax burden lay

---

[2] Germany had eight currencies until 1873, when the mark was introduced. Until then, Prussia used the taler. Throughout this article, all currencies are converted into marks (1 mark equals one-third of a taler).

heavily on day laborers – there was no exemption for low-income brackets until 1875 – large estate owners paid no more than the maximum tax amount of 432 marks annually. To compare, throughout the first half of the nineteenth century, annual wages of German builders were about 300 marks.[3]

The graduated capitation tax remained unchanged until the aftermath of the 1848 revolutions. In the tax reform of 1851, the tax base changed from socioeconomic status to actual income, and the graduated capitation tax was limited to income brackets of up to 3,000 marks annually. Taxpayers whose income was more than 3,000 marks were subjected to the graduated income tax. This new tax, which also tapped the cities, stood for a burden of around 3 percent on income up to a tax ceiling of 21,600 marks.

While the graduated income tax imposed a much higher tax burden on wealthy taxpayers, it increased their political voice enormously. The three-class suffrage introduced in 1849 linked the voting power of taxpayers to the amount of direct taxes they paid. The system divided the voters into three electoral classes depending on direct state taxes paid (graduated income tax, graduated capitation tax, and impersonal taxes). The first class comprised the largest taxpayers until their combined direct taxes made up one-third of the total direct tax revenues of the voting district. The second class was formed by the next group of taxpayers and filled the second third of the total direct tax revenues. In the first class, the share of voters did usually not exceed more than 5 percent of the electorate; in the second, the share ranged from 12–16 percent and the rest of the electorate was to be found in the third class (80–85 percent). However, each class provided the same amount of delegates who voted on the candidates for the lower house. Hence wealthy taxpayers were extraordinarily privileged by this procedure (Nützenadel 2007: 119–21). Although nearly everywhere in Germany franchise was tied to the amount of direct taxes paid (by men), this amount usually served merely as a threshold. Tying the weight of the vote to the economic position of the voter was a Prussian peculiarity (copied only by some small states and by Saxony between 1896 and 1909) that evoked much criticism at the time. The three-class suffrage, however, was not repealed until 1918.

### 4.2.3 The Fiscal Structure of Unified Germany

The predecessor of the German Empire, which was founded in 1871, is – not only in fiscal terms – the German *Zollverein* (customs union), which

---

[3] For wages, see Gömmel (1979: 27).

was created in 1833 and became effective on January 1, 1834. It is generally assumed that two motives propelled the formation of the *Zollverein*. First, the German states realized that customs were barriers to trade. Prussia, for example, abolished all domestic customs in 1818. A geopolitical problem for Prussia was that its territory was divided and that it lacked a territorial link between its new and comparably rich provinces in the West and the mainland in the East. Hence, Prussia tried to convince the neighboring states to form a customs union. This, second, was also a means of expanding Prussia's political influence in central Europe and pushing back that of Austria, its major rival. The agreements that finally led to the *Zollverein* stipulated that the customs revenues of the *Zollverein* were to be distributed among the states on a per capita basis. As the ratio of gross revenues and costs of maintaining a customs line increases with the size of the population, this was an important incentive for the smaller states to join the *Zollverein* and a remarkable financial sacrifice of Prussia (Dumke 1976: chaps. 1 and 3).

Nearly four decades later, Germany was unified and dominated by Prussia, which accounted for roughly two-thirds of German territory and population. The main other member states were, by population, Bavaria, Saxony, Württemberg, and Baden. For their consent to join the empire, the south German member states reserved a number of exceptions, among which figured the right to continue to levy the beer tax and the liquor tax.

The distribution of tasks between the newly formed *Reich* and the member states was typical for a federal state. The *Reich* was responsible for defense, international relations, and the government of Alsace-Lorraine, which was annexed in 1871. Moreover, it ran a number of monopoly establishments, like the *Reichspost* and the railways in Alsace-Lorraine. The revenues of the *Reich* were – apart from profits of the monopolies – confined to the customs duties, a number of other indirect taxes that were transferred from the member states, mainly on the consumption of salt and of staple luxury goods like liquor, beer, sugar, and tobacco, and to some indirect transaction taxes.

A very peculiar institution was the financial settlement between the *Reich* and the member states. The *Reich*'s constitution of 1871 stipulated that, should the *Reich* not be able to finance its activities by its own means, the member states would have to pay so-called matricular contributions, which were allocated among the member states on a per capita basis. When the *Reich* introduced protectionist tariffs in 1879, the member states feared that its financial position would increase much more than they wished it to. Hence, the *Reichstag* (the lower house) pushed through a law that committed the *Reich* to remit customs duties and tobacco taxes that exceeded a fixed sum of 130 million marks (raised to 143 million marks in 1896 and 180 million marks in 1897) to the member states (Kruedener 1987). Hence, since 1880, matricular contributions and remittances flowed back and forth between the *Reich* and the member states. This considerably complicated the planning of the budget for the member states. Well-known public economists like Adolph Wagner and Wilhelm Gerloff pleaded for a thorough fiscal reform. The reforms that actually took place, however, did not fundamentally change the structural imbalances between the *Reich* and the member states.

The assessment of these imbalances has recently come under discussion. The traditional view holds that the *Reich* was financially weak and a *Kostgänger* (boarder) of the member states and that the reluctance of the member states to improve the financial position of the *Reich* was responsible for the increased accumulation of central government debt in the run-up to the First World War (Schremmer 1989: 464–70; Hefeker 2001). Niall Ferguson has taken the theory of underendowment to the extreme. He argues that it was the weak financial position of the *Reich* that made an armaments race against Germany's main adversaries (France, Russia, and Britain) hopeless in the long run and thus induced the imperial military to conduct a preemptive strike in the summer of 1914 (Ferguson 1994; 1998: 135–48). Charles Blankart (2007), in contrast, has taken issue with the underendowment hypothesis. The fact that the *Reich* was able to overdraft its budget allocations and accumulated debt is considered a consequence of a soft budget constraint. What followed was a reverse bailout from the bottom up, that is, from the member states that had to increase their matricular contributions (Blankart 2007: 51–4).

## 4.3 The Increase of Public Expenditure and Wagner's Law

The expenditure side of the classical early modern princely budget was dominated by three items that helped the prince gain, keep, and demonstrate his power: the military, the public administration, and the court. As mentioned before, however, besides the prince, a number of other subcentral institutions collected taxes and duties and spent them for collective purposes such as municipal administration and maintenance of local roads and bridges.

In the course of the nineteenth century, a number of expenditure items gained particular importance: education, administration, utilities, transport, and welfare. The military, which lost importance throughout the nineteenth century, regained shares only in the last years before the First World War.

The expenses for education, which were primarily borne by the municipalities, increased because of three factors. First, compulsory education, introduced in Prussia as early as 1717, was increasingly enforced. Second, Germany experienced population growth rates in the nineteenth century that were never attained before or after (Guinnane 2003). Whereas the aforementioned factors are of quantitative nature, a third factor concerned the quality of schooling. Teachers used to be employed on a part-time basis and were paid accordingly, yet in the course of the nineteenth century, the occupation experienced a professionalization that was reflected in higher salaries. In Prussia, expenditure on elementary education devoured 66 percent of total public expenditure on education in 1891 (and 69 percent in 1911). Whereas the Prussian municipalities and the state spent 33 million marks for elementary education in 1864, this amount increased to 421 million in 1911. Expressed in real terms (1913 prices), Prussia spent 20 marks per elementary school student in 1864 and 65 marks in 1911 (Lundgreen 1973: 111).

The expenses for the administration increased because most states undertook large administrative reform projects. Although one aim was to unify the old core territory with the territories gained before and in 1815, the other was to strengthen the grip on the country in general. The outdated land registers had to be updated (not least for the purpose of allocating the land tax), and the states were increasingly active in improving the infrastructure.

Public utilities – for the production and distribution of water, gas and electricity, or sewerage – was another important field of activity for the municipalities. The reason so many municipalities engaged in the new industry of utilities is to be found in the fact that the cost structure made them natural monopolies. Once a network that links production (of water, gas, or electricity) and consumption is established, a second one is usually inefficient. The activities of so many municipalities in costly but potentially profitable public enterprises led contemporary liberal observers to create the dictum of 'municipal socialism.'

Another monopoly played an important role in the fiscal history of Prussia, the railways. Following a liberal decade in the 1860s, the mixed system of public and private railways came increasingly under public criticism in Germany. The pricing policies of the private railways were a particular source of criticism. After the stock market crisis of 1873, which was followed by a real economic crisis until 1879, the states, especially

Prussia, nationalized most of the German private railways at comparably low cost (Ziegler 1996: 211–29). Maintaining and expanding the railways was very costly and inflated the Prussian state budget enormously. Yet the revenues were huge as well. Rather than passing on efficiency gains to their customers, the Prussian state railways took advantage of the monopoly and generated huge profits (see the subsequent section).

Welfare costs had always been important items in municipal budgets. But whereas supporting the poor used to be discretionary, welfare support became an entitlement with the much-praised social security legislation of Reich Chancellor Otto von Bismarck. By inaugurating the statutory health insurance in 1883, the accident insurance in 1884, and what later became old-age insurance in 1889, Bismarck intended to take the wind out of the socialists' sails. His aim was to make the laborer a dependent of the state, someone who feared that he risked his pension should the socialists overthrow the bourgeois order. As the branches of the social insurance system, which was partly financed by employers and employees, needed start-up financing, the *Reich* had to supply funds.

Table 4.1 illustrates the expenditure shares of Prussia and the *Reich*. Because the *Reich* took over the responsibility for the military, the data for Prussia are affected by a structural break in 1871.

As complete public finance data including the municipalities were compiled and published only in the very last years of the empire, it is not possible to trace the breakdown of total public expenditure (*Reich*, member states, and municipalities) over time.[4] However, the data are sufficient to give an impression of total public expenditure in Germany prior to and after the First World War (Table 4.2).

The increase of public expenditure (see also Table 4.1) was acknowledged by contemporaries. As early as 1863, the public economist Adolph Wagner (1835–1917) formulated what later became famous as Wagner's law: the wealthier a country becomes, the more the share of public activity (and thus expenditure) will increase (Wagner 1863: 2–5). In other words, public expenditure will increase faster than national income. Although Wagner never expressed his opinion on whether or at what level the rise of the public share would end, he and his contemporaries, who considered high a state quota of 10 percent, would certainly have been astonished had they been able to anticipate the figures of the interwar period and especially the second half of the twentieth century.

---

[4] Below the level of the states were, apart from the municipalities, also municipal associations. These two governmental levels are counted together throughout this article.

Table 4.1. *Public Expenditure Shares of Prussia and the Reich, 1847–1913 (shares in percentage)*

| | Military | Administration | Welfare | Public Enterprises | Debt Service | Transfers | Total (mio. M) |
|---|---|---|---|---|---|---|---|
| Prussia | | | | | | | |
| 1847 | 30.3 | 39.7 | 0.0 | 19.0 | 11.0 | 0.0 | 254.7 |
| 1867 | 25.4 | 39.1 | 0.0 | 26.0 | 9.5 | 0.0 | 513.0 |
| 1875 | 0.0 | 48.0 | 0.0 | 31.7 | 15.0 | 5.3 | 812.6 |
| 1892 | 0.0 | 30.1 | 0.0 | 40.1 | 19.0 | 10.7 | 1,993.6 |
| 1913 | 0.0 | 21.3 | 0.0 | 53.6 | 21.3 | 3.8 | 5,917.9 |
| Reich | | | | | | | |
| 1872 | 96.0 | 2.2 | 1.6 | 0.1 | 0.0 | 0.0 | 1,380.3 |
| 1893–4 | 53.8 | 6.7 | 5.7 | 1.9 | 5.1 | 26.7 | 1,269.9 |
| 1912 | 44.8 | 8.9 | 5.0 | 30.0 | 8.0 | 3.4 | 2,893.4 |

*Note:* Transfers are either matricular contributions to or remittances from the Reich.
*Source:* Prussia: Schremmer (1989: 458, 462); Reich: *Statistisches Jahrbuch für das Deutsche Reich* (1880: 156–9; 1897: 158–63; 1914: 353–5).

Table 4.2. *Aggregated Public Expenditure in Germany, 1913–14 and 1927–8 (percentage)*

|  | 1913–14 | 1927–8 |
|---|---|---|
| General administration | 5.8 | 6.0 |
| Fiscal administration | 3.5 | 4.8 |
| External and internal security | 33.5 | 14.8 |
| Of which military | 25.6 | 5.1 |
| Education | 19.6 | 19.1 |
| Welfare | 9.7 | 20.8 |
| Housing | 0.4 | 10.8 |
| Economy and transport | 14.3 | 14.2 |
| Other expenditure | 13.2 | 9.5 |
| Total (mio. M or RM) | 8,063 | 18,771 |
| As share of gross domestic product | 14.2 | 22.7 |

*Notes:* Excluding war burdens (in 1927–8, mostly reparations). Total public expenditure for 1913–14 rebased to prewar territory.

*Source:* Statistisches Reichsamt (1930: 5, 16, 103); GDP: Ritschl and Spoerer (1997: 53–4 ff.).

## 4.4 New Tasks Require New Sources of Revenue

### 4.4.1 Traditional Taxes

Apart from revenues from traditional activities, like domains and forests, impersonal taxes were the backbone of most states' finances, usually on land and buildings, and excises. In contrast to direct taxes, which at least before the age of absolutism required the consent of the estates, excises originated from regal rights and were usually not subject to restrictions. Many princes followed the principle of defining a broad tax base and low excise rates. Prussia's move from broad excises to the milling and butchery tax in 1820 with high tax rates on flour and meat products was thus an exception that found few epigones (Spoerer 2008a).

Impersonal taxes had emerged from extraordinary contributions in times of war and penury, for which the prince had been forced to win the consent of the estates. Whereas princes aimed to make the tax permanent, they often had to accept that the total amount of the tax was capped. The fixed tax amount was then allocated to individual taxpayers according to the estimated revenue of the soil or the building according to historical averages. That is, the tax amount did not depend on the actual efforts of the taxpayer. Although this type of tax was increasingly regarded as outdated, modern public economists would find it interesting, as the separation of taxpayers' tax duty and their ability to pay did not create incentive problems. The same holds, with a few reservations, for the graduated capitation tax that was levied in Prussia since 1820 (see Section 4.2.2). Until the introduction of the graduated income tax in 1851, economic success would transform into a higher tax duty only if taxpayers changed their profession.

As the economic importance of the nonagricultural sectors grew, the states introduced business taxes or reformed existing ones. In the early nineteenth century, businesses were usually assessed by items that were easily identified: employees, horses, and so on. Some states, like Baden, developed assessment schemes so sophisticated that they can be interpreted as production functions (Schremmer 1987).

There are two sources of income that the German states found difficult to tax. On the one hand, interest from financial assets remained largely untaxed. On the other hand, the rise of professions enabled individuals to earn large incomes independent of visible assets like soil, buildings, or machinery. Income from human capital thus was underproportionally taxed before the rise of the income tax.

### 4.4.2 The Fall and Rise of the Income Tax

When German bureaucrats and politicians discussed the introduction of the income tax, they always looked at the British experience. After William Pitt introduced the income tax in 1798 to finance the war against Napoléon, Prussian reformers were keen to follow the British example. Following the defeat against France in 1807, Prussia had to pay hefty reparations and tried to reorganize its revenues. In 1808, Prussia introduced an income tax that it declared as an extraordinary direct emergency measure – to no avail, the taxpayers' resistance forced the administration to suspend the tax collection. A second effort in 1811–12 produced no better results (Schremmer 1989: 329, 428–9). When Britain abolished the income tax in 1815, the discussion in Germany fell silent.

After Britain reintroduced the income tax in 1842 – and this time permanently – an increasing number of commentators urged the German states to follow the British example. The income tax, however, raised concerns and emotions. Liberal economists, in particular, denounced the income tax as intrusive, confiscatory, or even terrorist. In contrast, an influential group of public finance economists spoke in favor of the income tax because it allowed integrating redistributive elements into the tax system by means of progressive taxation. Moreover, once introduced, the positive financial results of the income tax attracted bureaucrats and politicians alike. Most other direct taxes were income inelastic; that is, revenues increased less than proportionally with income. The income tax, by definition, kept pace with increasing incomes and even offered the possibility to siphon off more via progressive tax rates.

Hence, a number of German states followed the British example, among them Saxony, then the economically most advanced German territorial state, in 1878, and Baden, in 1884. The other southern states, however, stuck to their quite sophisticated impersonal tax systems for the time being. The breakthrough of the income tax in Germany came with the famous tax reform of the Prussian finance minister Johannes von Miquel. After Bismarck, a fervent enemy of direct taxes in general and the income tax in particular, had left the helm in 1890 (both as German chancellor and as Prussian prime minister), the way was cleared for the income tax. The Prussian income tax was introduced in 1891 (effective from 1893) and raised more revenues than even its proponents had hoped for. It was followed by a property tax that, in contrast to the existing ones, also targeted financial assets. The existing impersonal taxes on land, buildings, and businesses were transferred to the municipalities.[5]

For a number of reasons, Prussian politicians were keen to retain the income tax and rejected proposals to transfer it to the *Reich*. The first was simply its profitability. Second, the income tax, especially if enhanced with progressive elements, was considered a precarious tool that should not fall into the hands of the socialists, who were much more successful in elections for the *Reichstag* than for the Prussian lower house, which was easier to control for the ruling elite because of the three-class suffrage. Hence, in contrast to Britain, the German *Reich* did not dispose of a central income tax at the eve of the First World War.

### 4.4.3 Public Enterprises, Railways, and State Finance

Another peculiar feature of the German budgets in the nineteenth century – at the level of the states and, after 1871, of the *Reich* – was the large share of revenues from public enterprises. Among them figured traditional establishments like those responsible for domains, forests, salt and coal mines, and so on. Postal services expanded in parallel to the emerging manufacturing and service sectors. The traditional public establishments were increasingly joined by public enterprises already described in Section 4.3: utilities, public transport, and railways.

Expenditure for and revenues from public enterprises extended the budget, of course. If one is interested in the fiscal burden of the taxpayer, however, it is more meaningful to look at the surplus (or losses)

---

[5] See Schremmer (1989: 443–8); Thier (2009).

Table 4.3. *Public Revenue Shares of Prussia and Württemberg, 1819–1913*

| | Shares (percentage) | | | Million Marks | | | |
|---|---|---|---|---|---|---|---|
| | Operating Surplus | Direct Taxes | Indirect Taxes | Operating Surplus | Direct Taxes | Indirect Taxes | Total |
| Prussia | | | | | | | |
| 1857 | 12.7 | 39.6 | 47.7 | 35.3 | 110.4 | 133.0 | 278.7 |
| 1869 | 20.0 | 37.9 | 42.1 | 104.2 | 197.6 | 219.7 | 521.5 |
| 1876 | 19.2 | 44.8 | 35.9 | 132.5 | 308.7 | 247.4 | 688.6 |
| 1883 | 25.4 | 42.0 | 32.6 | 220.8 | 364.1 | 282.7 | 867.6 |
| 1895 | 35.2 | 29.9 | 34.9 | 546.2 | 464.0 | 541.2 | 1,551.4 |
| 1902 | 31.7 | 35.0 | 33.2 | 664.8 | 734.3 | 696.8 | 2,095.9 |
| 1913 | 18.9 | 45.0 | 36.2 | 664.4 | 1,581.5 | 1,271.7 | 3,517.6 |
| Württemberg | | | | | | | |
| 1819–20 | 36.5 | 39.6 | 24.0 | 7.0 | 7.6 | 4.6 | 19.2 |
| 1831–2 | 40.2 | 35.6 | 24.2 | 7.8 | 6.9 | 4.7 | 19.4 |
| 1843–4 | 41.8 | 28.5 | 29.7 | 10.0 | 6.8 | 7.1 | 23.9 |
| 1860–1 | 42.9 | 31.1 | 25.9 | 14.9 | 10.8 | 9.0 | 34.7 |
| 1869–70 | 32.7 | 32.5 | 34.8 | 13.8 | 13.7 | 14.7 | 42.2 |
| 1879–80 | 31.9 | 38.5 | 29.6 | 21.1 | 25.5 | 19.6 | 66.2 |
| 1895–6 | 25.1 | 35.9 | 39.0 | 28.9 | 41.3 | 44.8 | 115.0 |
| 1911 | 13.8 | 44.0 | 42.2 | 27.0 | 86.3 | 82.7 | 196.0 |

*Note:* Includes revenues from the *Zollverein/Reich* and municipalities (in contrast to Table 4.4).
*Source:* Spoerer (2004: 108–11).

of the public enterprises. The revenues are not pure fiscal income like taxes (less tax collection costs, which usually amounted to 3–10 percent) but have to be set off against the costs. Insofar as there is a monopoly rent that exceeds normal profits (covering capital costs and an imputed owner's salary), the operating surplus of public operations should be interpreted economically as indirect taxes (Fremdling 1980: 38) and thus might be called "indirect indirect taxes" (Spoerer 2004: 106).

The increase of the operating surplus generated by public enterprises was a welcome revenue source for the Prussian Prime Minister Bismarck. As he was often in conflict with the parliament, which was not willing to consent to new taxes without political concessions, the railway profits were a comfortable extraparliamentary substitute for tax revenues (Fremdling 1980; Spoerer 2007: 51–65).

The *Reich* and the municipalities profited from public enterprises as well, but not on the same scale as Prussia. Table 4.3 illustrates the total fiscal burden on the populations in Prussia and Württemberg, that is, the operating surplus of public enterprises and the gross revenues of direct taxes and indirect taxes of all three governmental levels (*Zollverein/Reich*, member states, and municipalities). In both countries, the share of the operating surplus was still more than a quarter at the end of the nineteenth century.

## 4.5 The Economic Effects of Taxation

### 4.5.1 The Public-Sector Share

When Adolf Wagner formulated his law of increasing state activity, he was not able to support his thesis with hard data. Public economists in the late twentieth century who calculated the public-sector share in Germany even came to the conclusion that it fell throughout the period from 1815 to the First World War or remained constant (Weitzel 1967; Recktenwald 1970; 1977: 733).[6] Past research on the public-sector share, however, considered only two of the three German governmental levels, the two for which published data are easily available: the Reich and the member states. Thus the enormous increase of municipal finances, especially since the 1870s, has been overlooked. Table 4.4 illustrates this from the revenue side of the public budgets.

If the tax revenues of all three governmental levels are taken into consideration, it emerges that the overall tax burden, both absolute and compared to national income, increased at least since the mid-nineteenth century both in Prussia and in Württemberg.

Whereas the outlined symbols in Figure 4.2 represent the taxes as measured conventionally, the bold symbols also include the operating surplus of public enterprises (both in the numerator and in the denominator of the tax-load ratio).

As Figure 4.2 shows, the tax burden increased in both absolute and relative terms. Because public debt played a significant role only shortly after the Napoleonic Wars and shortly preceding the First World War (see Section 4.7), we can safely conclude that Wagner's law, which in its original formulation pertained to public expenditure, is a valid empirical description of the development of the public-sector share during his time.

How was that increasing burden distributed among taxpayers? The following two sections focus on the class-specific distribution of the tax burden and on how – as early as around 1900 – evasive reactions of wealthy taxpayers forced Prussian municipalities in the Berlin area into tax competition.

---

[6] For the conventional wisdom confirming Wagner's thesis, see Andic and Veverka (1964).

Table 4.4. *Government-Level Shares of Total Tax Revenues in Prussia and Württemberg, 1819–1913 (percentage)*

|  | Prussia | | | Württemberg | | |
|---|---|---|---|---|---|---|
|  | *Zollverein* Reich | State | Municipalities | *Zollverein* Reich | State | Municipalities |
| 1819 |  |  |  |  | 79.7 | 20.4 |
| 1831 |  |  |  |  | 82.8 | 17.2 |
| 1843 |  |  |  | 32.4 | 46.0 | 21.6 |
| 1857 | 21.2 | 60.4 | 18.4 |  |  |  |
| 1860 |  |  |  | 24.1 | 53.3 | 22.6 |
| 1869 | 33.8 | 45.6 | 20.6 | 24.7 | 54.4 | 20.8 |
| 1876 | 35.6 | 35.2 | 29.1 |  |  |  |
| 1879 |  |  |  | 22.6 | 47.9 | 29.5 |
| 1883 | 34.9 | 30.8 | 34.2 |  |  |  |
| 1890 |  |  |  | 35.9 | 37.7 | 26.3 |
| 1895 | 44.5 | 22.8 | 32.7 | 32.3 | 36.1 | 31.6 |
| 1902 | 39.1 | 22.4 | 38.6 |  |  |  |
| 1908 |  |  |  | 31.1 | 32.8 | 36.2 |
| 1911 | 40.1 | 20.3 | 39.6 | 35.2 | 32.4 | 32.4 |
| 1913 | 37.7 | 20.4 | 41.9 |  |  |  |

*Source:* Spoerer (2004: 109, 117–18).

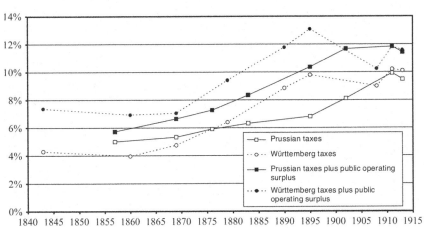

Figure 4.2. Tax load ratios in Prussia and Württemberg, 1843–1913 (percentage of national income). *Source:* Spoerer (2004: 109, 112, 115). *Note:* Taxes of all governmental levels included.

### 4.5.2 *Taxation and Distribution*

If, as financial sociologists argue, the public budget is a mirror of the power relations in a country, then we should assume that the process of democratization in nineteenth-century Germany is reflected in the fiscal system. From a theoretical point of view, one should have to estimate the budget incidence, that is, the redistributive effects that emerge from the revenue side (people pay taxes to the state) and the expenditure side (people value the public and private goods provided by the state). Such a general assessment of the distributional effects of public activity, however, is not feasible even for today. As the distributional effects of the revenue side are easier to assess than those of the expenditure side, we have to focus on the former.

Eckart Schremmer (1989: 452–4, 483–5) finds that the tax system at the beginning of the nineteenth century was very favorable to wealthy members of society. He rightly argues that the reforms of direct taxes had an increasingly progressive stance throughout nineteenth-century Germany. However, the share of the indirect taxes increased in the last quarter of the nineteenth century in both Prussia and Württemberg, especially if the public operating surplus is taken into account (Figure 4.3). Because the propensity to save increases with rising incomes, indirect taxes have a regressive distributional effect.

In the 1880s, the decade following Germany's return to high tariffs, the share of indirect taxes increased in Prussia by ten percentage points,

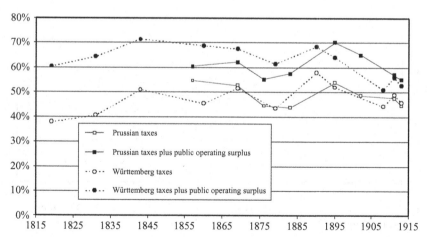

Figure 4.3. Share of indirect taxes of total tax revenues in Prussia and Württemberg, 1819–1913 (percentage). *Source:* Spoerer (2004: 109, 120). *Note:* Operating surpluses and taxes of all governmental levels included.

and in Württemberg by fifteen. In 1886, when grain and meat imports contributed 15 percent of total customs revenues, and imports of typical luxury goods of the common people like coffee, coffee substitutes, and tobacco made up another 34 percent (*Statistisches Jahrbuch für das Deutsche Reich* 1887: 185–7), the effects of the tariffs were probably regressive as well. Hence, the fiscal burden put on ordinary German households remained high even in the late nineteenth century. Only around the turn of the century did the share of indirect taxes decrease considerably.

### 4.5.3 Tax-Induced Migration and Tax Competition

Taxation always leads to evasive measures on the part of the taxpayers: tax avoidance, tax fraud, tax revolts – or peaceful migration into a jurisdiction with lower taxes. This, in turn, gives incentives for jurisdictions to lower the tax load on mobile factors so that wealthy taxpayers move in. Tax breaks offered by medieval or early modern merchant cities to attract wealthy, far-distance traders were an early example of tax competition.

The idea behind tax competition is fairly simple. If a jurisdiction decreases its marginal tax rate to slightly less than that of a competing jurisdiction, it might attract wealthy taxpayers from the other. If the jurisdictions do not harmonize their tax rates but instead compete by undercutting the opponent's rate, they are in a vicious circle, a race to the bottom. What may emerge from such a race is a suboptimal provision of public goods and empty public coffers that no longer allow for the sustaining of redistributive measures (Sinn 1990).

In nineteenth-century Germany, which experienced a much stronger vertical and horizontal mobility than ever before, tax-induced migration and tax competition became increasingly important. When Prussian bureaucrats discussed measures to reform the graduated capitation tax, which had been introduced only a few months before, tax-induced migration was apparently a credible threat, especially in a country with many states of the same language. The director of the Prussian statistical office warned in a confidential memorandum to the finance ministry in late 1820: "How dangerous it is to give capital an incentive to emigrate in regions where its consumption is taxed less. The German will be able to find his fatherland outside the Prussian state as well, and the migration from a German state to the next is much easier than migration from England to France or Germany" (qtd. in Spoerer 2004: 169; my translation). In fact, although the burden of the graduated capitation tax, which

was levied mainly on the countryside, for the highest-income bracket
was a mere 432 marks (between 1821 and 1851), many wealthy estate
owners acquired a domicile in a nearby city that was subjected to the
milling and butchery tax, which was negligible for them. If they were
able to convince the tax authorities that they spent at least half a year in
their urban domicile, they were exempted from the graduated capitation
tax.

As the tax load increased in the further course of the nineteenth century, the problem of tax-induced migration and tax competition became
increasingly relevant. In the late German Empire, jurisdictions competed
not for multinational firms on an international scale as they do today
but for wealthy rentiers and on a local or a national level. They did
so because the Prussian local tax reform of 1893 entitled municipalities
to levy individual surtaxes on top of the state's direct taxes. When the
local tax reform became effective in 1895, each Prussian city was entitled
to levy surtaxes on the land tax, the business tax, and the income tax.
Whereas land is immobile and businesses were less mobile than they are
today, many wealthy income taxpayers, especially the rentier class, were
highly mobile.

Figure 4.4 illustrates tax competition in the Berlin area. The lower
panel shows the dispersion (measured by the coefficient of variation) of
the surtaxes to the state income tax of thirty municipalities in the Berlin
area. After some years of local fiscal experiments with the new surtaxes,

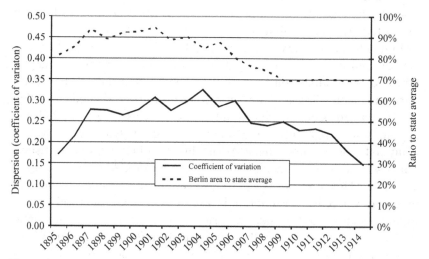

Figure 4.4. Municipal surtaxes to the Prussian income tax in the Berlin area: Dispersion and ratio to state average, 1895–1914. *Source:* Spoerer (2007: 64).

the coefficient of variation of the municipal income surtaxes hovered around 30 percent. But shortly after the turn of the century, the surtax rates increasingly converged, indicating tax competition. Even more informative, the average ratio of the income surtax rates around Berlin to the average of all Prussian cities, which around the turn of the century had been close to 100 percent, fell sharply between 1901 and 1909 to a much lower level of around 70 percent (upper panel), though Berlin was much richer. Of course, the revenue gaps had to be filled. Hence, in contrast to the falling surtaxes on the income tax, those on the land tax and the business tax increased in the Berlin area (Spoerer 2002).

In other words, wealthy taxpayers seized the opportunity to decrease their income tax load by choosing a different place of residence, and in doing so, they forced the municipalities to react. For example, municipalities in the Berlin area actively promoted their low income tax surtaxes in the press. Adolf Wagner (1904: 63), in 1904 the grand old man of German public finance, called this race to the bottom an 'endless screw-thread.'

For this reason, local politicians opted for a merger of the cities around Berlin to form a larger entity called 'Gross-Berlin,' with the express purpose of stopping the tax competition between them. It was not without reason that Matthias Erzberger, the Weimar Republic's first minister of finance, centralized the income tax and explained ironically in 1919: 'The German taxpayer will no longer have to bother about calculating whether he can ease his tax burden by moving to Berlin, Grunewald, Coburg or Lake Constance' (qtd. in Möller 1971: 39).[7]

By centralizing the income tax, Germany solved the problem of increasing tax competition among its municipalities. In the early twentieth century, when international migration was hampered by language problems, high transaction costs, and nationalism, harmonization from above was still a feasible policy option.

## 4.6 Taxation and Industrialization

Conventional wisdom has it that the German tax systems were, in general, quite favorable for industrialization.[8] The impersonal taxes that formed the backbone of tax revenues in nearly every German state had been created in times when agriculture accounted for the largest share of value-added and in which economic growth was hardly visible. In a

---

[7] Grunewald is now part of Berlin.
[8] My translation. For Prussia, see Lee (1975); for Germany as a whole, see Schremmer (1985).

static society, it may have made sense to subject the direct taxes to an allotment system with capped revenues and fixed sectoral shares such as the one in Württemberg (see Section 4.2.1).

In a dynamic society driven by an emerging manufacturing sector, however, the traditional tax system was outdated. The new business taxes that many German states established in the 1810s and 1820s taxed businesses according to characteristics that were visible (e.g., industry, number of employees) but that were correlated only loosely with productivity or profitability. The business tax systems in Prussia and Württemberg were regressive and rewarded the substitution of capital for labor.

Hence, it has been argued, the tax systems lay heavier on the agricultural sector than on the manufacturing sector, and in the latter, they favored capital-intensive firms. Although this was certainly conducive for the manufacturing sector and industrialization, it is not clear whether this was really beneficial for the German economy. International comparisons show that the share of the manufacturing sector in German aggregated output was unusually high. No European economy had as large a manufacturing share as Germany, with 44 percent before the First World War (Mitchell 1993: 912–17; Maddison 1992: 248–50). Hence, Germany has been characterized as overindustrialized in the late twentieth century.

It is, however, not totally clear whether the tax system put a larger burden on agricultural production than on manufacturing and services. After 1815, every major Prussian tax reform (except that of 1861) reallocated the tax burden toward the west, and hence toward the more industrialized provinces. To assess whether the taxes lay more heavily on agricultural rather than manufacturing activities, one would need regional value-added data broken down by sectors. These data are not available. Hence, it is not clear which forces prevailed, the political influence of the landed gentry east of the Elbe River or the economic dynamics of the manufacturing sector. The former tried to shift the tax burden to manufacturing, whereas the latter dissimulated the burden through economic growth.

For Württemberg, the data do allow for a comparison between sectoral economic growth and sectoral tax burden. If one includes the local taxes, it becomes clear that they put an additional burden on manufacturing and thus may have outweighed the effects of the state taxes, which lay heavily on agriculture. The analysis of the combined effects of state and local taxes corroborate the hypothesis that the tax system favored manufacturing before Württemberg's industrialization set in, that is, for the second quarter of the nineteenth century. After midcentury, the state

Table 4.5. *Public Debt of Prussia and the Reich, 1794–1913*

| | Prussia | | | *Reich* | | |
|---|---|---|---|---|---|---|
| | Millions of Marks | Per Capita | Debt Ratio | Millions of Marks | Per Capita | Debt Ratio |
| 1794 | 144 | 16.8 | | | | |
| 1807 | 160 | 32.7 | | | | |
| 1815 | 863 | 83.7 | 42.5 | | | |
| 1820 | 652 | 58.5 | 27.9 | | | |
| 1848 | 475 | 29.4 | 10.8 | | | |
| 1866 | 870 | 44.4 | 14.7 | | | |
| 1872 | 1,248 | 50.3 | 14.2 | 39 | 0.9 | 0.4 |
| 1882 | 2,686 | 97.0 | 26.7 | 488 | 10.7 | 4.9 |
| 1892 | 6,240 | 204.0 | 48.2 | 1,806 | 35.9 | 14.0 |
| 1902 | 6,721 | 189.0 | 38.0 | 2,934 | 50.8 | 16.6 |
| 1913 | 9,421 | 226.0 | 31.2 | 5,017 | 74.9 | 16.6 |

*Note:* Debt ratio = debt/net national product.
*Source:* Prussia, debt: Schremmer (1989: 454); net national product: Hoffmann and Müller (1959: 86–7); *Reich*, debt: *Statistisches Jahrbuch* (1880–1914); population and net national product: Hoffmann et al. (1965: 173–4, 825–6).

and local tax systems were quite successful in catching up with the booming manufacturing sector. Hence, it is doubtful whether the tax system in Württemberg actually favored manufacturing (Spoerer 2004: 97–100).

In general, it seems fair to say that some German tax systems favored the substitution of capital for labor. Whether they also favored manufacturing and services to the detriment of agriculture would require an analysis of more detailed data.

## 4.7 The Recurrence of Public Debt

After the Napoleonic Wars, most surviving German states were deep in debt and would require decades to redeem it. As the example of Prussia shows (Table 4.5), this attempt was successful. It was only after mid-century that there was more new debt being issued than old debt being repaid, at both state and municipal levels. The main reason for this was the opportunity offered by existing (e.g., mining, smelters) or new (e.g., utilities, railways) public enterprises. Hence, the function of the funds raised by public loans was not to fill gaps between ordinary revenue and ordinary expenditure but to serve as means for potentially profitable investment projects.

The situation was different for the *Reich*. Because the inflow of matricular contributions was paralleled by an outflow of remittances, the

*Reich* was often a net payer to the member states (1888–98, 1912–19) (Schremmer 1989: 468). Hence, it lacked the ordinary revenues to keep a strong army and to build a navy that should have been second only to the British. As Table 4.5 shows, the *Reich* rapidly accumulated considerable debt. Not shown in Table 4.5 is the debt of the non-Prussian member states and the municipalities, which, like Prussia, issued most of their debt to finance infrastructure and utilities.

On the eve of the First World War, total public debt in Germany amounted to 29.5 billion marks: the *Reich*, 5 billion marks; the member states, 17 billion marks; and the municipalities, 8 billion marks (Schremmer 1989: 470).[9] In relation to net national product, this amounted to a total public debt ratio of 59 percent. Although the ratio of debt to gross domestic product was around 52 percent, which is not far from the European Union's Maastricht criterion of 60 percent, the situation was different. Grosso modo, only the debt of the *Reich* was unproductive, whereas the member states and municipalities mostly had balanced ordinary budgets and issued debt mainly for investment projects.

## 4.8 Conclusion

Without any doubt, the German tax systems underwent a process of profound modernization throughout the long nineteenth century. In formal terms, the whole process of preparation, enforcement, and control of the budget became rationalized. The assessment of the change in material terms is not as straightforward. Although at the beginning of the century horizontal tax equity (in which the same ability to pay leads to the same tax amount) was by no means standard even within a particular member state, it was generally achieved prior to the First World War, except for differences due to different tax laws between member states.

The realization of principles of vertical tax equity (greater ability to pay leads to a higher taxation) was, however, far more difficult (Buchanan and Musgrave 1999). Redistribution via the tax system proved a much-contested principle and, naturally, found many political obstacles. This is best shown by the revenue side of public finances, which allows for discussion of recent theories of fiscal stage models as a conclusion.

Shortly before the end of the First World War, the Austrian economist Joseph A. Schumpeter (1918) published the article "The Crisis of the Tax State," in which he developed a three-stage model to describe the

---

[9] Slightly higher figures are found in Ullmann (2005: 71).

development of fiscal systems. For antiquity, he used the term *domain state*, which degenerated into a domain economy in the Middle Ages. Increasing military costs forced the sovereigns in the early modern period to pile up debts. To serve the debts, they expanded the tax system, which soon became the backbone of their finances: the tax state had evolved. For Schumpeter (1918/1954: 19), "'tax' has so much to do with 'state' that the expression 'tax state' might almost be considered a pleonasm." Schumpeter's model is generally considered the starting point for fiscal stage models, though other authors like Gustav Schmoller (1877: 113) had formulated similar ideas four decades earlier.[10]

Schumpeter's concept of the domain state and the tax state was particularly advocated by Kersten Krüger (1987), who elaborated criteria to characterize the domain state and the tax state, respectively. This, in turn, inspired Richard Bonney and W. Mark Ormrod (1999: 10, 16; see also Bonney 1995: 451) to expand this stage model. They distinguished four stages in fiscal history: the tribute state, the domain state, the tax state, and the fiscal state. Although they did not make explicit which criteria they consider essential, the very fact that they stuck to the notions created by Schumpeter – domain state and tax state – indicate that the revenue structure is of pivotal importance in their stage model (see also Petersen 1975).

According to Bonney and Ormrod (1999), the fiscal state is characterized by a number of features for which Prussia certainly qualified at the end of the nineteenth century. On the revenue side, which is so central for the Bonney-Ormrod model, however, Prussia remained at the level of a domain state, as illustrated by Figure 4.5.

Figure 4.5 illustrates the revenue shares of the Prussian budgets since the mid-seventeenth century. Although the share of the public operating surplus fell in the third quarter of the seventeenth century, it strongly bounced back afterward. Throughout the nineteenth century, the share of the operating surplus increased tremendously, as mines, iron- and steelworks, postal services, and particularly railways generated large profits. Andreas Thier (2000: 316) even dubbed this process the transition to a railway state. Thus, it is doubtful whether Prussia (or other German states; Spoerer 2008b) was ever a fiscal state.

Figure 4.5 and Table 4.3, though not fully representative of other German states or the Reich, also mirror the slow process of democratization in nineteenth-century Germany. At least in Prussia, most of the revenues

---

[10] In generalizing the Prussian experience, Schmoller (1877) distinguished the tribute economy, the domain economy, the regal economy, and the tax economy.

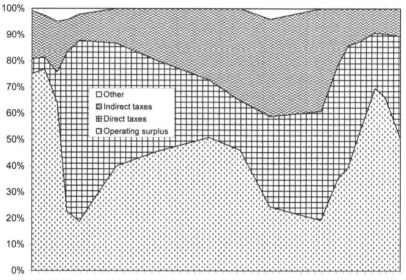

Figure 4.5. Public revenue shares in Brandenburg-Prussia, 1653–1913. *Source:* Spoerer (2008b: 792). *Notes:* State budget only. Benchmark years are 1653, 1662, 1671, 1678, 1687, 1713, 1740, 1778, 1800, 1821, 1857, 1869, 1876, 1883, 1895, 1902, and 1913. Shares split between direct and indirect taxes in 1713 were extrapolated from values in adjacent benchmark years.

came from indirect taxes and the public operating surplus, which in economic terms is equivalent to an indirect tax (see Section 4.4.3). Even the taxation of the Reich increased the relative burden of the poor, as a large share of the custom duties was paid via their consumption of grain, meat, and staple luxury goods. The share of direct taxes, which were mostly paid by the wealthy, increased only toward the end of the nineteenth century, when Saxony, Baden, and Prussia introduced the general income tax. These tax reforms increased vertical tax equity and paved the way for the breathtaking increase of taxation in the twentieth century.

## References

Andic, S. and Veverka, J. (1964) "The growth of government expenditure in Germany since the unification," *Finanzarchiv*, 2nd ser., 23, 169–278.

Blankart, C. B. (2007) *Föderalismus in Deutschland und in Europa*. Wiesbaden: Nomos.

Bonney, R. (1995) "Revenues," in R. Bonney (ed.) *Economic Systems and State Finance*. Oxford: Clarendon, 423–505.

Bonney, R. and Ormrod, W. M. (1999) "Crises, Revolutions and Self-Sustained Growth: Towards a Conceptual Model of Change in Fiscal History," in W. M. Ormrod, M. Bonney, and R. Bonney (eds.) *Crises, Revolutions and Self-Sustained Growth*. Stamford, CT: Shaun Tyas, 1–20.

Buchanan, J. A. and Musgrave, R. A. (1999) *Public Finance and Public Choice: Two Contrasting Visions of the State*. Cambridge, MA: MIT Press.

Dumke, R. H. (1976) "The Political Economy of Economic Unification: Tariffs, Trade and Politics of the Zollverein Era." Ph.D. dissertation, University of Wisconsin, Madison.

Ferguson, N. (1994) "Public Finance and National Security: The Domestic Origins of the First World War Revisited," *Past and Present*, 142, 141–68.

Ferguson, N. (1998) *The Pity of War*. London: Allen Lane.

Fremdling, R. (1980) "Freight rates and state budget: The role of the national Prussian railways 1880–1913," *Journal of European Economic History*, 9, 21–39.

Gerloff, W. (1916) *Die steuerliche Belastung in Deutschland während der letzten Friedensjahre. Gutachten dem Staatssekretär des Reichsschatzamts erstattet*. Berlin: Reichsdruckerei.

Gerloff, W. (1929) "Der Staatshaushalt und das Finanzsystem Deutschlands," in *Handbuch der Finanzwissenschaft*, vol. 3. Tübingen: Mohr Siebeck, 1–69.

Goldscheid, R. (1926) "Staat, öffentlicher Haushalt und Gesellschaft. Wesen und Aufgabe der Finanzwissenschaft vom Standpunkte der Soziologie," in *Handbuch der Finanzwissenschaft*, vol. 1. Tübingen: Mohr Siebeck, 146–84.

Gömmel, R. (1979) *Realeinkommen in Deutschland. Ein internationaler Vergleich (1810–1914)*. Nuremberg.

Guinnane, T. W. (2003) "Population and the economy in Germany, 1800–1990," in S. Ogilvie and R. Overy (eds.) *Germany: A New Social and Economic History, Vol. 3, Since 1800*. London: Arnold, 35–70.

Hefeker, C. (2001) "The agony of central power: Fiscal federalism in the German Reich," *European Review of Economic History*, 5, 119–141.

Hoffmann, W. G. and Müller, J. H. (1959) *Das deutsche Volkseinkommen 1851–1957*. Tübingen: Mohr.

Hoffmann, W. G. et al. (1965) *Das Wachstum der deutschen Wirtschaft seit der Mitte des 19. Jahrhunderts*. Berlin: Springer.

Kruedener, J. (1987) "The Franckenstein paradox in the intergovernmental fiscal relations of imperial Germany," in P.-C. Witt (ed.) *Wealth and Taxation in Central Europe: The History and Sociology of Public Finance*. New York: Berg, 111–23.

Krüger, K. (1987) "Public Finance and modernisation: The change from the domain state to tax state in Hesse in the sixteenth and seventeeth centuries," in P.-C. Witt (ed.) *Wealth and Taxation in Central Europe: The History and Sociology of Public Finance*. New York: Berg, 49–62.

Lee, W. R. (1975) "Tax structure and economic growth in Germany (1750–1850)," *Journal of European Economic History*, 4, 153–78.

Lundgreen, P. (1973) *Bildung und Wirtschaftswachstum im Industrialisierungsprozeß des 19. Jahrhunderts. Methodische Ansätze, empirische Studien und internationale Vergleiche*. Berlin: Colloquium.

Maddison, A. (1992) *Dynamic Forces in Capitalist Development: A Long-Run Comparative View*. Oxford: Oxford University Press.

Mitchell, B. R. (1993) *International Historical Statistics: Europe 1750–1988*, 3rd ed. New York: Stockton, 912–17.

Möller, A. (1971) *Reichsfinanzminister Matthias Erzberger und sein Reformwerk*. Bonn: Stollfuss.

Nützenadel, A. (2007) "Taxation, electoral system, and citizenship in nineteenth-century Germany," in A. Nützenadel and C. Strupp (eds.) *Taxation, State and the Civil Society in Germany and the United States, 1750–1950*. Wiesbaden: Nomos, 113–24.

Petersen, E. L. (1975) "From domain state to tax state: Synthesis and interpretation," *Scandinavian Economic History Review*, 23, 116–48.

Recktenwald, H. C. (1970) "Staatsausgaben in säkularer Sicht," in H. Haller et al. (eds.) *Theorie und Praxis des finanzpolitischen Interventionismus: Fritz Neumark zum 70. Geburtstag*. Tübingen: Mohr Siebeck, 407–30.

Recktenwald, H. C. (1977) "Umfang und Struktur der öffentlichen Ausgaben in säkularer Entwicklung," in *Handbuch der Finanzwissenschaft*, vol. 1, 3rd ed. Tübingen: Mohr Siebeck, 713–52.

Reichsschatzamt (1908) *Denkschriftenband zur Begründung des Entwurfs eines Gesetzes betreffend Änderungen im Finanzwesen*, 3 vols. Berlin: Reichsdruckerei.

Ritschl, A. and Spoerer, M. (1997) "Das Bruttosozialprodukt in Deutschland nach den amtlichen Volkseinkommens- und Sozialproduktsstatistiken 1901–1995," *Jahrbuch für Wirtschaftsgeschichte*, no. 2, 27–54.

Schissler, H. (1982) "Preußens Finanzpolitik nach 1807. Die Bedeutung der Staatsverschuldung als Faktor der Modernisierung des preußischen Finanzsystems," *Geschichte und Gesellschaft*, 8, 367–85.

Schmoller, G. (1877) "Die Epochen der preußischen Finanzpolitik," *Jahrbuch für Gesetzgebung, Verwaltung und Volkswirtschaft*, 1, 33–114.

Schremmer, E. (1985) "Föderativer Staatsverbund, öffentliche Finanzen und Industrialisierung in Deutschland," in H. Kiesewetter and R. Fremdling (eds.) *Staat, Region und Industrialisierung*. Ostfildern: Scripta Mercaturae, 3–65.

Schremmer, E. (1987) "Die badische Gewerbesteuer und die Kapitalbildung in gewerblichen Anlagen und Vorräten in Baden und Deutschland, 1815 bis 1913," *Vierteljahrschrift für Sozial- und Wirtschaftsgeschichte*, 74, 18–61.

Schremmer, E. (1989) "Taxation and public finance: Britain, France, and Germany," in *Cambridge Economic History of Europe*, vol. 8. Cambridge: Cambridge University Press, 315–494.

Schumpeter, J. A. (1918) "Die Krise des Steuerstaates," *Zeitfragen aus dem Gebiet der Soziologie*, 4, 3–74. (English translation: "The Crisis of the Tax State," *International Economic Papers*, 4 [1954], 5–38).

Sinn, H.-W. (1990) "Tax harmonization and tax competition in Europe," *European Economic Review*, 34, 489–504.

Spoerer, M. (1997) "Taxes on production and on imports in Germany, 1901–13," *Jahrbuch für Wirtschaftsgeschichte*, no. 1, 161–79.

Spoerer, M. (2002) "Wann begannen Fiskal- und Steuerwettbewerb? Eine Spurensuche in Preußen, anderen deutschen Staaten und der Schweiz," *Jahrbuch für Wirtschaftsgeschichte*, no. 2, 11–35.

Spoerer, M. (2004) *Steuerlast, Steuerinzidenz und Steuerwettbewerb: Verteilungswirkungen der Besteuerung in Preußen und Württemberg (1815–1913)*. Berlin: Akademie. [English summary: "The political economy of taxation in 19th century Germany," in A. Nützenadel and C. Strupp (eds.) (2007) *Taxation, State and the Civil Society in Germany and the United States, 1750–1950*. Wiesbaden: Nomos, 51–65].

Spoerer, M. (2008a) "The Laspeyres-paradox: Tax overshifting in nineteenth century Prussia," *Cliometrica*, 2, 173–93.

Spoerer, M. (2008b) "The revenue structures of Brandenburg-Prussia, Saxony and Bavaria (fifteenth to nineteenth centuries): Are they compatible with the Bonney-Ormrod model?" in S. Cavaciocchi (ed.) *Fiscal Systems in the European Economy from the Thirteenth to the Eighteenth Centuries*. Prato: Istituto Datini, 785–95.

*Statistisches Jahrbuch für das Deutsche Reich* (1880–1914). Ed. by Kaiserliches Statistisches Amt. Berlin: Puttkammer.

Statistisches Reichsamt (1930) *Die deutsche Finanzwirtschaft vor und nach dem Kriege nach den Hauptergebnissen der Reichsfinanzstatistik*. Berlin: Hobbing.

Thier, A. (1999) *Steuergesetzgebung und Verfassung in der konstitutionellen Monarchie. Staatssteuerreformen in Preußen 1871–1893*. Frankfurt: Klostermann.

Thier, A. (2000) "Steuergesetzgebung und Staatsfinanzen in Preußen 1871–1893," in G. Lingelbach (ed.) *Staatsfinanzen, Staatsverschuldung, Staatsbankrotte in der europäischen Staaten- und Rechtsgeschichte*. Cologne: Böhlau, 311–33.

Thier, A. (2009) "Traditions of wealth taxation in Germany," in J. Tiley (ed.) *Studies in the History of Tax Law, Vol. 3*. Oxford and Portland: Hart, 73–88.

Ullmann, H.-P. (2005) *Der deutsche Steuerstaat. Geschichte der öffentlichen Finanzen vom 18. Jahrhundert bis heute*. Munich: Beck.

Wagner, A. (1863) *Die Ordnung des österreichischen Staatshaushaltes, mit besonderer Rücksicht auf den Ausgabe-Etat und die Staatsschuld*. Vienna: Gerold.

Wagner, A. (1904) *Die finanzielle Mitbeteiligung der Gemeinden an kulturellen Staatseinrichtungen und die Entwickelung der Gemeindeeinnahmen: Mit besonderem Bezug auf preussische Verhältnisse*. Jena: Fischer.

Weitzel, O. (1967) "Die Entwicklung der Staatsausgaben in Deutschland: Eine Analyse der öffentlichen Aktivität in ihrer Abhängigkeit vom wirtschaftlichen Wachstum," Ph.D. dissertation, University of Erlangen-Nuremberg.

Ziegler, D. (1996) "Eisenbahnen und Staat im Zeitalter der Industrialisierung." *Die Eisenbahnpolitik der deutschen Staaten im Vergleich*. Stuttgart: Steiner.

# 5

# Public Finance in Austria-Hungary, 1820–1913

## Michael Pammer

## 5.1 Introduction

Austria-Hungary, which included the complete territories of today's Austria, Hungary, the Czech Republic, Slovakia, Slovenia, Croatia, Bosnia and Herzegovina (from 1878 to 1908 onward), and parts of Poland, Ukraine, Romania, and Italy, was a monarchical union of otherwise separate lands at the beginning of the nineteenth century, and it was a dual monarchy consisting of two constitutional countries (in short, Austria and Hungary) and a common land (Bosnia and Herzegovina) at the eve of the First World War. In 1910, Austria had about 29 million inhabitants; Hungary, 21 million; and Bosnia and Herzegovina, 2 million. Up to 1867, the then so-called Austrian Empire (*Kaisertum Österreich*) passed through a process of centralization and unification opposed by regional forces that worked toward autonomy or independence, notably in the Italian provinces and Hungary, and led to fundamental changes in territory and constitution in the 1860s. Throughout the period, conflicts between the dominating ethnicities (Germans and Hungarians) and other nationalities remained a disintegrating force, which eventually led to the end of Austria-Hungary.

The territorial and constitutional changes of the 1860s were most important for the fiscal history of Austria. In 1860 and 1866, respectively, following the Italian war of 1859 and the Austro-Prussian war of 1866, Austria lost its Italian provinces of Lombardy and Veneto, which together had formed the Lombardo-Venetian Kingdom. This meant that the Lombardo-Venetian state debt disappeared from the Austrian state debt, but it also meant that the country lost two large and affluent provinces that had contributed disproportionately to state revenues.

Another and even more important effect of the war of 1866 was the so-called compromise (*Ausgleich*) of 1867 between Austria and Hungary. The compromise created Austria and Hungary as two more or less independent countries, which had their own constitutions, parliaments, and governments, and were fiscally independent as well, apart from foreign and defense policy matters, which were subject to a common government and a common budget. The Austrian head of state, the emperor, was king of Hungary in personal union. The customs union between the two parts of the empire remained in existence, and the pre-1867 state debt formed a common debt of both Austria and Hungary.

The last major territorial change, the occupation of Bosnia and Herzegovina in 1878 as a result of the Congress of Berlin, and its annexation in 1908, was fiscally relevant mainly because of an expansion of military expenditure.

Data on the fiscal history of Austria-Hungary are abundant insofar as they were produced by the administration. Information on the state debt is virtually complete; we dispose of yearly or (from 1861) half-yearly lists containing every single state loan in its nominal and interest-standardized values at a given point in time. The internal or published statements of revenues and expenditures differ from period to period but are good enough to allow a description of net revenues and expenditures in the single departments and the details of the tax system on the national level. In addition, depending on the period, we have information on gross revenues and expenditures or on fiscal management at the provincial level. Much more unsatisfying is the quality of general data on the society and the economy. There had been censuses from the eighteenth century onward, but the first adequate statistics of the labor structure date from 1867. Although we dispose of comprehensive and reliable agricultural statistics and adequate estimates of industrial production, data on gross domestic product are unsatisfying. In the absence of comprehensive income statistics, we have only crude estimates of the production in the service sector, and we know little about income distribution. Estimates of GDP established by several historians, though differing to some extent, allow for calculations of relations between financial indicators and state income.

## 5.2 Background

### 5.2.1 Economic and Social Trends
In Austria-Hungary, sustained economic growth started not later than in the 1820s and proceeded at a slow pace. The development in Austria

and Hungary followed different patterns: in every business cycle of the
decades from 1860 to the First World War, Austria enjoyed high growth
rates when Hungary fared badly, and vice versa.[1] In 1830, Austria-
Hungary was already among the least developed countries of Europe,
with a real GDP per capita comparable to that of Russia. Even the most
advanced parts of Austria-Hungary, the alpine lands, lost ground compared to most Western European countries and had a lower income per
capita than practically all countries of Western and Northern Europe in
1913. Estimates of GDP per capita yield a growth rate of around 0.5 percent annually between 1830 and 1870 with little difference between the
Hungarian lands and the rest of the empire. Between 1870 and 1913, the
growth rates were higher and remained around 1.15 percent per year
according to more recent estimates. Generally, growth rates in Austria
are estimated lower than in Hungary in this period, that is, at 1.0–1.3
percent in Austria versus 1.4–1.7 percent in Hungary.

As the growth rates suggest, Austria-Hungary was a heterogeneous
empire in both economic and ethnic terms. In 1910, 57 percent of the
Austrian and 67 percent of the Hungarian population still worked in
agriculture. The more industrialized regions lay in modern-day Austria
and the Czech Republic, while the northern, eastern and southeastern
parts of the empire had extremely high proportions of agriculture. In the
last decades prior to the First World War, the Czech lands became the
center of Austria-Hungary's industry, forming a large industrial region
in the north and northwest of today's Czech Republic. Altogether, the
share of Lower Austria and the Czech lands in the Austro-Hungarian
population was less than 30 percent, but their share in the industrial population remained more than 50 percent until the First World War. In the
other alpine lands, the small land of Vorarlberg became the most heavily
industrialized province, with a share of industry around 45 percent. In
Hungary, no major region and only one mining city had a similar proportion of industrial population.

Lower Austria was also the land with the largest commercial and
banking sector, as might be expected considering that the city of Vienna
alone comprised more than half of the Lower Austrian population in

---

[1] For economic development and financial policy see Mülinen (1875), Matis (1972),
Komlos (1983a), Good (1984), Eddie (1989), and Sandgruber (1995). For sectoral pro-
duction and GDP growth see Gross (1966), Katus (1970), Gross (1971), Rudolph (1975),
Wysocki (1975), Rudolph (1976), Bairoch (1976), Good (1978), Komlos (1978), Sand-
gruber (1978), Kausel (1979), Good (1980), Komlos (1983b), Good (1991), Good (1994),
Schulze (1996), Good (1997), Pammer (1997), Schulze (1997), Good and Ma (1998),
Good and Ma (1999), and Schulze (2000).

1910. Vienna was Austria-Hungary's financial center and largest urban center, with more than 2 million inhabitants in 1910, followed by Budapest (about 880,000). Apart from Vienna, only six cities in the Austrian part of the empire had more than one hundred thousand inhabitants, and none had more than three hundred thousand; in Hungary, just one city apart from Budapest had slightly more than one hundred thousand inhabitants. Both capitals had grown by migration mainly from the interior; Budapest, which had a German-speaking majority in the first half of the nineteenth century, attracted many Hungarian-speaking citizens, and the new Viennese came primarily from Moravia and the other Czech lands.

The ethnic tensions and the treatment of minorities worked as the most important disintegrating factor of the dual monarchy. None of the ethnicities (including Germans, Hungarians, Czechs, Slovakians, Poles, Ukrainians, Italians, Slovenians, Croatians, Serbs, and Romanians) ever represented an absolute majority of the population of the empire as a whole, but almost all lands and major Hungarian regions and 95 percent of the districts and counties had such a majority of any of the ethnic groups (but also often strong ethnic minorities). Thus, regional economic specifics coincided with ethnic differences; consequently, economic integration had the potential to either strengthen or mitigate ethnic tensions. However, there is no clear answer to the question of whether the economy worked as an integrating factor or in the opposite way. Unfortunately, we do not dispose of income data that would allow any distinction of the kind, but sectoral change and productivity growth do not generally suggest a catching-up process of late-coming regions.

Ethnic tensions had a direct impact on economic policy whenever economic measures concerned specific regions. A typical example was the 1 billion crowns program, introduced by the Austrian government in 1901, which aimed to modernize transport infrastructure, including railway construction, regulation of riverbeds, and the building of canals. Although the program was eventually accepted by the Austrian parliament, the political debate around it illustrates Hungarian fears concerning Austrian influence on the Balkans, Czech fears concerning a program that might be an advantage to the German-speaking provinces, and the needs of Polish- and Ukrainian-speaking provinces to be included in the program. The government consciously designed, for instance, one part of the railway program in a suboptimal way in both technical and economic terms simply to satisfy the demands of the Slovenian populations (Gerschenkron 1977: 71–5).

The increasing importance of industry and commerce led to the formation of private and public corporations that were to represent the interests of entrepreneurs. Before 1848, several private industrial corporations were founded, the first of them in Prague. In 1848, in imitation of the French example, a law introduced chambers of commerce with general franchise of entrepreneurs and consultative rights in all matters concerning industry and commerce.[2] The chambers of commerce remained in existence under the absolutist government of the 1850s, but their rights of participation in the legislation became precarious. Only in the constitutional era (i.e., from the 1860s) could they secure a stable and strong position, including the right to examine bills and, from 1873 to 1907, the representation in one of the four separate curiae in parliament. The unification of the social democratic movement in 1888–9 induced industrialists to seek more efficient cooperation in several industrywide federations. In the constitutional era, the relation between labor organizations and the authorities was ambiguous, with both freedom of association and freedom of the press on the one hand, and manifest successes of the labor movement (like the introduction of the eleven-hour day in 1885 and health and accident insurance in 1888) on the other hand.

### 5.2.2 Political Development
The Austrian Empire was a heterogeneous state not only economically and ethnically but also in political and constitutional terms. A common head of state united its lands, whereas the constitutional structure differed from case to case. The largest land, the Kingdom of Hungary, occupied a special position for most of the time, especially before 1848. Traditionally, the Hungarian imperial diet had the right to approve new taxes; between 1815 and 1825, however, the king refused to summon the diet and tried to collect taxes for military matters independently, which proved unfeasible. In 1825, the diet had to be summoned again, and it approved the taxes under the condition that it be summoned every three years at least from then on. In the other lands, the absolutist rule proved much more successful. Their provincial diets remained in existence during the pre-March era as well, but their rights were more limited and did not include the approval of taxes or legislation.

This remained so until 1848, when the report of the national bank about the debt status of the state led to a run on banks and in the sequel to the announcement of, among others, a constitution for the Austrian

---

[2] Imperial Order, December 15, 1848, Reichsgesetzblatt (RGBl) 27/1849.

Empire; a new constitution for Hungary followed immediately in April 1848. In view of the policy of the government in the following months, the newly elected Hungarian diet declared the land an independent republic in 1849. After the defeat of the revolution, the government declared the Hungarian constitution forfeited and Hungary an ordinary land under absolutist rule. The constituent diet for the other lands had been opened in July 1848; it lasted until the emperor imposed his own constitution on the whole empire (including Hungary) in March 1849, which he revoked in December 1851. This constitution provided for a general legislative right of the imperial diet, which included taxation, and a right of provincial diets to introduce provincial taxes for provincial purposes. From 1852 on, the whole empire remained under the so-called neo-absolutist regime, which ended in February 1861 when a new constitution came into effect. Its basic features were adopted by the constitutions for Austria and Hungary that were issued in connection with the compromise and the creation of the two countries in 1867.

Although the revolution of 1848–9 led to a constitution only temporarily, it had a profound and lasting effect on the administrative structure of the Austrian Empire. Until 1848, local government and local justice had still been administered by seigneuries and municipal magistrates. One of the lasting reforms of the short-lived revolutionary parliaments was the abolition of the seigneuries, which led to the creation of district authorities and district courts as the first instance of a comprehensive and centrally directed administration by the state. Another effect of this reform was the end of the feudal relation between lords and peasants. In part, the costs of the indemnification of lords were shouldered by the state and financed by raising taxes. The onetime effect of this act on agricultural productivity lay in the range of a 1.2 percent increase in Hungary and 2.4 percent in Austria at most. Thus, this reform was important for political and mental reasons and not simply in economic terms.[3]

The imposed constitution provided also that the whole empire was to form a single customs district. So far, the empire had passed through a lengthy process of unification in which customs lines within and between provinces were removed step by step, but the customs line between Hungary and the rest was still in existence. Pursuant to the constitution, a customs union in the whole Austrian Empire was created by imperial order in 1850. The economic effects of this reform, however, were limited

---

[3] September 7, 1848, RGBl; Imperial Order, March 3, 1849, RGBl 152; Imperial Order, August 15, 1849, RGBl 361; Komlos (1983b: app. B).

and amounted to a one-time income gain of 2.7 percent in Hungary and 0.8 percent in Austria at most.[4]

The heterogeneity of the Austrian Empire in the pre-March period becomes visible also in the structure of the tax systems in the different lands. Again, the great difference lay between Hungary and the other lands: before 1848, Hungarian revenues were mostly custom duties and revenues from the salt and other monopolies. The state began to collect both direct taxes and consumption taxes in Hungary in earnest only after 1849. Then, with Hungary being treated like an ordinary Austrian province, direct taxes rose to more than 40 percent of the Hungarian tax revenues in a few years and the consumption tax to another 15 percent. Other regional specifics in various provinces were the Jewish tax (a tax collected only from the Jewish population), which existed only in Lower Austria, the Bohemian lands, Galicia, and Hungary; or the *diritti uniti*, a leftover from the French rule of the Italian provinces that was a combination of transport tolls and other fees.

Military concerns were among the most effective forces in fiscal policy both for expenditure and for revenues of the state. Military expenditure always comprised a major share in the state budget and exploded in times of internal and external crises. In some cases, expenses were made preventively, such as in the revolutions of 1830 and in the Crimean War, in which the Austrian military was not actually engaged. Apart from these events, however, Austria was involved in a number of wars, such as the Italian war of 1859, the Danish war of 1864, and the German war of 1866. In 1878, after a decision by the Congress of Berlin, Austria occupied Bosnia and Herzegovina, which proved a lasting reason for extraordinary military expenditure. In some of these occasions, as wars ended military expenditure was reduced to its prior level, as, for example, happened after the wars of 1864 and 1866. In other cases, however, military expenditure decreased but remained higher than in the prewar period, for example, after 1849 and 1859. Wars had also a profound effect on revenues, as Austria-Hungary usually lost its wars, which cost two of its richest provinces, Lombardy and Veneto, in 1860 and 1866. The occupation (in 1878) and annexation (in 1908) of Bosnia and Herzegovina, though demanding high military expenditures, added just another backward and fiscally unattractive province to the empire.

The variable role of the state as an entrepreneur was closely connected with the situation of the state budget in a given time period.

---

[4] June 7, 1850, RGBl 220; Komlos (1983b: app. A).

Factories and mines owned and operated by the state had a long tradition but had minor importance in the nineteenth century. The focus lay now on the railways, which demanded enormous amounts of capital (Baltzarek 1993: 229). The first railway companies, founded in the 1820s and 1830s, quickly got into financial troubles, which led to the acquisition of ever more railway shares by the state in the 1840s. In 1854, the state railway administration owned 70 percent of the railway system, and the state had shouldered 78 percent of all railway expenditure accumulated in the country (Bachinger 2005: 282). When, in the 1850s, the budgetary situation of the government became exceedingly difficult, the state privatized its railways again, starting with a privatization law in 1854 and the sale of the northern and southeastern railways to the French Societé General du Crédit Mobilier in the same year. Other railways followed in the ensuing years. A new wave of nationalization was announced by the acquisition of several small railway companies in the 1870s, and it began in earnest after 1880, when the state nationalized first the Western Railway Company and then several other major companies. From that time on, almost up to the First World War, the state nationalized additional railway companies every few years. In the railway sector, which doubled in size between 1880 and 1913, the state held mostly one-third of the capital from the late 1880s, and 60 percent from 1910. In addition, a large part of the privately owned companies were operated by the state so that, effectively, 82 percent of the Austrian railways were run by a state agency. A similar development happened in Hungary, where the state nationalized a number of railway companies from 1876 onward and partly operated private lines; eventually 84 percent of the Hungarian railway system was run by the state.

## 5.3 Public Finance

Following the constitutional development, the framework of public finance changed fundamentally in the course of the nineteenth century. Until 1867, the Austrian Empire had one state budget without any distinction between Austrian and Hungarian affairs. From 1868, Austria and Hungary, being essentially two countries, had separate budgets. However, some policy fields, notably defense and foreign policy, were subject to a common government with its own budget, consisting of expenditures mostly for military purposes and some revenues that were comparably negligible. The net expenditure of the common government had to be covered by Austria and Hungary according to a quota that was negotiated anew every ten years, and it appeared again in the Austrian and Hungarian budgets in the form of contributions to common affairs. Similarly, the pre-1867 state debt remained in existence, and the respective contributions to interest and amortization were also subject to the negotiations between the Austro-Hungarian delegations.

The contributions to common matters consisted of customs duties, which came mostly from Austria; the Austrian share usually was more than 85 percent and never less than 80 percent; until 1900, a small amount of these revenues were transferred to the government of occupied Bosnia and Herzegovina. Until 1887, the proportion of customs contributions to the common budget was less than 20 percent (and in 1881 even below zero) because governments deducted reimbursements of consumption taxes for exported goods from the customs revenues.[5] From 1888, the proportions of customs revenues in the common budget came close to 40 percent in some years.

The remainder of the contributions to common affairs had to be paid out of other funds. Theoretically, the Austrian and Hungarian shares in the common expenditure remained invariant for each ten-year period. Their size was supposed to be based on the size of the two economies; as the Austrian population was almost 40 percent greater than that of the Hungarian, and per capita income in Austria was higher, the Hungarian share in the common expenditures was initially only 30 percent but rose to 31.4 percent in 1871; 34.4 percent, in 1900; and 36.4 percent, in 1907 (in fact, the shares deviated from the negotiated values by a few percentage points because of extraordinary budgets and technical aspects of accounting).[6] Per capita, the Austrian share was about 50 percent (until 1899), 40 percent (1900–6), or 31 percent (from 1907) greater than the Hungarian share.

Given the large Austrian share in customs duties, the Austrian share in the overall contributions to common matters was almost always greater than 70 percent and grew from 1888 onward. Because of the greater proportion of customs duties in the combined income, Austria paid henceforward 74–75 percent of the common expenditure.

### 5.3.1 Public Expenditure
The common budget was dominated by military expenses, which always constituted about 95 percent of the common expenditure; the rest were mostly expenses of the common Ministry of Foreign Affairs (Austria

---

[5] Law, June 27, 1878, RGBl 62; Law, May 21, 1887, RGBl 47.
[6] Law, June 8, 1871, RGBl 49; Law, December 30, 1907, RGBl 280.

and Hungary had no foreign ministries of their own). In addition to the common military expenses, both Austria and Hungary had defense budgets for their territorial reserves and other military purposes, which amounted to up to 10–15 percent of overall military expenditure in the first two decades and 20–25 percent from the 1890s. With Austrian and Hungarian budgets combined, military spending basically followed a long-term upward trend, increasing by 2.44 percent per year from the 1820s to 1907, or an increase from about 70 million crowns in the 1820s to 500 million crowns after the turn of the century (see Figure 5.1). This estimate excludes the early 1830s, the period 1848–66, the two Bosnian incidents (occupation and annexation) and Balkan crises of 1878 and 1908, and the remaining years up to the Great War. In all of these periods, defense expenditure increased enormously, especially in the 1850s and 1860s, when in a number of years military spending was two or three times greater than normal. The Bosnian incidents also had strong effects, especially the annexation crisis of 1908, which led to an increase in military spending by about 50 percent; in 1878, the effects were limited to one year, and 1908 was the start of a period of armament that continued into wartime. These figures stand for net expenditure, which differs little from gross expenditure (the own revenues of the military amounted to only about 3 percent of gross expenditure). In normal years, military expenditure remained remarkably constant, fluctuating closely around 2 percent of the GDP. However, in the peak years (1848, 1854–5, 1859, and 1866), Austria-Hungary spent 5–6 percent of its GDP on military expenses. In the context of overall gross expenditure, military spending did not decline dramatically: in the first four years after the compromise, Austria dedicated almost 25 percent of its gross expenditure to the military; from 1872, this share fluctuated around 20 percent (with the exception of the 1880s, when it was close to 15 percent for a few years). In Hungary, because of the more limited Hungarian contribution for common expenses, the share of military spending in overall expenses fluctuated around 10 percent. In the early 1890s, with smaller Hungarian state budgets, the share of military spending rose briefly to about 15 percent. The net results in the single departments clearly yield a larger share of military expenditure. Although in Hungary it reached only 20 percent of net expenditure after 1900, in Austria it was about 50 percent in the revolution and war years after 1848 and dropped to between 25 percent and 30 percent in the first decades after the compromise, only to rise again to 30–35 percent in the 1890s and 1900s.

The second major portion of state expenditures was the cost of the state debt, which was at the same order of magnitude as military expenses

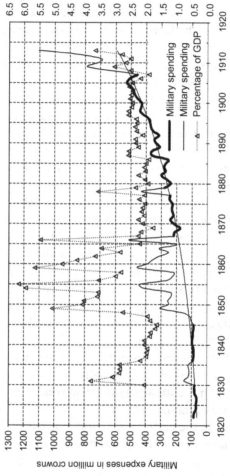

Figure 5.1. Military spending in Austria-Hungary. *Sources:* Military expenditures: Central-Rechnungs-Abschlüsse; *Compass. Finanzielles Jahrbuch;* Liese 1993. GDP: Bairoch 1976; Kausel 1979; Schulze 2000. *Note:* Military spending includes common expenditures for the military and Austrian and Hungarian spending for territorial reserves.

throughout the period except during war years. During peaceful times, in both Austria and in Hungary, 20–25 percent of gross state expenses were used to pay the interest of state loans and (to a much lesser degree) pay off the debt; in the decade before the Great War, this share fell to about 15 percent. This represented about 30–35 percent of the net expenses. These numbers include the costs of the railway debt, that is, the debt of private railway companies assumed by the state in the course of the nationalization of railways. The costs of the railway debt were about one-fifth of the overall Austrian state debt around 1890, one-quarter around 1900, and 45 percent in 1911. Conversely, in Hungary, where the railway debt did not change much after 1890 (except for its conversion into perpetual state bonds), this share decreased and was close to 20 percent after the turn of the century.

These numbers leave little room for other expenses. Leaving aside state business enterprises like railways and the postal service (see Section 5.3.3), only minor portions of state expenditure went to the departments of justice, education, commerce and public works, the interior (including general administration on all levels), financial administration, and state pension funds. In most of these fields, spending grew in absolute terms but at a different pace: in Austria, the shares of the general and financial administration, and the share of the justice department, in overall net expenses remained fairly constant around 15 percent. The two winners were the education and the pension systems. The education department received just 2 percent of net expenses after the compromise and more than 6 percent after the turn of the century, whereas the share of the pension fund, which paid pensions to the state officials, grew from 4 percent to more than 7 percent in the same period. There was one field in which public spending diminished even in absolute terms: in the 1870s, the state had paid considerable subsidies to private firms, which amounted to more than 9 percent of net expenditure in some years. These subsidies became unnecessary in the course of the following period because the firms that were concerned were mostly the very railway companies that were to be nationalized starting in the 1880s; therefore, subsidies to private firms shrank to less than 2 percent in the mid-1890s and continued to fall. Similarly, the Hungarian education system received a growing share of state expenditure; this process started later than in Austria but proceeded quickly, and in the last years before the First World War, Hungarian schools and universities received as much money (in absolute terms) from the state as did their Austrian counterparts, which means that per capita spending in the field eventually was higher in Hungary.

The shares of other departments, like justice or the interior, in the Hungarian state budget showed no such change.

### 5.3.2 Public Revenues

State gross revenues consisted of the income derived from state monopolies and state-owned enterprises (treated in the next section) and of revenues obtained in the single departments in connection with their specific activities. The most important source of revenue, however, was direct and indirect taxes. In the period from the early 1820s to the 1860s, the Austrian state revenues derived from these sources (not counting earnings from the sale of state property) grew from 220 million to more than 500 million crowns, and in 1910, Austria and Hungary combined delivered about 2.2 billion crowns to their governments.[7] Although the annual growth rate was less than 2 percent before 1848 and around 5 percent in the 1850s, after the compromise, the long-term growth rate was 3–3.5 percent. The proportion of direct and indirect taxes, including customs duties, in the gross domestic product rose from about 4 percent in the pre-March period to 6–8 percent after the compromise, with Austrian values ranging from 5–7 percent and Hungarian values from 7–9.5 percent (Figure 5.2).

Changes in the tax system were driven both by ad hoc measures that lasted indefinitely and by systematic evaluation and comprehensive reform efforts. A typical example for the former pattern was the extraordinary one-fifth tax increase introduced in 1859, initially meant as a temporary measure to finance the war in Italy in that year. A true example of Wagner's law, the additional tax remained in existence further on. Moreover, in the following recession the surtax on direct taxes was even doubled (1863), which led to tax rates that were extraordinarily high according to contemporary standards and amounted to up to 26.67 percent on property income and 20 percent on personal income; in 1868, direct tax rates were raised again (Gratz 1949 250, 258). In 1859, as the Austrian Empire was still ruled by a neo-absolutist monarchy, no parliamentary approval was necessary. But in 1863 and 1868, when the initiative for tax increases belonged to the government as well, Austria had already a parliament (*Reichsrat*) that had to approve of new taxes.

For the decades after the compromise, a comprehensive reform of direct taxes remained a core project of Austrian financial policy. Again, the government stepped forward with various plans, but it had now to

---

[7] For the pre-March tax system see Hauer (1848), Hübner (1849).

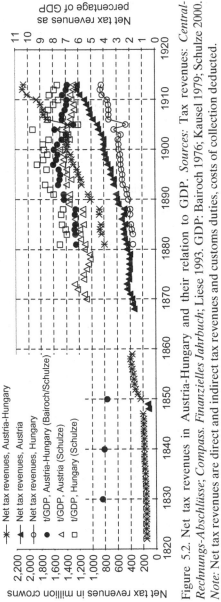

Figure 5.2. Net tax revenues in Austria-Hungary and their relation to GDP. *Sources:* Tax revenues: *Central-Rechnungs-Abschlüsse; Compass. Finanzielles Jahrbuch;* Liese 1993. GDP: Bairoch 1976; Kausel 1979; Schulze 2000. *Note:* Net tax revenues are direct and indirect tax revenues and customs duties, costs of collection deducted.

145

deal with a number of self-confident counterparts, not only in the parliament but also in the chamber of commerce, which had the right to review legislation. The chamber of commerce, not surprisingly, aimed to abolish tax privileges of any kind and to create a stable legislation to create conditions that tax payers could rely on. Both aims were reached only in 1896, when the reform of direct taxes determined financial policy for the remaining years until the war.

The legislation of 1896 became the most important tax reform of the period. It shows a most interesting feature in Austrian financial policy making, namely the involvement of economists in fiscal policy, not just as government consultants but also as members of the administration itself. The most famous example is Eugen Böhm von Bawerk, a leading representative of the Austrian school of economics, who acted as head of the department of the Austrian Ministry of Finance that was responsible for the tax reform and several times as minister of finance (before and after, Böhm was a university professor of economics). Böhm and other representatives of the Austrian school, like Robert Meyer, were personally involved in the tax reform of 1896, whose central feature was a progressive income tax, with *income* meaning all sources of individual income. Other kinds of direct taxes were adapted to the new system. Although the parliament had to consent, this reform clearly was a product of the bureaucracy and of its expert members with academic backgrounds (Gratz 1949: 262–3; Blumenthal 2007: 107).

Direct taxes were the most important source of revenue throughout the nineteenth century. Their share was highest at the beginning of the period, when direct taxes made up 45 percent of the state revenues. As the absolute amount of direct taxes remained more or less stable up to 1848, their share fell to one-third of revenues in 1847. In the 1850s, direct taxes doubled as a result of higher proceeds of property taxes in most provinces and the introduction of the property tax system in Hungary. Property taxes were, in fact, taxes on the estimated yields of agricultural estates and potential rent value of houses according to the data in land registers. Taxes on agricultural property constituted about 90 percent of property taxes in the 1820s and 80 percent at the end of the 1850s.

In comparison with property taxes, personal taxes were of minor importance in the period of the Austrian Empire, fluctuating between 15 percent and 20 percent of direct taxes in the 1820s and about 10 percent in the following decades. In the pre-March period, there was no comprehensive system of personal taxes but a combination of regular taxes on the income of selected professions and irregular taxes that had to be imposed anew every year. They were accompanied by the Jewish tax, a mixture of an income tax and tolerance fees. Both irregular personal taxes and the Jewish tax lost their importance or disappeared completely after 1848, when the government introduced a general income tax on income from liberal professions, wages, and capital income of more than 1,260 crowns, which was already a progressive tax.[8]

The relation between property and personal taxes changed only after the compromise. In both Austria and Hungary, the relative weight of personal taxes increased. In Austria, the share of personal taxes grew to about one-third within a few years but increased slowly afterward. The fundamental change came with the tax reform of 1896.[9] Its main effect was an increase in absolute revenue from income taxes by 50 percent within three years. Revenues from income taxes immediately equaled proceeds from property taxes, and on the eve of the First World War, the share of property taxes had diminished to little more than 40 percent. Changes in Hungary went into the same direction, but income taxes delivered a larger share than in Austria from the beginning, and eventually less than 40 percent of Hungarian direct tax revenues were property taxes.

All other direct taxes brought only limited revenues to the state. Inheritance tax furnished just 2 million crowns even in the best years around 1835 and became completely irrelevant after 1848. The Jewish tax, still at 3 million crowns in the early 1820s, and 2 million from 1830, was canceled after 1848.

Excise and customs duties together yielded about 45 million crowns in the early 1820s, doubled in the pre-March period, and grew by another 30 percent in the 1850s, which meant that their share in the total of direct and indirect taxes grew from 30 percent in 1822 to 50 percent in 1848 and was lower again in the 1850s. After the compromise, the share of indirect taxes in the state revenues rose continuously, and from the mid-1890s, it accounted for more than 70 percent of all taxes (Austria and Hungary combined). Revenues from excise duties were always greater than from customs duties. Excise duties were mostly duties on alcoholic beverages and on different kinds of food, like meat and sugar. In Austria (less so in Hungary), the sugar tax eventually proved particularly profitable, given the fast rise of sugar beet production and consumption; in 1913, almost 40 percent of the excise was derived from the sugar tax.

[8]  Order, October 29, 1849, RGBl 439.
[9]  Law, October 25, 1896, RGBl 220.

The loss of Lombardy and Veneto in 1860 and 1866, respectively, deprived Austria of two of its most affluent provinces. In 1858, the Italian provinces together delivered to the Treasury 17 percent of the net tax revenues and 19 percent of the revenues from state monopolies. Given the fact that the most of public expenditure was central expenditure for the military and for debt servicing, with only a small part spent in the provinces, the wars of 1859 and 1866 brought about a considerable loss in state revenues that was not accompanied by a similar drop in expenditure.

### 5.3.3 State Monopolies and Firms in Public Ownership

Apart from direct and indirect taxes, state monopolies and firms owned by the state formed the third-largest part of state revenues, yielding the same amount as excise and customs duties, and sometimes more. In general, the relative weight of monopolies in all revenues gained from taxes and monopolies together diminished from about 30 percent in the pre-March era to 18 percent in Austria and 13–15 percent in Hungary after the turn of the century.

The state held monopolies on the production of salt and tobacco, on lotteries, and on postal services. The salt retail trade, which the state originally had monopolized as well, became free in different provinces between the 1780s and the 1820s, whereas tobacco remained a monopoly both in production and in trade. Mining was subject to state regulation as well; the state-owned mines and private mining companies operated on privilege by the state and paid special fees. The state also owned a number of demesnes and a few industrial enterprises, but it was far from having a monopoly in those fields. Nor had the state a monopoly in the (intermittently completely private) railway sector, but it eventually owned a majority of the railway capital and ran a number of private railway companies. Of course, in every one of these fields, net revenues were considerably less than gross revenues.

By far most important to 1848 in terms of gross and especially net revenues was the salt monopoly, which yielded about one-sixth of state net revenues. Yet in the following decades, tobacco became an ever more important source of revenue. The net result of the salt monopoly was about 40 million crowns in 1822, rose to 53 million in 1847, and fluctuated around 60 million in the last decades of the Austria-Hungarian union (Austrian and Hungarian revenues combined). Tobacco revenues started at a moderate 11–12 million crowns in the 1820s and doubled every twenty years. In 1913, Austria and Hungary together collected a net 340 million crowns (gross 545 million) from the tobacco monopoly, a sum that represented about one-tenth of all ordinary state revenues in both Austria and Hungary.

The state also held a monopoly in postal and telegraph services, a relatively fast-growing sector in the last decades of the Austria-Hungarian union. Gross postal revenues were about 25 million crowns in the 1850s, doubled until the early 1880s, and then doubled every ten years. In 1913, they amounted to 340 million crowns, which was about 6.5 percent of overall ordinary gross revenues (Austria and Hungary combined). Their net revenues were much less and, though mostly positive, accounted for around 1 percent of total net revenues.

State demesnes, mines, and industrial enterprises in public ownership were more important in Hungary than in Austria, at least as much as the absolute size of the business is concerned. In terms of net revenues, their contribution was minimal both in Austria and in Hungary. In Austria, gross revenues from the sources were about 2–3 percent of overall gross revenues, the same order of magnitude as, for instance, gross salt revenues. In Hungary, about 10 percent of gross revenues were gathered in state enterprises. Net revenues, however, were close to zero in both parts of the empire, in Austria mostly positive and in Hungary slightly negative. In the short run, state demesnes had some importance for balancing the state budget by increased sales in the fiscally tight 1850s. In 1859, for instance, the state earned 190 million crowns from the sale of demesnes, which was one-sixth of gross state revenues and one-quarter of net revenues in that year. After the compromise, the sale of state demesnes, though continual, brought in only irrelevant gains.

The nationalization of railways brought about the single most important change in state budgets (Figure 5.3). In the first period of nationalized railways in the 1840s and 1850s, the sector had been too small to gain the same importance in state budgets as it would half a century later, but the share of railway operation and construction still equaled almost 9 percent of gross expenditures in 1856 (Dirninger 1993: 194–8). From then, it decreased following the privatization of the railways. In the second era of nationalization, the railway system had become much larger and continued to grow, and the share of the state rose accordingly. Although railways were almost completely absent from Austrian state budgets in 1870, the share of railways in gross expenditures amounted to 2 percent in 1879, 15 percent in 1884, 19 percent in 1897, 20 percent in 1908, and 32 percent in 1909. Between the peak years, when additional companies were nationalized, the railway share in state expenditures

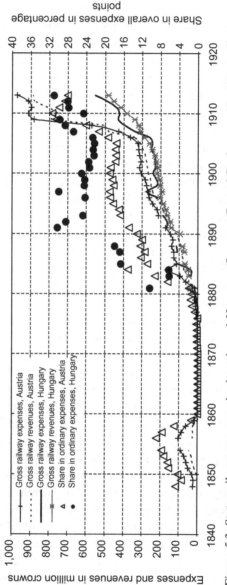

Figure 5.3. State railway expenses in Austria and Hungary. *Sources: Central-Rechnungs-Abschlüsse; Compass. Finanzielles Jahrbuch. Note:* Railway expenses include expenses for the state railway debt.

decreased slightly. These numbers include ordinary railway expenses for the operation of railways, maintenance costs, fleet-enlargement costs, construction of new lines, and payments to former owners and other capital costs. In addition, the annual costs of the railway state debt (bonds issued by private railways and shouldered by the state in the course of nationalization), mentioned earlier in connection with public expenditures, are included. The share of railway revenues in the overall state revenues was equally high and peaked at 28 percent in 1909. Excluding the railway state debt, the nationalized railways showed deficits in the first ten years and surpluses from 1889 onward, which equaled 1–4 percent (in 1912, almost 8 percent) of net tax revenues. Taking into account the railway state debt, the state railway system showed a deficit of about one-third of railway revenues in the mid-1880s and about 10 percent after the turn of the century.

The Hungarian state railways were less profitable than the Austrian ones. Revenues and ordinary expenses were normally approximate to each other, but if the annual costs of the railway debt resulting from the period before nationalization are included, Hungarian state railways usually show deficits.[10] The share of railways in the overall state expenditure was even higher in Hungary, amounting to 30 percent as early as 1891, decreasing to just 23 percent in 1905, and returning to 30 percent in 1909. The absolute size of the Hungarian state railway system was not much smaller up to 1906; it was only after the last wave of nationalization in Austria in 1907–9 that the Austrian state railway system became about twice the size of the Hungarian one.

### 5.3.4 The State Debt

As a result of the constitutional changes, the Austrian and Hungarian national debt had several elements that were raised and paid back separately.[11] Until 1866, the debt was divided into the debt of the Austrian Empire and the less important debt of the Lombardo-Venetian Kingdom. When Lombardy and Veneto were lost, in 1860 and 1866, respectively, their debt was accordingly transferred to Italy in 1867. After the compromise of 1867, the debt of the previous decades remained in existence as an undivided, so-called general debt. Both Austria and

---

[10] Values of Hungarian railway expenses from 1903 to 1913 include the value of railway bonds that had been converted into perpetual state bonds in 1902.

[11] For the state debt in general see Körner (1893), Körner (1899), and Püregger (1912). For the different parts of the state debt, see Pammer (2002: 119–41).

Hungary contributed to amortization and interest, with Hungary paying a certain amount that remained practically stable for the period up to the First World War. Thus, with annuities varying slightly in the short run because of exchange-rate fluctuations and shifts between amortizable debts and perpetual bonds, Hungary contributed between 24 percent and 29 percent to the costs of the general debt.

The general debt consisted of a large number of loans raised either directly by the Treasury or by way of the Vienna City Bank (Wiener Stadt-Banco) or the provincial diets. Most of them were perpetual bonds (i.e., not regularly redeemed) but converted into bonds of a different type from time to time. The largest conversion happened after the compromise, when Austria-Hungary issued so-called unified bonds (Einheitliche Rente) in silver and in paper money, respectively, which replaced most of the former bonds of the same denomination (Beer 1877: 372–85). The unified bonds eventually made up more than 85 percent of the long-term general debt. A minor part of the long-term debt originated from the emission of the highly popular lottery loans, which combined normal or low rates of interest (or even no interest at all) with raffled bonuses.[12]

The long-term general debt rose relatively steadily from about 1.6 billion crowns around 1820 to 4.8 billion crowns in 1867. A major increase happened in the 1850s, when the government issued the largest single loan that had been raised so far. It was called the National Loan (Nationalanlehen) and amounted to 1,340 million crowns raised in five years, beginning in 1854, and increased the long-term debt by half of its 1853 value (Brandt 1978: 692–704). From 1868, the general debt rose but moderately, mostly because of the emission of additional unified bonds for the payment of interest. After the peak in 1896, the general debt slightly decreased, amounting to 5.3 billion crowns in 1913.

Thus, short-term fluctuations of the general debt were normally generated not by the emission of perpetual bonds but by a variety of refundable short-term loans, such as short-term treasury bonds and three- to six-month bonds that were mortgaged on the Upper Austrian saltworks. The short-term debt typically increased in times of political crises and military measures, such as 1848–9, when the Austrian government fought

[12] Following the periodical statements of the Treasury and the State Debt Commission, the values of the state debt were recalculated according to an interest rate of 5 percent for perpetual bonds denominated in convention currency and Austrian currency, and 2.5 percent for bonds denominated in Vienna currency. Amortizable loans and non–interest-bearing securities were calculated at nominal value.

revolutionaries and separatists, and issued almost 400 million crowns in short-term loans, and 1859, when the war in Italy required new loans of half a billion crowns, most of them short term. In 1866, when the government had to finance the war against Prussia, it chose a different path, issuing government money (actually the small banknotes were declared state notes, and the central bank had to hand over large bills in equal amount; that is, the central bank had to issue a forced loan to the state).[13]

After the compromise, the Austrian part of the empire, while paying for its share of the general debt, did not raise its own new loans immediately. Only in 1876 did Austria start to issue perpetual gold bonds, which were accompanied by paper bonds from 1881. Apart from the conversion of florin bonds to crown bonds, all bonds once issued remained in circulation indefinitely. The state issued new bonds almost every year, and in three years, about half a billion crowns of gold bonds had been emitted. In 1888, Austrian perpetual bonds amounted to 1 billion crowns; in 1901, to 2 billion; and in 1913, to 3.6 billion. These means were used for all kinds of state expenditure, for infrastructural investments, for amortization of other parts of the state debt, for military expenses, for emergency measures, and so on.

From 1885 onward, the Austrian debt contained an increasing share of refundable loans, most of them belonging to the debt of the nationalized railways. The nationalization of the railways followed a variety of arrangements depending on the capital structure of the companies. The state took over some smaller companies, paying annuities to the previous owners for several decades (actually most such claims were effectively reduced to nil in the hyperinflation after the First World War). These claims were paid out of the annual state budget but did not appear in the debt statements of the state. The loans that had been raised in previous years by other railway companies, including all the large ones, became part of the public debt by way of nationalization, and railway shares were converted into state railway bonds (Eisenbahnstaatsschuldverschreibungen). Railway bonds were sometimes converted into state bonds as well

---

[13] The currency to 1858 was the silver florin *Conventionsmünze*, which was substituted by the silver florin Austrian currency (1 florin *Conventionsmünze* equalled 1.05 florins Austrian currency). In 1892, Austria-Hungary adopted de facto the gold standard, issuing the crown as the monetary unit. One crown was equal to two florins Austrian currency. The crown remained in a stable relation to the other gold currencies. The legal parity was 100 mark = 117.5627 crowns; 10 pounds = 240.1742 crowns; 100 francs = 95.2258 crowns. Throughout this chapter, all monetary values of state revenues and expenditures, and of the state debt, are given in crowns (Wysocki 1993).

and followed otherwise the original amortization scheme, which the companies had drawn up when issuing them. Thus, basically, the railway debt would have slowly decreased, but given the nationalization of additional companies every few years, it rose from 20 million crowns in 1880 to 900 million in 1888, 1.4 billion in 1895, 1.8 billion in 1907 and 3.1 billion (or 47 percent of the Austrian state debt) in 1910. The state's share in the overall nominal capital of Austrian railways rose from zero in 1883 to 25–30 percent from 1887 and to 60 percent in 1910.

In the emission of perpetual bonds, Hungary followed the same timing as Austria, issuing gold bonds in 1876 and paper bonds in 1881, and converting the paper bonds from florins to crowns in 1892. However, the share of perpetual bonds in the Hungarian debt became much larger in the course of time, reaching 80 percent in 1913, and the absolute value of Hungarian perpetual bonds exceeded the value of the Austrian counterparts. In 1913, 5 billion crowns of Hungarian bonds were in circulation, a sum that was one-third more than the total of equivalent Austrian securities, despite that the Hungarian economy and state budget was much smaller than those of Austria. One reason for this development was the limitation of refundable loans in Hungarian debt. Like Austria, Hungary nationalized railways, but contrary to its western neighbor, it withdrew a number of the loans that had been raised by the railway companies or by the state itself in connection with the takeover. Part of the returns of perpetual bonds was used to pay off these railway debts.

Investments into the Hungarian debt came mostly from abroad. For most of the time, the Hungarian-held share was in the range of 30–40 percent, only to reach 45 percent in the last years before the First World War. The biggest investors were Austria, during the Great Depression, and Germany, from the late 1890s. Because of the asynchronous course of the business cycles in Austria and Hungary, Austrian investments were particularly high in the early 1890s, when the Austrian economy grew only slowly and Hungary enjoyed high growth rates. In 1893, Austrians held 60 percent of Hungarian state securities. After the turn of the century, Germany overtook Austria as the biggest investor in the Hungarian economy, and between the late 1890s and the First World War, Germany's share in Hungarian state securities lay between 25 percent and 30 percent. Among the Western European economies, only France remained a major investor in Hungary throughout the period, holding 5–10 percent of the bonds. Great Britain and the Netherlands, which had participated largely in the 1870s, pulled out almost completely in the following decades (Komlos 1983b: table 4.28; Pammer 1998).

As mentioned previously, the abolition of seigneuries was connected with an indemnification of their lords. This indemnification was made by the newly created emancipation funds (*Grundentlastungsfonds*), which issued emancipation bonds (*Grundentlastungsobligationen*). Every crown land had its own emancipation fund. The payments and services that the lords had received previously were capitalized on the basis of an interest rate of 5 percent. The funds issued bonds valued at two-thirds of the capitalized value to the lords and redeemed them within forty years (the remaining third was regarded as an equivalent of lords' former expenses for local administration and justice, and it lapsed). The necessary means came from the peasantry and from the respective crown lands, as the state guaranteed the debt (therefore, the emancipation debt was always listed in the state debt reports). Because the emancipation process took some time, the corresponding debt rose, peaking in 1861 in Austria at 565 million crowns and in Hungary in 1867, when it totaled 514 million crowns. In the 1880s and 1890s, the Austrian lands and Hungary converted the emancipation bonds to ordinary provincial bonds. A significant portion of the converted bonds circulated to the end of Austria-Hungary and represented a large part of the provincial debts at the time.

Altogether, the weight of the state debt in the Austro-Hungarian economy was greater in the time after the compromise than it was before, and it differed between Austria and Hungary (Figure 5.4). In the pre-March period, the debt equaled about 57 percent of GDP in the early 1830s, decreasing to less than 40 percent a decade later. Heavy borrowing the 1850s resulted in a state debt of about 75 percent of GDP at the time of the compromise. The peak was in 1890, when debt had increased for various reasons and GDP growth had been moderate in the Great Depression years. In the last two decades before the First World War, high GDP growth reduced again the relative weight of the state debt to 60 percent of GDP. The Hungarian state was relatively more indebted than the Austrian state: the Hungarian debt equaled up to 108 percent of Hungarian GDP (in 1892), whereas in Austria, the respective value was just 83 percent (in 1888), following Kausel's (1979) rather low GDP estimates, and less than 80 percent according to the Schulze's (2000) GDP estimates.[14] In 1908, prior to the last wave of railway nationalization, the

---

[14] Compared to Schulze (2000), Kausel (1979) assumes low GDP values for Austria in the Great Depression. From the 1890s, the estimates of both are close to each other.

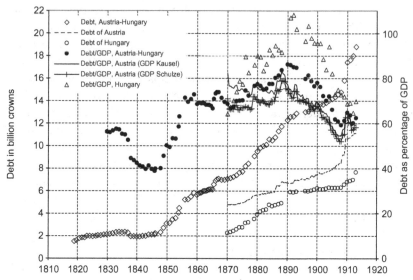

Figure 5.4. The Austro-Hungarian state debt and its relation to GDP. *Sources:* Debt: *Ausweise/Nachweisungen über den Stand der Staatsschulden; Compass. Finanzielles Jahrbuch.* GDP: Bairoch 1976, Kausel 1979, Schulze 2000. *Notes:* Debt, Austria-Hungary = debt of the Austrian Empire to 1867, and sum of debt of Austria and debt of Hungary from 1867. Debt of Austria = debt of the kingdoms and lands represented in the parliament and Austrian share in the common debt from 1867. Debt of Hungary = debt of the Hungarian lands and Hungarian share in the common debt from 1867. Nonrefundable debts are revalued to a standardized 5-percent interest rate. Debt/GDP, Austria-Hungary = Austro-Hungarian debt as percentage of Austro-Hungarian GDP (Bairoch [1976] GDP estimates 1830–60, intermediate years interpolated; Schulze [2000] estimates 1870–1913). Debt/GDP, Austria (GDP Kausel [1979]) = Austrian debt as percentage of Austrian GDP (Kausel GDP estimates). Debt/GDP, Austria (GDP Schulze) = Austrian debt as percentage of Austrian GDP (Schulze GDP estimates). Debt/GDP, Hungary = Hungarian debt as percentage of Hungarian GDP (Schulze GDP estimates).

Austrian state debt was equivalent to less than 55 percent of Austrian GDP.

## 5.4 Conclusion

Changes in taxation and public finance in nineteenth-century Austria-Hungary were determined in the first instance by the will to centralize and unify the system of taxation and to react to needs in infrastructure and education of an industrializing country. The centralization of the tax system was successful insofar as, following the revolution of 1848 and the neo-absolutist rule over Hungary and other lands, previously different regional conditions in taxation could be substituted by an ever more uniform tax system. Even after the political breakup of the Austrian Empire and the creation of Austria and Hungary as two separate entities, taxation remained similar in both halves of the empire. In contrast, the political system in which financial policy was conducted tended toward disintegration rather than unification. In 1867, the Austrian Empire was divided into Austria and Hungary, and the relative strength of a number of ethnic groups in Austria kept ethnic tensions alive and influenced fiscal policy as well as other fields.

Economic growth and sectoral change came apart rather independently of these political processes. There is little evidence that income growth and sectoral change worked as integrative forces to close the gap between more and less advanced regions; regional disparities probably remained as strong as ever until the end of Austria-Hungary. Fiscal policy, spending on education, and infrastructure policy, however, worked toward integrating regions at different levels of development, either as a political end in itself or for the rather practical necessity of recruiting political support.

## Sources

*A magyar korona országainak állami zárszámadása*, 1868–1913, Budapest 1869–1914.

*Ausweis über den Stand der allgemeinen Staatsschuld*, verfasst von der Staatsschulden-Commission des Reichsrathes, 1879–86, Beilagen zum amtlichen Theile der "Wiener Zeitung," Wien 1879–87.

*Ausweis über den Stand der gesammten consolidirten Staatsschuld, dann der nicht gemeinsamen schwebenden Schuld und der Grundentlastungs-, endlich der consolidirten garantierten Landesschulden von den im österreichischen Reichsrathe vertretenen Königreichen und Ländern,* verfasst von der Staatsschulden-Commission des Reichsrathes, 1868–78, Beilagen zum amtlichen Theile der "Wiener Zeitung ," Wien 1868–79.

*Ausweis über den Stand der gesammten österreichischen Staatsschuld,* verfasst von der Staatsschulden-Commission des Reichsrathes, 1860–7, Beilagen zum amtlichen Theile der "Wiener Zeitung," Wien 1860–7.

*Ausweis über den Stand der gemeinsamen schwebenden Staatsschuld,* verfasst von der Staatsschulden-Commission des Reichsrathes, 1868–86, Beilagen zum amtlichen Theile der "Wiener Zeitung," Wien 1868–87.

*Ausweis über den Stand der Schulden von den im Reichsrathe vertretenen Königreichen und Ländern,* verfasst von der Staatsschulden-Commission des Reichsrathes, 1879–86, Beilagen zum amtlichen Theile der "Wiener Zeitung," Wien 1879–87.

*Central-Rechnungs-Abschluß über den Staats-Haushalt der im Reichsrathe vertretenen Königreiche und Länder*, 1868–1913, vom k. k. Obersten Rechnungshofe für die im Reichsrathe vertretenen Königreiche und Länder, 1869–1914.

*Compass. Finanzielles Jahrbuch für Oesterreich-Ungarn*, Wien 1868–1918.

*Ergebnisse der Volkszählung und der mit derselben verbundenen Zählung der häuslichen Nutzthiere vom 31. December 1880*, vols. 3–4 (Oesterreichische Statistik, vols. 1.3, 2.1), k. k. Direction der administrativen Statistik, Wien 1882.

*Die Ergebnisse der Volkszählung vom 31. December 1890 in den im Reichsrathe vertretenen Königreichen und Ländern*, vols. 32/3, 33.2–5, 7 (Österreichische Statistik vols. 32.3, 33.2–5,7), Bureau der k. k. Statistischen Central-Commission, Wien 1892–4.

*Die Ergebnisse der Volkszählung vom 31. Dezember 1900 in den im Reichsrate vertretenen Königreichen und Ländern*, vols. 63/3, 66.2–5, 7 (Österreichische Statistik vols. 63.3, 66.2–5, 7), Bureau der k. k. Statistischen Zentral-Kommission, Wien 1903.

*Die Ergebnisse der Volkszählung vom 31. Dezember 1910 in den im Reichsrate vertretenen Königreichen und Ländern*, vols. 1/3, 3/2–5/7 (Österrreichische Statistik, vols. N.F. 1.3, 3.2–5,7), bearb. von dem Bureau der k. k. Statistischen Zentralkommission, Wien 1914–15.

Mitchell, B. R. (1998) *International Historical Statistics. Europe 1750–1993*, London: Macmillan.

*Nachweisung über den Stand der Staatsschulden*, verfasst von der Staatsschulden-Commission des Reichsrathes, 1887–1903, Beilagen zum amtlichen Theile der "Wiener Zeitung," Wien 1887–1903.

*Nachweisung der Staatsschulden-Kontroll-Kommission des Reichsrates über den Stand der Staatsschulden*, 1903–17, Beilagen zum amtlichen Theile der "Wiener Zeitung," Wien 1904–18.

Rechnungs-Abschluß (Haupt-Rechnungs-Abschluß, Central-Rechnungs-Abschluß) über den gesammten Staatshaushalt der österreichischen Monarchie, 1848–54, 1856–9, Bundesministerium für Finanzen, Bibliothek, XV 777.

*Schluß-Rechnung über den allen Königreichen und Ländern der österreichisch-ungarischen Monarchie gemeinsamen Staatshaushalt*, vom k. u. k. gemeinsamen Obersten Rechnungshofe, Wien 1868–1913.

*Staats-Voranschlag für die am constituirenden Reichstage vertretenen Länder der österreichischen Monarchie für das Verwaltungsjahr 1849*, Wien 1848.

[Tafeln zur Statistik der österreichischen Monarchie]: *Versuch einer Darstellung der Oesterreichischen Monarchie in statistischen Tafeln* (1828), Wien 1829. *Darstellung der Oesterreichischen Monarchie in Statistischen Tafeln*, 2. Jg, (1829), Wien 1830. *Tafeln zur Statistik der österreichischen Monarchie*, Jg. 3–21 (1830–1848), Wien 1831–53, Neue Folge 1–5 (1849–65), Wien 1856–71.

Voranschlag des Staatserfordernisses und der Bedeckung, Militärjahre/ Verwaltungsjahre 1821–48, Bundesministerium für Finanzen, Bibliothek, XV 777.

# References

Bachinger, K. (2005) "Das Verkehrswesen," in A. Brusatti (ed.) *Die Habsburger-monarchie 1848–1918. Bd. 1: Die wirtschaftliche Entwicklung*, 2nd ed. Vienna: Österreichische Akademie der Wissenschaften, 278–322.

Bairoch, P. (1976) "Europe's gross national product 1800–1975," *Journal of European Economic History*, 5, 273–340.

Baltzarek, F. (1993) "Die Finanzierung des Eisenbahnsystems in der Donau-monarchie," in R. G. Plaschka, A. Drabek, and B. Zaar (eds.) *Eisenbahn-bau und Kapitalinteressen in den Beziehungen der österreichischen mit den südslawischen Ländern*. Wien: Österreichische Akademie der Wissenschaften, 221–231.

Beer, A. (1877) *Die Finanzen Oesterreichs im XIX. Jahrhundert. Nach archivali-schen Quellen*, Prag: Tempsky.

Blumenthal, K. v. (2007) *Die Steuertheorien der Austrian Economics. Von Men-ger zu Mises*. Marburg: Metropolis Verlag.

Brandt, H.-H. (1978) *Der österreichische Neoabsolutismus. Staatsfinanzen und Politik 1848–1860*, 2 vols. Göttingen: Vandenhoek Ruprecht.

Dirninger, C. (1993) "Staatskredit und Eisenbahnwesen in den österreichischen Ländern im Verlauf des 19. Jahrhunderts," in R. G. Plaschka, A. Drabek, and B. Zaar (eds.) *Eisenbahnbau und Kapitalinteressen in den Beziehungen der österreichischen mit den südslawischen Ländern*. Wien: Österreichische Akademie der Wissenschaften, 191–219.

Eddie, S. (1989) "Economic policy and economic development in Austria-Hungary, 1867–1913," in P. Mathias (ed.) *The Cambridge Economic History of Europe*, vol. 8. Cambridge: Cambridge University Press, 814–86.

Gerschenkron, A. (1977) *An Economic Spurt that Failed*. Princeton, NJ: Prince-ton University Press.

Good, D. F. (1978) "The Great Depression and Austrian growth after 1873," *Economic History Review*, 2nd ser., 31, 290–4.

Good, D. F. (1980) "Modern economic growth in the Habsburg monarchy," *East Central Europe*, 7, 248–68.

Good, D. F. (1984) *The Economic Rise of the Habsburg Empire, 1750–1914*. Berkeley: University of California Press.

Good, D. F. (1991) "Austria-Hungary," in R. Sylla and G. Toniolo (eds.) (1991) *Patterns of European Industrialization: The Nineteenth Century*. Lon-don: Routledge, 218–47.

Good, D. F. (1994) "The economic lag of Central and Eastern Europe: Income estimates for the Habsburg successor states, 1870–1910," *Journal of Economic History*, 54, 869–91.

Good, D. F. (1997) "Proxy data and income estimates: Reply to Pammer," *Jour-nal of Economic History*, 57, 456–63.

Good, D. F. and Ma, T. (1998) "New estimates of income levels in Central and Eastern Europe, 1870–1910," in F. Baltzarek, F. Butschek, and G. Tichy (eds.) *Von der Theorie zur Wirtschaftspolitik – ein österreichischer Weg. Festschrift zum 65. Geburtstag von Erich W. Streissler*. Stuttgart: Lucius und Lucius, 147–68.

Good, D. F. and Ma, T. (1999). "The economic growth of Central and Eastern Europe in comparative perspective, 1870–1989," *European Review of Economic History*, 3, 103–37.

Gratz, A. (1949) "Die österreichische Finanzpolitik von 1848 bis 1948," in H. Mayer (ed.) *Hundert Jahre österreichischer Wirtschaftsentwicklung 1848–1948*. Vienna: Springer, 222–309.

Gross, N. T. (1966) "Industrialization in Austria in the nineteenth century," Ph.D. dissertation, University of California, Berkeley.

Gross, N. T. (1971) "Economic growth and the consumption of coal in Austria and Hungary 1831–1913," *Journal of Economic History*, 31, 898–916.

Hauer, J., Ritter v. (1848) *Beiträge zur Geschichte der österr. Finanzen*. Vienna: Wallishauser.

Hübner, O. (1849) *Oesterreichs Finanzlage und seine Hilfsquellen*. Vienna: Jasper, Hügel und Manz.

Katus, L. (1970) "Economic growth in Hungary during the age of dualism (1867–1913): A quantitative analysis," in E. Pamlényi (ed.) *Sozial-ökonomische Forschungen zur Geschichte von Ost-Mitteleuropa*. Budapest: Akadémiai Kiadó.

Kausel, A. (1979) "Österreichs Volkseinkommen 1830 bis 1913. Versuch einer Rückrechnung des realen Brutto-Inlandsproduktes für die österreichische Reichshälfte und das Gebiet der Republik Österreich," *Geschichte und Ergebnisse der zentralen amtlichen Statistik in Österreich 1829–1979*. Vienna: Österreichische Staatsdruckerei, 689–720.

Komlos, J. (1978) "Is the Depression in Austria after 1873 a 'myth'?" *Economic History Review*, 2nd ser., 31, 287–9.

Komlos, J. (ed.) (1983a) *Economic Development in the Habsburg Monarchy in the Nineteenth Century: Essays*. Boulder, CO: East European Monographs.

Komlos, J. (ed.) (1983b) *The Habsburg Monarchy as a Customs Union: Economic Development in Austria-Hungary in the Nineteenth Century*. Princeton, NJ: Princeton University Press.

Körner, A. (1893) *Staatsschuldentilgung und Staatsbankerott. Mit besonderer Berücksichtigung der fundirten Staatsschuld*. Vienna: Manz.

Körner, A. (1899) *Grundriss des Österreichischen Staatsschuldenwesens*. Vienna: Manz.

Liese, J. (1993) *Staatskredit und Defizitfinanzierung in der ersten konstitutionellen Periode der Habsburger Monarchie 1860–1867*. Frankfurt: Peter Lang.

Matis, H. (1972) *Österreichs Wirtschaft 1848–1913. Konjunkturelle Dynamik und gesellschaftlicher Wandel im Zeitalter Franz Josephs I.* Berlin: Duncker und Humblot.

Mülinen, Comte de (1875) *Les finances de l'Autriche. Étude historique et statistique sur les finances de l'Autriche-Cisleithanienne comparées avec celles de la France*. Vienna: Braumüller.

Pammer, M. (1997) "Proxy data and income estimates: The economic lag of Central and Eastern Europe," *Journal of Economic History*, 57, 448–55.

Pammer, M. (1998) "Austrian private investments in Hungary, 1850–1913," *European Review of Economic History*, 2, 141–69.

Pammer, M. (2002) *Entwicklung und Ungleichheit. Österreich im 19. Jahrhundert.* Stuttgart: Franz Steiner Verlag.

Püregger, J. (1912) *Fünfzig Jahre Staatsschuld 1862–1912.* Vienna: Staatsdruckerei.

Rudolph, R. L. (1975) "The pattern of Austrian industrial growth from the eighteenth to the early twentieth century," *Austrian History Yearbook,* 11, 3–25.

Rudolph, R. L. (1976) *Banking and Industrialization in Austria-Hungary: The Role of Banks in the Industrialization of the Czech Crownlands, 1873–1914.* Cambridge: Cambridge University Press.

Sandgruber, R. (1978) *Österreichische Agrarstatistik 1750–1918.* Vienna: Verlag fur Geschichte und Politik.

Sandgruber, R. (1995) *Ökonomie und Politik. Österreichische Wirtschaftsgeschichte vom Mittelalter bis zur Gegenwart.* Vienna: Ueberreuter.

Schulze, M.-S. (1996) *Engineering and Economic Growth: The Development of Austria-Hungary's Machine-Building Industry in the Late Nineteenth Century.* Frankfurt: Peter Lang.

Schulze, M.-S. (1997) "The machine-building industry and Austria's Great Depression after 1873," *Economic History Review,* 50, 282–304.

Schulze, M.-S. (2000) "Patterns of growth and stagnation in the late nineteenth century Habsburg economy," *European Review of Economic History,* 4, 311–40.

Wysocki, J. (1975) *Infrastruktur und wachsende Staatsausgaben. Das Fallbeispiel Österreich 1868–1913.* Stuttgart: G. Fischer.

Wysocki, J. (1993) "Die österreichisch/ungarische Krone im Goldwährungsmechanismus," in E. Schremmer (ed.) *Geld und Währung vom 16. Jahrhundert bis zur Gegenwart. Referate der 14. Arbeitstagung der Gesellschaft für Sozial- und Wirtschaftsgeschichte vom 9. bis 13. April 1991 in Dortmund.* Stuttgart: Franz Steiner Verlag, 143–56.

# 6

# The Rise of the Fiscal State in Sweden, 1800–1914

## Lennart Schön

### 6.1 Introduction

In the period 1800–1914, Sweden developed from a rather poor agrarian society to a modern industrializing nation with growth rates at the top of international standards of the time. In the same period, the Swedish state was modernized and its fiscal basis transformed in a way that corresponded to the new structure of the economy and to the new demands put on the state. Thus, in the beginning of the nineteenth century, the state was heavily dependent on a tax base whose origins were largely medieval. Land rents for the state administration and the provision for the military forces were provided locally and primarily due in kind. This system created a stable basis for the state but was not very flexible. It was complemented by temporary taxes mainly levied at wartime. Such pressures on state finances also induced short-term lending by different means. At the end of the period, the fiscal basis had shifted completely. On the one hand, there were income taxes and indirect taxes on monetary streams, and on the other hand, state borrowing was long term with a large funded debt.

This chapter will present the major trends in the relation between economic growth and the finance of state activities. It will also present the traditional fiscal structure of the early nineteenth century and give a particular emphasis on the construction of the new fiscal basis in the second half of the nineteenth century. This development involved not only technical and fiscal questions but also wider political questions, as the fiscal system was very much integrated with other economic and social issues of the industrializing nation.

Table 6.1. *Annual Growth Rates Per Capita of GDP, Public Services and State Revenues in Sweden 1800–1914. Constant Prices (GDP deflator)*

|           | GDP | Public Services | State Revenues |
|-----------|-----|-----------------|----------------|
| 1800–20   | 0.5 | −1.4            | −0.8           |
| 1820–50   | 0.6 | 0.0             | 0.0            |
| 1850–90   | 1.4 | 1.9             | 2.4            |
| 1890–1914 | 2.6 | 2.8             | 2.4            |
| 1800–1914 | 1.2 | 1.0             | 1.1            |

*Sources:* Krantz and Schön (2007); Fregert and Gustafsson (2005).

## 6.2 An Overview of Swedish Economic Growth and the Fiscal State, 1800–1914

The performance of the Swedish economy and Swedish growth in the nineteenth century and up to the First World War can be divided into four periods of different character (see Table 6.1). During the first two decades, successive wars crippled the economy, resulting in sharp fluctuations in economic activity and in slow growth. From the 1820s, economic performance became much more stable for some three decades, but growth rates were still rather low. The period was dominated by the transformation of agriculture and by some growth in the domestic market. From the mid-nineteenth century, economic activity fluctuated heavily once again but this time because of more economic stimulus. In the 1850s and then in the 1870s, there were very strong spurts of growth, originating mainly from the exports of natural resources–based industries. These put their imprint on the acceleration in growth rates. The growth rate increased even further from the 1890s with the breakthrough of new industries in the so-called second Industrial Revolution. In these decades up to the First World War, economic activity once again became less volatile.[1]

In the very long term, over the long nineteenth century, public activities and state revenue developed at a fairly similar pace and on par with economic growth. However, the pattern of change differed considerably between the economy at large, on the one hand, and the state, on the other hand. This is evident from the different growth rates shown in Table 6.1 and Figure 6.1, which present public-sector production and state revenues in relation to gross domestic product. The broad

---

[1] Major trends in the economy are analyzed in Schön (2000).

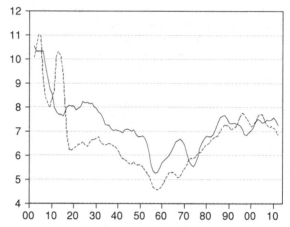

Figure 6.1. Public services (full line) and state revenue (dotted line) as percentage shares of GDP, 1800–1914 (current prices and five-year moving averages). *Sources:* Krantz and Schön (2007); Fregert and Gustafsson (2005).

periodization also comes out very clearly in Figure 6.2, which shows the state debt in relation to GDP. Very briefly, the following picture emerges.

In the first decades of the nineteenth century, all indicators of state financial activity fluctuated strongly at rather high levels. Both revenues and public services corresponded to some 10 percent of GDP. Also, the public debt was high, corresponding to about 20 percent of GDP. From

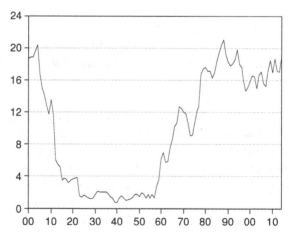

Figure 6.2. Public debt as share of GDP, 1800–1914. *Sources:* Krantz and Schön (2007); Fregert and Gustafsson (2005).

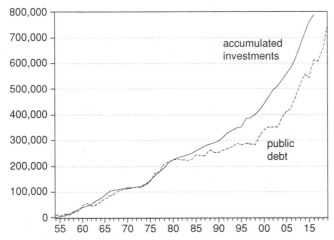

Figure 6.3. Accumulated public investments, 1854–1911, and public debt, 1854–1914 (in thousands of Swedish kroner). *Source:* Fregert and Gustafsson (2005).

the end of the 1810s to the 1850s, state finances were consolidated and levels of state activity decreased relative to GDP. Thus, over the first half of the century, public services and state revenues decreased in volume and, of course, even more so in relation to GDP. In the 1850s, both public services and state revenues had fallen to some 5 percent of GDP, and the state debt had been brought down to an even lower level. In the late 1850s, the tide turned. A new period followed characterized by a more expansionist public sector and by state revenues that increased their share of GDP. (See also Figure 6.3.) In the last two decades before the First World War, a new stability followed. Thus, from the 1890s, the growth of state activities was on par with the expanding economy.

Evidently, there were marked breaks in trends in the mid-nineteenth century. At that time, economic growth accelerated, but so did state activities and, even more so, state revenues. Thus, the expansion of the public sector – and in particular the expansion of state revenues – soared ahead of the stronger acceleration in economic growth that was to come from the 1890s.

The expansion of the state is a remarkable feature of the second half of the nineteenth century, particularly when one takes into account that it coincided with a shift to liberalization of the market economy. Although liberalization meant weaker state control of the economy, industrialization provided a number of new issues for the political agenda. In the same period, there were reforms of the parliament that paved the way for the principles of parliamentarism in Sweden and for a broader popular influence on politics. Even if there were still a long way to go to general suffrage to the parliament, these reforms created scope for new social classes and a new platform for debate and decision making.

Some notes on basic features of the political structure in Sweden ought to be made at the outset of this analysis of the rise of a modern fiscal state. In a comparative European perspective, the prominent role of the peasants in Swedish policy in the nineteenth century is possibly its most conspicuous feature. The position of the peasantry was ingrained in a distant past. Already in late medieval times, the peasants constituted one of the four estates in the Swedish parliament. As an estate – though not as individuals – the peasants were on par with the nobility, the clergy, and the urban bourgeoisie. At many times, the peasants were able to form an informal alliance with the king, primarily against the nobility. Because the king could guarantee freedom and independence from any bondage for the taxpaying peasants, the support from the latter estate gave the king a greater room of maneuvers in relation to the nobility. To the strength of the peasantry was added that tenants of the Crown were able to buy the landholdings as their private property during the eighteenth century, and by this means, the class of independent peasant landowners became numerous in the nineteenth century. Commercially oriented peasants holding family farms constituted one of the driving forces in the agrarian revolution in the first half of the nineteenth century, and they became very influential, as we will see, in the new parliament from the mid-nineteenth century onward. Thus, the restructuring of the state revenues for a long time became intricately connected with the state of affairs in agriculture.

### 6.3 The War Economy in the Early Nineteenth Century

In the first decades of the nineteenth century, public finances were heavily strained by the series of wars plaguing the Swedish, and indeed European, economy. The public debt increased and the wealth of the population was tapped by extraordinary taxation, with state revenues and expenditures rising sharply during the wars against Russia and France. Consequently, military expenses made up for some 50 percent of the provision of public services in Sweden in this period.

Up to 1809, the king (and thus the Crown) had a very strong hold on the state finances. In the last decades of the eighteenth century, a royal dictatorship was proclaimed, giving the king direct access to the Bank of Sweden and to the National Debt Office, something that was contrary to the Swedish tradition of parliamentary control of these institutions. Thus, the king could more easily finance warfare both by borrowing abroad and by printing of domestic debt obligations. The domestic credit notes were printed in large volumes and soon became non–interest-bearing and in practice irredeemable, although they could be used as legal tender in tax payments. In practice, the note-printing presses had to pay for the military expansionism with strong inflation and monetary disorder in their wake.

The military defeat against Russia meant the loss of Finland. This was a heavy blow to Swedish national pride and in particular to the economy of Stockholm, which had been the center of the Swedish Empire in the Baltic. In turn, this military catastrophe ended the sovereign royal rule in 1809. A new constitution was adopted and new institutions were to govern state finances. In principle, the parliament regained its strong hold of taxation, of the central bank and of the National Debt Office. Furthermore, the bank and the National Debt Office were independent of each other and formally independent of the executive power of the state, as both institutions were to be controlled by parliamentary committees. These institutional changes were important for the further development of the fiscal state in the nineteenth century, in particular because the peasantry became increasingly influential in the parliament. The peasants were relatively benign to the king and opposed the nobility, but they were also opposed to any increase in taxes that rested heavily on land.

One should also notice that the monetary turmoil created by the wars may have ameliorated the diffusion of fundamental changes in Swedish agriculture. Inflation in conjunction with demand shifts from population increases meant a sharp increase in the price of grain, which in turn relieved the tax pressure on land. This resulted in a redistribution of income that favored commercially minded landowners and tenant farmers. While the monetization of the economy improved, investments were encouraged. The enclosure movement gained momentum, commercialization increased, and these trends were to set their imprints on the first half of the nineteenth century.

## 6.4 Financial Consolidation and Restrictive Policies

The full effect of the new institutional rule of 1809 was not felt, however, until after the end of the Napoleonic Wars, when Sweden managed

Figure 6.4. Military expenditure as part of public expenditure, 1800–1914. Five-year moving averages. *Source:* Krantz and Schön (2007).

to acquire by force leadership in a union with Norway, which rendered some national consolation for the loss of Finland. By the end of the 1810s, a new period commenced with new goals set up for the monetary and fiscal policy of the state.

First of all, the European peace settlement meant a peace that was to be long lasting in Sweden. It has not been broken yet: since the Napoleonic Wars, Sweden has managed to stay out of every conflict. As a consequence, military expenditure decreased over the long run as a portion of public affairs (see Figure 6.4). The military share of public expenditure fell quite rapidly from close to half to one-third in the mid-nineteenth century. It is also fair to conclude that one of the mechanisms for state expansion – the financing of war efforts that later were turned into permanent taxes – was largely absent in Sweden during the nineteenth century up to the First World War.

Second, the public debt was more or less obliterated by a few political strokes. At the turn of the century, the public debt corresponded roughly to 20 percent of GDP and amounted to twice the annual state revenues. The foreign part of the debt disappeared very rapidly. The war with France at the end of the Napoleonic Wars became a pretext for, very one-sidedly, the writing off of all public debts to citizens of the so-called enemy country and of its possessions – this made up the larger part of the foreign debt, whereas the remainder was paid off by the sale of the last Swedish colonial possession, the island of Guadeloupe. A few years after the war, domestic debt taken by the prolific issuing of credit notes was also entirely written off. Credit notes and banknotes were formally declared irredeemable and a paper standard was introduced (Ahlström 1989).

Earlier, paper standard had been considered merely as a temporary expedient while state finances were improving. In the 1820s, parliamentary debates formulated the goal to reintroduce the silver standard. This issue of the paper notes led to a very restrictive financial policy to enlarge the treasury reserves of silver and foreign currency. A return to a silver standard was achieved in the 1830s (Brisman 1908). The trend from the 1820s to the 1850s was, however, the consolidation of state finances and a strong restriction of state activities – the parliament hardly approved new debt. The public sector even regressed in absolute terms as state revenues stagnated and, consequently, decreased as a share of total GDP.

During these decades, however, a fierce debate raged between proponents of the restrictive monetary policy and proponents of more expansionist policies to increase the supply of credit and to serve the interest of advancing commercial activities in all sectors. To the commercially oriented landowners, including new layers of the peasantry, this restrictive policy was a mixed blessing. On the one hand, nominal land taxes were kept low. On the other hand, the supply of domestic credit dwindled with export downswings or bad harvests, even if new mortgaging institutions provided access to long-term funding through privately organized capital imports in the 1830s and 1840s.

## 6.5 The Structure of Swedish Taxes to 1860

At the beginning of the nineteenth century, the structure of revenues kept a largely medieval character, relying heavily on payments in kind in a local context. To a great extent, this was the result of a conservative reaction of King Charles XI at the end of the seventeenth century. In the early seventeenth century, Swedish state administration and finances had been modernized to provide a more flexible basis for the Swedish Empire and to enhance the Swedish military strength. Two major assets were used to this end. The first asset of great importance for military flexibility in the imperial era was copper. The state controlled the great Swedish copper mines for export on the European market. This provided the state with a regular income flow of foreign currency and the means to sustain a mercenary army during long periods of war. When foreign demand for copper faltered and prices fell, the Swedish state tried to bolster demand by introducing a copper standard for its currency. As copper coins were much too heavy to circulate easily, early experiments with paper tokens took place, along with ensuing financial turmoil and reactions to this modernization. The second asset was Crown land, which was donated to the nobility in exchange for military and administrative services. This policy was successful in the short run, particularly as long as the Swedish imperial power was on the rise and new land was conquered around the Baltic – particularly as these conquests also gave control over the Baltic ports and an income stream from grain exports. In the longer run, however, as free peasants were turned into tenants under the nobility and taxes reverted from the Crown to the nobility, both the financial stability of the state and the freedom of the peasantry were at stake. Charles XI put an end to this trend by a very determined restoration of the royal domain with the support of the peasants against the nobility. With the restored possessions, the king constructed the meticulous scheme that locally distributed tax revenues in kind to the state administration and military. To each item of state expenditure, a specific source of revenue (mostly in kind and in a local or regional setting) was allotted.

This structure of earmarked taxation remained largely stable through the first half of the nineteenth century to the reforms of the early 1860s.[2] Most taxes were made up of land rents and payments to the military, which also were based on land holdings. These made up more than two-thirds of total direct taxes. The remainder comprised personal taxes and so-called contributions, based on estimates of property and income and more specific fees due to the state.

### 6.5.1 Fixed Land Rents

In 1789, the peasantry in the parliament and the king had reached an agreement that would become a mainstay in Swedish taxes to the mid-nineteenth century. All taxes on land holdings should be fixed, whether in money or in kind, and constant over time. Furthermore, reclamations of new land were to be exempted from taxes. These decisions were regarded as privileges of the Swedish peasantry and as a sign of their strong position in Swedish politics.

The introduction of the land taxes played a prominent role in the transformation of the Swedish economy and society in the period from the 1790s onward. They were not elastic enough to follow the increase in agrarian productivity in lieu of the enclosure movement and the reclamations of new land that gained momentum from the turn of the

---

[2] The description of the tax system is primarily based on Eberstein (1929), Gårestad (1982, 1985) and Olsson (2005).

century onward. The flow of the agrarian surplus production shifted from the state to the peasants, most of all to the growing numbers of commercially oriented farmers. The population growth in the first half of the nineteenth century, with wages lagging behind grain prices, was a further stimulus to the agrarian transformation and to capitalist relations in farming.[3] Furthermore, the structure of land taxes increased differentiation among the peasantry. The fact that the taxes were fixed in relation to the size of the original land holding regardless of any changes in productivity made them regressive in character. Farmers investing in new methods to increase productivity and to reclaim additional acreage were rewarded with a decisively decreased tax share of their income. Thus, the tax burden increasingly fell on peasants who did not modernize production or were more traditional.

The regressive character of taxation was further emphasized by the personal tax, the *mantalspenning*. This tax began as a milling toll, but in the seventeenth century, its burden was transferred to each adult citizen, though women paid half the amount of men. Although low, its value was fixed regardless of income. Only three categories were exempted from the personal tax, namely the destitute supported by the parishes, the military, and the indigenous people of Lapland, the Samis.

### 6.5.2 General Contributions

The fixed land rents and the fixed personal tax were supplemented by general contributions. The basic idea of the contributions was that they should be based on income. However, for the major part of the population – which lived off agriculture and its subsidiaries of fishery, forestry, and domestic crafts – no income assessment was available. In 1810, the parliament attempted to make the contributions dependent on actual income, but difficulties in assessing income proved insurmountable, and the experiment was curtailed in the following parliamentary meeting of 1812. The contributions returned to the basic structure of different payments in defined categories, with a mixture of fixed and variable payments.

For the great majority of taxpayers, namely agricultural landowners, the contribution became a supplement to the land rent following much the same principle. The contribution was set at two per mill of the taxation value of the estate. The same principle was extended to the owners of real estate in towns.

---

[3] For grain prices and wages, see Jörberg (1972).

The ambition was to apply a system of income-related taxes for all urban income earners of services and enterprise. Civil servants were, however, the only category that paid contributions as a function of income. The tax rate was 5 percent on a medium income range of 200–1,200 riksdaler annually and 3 percent on income greater than that range. Income earners from private business, such as merchants, manufacturers, and craftspeople, were to pay 5 percent of total earnings with wage labor costs deducted. No deduction for interest on capital was admitted. However, because of the great difficulties in determining actual income, a minimum tax was fixed for each category of profession. Furthermore, the tax was differentiated between towns in five classes according to income-earning potentials (e.g., Stockholm and Gothenburg were in the first class), and contributions were largely paid according to a fixed minimum rate.

Furthermore, specific contributions were to be paid by manufacturers in the countryside, owners of ironworks, mill owners and so on. Also in these areas, the tax system developed into a number of specific cases with fixed payments in relation either to the occupation or to the taxation value of the enterprise.

Because contributions were estimated in relation to income flows, they were to be paid not in kind but in cash directed to the Bank of Sweden. Thus, they were to bring in monetary funds that were used to finance state activities as well as for other purposes (Pettersson 1989).

The contributions played some particular roles in the fiscal and financial system of the early nineteenth century. First, contributions became part of the restrictive monetary policy of the decades to the 1830s to deflate prices and to augment the value of the Swedish paper notes. A substantial part of the monetary contributions were drawn out of circulation at the bank to enable the bank to perform the currency realization and to achieve full convertibility to silver – a goal that was reached in 1834.

Second, the policy meant draining credits from the market, a process that particularly hit debt-burdened agricultural innovators of the earlier enclosures movement and capitalist owners of manufactories. The political pressure on the Bank of Sweden to come to their relief in the parliament was great; thus, the bank diverted funds into such rescue operations in what was a slight but patent contradiction of the first policy objective.

Third, the contribution funds of the Bank of Sweden were used to finance infrastructural investments that were considered of specific strategic importance from economic, administrative, and military perspectives. The parliament starkly opposed new debt taken by the state, and therefore even long-term investments were to be financed out of current tax revenues. Only thusly could public investments be harmonized with the restrictive monetary policy. During the 1820s and 1830s, the major public infrastructural investment was the construction of the Göta Canal that cut through the agricultural regions of southern Sweden, connecting the Baltic Sea and the North Sea as a new water trunk line between the capital city of Stockholm and the expanding western port of Gothenburg. The long-term effects of this investment were weak, however, as the canal was soon to be superseded by railways in a distinctly new era.

### 6.5.3 Payments in Kind

Taxes were only partly set in monetary terms. In the eighteenth century and still in the first half of the nineteenth century, a large part of the taxes were paid in kind (e.g., in the form of grain, butter, fuel wood, or even labor days). In the case that payments in kind were converted to money payments, the monetary value of all different items was fixed each year in close relation to the regional market value by means of negotiations between representatives of producers and consumers. Thus, although payments in kind were rather neutral to fluctuations in price levels, fixed monetary taxes meant that taxpayers would gain from inflation and lose from deflation.

Thus, in periods of inflation during the wars, state revenues shrank in real terms; accordingly, revenues were largely stable in the period of monetary stability from 1820 to 1850. However, the share of the state diminished substantially in relation to GDP and in relation to the rather thin but increasing layer of agrarian surplus production over subsistence, while both agrarian investments and consumption in a new middle class increased, adding to the new dynamism of the economy. An example of the new dynamics was a shift in the regional concentration of economic activity. In the eighteenth century, much of the agrarian surplus had been directed to the expanding capital city of Stockholm, where conspicuous consumption and, consequently, sophisticated industrial production had flourished. In the first half of the nineteenth century, Stockholm stagnated, however. New industrial centers appeared in the countryside and in growing urban areas that introduced a wider spectrum of consumption goods for the growing markets of upper- and middle-class farmers.

The system of payments in kind had another consequence. Transaction costs were kept relatively low as long as these taxes were consumed locally by military personnel or civil servants, as intended by the original seventeenth-century plan implemented during the reign of Charles XI.

Over time, however, the intended balance between revenue and expenditure on the local level was broken, particularly when the activity of the central authority grew. Thus, the state and even civil servants of the state became involved in trading local surpluses to receive much more flexible monetary revenues. Hence, a bishop could complain about the low grain prices in the 1820s devaluing his salary. As a more general effect, the state became an important actor in domestic trade and in early market integration. Furthermore, the state set up regional storage facilities to balance fluctuations in harvests and in tax payments. The state even took on an entrepreneurial industrial function and founded public bakeries to make use of the inflow of grain.

In conclusion, it is evident that the fiscal base of the state, as far as direct taxes are concerned, was poorly adapted to the dynamic character of economic and social development in the first half of the nineteenth century. Taxes rested heavily on agriculture as the main sector of production and employment, and these taxes as well as many others were fixed as part of a social contract drawn up between the king and the parliament in the late eighteenth century.

In addition to taxes, there was only one other item of importance in the state revenues: the tariffs on foreign trade, which corresponded to roughly one-third of revenues until the 1840s. In relation to the fiscal revenues based on agriculture, this source of revenue was of secondary importance for the state in the early nineteenth century. Indeed, given that tariffs were high or even prohibitive to protect domestic industries in accordance to mercantilist protectionism, foreign trade was small in volume.

During the 1840s, this situation started to change. While tax income from agriculture stagnated, foreign trade started to expand. Tariffs increased as a share of total state income. At the end of the decade, tariffs reached more than 50 percent of the tax revenues. Parallel to the growth of foreign trade, economic liberalism gained momentum in Sweden during the 1840s as a precursor to new trends in Swedish industrial development.

## 6.6 The Trend Breaks of the 1850s

The decisive trend breaks in economic growth and in economic policy began in the mid-1850s. The Swedish economy was drawn into the European boom during the Crimean War, which occasioned a stiff increase in demand for the country's exports. The acceleration in European industrialization, in foreign trade, and in railway construction from this decade cleared the stage for new policies. In the same period, new interests were strengthened in Swedish politics. Representatives of advancing industrial, commercial, and agrarian capitalism entered into the increasingly intensive parliamentary debate about the role of the state in this development.

### 6.6.1 A New State Debt Policy

Sweden was a sparsely populated country with vast natural resources that became increasingly highly valued through the shift in demand. To exploit these possibilities, Sweden needed a more efficient infrastructure. However, the conservative and cautious opinion of keeping state expenditure at bay to prevent any tax increases was widespread. The position of the parliament was decisively turned by one man, the minister of finance, Johan August Gripenstedt. He delivered to the parliament what have been called flowering speeches that presented a bright picture of a future Swedish economy in full bloom, if the state engaged itself in developing a modern infrastructure of railways and telegraphs. He denounced all fears of future tax increases by vividly painting the dynamic effects of these investments on future income streams.

Gripenstedt managed to engage the state in the construction and running of modern infrastructure. The financing of a system of trunk lines by far outstripped the domestic supply of long-term capital. As such, the state had to borrow abroad. Swedish bonds were placed on the international capital market, mainly in Germany and France, despite the Swedish state's poor treatment of foreign creditors forty years earlier. The new parliamentary control of the National Debt Office may have paved the way for new loans, but perhaps more important was the close cooperation between the state and the commercial banks that appeared in the same period.

The loans from the late 1850s marked an epochal event, although one that occurred without much debate but as the logical outcome of the new undertaking. With the construction of railways, the state opened up an era of capital imports to Sweden that would last until 1910 (i.e., almost to the First World War; Schön 1989a, 1989b). The state's take on the economy was decidedly expansionist. Investments in railway construction were later followed by state investments in electrification and in the development of telecommunications, all financed by capital imports through the National Debt Office. The trend shift in the state debt policy stands out clearly in Figures 6.2 and 6.3. Although the debt, almost solely

foreign, increased strongly, so did the accumulated investments under-
taken by the state. Actually, the public foreign debt was exclusively for
infrastructural investments, which were almost exclusively financed by
the emission of Swedish bonds in Germany and France.

Servicing the debt was strictly separated from the fiscal finances of
the state, and this aspect was probably important for the long-term stability and success of the Swedish state debt policy. For one thing, the
National Debt Office was independent of both the Bank of Sweden and
the state treasury: neither the bank nor the state had any direct access
to the decision making of the National Debt Office on the issue of state
bonds. The National Debt Office was run by a parliamentary committee and thus controlled by the Swedish taxpayers, which certainly contributed to enhancing the legitimacy of the office in the eyes of creditors. For another thing, the servicing of the debt was restricted to the
means flowing from the investments. Thus, interests and amortizations
had to be paid out of the returns from the infrastructural investments of
the state, primarily from running the railways. The taxpayers were not
to bear the burden of servicing the debt. Furthermore, interest rates on
the Swedish debt were kept low thanks to the punctual servicing of the
debt and to cooperation with Swedish commercial banks in negotiations
on the international market when bonds were emitted and prior bond
issues converted. The Swedish state's abominable treatment of creditors
in the early nineteenth century was forgotten.

The flow of foreign funds to the National Debt Office had yet another
consequence: the office became temporarily very liquid and worked as
a central bank by placing long-term funds as short-term credits both to
commercial banks and to the state until the foreign loans were used to
finance investments. Thus, the National Debt Office contributed to the
liquidity of the Swedish capital market during the period of industrialization (Nygren 1989).

### 6.6.2 A New Structure of Contributions from the 1860s
The 1850s trend break in terms of investment policy and financing was
followed in the subsequent decade by a set of new legislation that
resulted in further integration and market liberalization, following the
Western European trends. A new state emerged, one that relieved markets from a series of old restrictions but at the same time was more interventionist in creating infrastructural growth prerequisites.

The tax structure was, however, still premodern in character and
unsuitable to a more dynamic economy. Thus, at the end of the 1850s,

state revenues plunged to a historical trough of only 4 percent of the gross domestic income. Furthermore, the revenues became increasingly dependent on regressive taxation of consumption by means of tariffs. With the intention of drawing the tax structure closer to new streams of income, a bill reforming the structure of contributions was taken by the parliament in 1861.

The 1861 reform abandoned the old system of dividing all tax subjects into different classes with a number of subgroups and with different regulations on mainly fixed contributions for each of them. The intention was once again to tap real income flows by means of contributions based on income from real estate and income from capital and labor. Thus, the reform was modeled on the basis of the three production factors in political economy – land, labor, and capital.

As in the earlier period, it proved too difficult to assess the income from real estate, so contributions in this class remained standardized with a fixed percentage of the tax rate. However, agricultural holdings were taxed doubly because the system of land rents still prevailed. For that reason, contributions from agricultural estates were set at a lower percentage than from urban estates.

Income from labor or capital of less than four hundred riksdaler was exempted from tax. A large part of the population fell below this level. Most of the landless classes in agriculture and unskilled or low-skilled workers in industry paid no income tax at all.

The tax structure had particular political significance after the parliamentary reform in 1866. The old parliament of the four estates was dissolved and replaced by the new parliament of two chambers, in which members of the politically more influential second chamber were directly elected by popular vote. Until 1900, the right to vote was limited to those paying taxes from income on land, labor, or capital – vast numbers of Swedish peasantry dominated the electorate. With this shift in the composition of the parliament, capitalist farmers and peasants became a most influential political group.

### 6.6.3 Local Authorities

The new institutional settings of the 1860s reorganized and modernized another important player: local authorities. Prior to the reforms, local authorities were relatively independent of the state in the sense that they had extensive rights to decide on local taxes to finance their activities. These activities comprised, for instance, basic education, health care, poor relief, and urban amenities. Thus, local authorities were in charge of some of the fundamental responsibilities of the new industrial labor force, such as building up and maintaining human capital and providing for the new social environment. Some of these tasks were stipulated and regulated by the state, but they were organized and largely financed locally (the state subsidized some of the stipulated undertakings). They all became increasingly important when industrialization took off. Locally supplied services increased the share of public services, and from the 1880s, the authorities of larger cities also resorted to bond issues on the international markets to finance long-term investments in urbanization.

From the 1860s, the revenue of local taxes grew at a somewhat higher rate than state revenues, contributing to the growth of the public sector. It is clear that there was a trend break not only in state activities but also in the activities of local authorities, which expanded from the mid-nineteenth century. Local taxation was made up of both contributions (which followed a similar logic as the tax ordinance of 1861) and specific taxes for items such as basic education, health care, and road maintenance. In the 1860s, local taxes corresponded to nearly half of state revenues, and by the outbreak of the First World War, local taxes were roughly even with state revenues (Gårestad 1985).

The right to set taxes locally for the provision of these services was a fundamental feature of the Swedish tax system and for the evolution of the Swedish welfare system, both from a fiscal point of view and from a political one.

### 6.7 Mounting Pressure for Reform of the Central Taxes

Despite the reforms of the early 1860s, the pressure to modernize the fiscal basis of the state built up in the following decades. The system of direct taxes became increasingly insufficient as a fiscal pillar for the state. Land rents actually decreased in nominal terms while contributions based on income grew slowly because of the great share of taxes with fixed rates and the low progression in tax rates. Accordingly, the means for state expansion came increasingly from custom dues and from other indirect taxes on consumption (e.g., distilled spirits, sugar; on the share of direct taxes in state revenues, see Figure 6.5). Despite the lowering of custom tariffs in the 1860s, the state revenues from foreign trade increased thanks to simultaneous spectacular growth in trade. The return to protectionism in the 1880s slowed down trade only marginally, and naturally boosted customs revenues even further. From the middle of

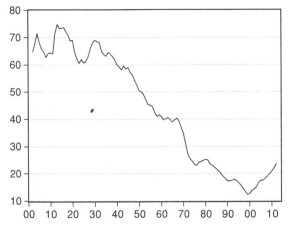

Figure 6.5. Direct taxes as share of State revenues, 1800–1914. Five-year moving averages. *Sources:* Krantz and Schön (2007); Fregert and Gustafsson (2005).

the 1860s to the late 1890s, tariffs and other indirect taxes increased as a share of state revenues from 60 percent to nearly 90 percent.

Low progression in the taxation of income and wealth, as well as the great dependence on mainly consumption taxation, made the whole taxation system very regressive, hitting low- and middle-income groups the hardest. This added to the political pressure for further reforms.

There were other shortcomings as well. The medieval construction of fixed land rents and locally organized military support became increasingly outdated. It was all the more so because these taxes were still, to a large extent, paid in kind. With the monetization of the economy, payments in kind were, however, generally converted into monetary payments. In the wake of this, the state abolished its medieval system of storing grain to counteract the effects of harvest failures and famines. This was also a reflection of greater reliance on market integration as a means to even out food consumption. Nevertheless, the system to support military forces locally by tax payments in kind did persist until the 1880s, when both the old system of fixed land rents and the local taxes for the armament, recruitment, and remuneration of the military forces eventually came to an end.

During the 1870s and 1880s, the parliament set up committees to prepare for the reformation of the tax system and to introduce taxes adapted to the income flows of commercial agriculture and industrial capitalism. Basically, the idea was to move from fixed estimates to the actual net income.

There was one shift in the principles in these decades that prepared the grounds for further reforms. The 1861 contributions system, which taxed separately the production factors of land, labor, and capital, was inspired by the theory of political economy and followed the example of English taxation. In the following decades, German influence became much more widespread in Swedish policy and economics at large, and in taxation. In this case, the focus shifted from the three production factors to the aggregated net income from all three, which became the target for the new system of taxation.

In the major political debates, the position of the dominant political force, the peasants, was contradictory. On the one hand, they favored reform because the bulk of traditional taxes fell on them; on the other hand, they feared, soundly, that a shift to actual income would result in even higher taxes. To add to their uncertainty, the concept of net income was still diffuse. In particular, it was not clear how to deal with interests on loans. To debt-burdened capitalist farmers – as well as to industrial capitalists – this was a crucial question. For both political and legal reasons, a major tax reform was slow to come.

The other major debate in the period was over trade policy and tariffs. When grain prices fell on the international market during the 1880s, the opposition to free trade policy became fiercer. Proponents of agricultural interests were certainly the mainstay of the opposition, which was not homogenous, however. Market-oriented farmers were divided regionally. In northern Sweden, which relied more on export-generated income from forestry, and in southern Sweden, with a greater shift to husbandry, the position regarding tariffs was more mixed. Interests from the dominant grain-producing regions in conjunction with home–market-oriented industrialists could effectuate the shift in trade policy at the end of the 1880s, thus aggravating the imbalance between the income basis and the consumption basis.

## 6.8 New Dynamism from the 1890s and a Modern Taxation System

In the 1890s, a new economy emerged. The second Industrial Revolution had a strong impact on the Swedish economy. Although dependence on natural resources diminished during the decades leading up to the First World War, more sophisticated and knowledge-intensive industries expanded. The expansion was particularly strong in some branches of the engineering industry and in chemical industries affiliated with the pulp and paper industry. In turn, social conditions changed.

Urbanization accelerated and the conditions of the industrial society became more widespread. The expansion of urban industries and services in combination with an income-based extension of suffrage to the parliament changed the political arena in Sweden. Social democrats and liberals entered as a new power bloc in many political questions, although the interests of the agricultural sector and of the rural areas remained strongly represented in the parliament.

The economic and social transformation placed the state in new circumstances. The need for infrastructural development reappeared and expansionist activities continued, still financed by capital imports, but as mentioned earlier, there was a new focus on electricity and telecommunications. Public investment in modern infrastructure became complementary to new industrial ventures, such as ASEA (ABB) and Ericsson in electrotechnical and telecommunications equipment, respectively, and gave a strong second wind to Swedish industrialization.

However, new concerns about social development and the tapping of new income streams arose. From the 1880s onward, the so-called social question, focusing on the situation of the urban proletariat, came to the forefront. The old provisions for social security inherited from rural conditions of poor relief became obsolete in the industrial urban society. Both social democrats and liberals acted for social reforms adapted to the industrial society. The political importance of this issue was reinforced by mass migration to North America, which was considered a national shame by conservatives and, of course, posed a threat to the interests of the landed classes through the rising wages of unskilled workers. In the early twentieth century – around 1910 – the first steps were taken toward a modern social security system run by the state. Because a public social security system would relieve local authorities of some expenditure on the poor and the elderly, these propositions gained support from some of the farmer-politicians. Thus, legislation was passed in the parliament on state contributions to sickness insurance, and general and public old-age insurance. The state also became more active in setting up institutions to solve conflicts in the labor market. This period established some of the principles that were later further developed and expanded into the so-called Swedish model.

The old state revenues, custom dues, land taxes, and proportional income taxes at low rates also became inadequate as the foundation of public finance in a period when new income streams were growing. Furthermore, the regressive character of the indirect taxes, with the heavy burden on the consuming masses of the population, led to growing discontent. With a new political situation in the parliament and after decades of official investigations and political debates, a new system was inaugurated in 1902. It followed the principle of progressive taxation of aggregated net income based on annual personal declarations of income to the state.[4]

The reform of 1902 was only provisional, however. Income from real estate was still estimated as a fixed share of the taxation value. Furthermore, the new income taxation coexisted with the older system of contributions as two parallel income taxes. The system of contributions was considered necessary as long as voting rights were attached to it. A reform of suffrage in 1909 untied this knot. In 1910, the parliament passed a new bill for a comprehensive tax on income and wealth that met the principles of progressive taxation of aggregated net income. The remainders of the old system, the contributions, were discontinued and eventually the transformation of the taxation system was completed.

These reforms extended the fiscal basis of the state. Taxes were directed at the sources of income and wealth of the modern industrial and urban society. The dependence on tariffs diminished. Already by 1912, the direct income tax had risen to comprise roughly a quarter of state revenues.

General expansion in the economy more or less balanced the growth of public expenses. In that sense, one can say that Gripenstedt's optimistic view on the dynamic effects of infrastructural investments and public debt was right. The dynamics did involve a major restructuring of public revenues following the example of European forerunners – from medieval dependence on land rents in kind to taxation of the flow of merchandise and the creation of a modern fiscal state with the instruments and muscles to tax income. In all this, a stable platform was created for further extension of public services and for the fiscal state in the ensuing growth of the industrial society.

## 6.9 Conclusions

Over the nineteenth century, the market economy expanded with great force in Sweden, with the economy becoming increasingly monetized. The commercialization of the economy developed by leaps and bounds, particularly in the second half of the century, when industrialization and

---

[4] On the principles, see Mattson (1982) and Rodriguez (1982).

foreign trade really took off. Thus, while the total supply of money corresponded to less than 20 percent of GDP in the mid-nineteenth century, this correspondence had increased to more than 70 percent in the beginning of the twentieth century. Under the pressure of this development, the imbalance grew between the fiscal system and the duties of the state. On the one hand, the fiscal system retained many medieval features, like payments in kind and sources of revenues assigned to local items of expenditure; on the other hand, the state had to cope with the tasks evolving in a modernizing and industrializing nation. This imbalance was not fully addressed until the first decade of the twentieth century. Over the long nineteenth century, however, the reforms of the fiscal system were presented and debated in wider frameworks of related political issues. These frameworks changed over time in a manner that partly explains the path of the reforms.

Over much of the century, direct taxes rested mainly on landholdings. This was a double blessing for the peasants. Taxes were a financial obligation to the state but also tokens of land proprietorship for the free peasantry in Sweden, and they conferred political voting rights as part of the pact that earlier had been established between the Crown and the peasantry. The system of taxes was therefore very much integrated into basic institutions of the agrarian society.

A constant dilemma was how to combine the land rents with a necessary flow of monetary income to give the state some flexibility. The contributions were, in part, a solution to this dilemma in the early nineteenth century. As such, they also became part of a heated debate on monetary policy that engaged a considerable number of political agitators and economic theorists. Debt-burdened agriculturalists propagated expansionist financial policies, but the political course of the state was largely decided by proponents of a new formulation of the monetary theory. Thus, the quantitative theory of money was expressed by Swedish intellectuals in the social sciences.[5] One difficulty was that the regent Charles XIV John (the first Bernadotte) took a different stand, so many theorists had to veil their arguments in front of their mighty opponent. Nevertheless, the new theorists set the path.

From the mid-nineteenth century, the role of the contributions was superseded by the new flow of cash from customs dues and from lending

---

[5] David Davidsson (1931) claims that the economic-theoretical debate in Sweden of the early nineteenth century was of very high standard internationally, with precursors to Wicksell and Cassel in the twentieth century.

on the foreign capital market. By these means, the revenues of the state were remarkably monetized. The sudden boom in foreign trade and capital imports drew liquidity into the Swedish fiscal system. At the same time, new income flows expanded, putting the fiscal system into a new economic and political context. Taxes based primarily on income rose to the forefront of a debate that appeared in different configurations. Step by step, the resistance to such a tax reform was broken down.

Tariffs were the great political issue in the 1870s and 1880s. The increased reliance of the state on tariffs was a problem for the liberals who advocated free trade and for whom a reformed income tax would provide a solution. Furthermore, to the growing number of industrialists, particularly in the export sector, regressive taxes on consumption meant an increased cost of living and upward pressure on wages. A fiscal system that, at the turn of the century, in 1900, rested almost exclusively on indirect taxes, mainly on consumption, added to the rapid wage increases in Sweden that threatened to undermine competitive power in many traditional branches. To this were added new issues on the political agenda. Liberals and the progressive labor movement demanded social security reforms to address the harsh conditions in the rapidly urbanizing industrial districts. With the advent of the social democrats, a new parliamentary situation arose, paving the way for income-tax reform. The political basis for such a reform was broadened when the modernization of the armed forces became urgent. To achieve this end, and inspired by the growing nationalist sentiments in the decades leading up to the 1910s, even conservatives supported a reform that introduced progressive taxes on income and property.

Thus, by the early twentieth century, a new fiscal structure had been settled with a large funded debt, with revenues completely monetized, and with progressive income taxes encroaching on the realms of tariffs and consumption dues.

## References

Ahlström, G. (1989) "Riksgäldskontoret och Sveriges statsskuld före 1850-talet," in E. Dahmén (ed.) *Upplåning och utveckling. Riksgäldskontoret 1789–1989.* Stockholm: Allmänna Förlaget, 91–134.

Brisman, S. (1908) *Realisationsfrågan 1808–1834. I. Frågans förhistoria och första framträdande 1808–1818.* Göteborgs Kungl. Vetenskaps- och vitterhets samhälles handlingar 4 följden, XII. Gothenburg.

Davidsson, D. (1931) *Riksbanken 1834–1860.* Sveriges Riksbank IV. Stockholm.

Eberstein, G. (1929) *Om skatt till stat och kommun enligt svensk rätt*. Stockholm: Förra Delen. PA Norstedt & Söner.

Fregert, K. and Gustafsson, R. (2005) "Fiscal statistics for Sweden 1719–2003," Working Paper 2005-40, Department of Economics, Lund University.

Gårestad, P. (1982) "Jordskatteförändringar under industrialiseringsperioden 1861–1914" [Changes in land tax during the period of industrialization 1861–1914], *Historisk tidskrift* 102(4), 516–39.

Gårestad, P. (1985) "Industrialisering och beskattning i Sverige 1861–1914," Ph.D. dissertation, Ekonomisk-Historiska Institutionen, Uppsala Universitet.

Jörberg, L. (1972) *A History of Prices in Sweden 1732–1914*, vols. 1–2. Lund: Gleerups.

Krantz, O. and Schön, L. (2007) *Swedish Historical National Accounts 1800–2000*. Lund: Almqvist and Wiksell International.

Mattson, N. (1982) "Hur bör en inkomstskatt utformas? En undersökning av motiven till de första moderna inkomstskatteförfattningarna" [How should income tax be constructed? An investigation into the first modern income tax enactments], *Historisk tidskrift*, 102(4), 557–73.

Nygren, I. (1989) "När lång upplåning blev korta krediter 1840–1905," in E. Dahmén (ed.) *Upplåning och utveckling. Riksgäldskontoret 1789–1989*. Stockholm: Allmänna Förlaget, 173–226.

Olsson, M. (2006) *Skatta dig lycklig. Jordränta och jordbruk i Skåne 1660–1900*. Hedemora: Gidlunds Förlag.

Pettersson, L. (1989) "Riksgäldskontoret, penningpolitiken och statsstödssystemet under tidigt 1800-tal," in E. Dahmén (ed.) *Upplåning och utveckling. Riksgäldskontoret 1789–1989*. Stockholm: Allmänna Förlaget, 135–72.

Rodriguez, E. (1982) "Den progressiva inkomstbeskattningens historia" [The history of progressive income tax], *Historisk tidskrift*, 102(4), 540–56.

Schön, L. (1989a) "Kapitalimport, kreditmarknad och industrialisering 1850–1910," in E. Dahmén (ed.) *Upplåning och utveckling. Riksgäldskontoret 1789–1989*. Stockholm: Allmänna Förlaget, 227–73.

Schön, L. (1989b) *From War Economy to State Debt Policy*. Stockholm: National Debt Office.

Schön, L. (2000) En modern svensk ekonomisk historia. Tillväxt och omvandling under två sekel. Stockholm: SNS Förlag.

# 7

## Always on the Brink

### *Piedmont and Italy*

### Giovanni Federico

## 7.1 Introduction

After the end of Napoleonic Wars, the Italian peninsula was divided into eight independent states, plus the Kingdom of Lombardy-Venetia, by then formally independent but belonging to the Austrian-Hungarian emperor. All these states but one, the Kingdom of Sardinia (which, in spite of its name, consisted mainly of Piedmont), pursued very conservative, small-state policies, with low taxation and low expenditure. By contrast, since the 1850s, Piedmont had been implementing an ambitious and expensive plan of modernization mostly funded with an increase in its sovereign debt to buttress its political ambitions. The latter were fulfilled in 1861, when Italy was unified for the first time since the fall of the Roman Empire. The king of Sardinia became king of Italy, and the Piedmontese constitution, institutions, and economic policies were extended to the whole new state, with few exceptions and in most cases without any delay. Also, the budget policy of the newborn kingdom featured a strong continuity with the Piedmontese one, at least at the beginning. In its first years, Italy spent lavishly on infrastructures and army, funding itself with imports of capital. Predictably, it soon ran into serious financial troubles. Italy extricated itself with about a decade of harsh fiscal measures and managed to keep its budget more or less balanced from the mid-1870s onward. The revenue-GDP ratio grew until the mid-1890s, and on this ground, Italy would qualify as a fiscal state. After that, however, the situation changed, and this ratio fell until the First World War, as the result of a noticeable slowdown in the rate of growth of revenues and an acceleration of GDP growth (known as the *boom giolittiano*). The situation would change dramatically with the outbreak of the war, which caused expenditure to jump to unprecedented levels.

The two next sections (7.2 and 7.3) describe the fiscal policy of pre-unitary states, focusing on Piedmont, and the adoption of Piedmontese tax system in the whole country. Section 7.4 outlines the rise of the fiscal state with macroeconomic data, and Section 7.5 discusses the structure of taxation and the process of policy making. Section 7.6 deals with local fiscal system, which funded many essential items of expenditure (notably education). Section 7.7 puts forward some tentative ideas about the political economy of taxation, while Section 7.8 concludes.

## 7.2 Before 1861: Piedmont and the Rest

The fiscal policy of preunification states used to be one of the favorite topics among Italian economic historians until the 1960s. Since then, it has totally slipped out of fashion, as has the whole economic history of that period (Federico 2001). Past interest has left us (incomplete) series on revenues and expenditures for most states. Table 7.1 reports the essential information on real revenues for all states, except Piedmont. From the early 1830s to the eve of unification, the increase in most states was modest if not negligible. Real revenues even declined in the Kingdom of Two Sicilies, which included all regions south of Rome and about a third of the Italian population.[1] Nitti (1958: 41), an economist and the Italian prime minister in the 1920s, praises the fiscal policy of that kingdom as 'the most suitable for the development of the South' and as based on 'a high tax on estates, collected in the cheapest possible way; some substantial monopolies; almost total exemption of non-landed wealth; and very low taxes on business transactions.' In 1856–8, indirect taxes (mostly on consumption) accounted for about 40 percent of total revenues and land tax for 25 percent (Ostuni 1992: app. 3). The South, as other Italian states, did not need much revenue because it spent little for the army and civil service and almost nothing for public works and other developmental items.[2] Indeed, the situation of the budget was good in almost all states. According to a contemporary estimate, on the eve of unification, Lombardo-Veneto, Tuscany, and the

---

[1] Population from SVIMEZ (1958: table 18).

[2] However, in the 1820s and 1830s, the kingdom had to pay huge sums to Austria as a contribution for its role in the restoration of the Bourbon monarchy after 1815 (Ostuni 1992). Part of the necessary funds was raised with loans.

Table 7.1. *Real Revenues in Preunitary States (1858 = 1)*

|                     | 1832–4 | 1845–7 | 1856–8 | % Δ   |
|---------------------|--------|--------|--------|-------|
| Lombardy*           | –      | 0.791  | 0.891  | 12.5  |
| Veneto*             | –      | 0.784  | 0.883  | 12.5  |
| Parma               | 0.922  | 0.865  | 0.936  | 1.5   |
| Modena              | 0.696  | 0.671  | 0.913  | 31.3  |
| Tuscany             | 0.72   | 0.72   | 0.882  | 22.5  |
| Regno Due Sicilie   | 0.988  | 0.906  | 0.891  | −9.7  |
| Stato Pontificio    | 0.816  | 0.863  | 0.902  | 10.5  |

\* Since 1845–47.

*Sources:* Nominal revenues in local currencies from Uggè (1956) for Lombardy and Veneto, from Falconi and Spaggiari (1959) for Parma, from Livi (1956) for Modena, from Parenti (1958) for Tuscany, from Rossi Ragazzi (1956) for the Papal States, from Ostuni (1992) for the South. All revenues have been deflated with price indexes from Malanima 2006, app. 1 ('Italy' for the South and the Papal States, 'North' for all others).

duchies (Parma and Modena) balanced their budget, whereas the South ran a modest deficit (Correnti and Maestri 1864: 609–93). Only the Papal States ran a sizable deficit, which, however, was balanced by substantial revenues from donations. From the 1830s to unification, total 'Italian' GDP, according to Malanima's (2006: app. 2) estimates, remained constant (or, more precisely, fell by 3 percent). These estimates, in 1911 Italian lire, are not easily comparable with the data on revenues, in local currencies, and above all, there are no data on GDP from preunitary states. Yet anecdotal evidence seems to rule out substantial changes in the distribution of GDP by region and thus also in the ratio of revenues to GDP by state. In other words, it seems highly unlikely that any of these states could have met the description of a fiscal state.

This statement does not hold true for Piedmont, which stood out among Italian states for its political ambitions. Since the late Middle Ages, the ruling dynasty (the longest serving in Europe) had been expanding its domains from its alpine homeland in Savoy toward the Po Valley, deftly siding with the winning coalition in most European wars. The Vienna Congress had compensated the king for his exile during the French wars by adding Liguria to his domain. The political climate during the restoration was not encouraging for further expansionary moves, but the king did not abandon all hopes, and he backed them with substantial investments in his army and, for the first time in the history of the country, navy. From the mid-1820s (when the available series begin) to the mid-1840s, real expenditure increased by a fifth and real revenues by a third. This growth, though modest, must have caused a rise in the revenue-GDP ratio. In fact, Italian GDP declined by 15 percent between

1825 and 1828 and between 1843 and 1845 (Malanima 2006). If the Piedmontese share had remained constant, the revenue-GDP ratio would have increased from 3.3 percent to 4 percent.[3] The European uprising in 1848 offered Piedmont what it considered a great opportunity. The king granted his subjects a constitution (the Statuto Albertino) and accepted the plea for help by Lombard insurgents against Austrian rule. This war was expensive (Table 7.2) and ended in total defeat.

Piedmont started a wide-ranging program of economic modernization, under the leadership of Camillo Cavour, minister for the economy since 1850 and prime minister since 1852. It liberalized trade (Di Gianfrancesco 1974) and invested huge sums in infrastructure, most notably railways. In just a decade, Piedmont built a fully developed railway network, which at the beginning of 1859 accounted for about half of the total railway lines in Italy, 850 out of 1707 kilometers (Corbino 1931–6: vol. 1, 181). The government also funded a further increase in the size of the army and the Piedmontese participation to the Crimean War. As a result, the expenditure in real terms in 1856–8 was 2.5 times greater than in 1843–7, possibly growing from about a twentieth to more than a tenth of the Piedmontese GDP (Table 7.2; Figure 7.1).[4]

The government tried to fund this surge in expenditure with a parallel increase in revenues. It reorganized the management of state finances, introducing a comprehensive yearly budget, subject to the parliamentary approval, and adopted a series of fiscal measures (Romeo 1984a: 483–97, 661–71, 723–27; Romeo 1984b: 341–5; Marongiu 1995: 107–8). It extended the consumption duties to Savoy and Nice and the land tax to previously exempt Sardinia; increased the rates of the personal tax; and introduced new taxes on coaches, buildings, and above all, on the mobile wealth. The new tax (*ricchezza mobile*) hit nonagricultural incomes, such as interest from capital, fees from liberal professions and wages (beyond a minimum). Beforehand, these sources of income did not pay any tax, in stark and unfair contrast with agricultural rents, which were subject to the land tax (*imposta fondiaria*). In its first version (approved in 1851), the *ricchezza mobile* had to be paid, as the British income tax, according to taxpayers' returns. However, the revenue did not meet

---

[3] Of course, this increase would be smaller if the Piedmontese share of Italian GDP grew. The Piedmontese revenue-GDP ratio would have remained constant if the share of the region had increased by two-thirds. Some relative growth of Piedmont cannot be ruled out a priori, but such a change is wholly implausible.

[4] The Piedmontese GDP is crudely estimated by assuming that the share of the kingdom on Italian GDP (Malanima 2006: app. 2) was equivalent to the combined share of Piedmont, Liguria, and Sardinia at the 1891 level (Felice 2005: table A8).

Table 7.2. *Piedmont 1825–60 (millions of 1860 lire)*

|      | Expenditures | Revenues | Deficit |
|------|--------------|----------|---------|
| 1825 | –            | 47.6     | –       |
| 1826 | –            | 44.9     | –       |
| 1827 | –            | 49.2     | –       |
| 1828 | –            | 57.3     | –       |
| 1829 | –            | 56.2     | –       |
| 1830 | 53.5         | 52.0     | −1.5    |
| 1831 | 59.2         | 52.2     | −7.0    |
| 1832 | 55.3         | 49.5     | −5.8    |
| 1833 | 52.5         | 50.7     | −1.8    |
| 1834 | 52.5         | 49.4     | −3.0    |
| 1835 | 53.2         | 50.7     | −2.5    |
| 1836 | 57.9         | 60.3     | 2.4     |
| 1837 | 66.8         | 67.7     | 0.9     |
| 1838 | 61.0         | 62.5     | 1.6     |
| 1839 | 66.0         | 65.7     | −0.3    |
| 1840 | 69.4         | 67.6     | −1.7    |
| 1841 | 63.3         | 63.9     | 0.6     |
| 1842 | 61.1         | 62.5     | 1.4     |
| 1843 | 64.3         | 66.8     | 2.5     |
| 1844 | 67.4         | 68.8     | 1.4     |
| 1845 | 66.3         | 66.9     | 0.6     |
| 1846 | 80.2         | 69.2     | −11.0   |
| 1847 | 102.6        | 74.1     | −28.5   |
| 1848 | 146.8        | 63.3     | −83.5   |
| 1849 | 173.8        | 68.3     | −105.5  |
| 1850 | 149.8        | 72.5     | −77.3   |
| 1851 | 127.2        | 76.1     | −51.2   |
| 1852 | 119.7        | 87.9     | −31.8   |
| 1853 | 140.8        | 100.1    | −40.7   |
| 1854 | 146.5        | 117.3    | −29.3   |
| 1855 | 168.2        | 130.3    | −37.9   |
| 1856 | 185.9        | 146.7    | −39.2   |
| 1857 | 160.0        | 136.5    | −23.5   |
| 1858 | 144.9        | 121.4    | −23.5   |
| 1859 | 269.2        | 161.1    | −108.1  |
| 1860 | 448.4        | 161.7    | −286.6  |

*Sources:* Expenditure and revenues from Felloni (1959a, 1959b), deflated with the northern price index by Malanima (2006: app. 1).

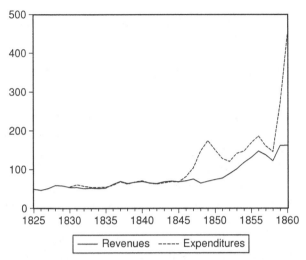

Figure 7.1. Revenues and expenditure, Piedmont (millions of 1860 lire).

expectations because of widespread elusion and the distinctly lukewarm attitude by the financial offices. Furthermore, the chamber of commerce complained loudly. Thus, in 1853, the government shifted to the French system of trade-specific rates, based on objective features (e.g., rental value of the premises). The reform achieved its aim: from 1850 to 1855, real revenues from direct taxation (including the land tax and the personal tax) increased by 120 percent. Yet even at their 1855 peak, they yielded barely a fifth of total revenues, marginally more than in the 1820s and early 1830s.

In spite of the government's efforts, the rise of the revenues did not match the growth in the expenditure. Real revenues in the 1850s were 80 percent greater than before 1845, and about 8 percent of GDP, so that the deficit-GDP ratio exceeded 3 percent. In just eight years, Piedmont cumulated some 1.2 billion lire of debt – equivalent to 75 percent of its GDP. This debt accounted for 54 percent of the Italian total, whereas the kingdom accounted for only 16 percent of the Italian population and 18 percent of GDP.[5] In other words, the modernization of Piedmont was largely financed with loans, mostly from abroad.

---

[5] Of a total of 2,374 millions, Piedmont owed 1,292 million lire, whereas 400 had been accumulated by the provisional governments during the war years (Corbino 1931: vol. 1, 210). Population from SVIMEZ (1961: table 18), GDP by region in 1891 from Felice (2005: table A8).

### 7.3 Patching Up an Italian Tax System

The so-called Second War of Independence (1859–61) was a triumph well beyond Cavour's wildest dreams, in which he fancied at most a kingdom of North Italy. After the war's end, the government faced the huge task of forging an Italian tax system out of nine (very) different ones. Given the speed of the process of unification and its political circumstances, the only realistic option was to extend the Piedmontese system to the whole kingdom. Indeed, the provisional governments of the new provinces adopted Piedmontese law for local finances and the customs tariff already in 1859–60, well before the official proclamation of the new kingdom in March 1861. In the subsequent two years, taxes on consumption and business transactions were harmonized without much discussion and with marginal adjustments to the Piedmontese system. These were easy steps: the harmonization of direct taxation proved much more difficult and met with much resistance.[6]

The South had no taxation on nonfarm income at all, and the Piedmontese *ricchezza mobile* was by far heavier than any comparable tax in other preunitary states. Indeed, in 1862, the *antiche provincie* (former kingdoms) yielded some 56 percent of its revenue (Parravicini 1958: 242). Such a concentration was politically untenable, but a simple extension of the Piedmontese law was impossible. In 1864, after two years of debate, it was decided to set a target revenue (*contingente*) for the whole country and to allocate first among regions, provinces, and cities according to a series of parameters (e.g., population, land tax, number of civil servants) and then among individual taxpayers in each city according to their tax returns. The target revenue was initially set at 30 million lire (i.e., about two times the 1862 yield), but in the next year, it was more than doubled to 66 million lire, equivalent to about 5 percent of the cumulated returns (the liable income was surely substantially higher). Notwithstanding this, the method of the *contingente* raised objections from a special parliamentary committee, which included all prominent members with expertise in financial issues, and from the minister for finance (the equivalent of the British chancellor). Thus, in 1866, it was substituted by an 8-percent flat tax.

The case of the land tax was largely similar. To be sure, unlike the *ricchezza mobile*, it existed in all states, and in all of them, it was paid on imputed rents, as estimated by cadastres. However, the latter were

---

[6] The narrative is based mainly on Parravicini (1958); see also the documents collected by Izzo (1962).

generally obsolete, with the majority dating back to the early eighteenth century – and not even then they had been accurate. In addition, tax rates differed as well – ranging from a maximum of 19.9 percent of the assessed rent in Lombardy to a minimum of 9.1 percent in Tuscany (Parravicini 1958: 216–18). As a result, in 1862, the South, with 47 percent of total cropland, paid only 39 percent of the total tax, while Lombardy paid a fifth, with less than a tenth of the land.[7] Land productivity was higher in the North, but the difference was not large enough to compensate northern landowners who duly called for the harmonization of taxation (*perequazione*). After three years of discussion, the parliament approved a new law in July 1864. This law set the target revenue 10 percent higher than the 1863 yield and allocated the additional revenue among the regions in what was a halfhearted effort to redress the disparities. For instance, Piedmont and Liguria paid 25 percent more (in nominal terms), and their share on revenue rose from 14.7 percent to 17 percent (Parravicini 1958: 216–18). The law was to last for three fiscal years, pending the search of a final, and more equitable, allocation.

## 7.4 The Macroeconomic Framework: Italy, 1861–1913

Unification also marked the onset of statistical age in Italy. It is thus easy to support the narrative with data on revenues, expenditures, and their ratio to GDP. Paradoxically, it is too easy. There are four different sets of budget data in current terms (Ercolani 1969; Ragioneria Generale dello Stato 1969; Brosio-Marchese 1986; Fratianni and Spinelli 1997), which can be deflated with three different price indexes: the ISTAT (1958) wholesale price index, the implicit price deflator by Ercolani (1969), and the consumer price index by Fenoaltea (2002). Real revenues (or expenditures) can be divided by any of the seven available estimates of GDP at constant prices (ISTAT 1956; Ercolani 1969; Fuá-Gallegati 1993; Bardini, Carreras, and Lains 1995; Maddison 1992; Fenoaltea 2005; Malanima 2006), yielding a total of eighty-four possible combinations. The best option is to use the budget data by the Ragioneria Generale dello Stato (1969), which have a somewhat official seal of approval, and then deflate them with the ISTAT (1958) prices and the GDP series by Fenoaltea (2005).[8] Although differences in short-term movements are

---

[7] Revenue (excluding the surcharges from local authorities) from Parravicini (1958: 216); acreage for 1870-4 from MAIC (1876: vol. 1, 471–3).

[8] When possible, graph(s) reports also an alternative estimate of revenue-GDP ratios, which uses data from Ercolani (1969), a standard reference in Italian macroeconomic history.

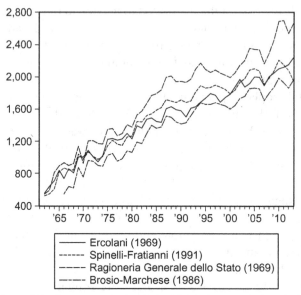

Figure 7.2. Revenues, Italy 1861–1913 (millions of 1911 lire).

substantial, long-term trends are reassuringly similar. In particular, all revenue series show a substantial increase in real terms (Figure 7.2).[9]

Both contemporaries and historians have interpreted Italian fiscal policy for the best part of the nineteenth century as a frantic effort to find money to prevent the deficit from increasing too much, given the relentless increase in expenditure. Indeed, Italian policy makers always talked about cutting expenditure, but this was clearly deemed an inferior solution. Not paying interest on debt was unthinkable, and military expenses were considered essential for the status of Italy as a great power.[10] The remaining expenses did not allow for significant savings: the civil service was very small (366,000 people of a total active population of 17.8 million as late as 1911), and productive expenditure (education and public works) fluctuated between 15 percent and 20 percent of the

[9] Over the period 1861–1913, the yearly growth rate of real revenues (deflated with prices from ISTAT 1958) was 1.86 percent, according to Ercolani and Brosio-Marchese or 1.95 percent according to the Ragioneria Generale dello Stato, but only 1.37 percent according to Fratianni-Spinelli.

[10] Military expenditures were the third rail of Italian politics. For instance, an attempt to cut the size of the army in 1896, after the Adowa disaster, caused a strong reaction from the king and the fall of the second Di Rudini Ministery (Marongiu 2002: 69–73).

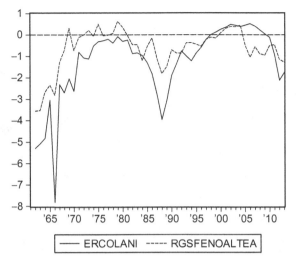

Figure 7.3. Deficit-GDP ratio, Italy 1862–1913. *Sources:* Ercolani (1969), Ragioneria Generale dello Stato (1969); Fenoaltea (2005).

total.[11] As a result, nominal expenditure declined only in thirteen years of fifty-one, and only twice, in 1867 and 1870, by more than 5 percent.[12] As Figure 7.3 shows, the struggle to match expenditures with new revenues was by and large successful. The deficit-GDP ratio averaged 0.64 percent over the whole period and exceeded 3 percent only in 1862–3. Thus, according to late twentieth-century standards, this was a great achievement. Of course, nineteenth-century standards were stricter, and so the situation was considered critical in the early 1860s and worrisome at the end of the 1880s, the early 1890s, and on the eve of the First World War. A closer look to ratios of GDP to expenditure (Figure 7.4) and to revenues (Figure 7.5) suggests the division of the whole period into four stages:

1. The postunification party: Expenditure largely exceeded revenue despite a massive sale of state assets.[13] The party was wild but

---

[11] Share of productive expenditures from Brosio-Marchese (1986: table 4A) and number of state employees from Zamagni (1987: table A1). This latter excludes schoolteachers and draftees for the army and navy.

[12] Data from Ragioneria Generale dello Stato (1969). Expenditures declined also in 1875, 1878–9, 1882, 1890–3, 1896–7, and 1907 by 2 percent on average.

[13] The state sold its railways network (1865), privatized the highly lucrative monopoly for tobacco products (1868), expropriated the church and the local authorities of the land they owned, and proceeded to sell it. The sales started in 1862 and lasted for about ten years, affecting some 3 million hectares – roughly an eighth of agricultural land in the whole country but a quarter in the South.

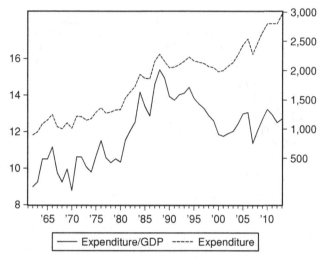

Figure 7.4. Real expenditure (millions of 1911 lire) and expenditure-GDP ratio.
*Sources:* Ragioneria Generale dello Stato (1969); Fenoaltea (2005).

lasted only a few years. The war with Austria (1866) caused the price of the main state bond (*rendita*) to collapse, effectively shutting Italy out from the world capital market. Thus, Italy was forced to balance its budget.

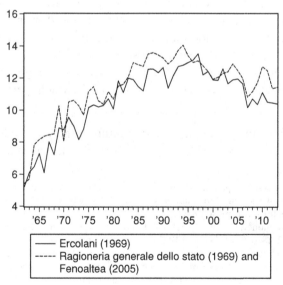

Figure 7.5. Revenue-GDP ratio, Italy 1862–1913.

2. The after-party hangover: The hangover lasted about ten years. The budget was officially declared as balanced in 1876. The adjustment was achieved almost exclusively from the revenue side. By 1876, expenditure was 50 percent greater in real terms than in 1862 and 10 percent greater than in 1866. In contrast, revenues were 2.3 times and 50 percent greater, respectively. The successful return to a balanced budget had far-reaching political consequences. The right (the *destra*), which had ruled Italy since unification, split and lost power for more than twenty years.

3. The unsteady equilibrium: From 1876, the budget appeared more or less balanced, with revenues and expenditures growing more quickly than GDP. However, the balance was permanently on the brink: the deficit reappeared in the second half of the 1880s, and most economists of the time suspected that official figures underestimated it by shifting some items of expenditure (e.g., pension liabilities) to special accounts. The period ended with a severe crisis at the end of the 1880s and in the early 1890s, which called for a massive increase in taxation. By 1894, total revenues were 70 percent greater than in 1877; they accounted, according to the baseline series, for 14 percent of GDP, the highest level in the whole period.

4. The golden age: After some years of respite in the second half of the 1890s, the real revenues went on growing throughout the 1900s: the average in 1910–13 was 20 percent greater than the previous 1894 peak. Yet the GDP grew even more quickly – so that the revenue-GDP ratio declined to slightly more than 11 percent. A new budget crisis might have been looming, as the deficit-GDP ratio had been inching upward since the late 1900s. The outbreak of the war changed everything. Balancing the budget was no longer an issue: the only real task was to find enough resources to wage the war.

Thus, unified Italy adopted the Piedmontese model of debt financing only for a few years: in just seven years, from 1861 to 1867, its nominal debt increased by 130 percent, from some 3 billion to 7.2 billion lire. Since then, debt continued to rise, if much more slowly: by 1913, nominal debt totaled almost 17 billion lire. However, the increase has to be compared with the growing total income: the debt-GDP ratio (Figure 7.6) peaked in 1897 at 117 percent and then declined to 71.5 percent in 1913. In addition, the share of debt owned by foreign investors,

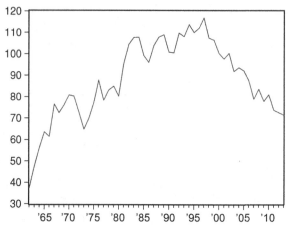

Figure 7.6. Public debt–GDP ratio, Italy 1861–1913. *Sources:* Debt: Zamagni (1998), deflated with price index from ISTAT (1958); GDP: Fenoaltea (2005).

allegedly more likely to flee, declined from about a third between the 1860s and 1890s to slightly more than a tenth on the eve of the First World War.[14] Some recent work on financial history has argued that the debt-GDP ratio is not the correct yardstick for assessing the creditworthiness of a country, as the concept of GDP was unknown to investors at that time (Flandreau and Zumer 2004). Flandreau and Zumer (2004) suggest instead focusing on the debt-revenue ratio. The Italian average ratio over the whole period 1861–1913 was 7.41, with a maximum of 9.47 in 1870 and a minimum of 5.85 in 1911. As a term of comparison, Ferguson and Schularick (2006) estimate that, in 1880–1913, the average ratio for fifty-seven political entities was 4.95, with a maximum of twenty. Thus, the Italian debt-revenue ratio was slightly on the high side, though not disproportionately so. But it was high enough to suggest that Italian policy makers tread carefully to avoid a financial crisis.

In summary, macroeconomic evidence shows that the Italian budget was never on firm ground, but contrary to the expectations of many people in those years, it never fell into the abyss. The contribution of fiscal policy was instrumental to this achievement.

---

[14] These figures are based on the percentage of coupons for the *rendita* paid abroad (Zamagni 1998). They are likely to overstate the actual share, as they omit other types of bonds and include coupons paid abroad to Italian citizens. Many Italian citizens tried to disguise themselves as foreign investors to be paid in gold while the lira was under par. The government actively tried to fight this behavior but not always successfully.

## 7.5 Italian Fiscal Policy, 1861–1913

The nineteenth-century Italian tax system was extremely complex, with dozens of different sources of revenue. As a first approximation, sources of revenue can be classified in four main categories: taxes on production and consumption (excises, taxes on market transactions, taxes on consumption, proceeds from state monopolies); custom duties; taxes on income (land tax, tax on dwellings, and the *ricchezza mobile*), and other sources. In the period 1861–1913, these categories accounted, on average, for 44 percent, 30 percent, 14 percent, and 12 percent of total revenue. The share of income taxes was surprisingly high for a nineteenth-century backward country, although a modern comprehensive income tax would be introduced only in the 1960s. As Figure 7.7 shows, the composition of revenues by macrocategories has remained remarkably stable in the long run. Indirect taxes and other sources of revenue fluctuated with no clear trend, duties increased from less than 10 percent in the 1870s to more than 17 percent on the eve of the First World War, and in the same period, taxes on income fell from about a third to a fifth of the total. In absolute terms, from 1862–4 to 1911–13, the proceeds from custom tariffs increased by 5.6 times, those of tariffs by 4.5 times and those from income taxes only by 3.3 times. Changes were much larger within each category. The revenue from land tax

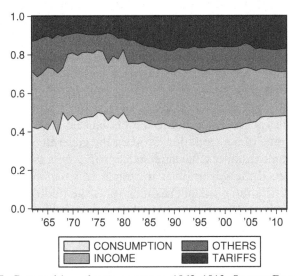

Figure 7.7. Composition of state revenues, 1862–1913. *Source:* Repaci (1962).

decreased from the 1880s onward, the only case of absolute decline of revenue of a tax in the whole period. Its share on total revenue collapsed from a sixth in the 1860s to 3 percent on the eve of the First World War. This decline was only partially compensated by the rise in the percentage of the *ricchezza mobile* from about 7 percent to about 15 percent (the share of taxes on dwellings remained constant at around 5 percent). The share of consumption taxes doubled from the 1860s to the 1870s and then slowly declined to 3 percent, whereas excises rose from few percentage points to almost 10 percent of revenues. The monopolies on tobacco, alcohol, and salt yielded about a fifth, and the taxes on transactions about a tenth, of total revenue for the period.

This contrast between the stability of shares by category and the changes in percentages of their components is, in itself, indirect evidence of the nature of Italian fiscal policy in those fifty years. In a nutshell, although long-term orientation of tax policy was the subject of many lofty debates, actual policies were dictated mainly by the pressing needs of the day. Tax issues were frequently on the parliamentary agenda. Each year the finance minister had to have a budget approved, and taxes could be changed within the fiscal year, should the need arise. The budget assessed the prospects for the next fiscal year and suggested the adjustments that the minister deemed necessary. If the minister forecasted a surplus, he might propose to reduce rates on or perhaps abolish some minor tax. If, on the contrary, the minister expected a high or growing deficit, he would suggest increasing the rate and/or creating a new tax. Usually, discussion in the budget sessions (*sessione di bilancio*) was rather lively, and often deputies harped on general principles of ideal taxation or put forward far-reaching proposals to reorganize the whole tax system. However, these were distractions rather than serious business. The real debate focused on the more mundane issue – whether to approve the budget as proposed or to suggest further changes. The latter almost always aimed to reduce the tax burden so that the final bill was the outcome of a negotiation between the government and the parliament. In some instances, the agreement proved impossible, and sometimes this forced the government to resign. It is plainly impossible to deal with all fifty-three budget sessions (plus the odd debate on additional tax changes). Here we consider just one of them, the 1871 budget (Parravicini 1958: 72–9), and two long-running issues, the harmonization (*perequazione*) of the land tax and the milling tax (*macinato*).[15]

---

[15] The narrative is based on Einaudi (1942: 13–75), Parravicini (1958: 222–33), Nieri (1976) Marongiu (1996: 226–86), Marongiu (2002: 97–8, 337–9), and Di Salvo (1995) for the

In March 1871, Italy was in the midst of its 'after-party hangover,' and the finance minister, Sella, wanted it to end as soon as possible. He proposed to cut expenditures by 25 million lire and to increase revenues by 75 million lire (about 0.7 percent of GDP). To this aim, Sella proposed increasing the rate of the *ricchezza mobile* to 12 percent (including local surtaxes) and to extend it to wages of civil servants, income from agricultural capital, and winnings from lotteries. He also suggested applying, in that year only, a 5-percent surcharge on all taxes on income. He also asked for a 10-percent increase in all taxes on business transactions and consumption taxes and the abolition of franchise on these taxes, which Venice enjoyed. Finally, he proposed introducing an excise on production of spirits, with a matching duty and a new stamp duty on all judicial acts. The parliament approved most of Sella's proposals, with two major changes, both favoring the landed interest group. The parliament restored the traditional exemption of the income from agricultural capital from the *ricchezza mobile* and substituted the proposed 5-percent increase to all direct taxes (including the land tax) for a 10-percent surcharge on tax on mobiles only. During the debate in the upper chamber, Marliani (qtd. in Parravicini 1958: 79) stated, 'in Sella's massive work, I have not been able to find a single spark of genius, a daring thought, not a single major idea; I have seen only the report of a modest and prudent superintendent,' and he warned, 'With these means the state finances have never been restored.' He proved wrong. Total revenues in 1871, with the contribution of additional tax measures later in the year, were a third greater than in 1870, and the deficit shrank from 0.7 percent to 0.1 percent of GDP. Yet Marliani had a point about the method. No budget in the next forty years would be as burdensome as the 1871 one, but most of them included lists of motley tax measures with little consistency and vision. Not by chance, fiscal laws were often called omnibus laws (general-purpose laws).

As mentioned in Section 7.3, the issue of land tax had been temporarily settled by the 1864 law. The absolute burden of the tax was not exactly crushing, even including the surtaxes by the local authorities and the three additional 10-percent surcharges (the so-called *decimi*), which had been imposed in 1867–8. The total revenue accounted for 5 percent of gross agricultural output in the early 1860s and for

perequazione; on Parravicini (1958: 35–6, 57–9), Marongiu (1995: 203–20), and Cammelli (1984: 21–9) for the institution of the *macinato*; and on Parravicini (1958: 128–30, 136–46) and Marongiu (1996: 93–104, 119–33) for its abolition.

7 percent in the 1880s.[16] However, the distribution among regions remained rather inequitable, despite repeated adjustments to the 1864 allocation in the 1860s and 1870s. By 1883, the ratio between shares on land tax and on gross agricultural output ranged from a maximum of 1.59 in Lombardy to a mere 0.59 in Sicily (i.e., the former paid 2.5 times more, in proportion to the output, than the latter).[17] On paper, everyone recognized that the regional disparities had to be eliminated and that the tax should be based on a new cadastre. As early as 1869, the government had introduced a bill that the parliament rejected without even discussing it. In the following years, other projects failed in the same way. The government tried again in 1882, and this time the lower chamber (Camera dei Deputati) appointed a committee to assess the proposal. The discussion in committee lasted two years, and the parliamentary debate on the report took two further years, all because of the stubborn opposition of southern landowners. They were eventually convinced with a massive cut in rates: the future rate was to be set at 7 percent of the estimated income, down from the current 16.25 percent, inclusive of the 10-percent surcharges or *decimi* that were to be abolished immediately. The new law stipulated that the cadastre had to be finished in twenty years' time, but this deadline was postponed time and again.[18] The Italian land cadastre was to be completed only in 1956.

Taxes on milling were not totally unknown in Italy. Before unification, they had existed in the Kingdom of the Two Sicilies as a local tax and, from 1826 to 1847, as a national one (Ostuni 1992: 29–32). However, the provisional governments had abolished the tax to win the peasants' support for the cause of a unified Italy. The milling tax was an ideal tax from the point of view of a government seeking to boost its revenues. Consumption of bread was highly inelastic and growing with population, so the tax was bound to yield substantial and growing revenues, provided a way to avoid taxpayers' elusion could be found. However, the tax was highly regressive and hit the staple food of the population.

[16] Yearly data land tax from Repaci (1962: table 13) for the state and Volpi (1962) for the local authorities; for gross output Federico (2003).

[17] Land tax (1862 and 1883) from Parravicini (1958: 216, 218, 232), gross output by region (in 1891) Federico (2003: table 5).

[18] The law stipulated also that the preliminary results of the cadastre by province could be immediately used to revise the tax rolls and that any province could volunteer to pay for the expenses to have the cadastre been implemented. Clearly, this opportunity was exploited by high-tax areas, which in this way hoped to have their fiscal burden reduced. Thus, the effect of the *perequazione* was asymmetrical, and jointly with the abolition of the *decimi* in 1887, it explains the absolute decline in the revenue of the land tax.

Its opponents were quick to call it a tax on hunger. The institution of the milling tax was first proposed in 1865 by Sella but was approved only three years later, after a long debate, which featured the appointment of an ad hoc parliamentary committee. The beginning of collection caused a lockout of many mills and popular revolts, especially in the region of Emilia. However, the initial consequences on welfare were less serious than feared. In some areas, the tax unleashed competition among mills, which reduced their fees (in other words, millers paid the tax). Elusion was widespread, so that in the first years the revenue fell much short of the forecasts. Those loopholes were closed by successive changes in the procedures of collection and by improvements in meters. The total proceeds doubled, and the burden on consumers correspondingly increased. In the mid-1870s, the milling tax had become an essential source of revenue, accounting for 7.7 percent of the total in 1876. Its abolition had been a key promise in the political manifesto of the left (or *sinistra*) in the 1876 elections, but it did not rush to keep its pledge after its crushing victory. Only in 1878 did the new government propose a phased-out abolition. The proposal met a widespread concern about its effects on the state budget. The legislative process dragged on for more than two years, causing the fall of three governments and the dissolution of the lower house in 1880. The milling tax was finally abolished by the newly elected parliament and effective only since January 1, 1884.

## 7.6 The Local Authorities: The Unsung Heroes of Italian Fiscal System?

By focusing on the central state, the discussion has so far neglected the local authorities, the counties (*provincie*), and the city councils (*comuni*). Counties and city councils played a major role in nineteenth-century Italy, as they funded local public works (including most roads) and provided essential services such as basic health assistance, subsidies to the poor, and, above all, primary education. They received the proceeds of surcharges on direct taxes (on buildings, land, and *ricchezza mobile*) and a substantial part of the sales taxes (*dazi consumo*), and they could cash rents from their properties (e.g., land, buildings). On average, for the period 1866–90, direct taxes accounted for half of their revenues, indirect ones for a quarter, and rents for a tenth (the rest was labeled 'miscellaneous'). This composition remained remarkably stable (Volpi 1962: table 5).

The relationship between state and local authorities was deeply asymmetrical, as the latter enjoyed little autonomy. The parliament had the right to force them to take care of some expenses and used this prerogative several times with the explicit goal of reducing its own outlays. For instance, the city councils were asked in 1865 to contribute to fund prisons and courts of justice; in 1868, the counties were requested to pay for secondary technical education; and so on (Volpi 1962: 111–26). But decisions by the parliament constrained the amount of revenues available to local authorities. They had no say on rates for direct taxes, and they were not allowed to raise their surcharge beyond a certain percentage of the state intake. The percentage was generous for the land tax (100 percent since 1866) but not for the *ricchezza mobile*. Actually, the maximum allowed surcharge was repeatedly reduced in the late 1860s and abolished altogether in 1873. The parliament similarly capped the rates on sales taxes, allegedly to prevent local authorities from squeezing (poor) consumers.

Thus, local authorities were caught between a rock and a hard place. How did they manage to remain afloat? Answering this apparently simple question is not easy, as different authors provide widely diverging data. Volpi (1962: tables 55–9) is fairly upbeat. On the eve of unification, local budgets were roughly balanced in all states except Piedmont, where expenditures exceeded revenues by a third (Volpi 1962: 9). In the mid-1860s, the income of local authorities totaled some 285 million lire (1911) lire and expenditure only 260 million. In the subsequent thirty years, expenditure increased by 2.5 times and income doubled. Thus, a modest surplus was turned into a deficit, which amounted to some to 0.6 percent of GDP in the late 1880s. To cover their deficits, from 1870 to 1889, the local authorities sold 380 million 1911 lire in assets and accumulated 340 million lire of new debt.

The conditions of local authorities were much more dramatic according to Brosio and Marchese (1986), who span the whole period to the First World War. The total local revenues grew from some 200–250 million lire (1911) in the late 1860s and early 1870s to some 700 million lire on the eve of the First World War (i.e., from about a quarter to more than a third of state revenues for the same years). Yet this growth was not enough to cope with expenditures, and local authorities' budgets were in deficit in all years from 1866 to 1913. As Figure 7.7 shows, the deficit worsened dramatically in the first years of the twentieth century, exceeding 3 percent of GDP in 1911–12. The difference between the two sets of estimates when they overlap is huge and not easy to explain with the

available information.[19] The puzzle can be solved only with a new estimate, starting from the original sources on local budgets. One point is
clear: many local authorities tried to wriggle out from their financial
straitjacket by saving on the services they were obliged to provide. The
poor quality of primary education in the South, as reflected in the low
level of literacy (41.4 percent versus 87 percent in the Northwest as late
as 1911), was among the main motivations for the 1911 Daneo-Credaro
Law, which shifted the funding and control of primary education to the
state.[20]

### 7.7 The Political Economy of the Italian Tax Policy

According to the Statuto Albertino, Piedmont was a parliamentary
democracy, but the king still wielded substantial power. Sometimes he
meddled directly in budgetary issues – especially to ask for greater funds
for the army and navy – but his influence in fiscal issues was mainly
indirect. He appointed all members of the upper chamber, the Senate,
which had to approve all fiscal laws. In most instances, the Senate rubber-
stamped the laws approved in the elected lower house (Camera dei Deputati), but sometimes it did not. As a rule, the Senate tended to be fiscally
more prudent than the Camera, as its members did not have to worry
about reelection. For instance, Senate opposition delayed the abolition
of the milling tax. Seldom were divergences solved by changes in the final
bills. But these were exceptions: as a rule, the Camera dei Deputati set
fiscal policy. According to Piedmontese law (Ballini 1988: 48–9, 92–5),
the suffrage was limited to literate people, who paid more than 40 lire in
direct taxes, and to some specific categories (e.g., university graduates,
most civil servants). Women were excluded. As a result, at the time of
unification, only 400,000 people of the total 22 million population (i.e.,
1.9 percent) had the right to vote. In 1881, the requirements for suffrage
were somewhat relaxed by extending the right to vote to all literate people (i.e., to the urban middle class and to some industrial workers). The
number of voters rose from 600,000 to 2 million (6.9 percent of the Italian
population). Universal suffrage was to be granted to all men only in 1912,

---

[19] Brosio and Marchese rely on a work by Cavazzuti, with some smoothing of the data.
The ratios between their estimates and those by Volpi are fairly constant over time
(0.75 for revenues and 1.25 for expenditure), but the difference does not correspond to
any specific item.

[20] On the Daneo-Credaro law, see Acquarone (1987: 134–54); on primary schools in general, see Vigo (1971). The figure on literacy is from Felice (2007: table 3.8).

and to women in 1945. Until then, peasants, who were mostly illiterate, had no say in the political process, barring the occasional revolt.

Thus, the fiscal policy of Piedmont, and later of unified Italy, especially in the crucial decade after 1861, was decided by the representatives of a small minority of the population. In addition, the members of the parliament had to support themselves for most of the year, as they had no emoluments (until 1912). The Socialist Party, established in 1892, paid its member a stipend, but it elected a few members before the war. As a result, the Italian parliament was full of landowners and rich rentiers who could directly protect their interests without the intermediation of organized lobbies. The landed interest was particularly active and successful. For instance, in 1852, the chamber blocked Cavour's proposal for a temporary 25-percent increase in the land tax. Forty years later, northern landlords asked for protection against imported wheat, and despite the lack of enthusiasm from the government and latent opposition from their southern colleagues, they succeeded in having a duty on wheat approved in 1887 (Sereni 1966: 101–35; Musella 1984; Lupo 1990). The subsequent increases of the duty in 1888 and (twice) in 1894, up to double its initial level, were proposed by the governments and motivated by the urgent needs of public finances. The duty was indeed a moneymaker, yielding some 3 percent of total revenues in the late 1890s and up to 5 percent in the 1900s.[21] Yet one suspects that the inclusion of increases in that duty in a tax package was a shrewd attempt to facilitate the parliamentary passage of the financial bill by pandering to the landed interest.

Given its composition and the interests of the voters, one would expect the parliament to shift most of the burden of the rising fiscal state to the working classes, most notably to the voteless peasants. This view was quite common among radical reformers in the nineteenth and early twentieth century and, in more recent times, was forcefully expressed by Marxist historian Emilio Sereni. He rails against the 'ruthless class character of the policies of the Right – especially of its fiscal policy' (Sereni 1947: 60), quoting the milling tax and the heavy taxation on salt as the first exhibit of his indictment. Brosio and Marchese (1986: 127–35) put forward a more modern version of this idea. Their model formally refers to expenditure, but given the low deficits in the period it covers (1866–1913), it can explain fiscal policy as well. They assume that the ruling class set the maximum revenue it could extract from the nonvoting

---

[21] The estimate is obtained multiplying the share of wheat on total custom revenue (Ministero delle Finanze, ad annum) by the share of customs on total state revenues from Repaci (1962).

population without causing a revolt and then decided on the amount of taxes the latter was ready to pay, given its income and the opportunity cost of public goods in terms of its own private consumption. In their empirical test, they use revenues from indirect taxes as a proxy for the maximum sustainable level of taxation on nonvoters and (economywide) implicit deflators for private and public goods as proxy of the opportunity costs of taxation for the rich. All these variables and total GDP are significant and have the predicted sign, whereas the share of voting population is not significant.

The model by Brosio and Marchese (1986) is rather crude, and some results could be interpreted otherwise (e.g., total GDP may affect directly the level of expenditure via the amount of revenues instead of being a proxy for the income of the elite). Yet the model could have been a good starting point for a more refined approach to the political economy of fiscal policy. Alas, as it often happens, it has been totally ignored by Italian historians. The issue of the fiscal policy is not prominent in the current discourse about Italian economic growth, but the prevailing opinion in the profession seems to lean toward a more benign view than Sereni's. The most ardent supporter of this position is Marongiu (1995: 222–40), who praises the governments of the right for their unselfish dedication to common good in the 1860s and 1870s. In the same vein, Vera Zamagni (1992: 39) writes about the 'ethical foundations of the action of the ruling class' in those years. She quotes approvingly the increases in the income taxes and especially the 10-percent surcharges on the land tax, which directly hit the core constituency of the government, the landowners.[22] Marongiu (1995) regards the milling tax as absolutely necessary to balance the budget, and its implementation under the guidance of Sella an example of successful fight against tax elusion. In the second volume of his work, Marongiu (1996) contrasts the strong and forward-looking leadership of the right with the mediocre and wavering fiscal policy of the governments of the left after 1876. The data (Figure 7.7) show that Marongiu has a point: the share of direct taxes on total revenues peaked under the allegedly reactionary rule of the right and then started to decline to their historical minimum under the comparatively liberal and left-leaning Giolitti ministries in the 1900s.[23]

---

[22] The minister for finance, Sella, was the scion of a family of industrialists in the woolen industry, with wide banking interests. He was thus personally hit by increases in the *ricchezza mobile* rather than the land tax.

[23] Clearly, the actual burden of direct taxes on the liable income of the rich depends on the share of this latter on GDP; unfortunately, there is no reliable evidence (although

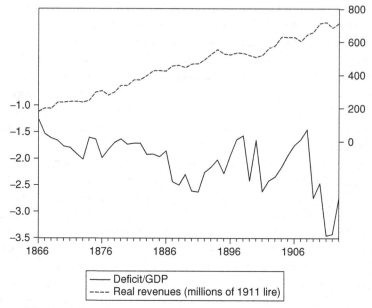

Figure 7.8. Local finances, 1866–1913. *Sources:* Brosio and Marchese (1986) deflated with wholesale price index from ISTAT (1958); GDP: Fenoaltea (2005).

## 7.8 Conclusions: An Open Issue

Although local authorities deserve much more attention, the main facts are well known, at least for the central administration. In the long run, Italy succeeded in meeting the financial needs to modernize the country and its ambitions of great-power status, with a limited resort to debt (unlike preunitary Piedmont). The growth in taxation was fairly modest for modern standards, and the years of the *boom giolittiano* featured a declining revenue-GDP ratio. The fiscal policy was hardly progressive, but the share of income taxes was fairly high for the nineteenth century, and the ruling elites showed some willingness to sacrifice to help the country out of financial crises.

Clearly, one could hypothesize a more equitable distribution of the tax burden or higher levels of development-fostering expenditures, but

Rossi et al. 2001 convincingly argue that the distribution of income did not change). If it remained constant at 40 percent (a figure as plausible as any other one), the rich-specific ratio would hover around 0.70–0.80 of the overall revenue-GDP ratio (Table 7.3) throughout most of the period, with a peak in the early 1870s, and would collapse to less than 0.6 in the early 1910s.

Table 7.3. *Italy, 1862–1913 (millions of 1911 lire)*

|      | Expenditures | Revenues | Deficit | Expenditure/GDP | Revenues/GDP |
|------|-------------|----------|---------|-----------------|--------------|
| 1862 | 897.6  | 541.3  | −356.3 | 8.98  | 5.41  |
| 1863 | 949.7  | 586.9  | −362.8 | 9.24  | 5.71  |
| 1864 | 1084.1 | 808.7  | −275.4 | 10.50 | 7.83  |
| 1865 | 1149.6 | 893.0  | −256.6 | 10.50 | 8.16  |
| 1866 | 1245.2 | 932.8  | −312.4 | 11.16 | 8.36  |
| 1867 | 1034.4 | 898.1  | −136.3 | 9.74  | 8.46  |
| 1868 | 999.8  | 922.2  | −77.6  | 9.23  | 8.51  |
| 1869 | 1102.4 | 1136.6 | 34.2   | 9.95  | 10.26 |
| 1870 | 1010.1 | 926.1  | −84.0  | 8.78  | 8.05  |
| 1871 | 1218.1 | 1204.6 | −13.6  | 10.62 | 10.51 |
| 1872 | 1206.9 | 1206.9 | 0.0    | 10.62 | 10.62 |
| 1873 | 1147.0 | 1170.6 | 23.6   | 10.07 | 10.28 |
| 1874 | 1173.8 | 1165.6 | −8.2   | 9.78  | 9.71  |
| 1875 | 1283.3 | 1344.9 | 61.6   | 10.66 | 11.17 |
| 1876 | 1363.8 | 1358.6 | −5.3   | 11.51 | 11.47 |
| 1877 | 1268.5 | 1267.6 | −0.9   | 10.59 | 10.58 |
| 1878 | 1287.4 | 1296.0 | 8.7    | 10.30 | 10.37 |
| 1879 | 1322.7 | 1403.8 | 81.1   | 10.51 | 11.16 |
| 1880 | 1328.9 | 1374.9 | 46.0   | 10.34 | 10.69 |
| 1881 | 1531.6 | 1526.1 | −5.5   | 11.54 | 11.50 |
| 1882 | 1633.7 | 1573.1 | −60.6  | 12.06 | 11.61 |
| 1883 | 1729.9 | 1667.5 | −62.5  | 12.52 | 12.07 |
| 1884 | 1935.0 | 1770.9 | −164.2 | 14.16 | 12.96 |
| 1885 | 1867.7 | 1792.4 | −75.4  | 13.37 | 12.83 |
| 1886 | 1859.0 | 1838.9 | −20.1  | 12.86 | 12.72 |
| 1887 | 2160.5 | 1996.0 | −164.4 | 14.62 | 13.51 |
| 1888 | 2278.7 | 2012.7 | −266.0 | 15.39 | 13.59 |
| 1889 | 2157.1 | 1943.4 | −213.7 | 14.93 | 13.45 |
| 1890 | 2048.0 | 1945.7 | −102.3 | 13.93 | 13.24 |
| 1891 | 2059.1 | 1931.7 | −127.4 | 13.73 | 12.88 |
| 1892 | 2100.1 | 1972.5 | −127.7 | 14.02 | 13.17 |
| 1893 | 2158.0 | 2101.6 | −56.4  | 14.11 | 13.74 |
| 1894 | 2230.1 | 2174.0 | −56.2  | 14.42 | 14.06 |
| 1895 | 2162.1 | 2093.9 | −68.2  | 13.83 | 13.39 |
| 1896 | 2141.2 | 2057.7 | −83.5  | 13.50 | 12.98 |
| 1897 | 2120.0 | 2087.0 | −33.0  | 13.28 | 13.07 |
| 1898 | 2066.4 | 2049.5 | −17.0  | 12.88 | 12.77 |
| 1899 | 2047.5 | 2022.8 | −24.8  | 12.58 | 12.43 |
| 1900 | 1978.2 | 1992.8 | 14.7   | 11.85 | 11.93 |
| 1901 | 2000.1 | 2051.6 | 51.6   | 11.74 | 12.05 |
| 1902 | 2077.1 | 2145.7 | 68.6   | 11.90 | 12.29 |
| 1903 | 2138.9 | 2206.3 | 67.4   | 12.02 | 12.40 |
| 1904 | 2274.2 | 2357.1 | 82.9   | 12.44 | 12.89 |

(*continued*)

Table 7.3 *(continued)*

|  | Expenditures | Revenues | Deficit | Expenditure/GDP | Revenues/GDP |
|------|------|------|------|------|------|
| 1905 | 2436.5 | 2343.9 | −92.6 | 12.97 | 12.48 |
| 1906 | 2540.4 | 2337.3 | −203.1 | 13.04 | 12.00 |
| 1907 | 2274.3 | 2163.4 | −110.9 | 11.36 | 10.81 |
| 1908 | 2474.6 | 2294.2 | −180.5 | 12.05 | 11.17 |
| 1909 | 2657.8 | 2458.2 | −199.6 | 12.69 | 11.73 |
| 1910 | 2800.1 | 2694.2 | −105.9 | 13.21 | 12.71 |
| 1911 | 2802.0 | 2703.0 | −99.0 | 12.92 | 12.46 |
| 1912 | 2801.5 | 2544.3 | −257.3 | 12.49 | 11.35 |
| 1913 | 2962.9 | 2667.4 | −295.4 | 12.70 | 11.43 |

*Sources:* Expenditure and revenues from Ragioneria Generale dello Stato (1969) deflated with the wholesale price index from ISTAT (1958), and GDP from Fenoaltea (2005).

radically different policies would have been implausible in the nineteenth century. Thus, Italian finances before 1913 could be qualified as successful, though with many qualifications. Italian finances surely do not deserve the very harsh assessment of Spinelli and Fratianni (1997), who blame the state deficit for the inflationary bias that allegedly has bedeviled Italy in all its postunification history. This allegation might be true for the 1970s and 1980s but seems far fetched for the years before the First World War (Cohen and Federico 2001). Fiscal policy may have affected Italy's economic performance, but the mechanism of this effect is surely more complex and involves the nature of taxation more than its absolute level (which Spinelli and Fratianni [1997] would have liked to be even higher to altogether avoid the deficit). So far, this line of research remains totally unexplored with analytical tools, but it is surely a promising one. Another potentially fruitful line of research is the analysis of policy making. We have information about the composition of the houses and some broad generalizations about interests, but we know little about the drafting of financial laws and actual voting patterns.

## References

Acquarone, A. (1987) *Tre capitoli sull'età giolittiana*. Bologna: Il Mulino.

Ballini, P.-L. (1988) *Le elezioni nella storia d'Italia dall'Unità al fascismo*. Bologna: Il Mulino.

Bardini, C., Carreras, A. and Lains, P. (1995) "The national accounts for Italy, Spain and Portugal," *Scandinavian Economic History Review*, 43, 115–47.

Brosio, G. and Marchese, C. (1986) *Il potere di spendere*. Bologna: Il Mulino.

Cammelli, S. (1984) *Al suono delle campane. Indagine su una rivolta contadina: i moti del macinato (1869)*. Milan: Franco Angeli.

Cohen, J. and Federico, G. (2001) *The Economic Development of Italy.* Cambridge: Cambridge University Press.

Corbino E. (1931–6) *Annali dell'economia italiana,* 5 vols. Città di Castello: Tipografia Leonardo da Vinci.

Correnti, C. and Maestri, P. (1864) *Annuario statistico italiano,* vol. 2. Turin: Tipografia Letteraria.

Di Gianfrancesco, M. (1974) "La politica commerciale degli stati sardi dal 1814 al 1859," *Rassegna Storica del Risorgimento,* 61(1), 3–36.

Di Salvia, B. (1997) "L'imposta fondiaria da Cavour a Magliani," in A. Guenzi and D. Ivone (eds.) *Politica economia amministrazione e finanza nell'opera di Agostino Magliani.* Naples: Editoriale Scientifica, 219–55.

Einaudi Luigi (1942) La terra e l'imposta. Turin: Einaudi [2nd ed. 1974].

Ercolani, P. (1969) "Documentazione statistica di base," in G. Fuà (ed.) *Lo sviluppo economico in Italia,* vol. 3. Milan: Franco Angeli, 380–460.

Falconi, E. and Spaggiari, P.-L. (1959) "Le entrate degli Stati Parmensi dal 1830 al 1859," *Archivio Economico dell'Unificazione Italiana,* vol. 3.

Federico, G. (2001) "L'economia della Restaurazione, *Contemporanea,*" 4–5, 541–5.

Felloni, G. (1959a) "Le entrate degli stati Sabaudi dal 1825 al 1860," *Archivio Economico dell'Unificazione Italiana,* vol. 3.

Felloni G. (1959b) "Le spese effettive ed il bilancio degli stati Sabaudi dal 1825 al 1860," *Archivio Economico dell'Unificazione Italiana,* vol. 3.

Felice, E. (2005) "Il valore aggiunto regionale. Una stima per il 1891 e per il 1911 e alcune elaborazioni di lungo periodo (1891–1971)," *Rivista di Storia Economica,* 21, 272–314.

Fenoaltea, S. (2002) "Production and consumption in post-unification Italy: New evidence, new conjectures," *Rivista di Storia Economica,* 18, 251–99.

Fenoaltea, S. (2005) "The growth of the Italian economy, 1861–1913: Preliminary second eneration estimates," *European Review of Economic History,* 9, 273–312.

Ferguson, N. and Schularick, M. (2006) "The empire effect: the determinants of country risk in the first age of globalization," *Journal of Economic History,* 66, 282–312.

Flandreau, M. and Zumer, F. (2004) *The Making of Global Finance, 1880–1913.* Paris: Organisation for Economic Co-operation and Development.

Fratianni, M. and Spinelli, F. (1997) *A Monetary History of Italy.* Cambridge: Cambridge University Press.

Fuá, G. and Gallegati, M. (1993) "Un indice a catena del prodotto 'reale' dell'Italia 1861 1989," *Rivista di Storia economicai,* 10, 281–306.

ISTAT (Istituto Centrale di Statistica) (1958) *Sommario di statistiche storiche.* Rome: ISTAT.

Izzo, L. (1962) *La finanza pubblica nel primo decennio dell'Unità d'Italia.* Naples: Giuffrè.

Livi, C. (1956) "Le entrate del ducato di Modena dal 1840 al 1859," *Archivio Economico dell'Unificazione Italiana,* vol. 1.

Lupo, S. (1990) "I proprietari terrieri nel Mezzogiorno," in P. Bevilacqua (ed.) *Storia dell'agricoltura italiana in età contemporanea,* vol. 2, *Uomini e classi.* Venice: Marsilio, 105–49.

MAIC (1876) Ministero di Agricoltura, Industria e Commercio, Divisione di agricoltura *Relazione intorno alle condizioni dell'agricoltura nel quinquennio 1870–1874*. Rome: Botta.

Malanima, P. (2006) "An age of decline. Product and income in eighteenth- and nineteenth-century Italy," *Rivista di Storia Economica*, 22(1), 91–133.

Maddison, A. (1992) "El crecimiento economico italiano 1861–1989: una revision," in L. Prados de la Escosura and V. Zamagni (eds.) *El desarrollo économico en la Europa del Sur: Espana e Italia en perspectiva historica*. Madrid: Alianza, 81–100.

Marongiu, G. (1995) *Storia del fisco in Italia, Vol. 1, La politica fiscale della Destra Storica*. Turin: Einaudi.

Marongiu, G. (1996) *Storia del fisco in Italia, Vol. 2, La politica fiscale della Sinistra Storica*. Turin: Einaudi.

Marongiu, G. (2002) *La politica fiscale nella crisi di fine secolo (1896–1901)*. Rome: Istituto per la Storia del Risorgimento Italiano.

Ministero delle Finanze (1861–1914) Ministero delle Finanze, Direzione Generale delle Gabelle. *Movimento commerciale del Regno d'Italia nell'anno*. Rome.

Musella, L. (1984) *Proprietà e politica agraria in Italia (1861–1914)*. Naples: Guida.

Nieri, R. (1976) "L'imposta fondiaria in Italia," *Annali della Fondazione Luigi Einaudi*, 10, 187–251.

Nitti, F. S. (1900) "Il bilancio dello stato dal 1861 al 1896–97," now in *Scritti sulla questione meridionale*, vol. 2. Bari: Laterza. 1958.

Ostuni, N. (1992) *Finanza ed economia nel regno delle Due Sicilie*. Naples: Liguori.

Parenti, G. (1956) "Le entrate del Granducato di Toscana dal 1825 al 1859," *Archivio Economico dell'Unificazione Italiana*, vol. 1.

Parravicini, G. (1958) *La politica fiscale e le entrate effettive del Regno d'Italia 1860–1890*. Turin: ILTE.

Ragioneria Generale dello Stato (1969) *Il bilancio dello Stato italiano dal 1862 al 1967*. Rome: Poligrafico dello Stato.

Repaci, F. A. (1962) *La finanza pubblica italiana nel secolo 1861–1960*. Bologna: Zanichelli.

Rossi, N., Toniolo, G. and Vecchi, G. (2001) "Is the Kuznets curve still alive? Evidence from Italian household budgets," *Journal of Economic History*, 61, 904–25.

Rossi Ragazzi, B. (1956) "Le entrate dello Granducato di Toscana dal 1825 al 1859," *Archivio Economico dell'Unificazione Italiana*, vol. 1.

Romeo, R. (1984a) *Cavour e il suo tempo, Vol. 2, 1842–1854*. Bari: Laterza.

Romeo, R. (1984b) *Cavour e il suo tempo, Vol. 2, 1854–1861*. Bari: Laterza.

Sereni, E. (1947) *Il capitalismo nelle campagne (1860–1900)*. Turin: Einaudi [2nd ed].

Sereni, E. (1966) *Capitalismo e mercato nazionale*. Rome: Editori Riuniti.

Spinelli, F. and Fratianni, M. (1991) *Storia monetaria d'Italia*. Milan: Mondadori.

SVIMEZ (1961) Associazione per lo sviluppo dell'industria nel Mezzogiorno (SVIMEZ) *Un secolo di statistiche italiane 1861–1961*. Rome: SVIMEZ.

Uggè, A. (1956) "Le entrate del Regno Lombardo-Veneto dal 1840 al 1864," *Archivio Economico dell'Unificazione Italiana*, vol. 1.

Vigo, G. (1971) *Istruzione e sviluppo economico nell'Italia del secolo XIX*. Turin: ILTE.

Volpi, F. (1962) *Le finanze dei comuni e delle provincie del Regno d'Italia 1860–1890*. Turin: ILTE.

Zamagni, V. (1987) "A century of change: trends in the composition of the Italian labour force, 1881–1981," *Historical Social Research*, 44, 36–97.

Zamagni, V. (1992) "Debito pubblico e creazione di un nuovo apparato fiscale nell'Italia unificata 1861–1876,' *Ente per gli studi monetari, bancari e finanziari L.Einaudi*," *Disavanzo pubblico in Italia: natura strutturale e politiche di rientro*, vol. 2. Bologna: Il Mulino, 9–94.

Zamagni, V. (1998) "Il debito pubblico italiano 1861–1946: ricostruzione della serie storica," *Rivista di Storia Economica*, 14, 207–42.

# 8

# Public Finance and the Rise of the Liberal State in Spain, 1808–1914

## Francisco Comín

## 8.1 Introduction

The wars and political changes that took place prior to 1840 created serious problems for the Spanish Treasury. Spain was affected by the Napoleonic Wars (War of Independence 1808–14) and by the subsequent restoration of the absolutist monarchy under Fernando VII. After General Riego's revolutionary uprising in 1820, Fernando VII was forced to swear fidelity to the Constitution of 1812 and thus became a constitutional monarch for three years during the so-called constitutional triennium (1820–3). A new absolutist coup in 1823, with the help of another French invasion, also called 'the hundred thousand sons of St. Louis', led to a second restoration of the ancien régime under Fernando VII and a period of absolutist stability known as the ominous decade. The death of Fernando VII was followed by widespread war, in the form of the First Carlist War (1833–40). The long transition from an absolutist regime to a liberal state was decided during these conflicts, which seriously affected fiscal issues. In this period, Spain lost a large empire and became a second-rate European power. Once Spain lost its colonies, it no longer received bullion remittances from the Americas and came to rely on its own revenues. Nevertheless, public expenditure increased more than receipts did, thereby raising the deficit and the public debt to alarming levels.

The end of the First Carlist War in 1840 consolidated the liberal state and allowed for greater political stability. There were both peaceful and revolutionary changes in government after 1840, but the liberal regime was never questioned. After the victory of the liberals supporting

Isabel II, the period from 1840 to 1844 was politically unstable and there were several rebellions. After a progressive coup on November 16, 1840, General Espartero seized power as regent. Espartero survived to three coup attempts between 1841 and 1843, and in 1844, there was a new phase of relative political stability with the government of General Narváez (the moderate decade). The legitimacy of the Constitutions of 1812 and 1820 was accepted, but the constitution was revised in 1845. Political instability returned briefly after the revolution in 1854–6 (progressive biennium) and once again in 1868–74 (democratic sexennium, after the so-called 'Glorious Revolution'). However, a conservative coup d'état in 1874 led to the restoration of the Bourbon monarchy in 1875 (Alfonso XII, the son of Isabel II) and returned the country to a phase of political stability that lasted until the beginning of the First World War. The two main political parties (conservative and liberal) alternated in power from 1875 under what was called the peaceful turn. Only the colonial wars, mainly the war that led to the loss of the remaining colonies in 1895–9 and the war in Morocco from 1909, disturbed this otherwise peaceful period.

The structure of this chapter is as follows: In the first section, I explore the efforts of tax reform before 1840 and the reasons for its failure. In the second section, I examine the 1845 tax reform, focusing on the changes that parliament introduced into the Ministry of Finance's proposal and on the breach of the fiscal principles in the Constitution of 1845. In the third section, I analyze the transition of the absolute monarchy's model of public expenditure that was replaced by that of the liberal state in the 1840s. In the fourth section, I examine the public deficit and financing mechanisms. Finally, in the fifth section, I evaluate the consequences of the fiscal policy on economic growth.

## 8.2 The Failure of Liberal and Absolutist Tax Reforms, 1813–40

After 1793, the wars against France and England further increased the deficit of the Royal Treasury. The state of the Spanish Treasury worsened as a result of incessant wars and regime changes. In the first place, the wars deteriorated the economy and the public finances. During the war of independence against Napoléon (1808–13), the junta of Cádiz (the patriotic government) managed to finance the expenditures of only that province. The armies of the other provinces took their supplies from where they were at the time, confiscating from the villages and paying them with promissory notes. Napoléon's armies resorted to the spoils of war, impoverishing local treasuries (Fontana and Garrabou 1986: 65–70). The finances of the Spanish monarchy also suffered because of the wars of independence of the colonies in America. The latter had consequences on the Spanish Treasury, including the disappearance of remittances of bullion from 1811, one of its main resources, and of credits from the colonies; the decrease of Spanish trade with America, thereby reducing the revenues from customs duties; and the incapacity to obtain lending in Europe without the guarantee of American bullion. Thus, deprived of the remittances and credits from the colonies, the Spanish governments had to resort to internal taxation.

The tax reforms also failed because of the political instability. The urgent and actual aim of the tax reforms of the parliament (Cortes) of Cádiz (1808–13) was to finance the war. The ideological and theoretical purpose, however, was to establish a fairer and more efficient liberal tax system. The direct tax (*contribución directa*) passed by the parliament in 1813 was abolished by Fernando VII in 1814, when he restored the old tax system. Given the tax-collection slump caused by the loss of the colonies, the difficult economic condition and the failure of the tax-collection mechanisms, the ministers of the absolutist Treasury suggested wide-reaching tax reforms to increase the revenues. Martín de Garay's (1817) reform stood out, but there was not enough time for it to take hold because it was repealed in the constitutional triennium (1820–3), when the parliament passed a new tax system put forward by Canga Argüelles. This new system, too, had insufficient time to consolidate because the second restoration of absolutism in 1823 repealed the liberal taxes. Once again, the penury of the Treasury led the absolutist minister López Ballesteros to carry out a tax reform (1824–7) that did not increase revenues. Despite the repeated failures, little by little, the reforms brought in taxes and tax-collection methods that would be integrated into the 1845 tax reform. Likewise, in 1845, the minister of the Treasury, Alejandro Mon, learned from these failures how to circumvent the obstacles that had prevented the liberal tax reform.

In the period of the Cádiz parliament (1808–13), the Constitution of 1812 established the principles of liberal taxation. The following features stand out. Every year, the parliament had to pass the budget of expenditures and receipts and, a posteriori, the government's Treasury accounts. The taxes had to be distributed among the Spanish people proportional to wealth and showing no preferential treatment to anyone. Customs duties (*rentas de aduanas*) and the provincial revenues (*rentas provinciales*) would have to be revoked, as they were compatible with neither the national freedom nor with the prosperity of the people. Under these guidelines, the Treasury's extraordinary commission presented to the Cádiz parliament in July 1813 a budget bill that abolished fiscal monopolies and provincial taxes at the same time that it created the direct tax (*contribución directa*). The various taxable yields were identified by external, indirect evidence rather than by a direct assessment conducted by the Treasury. Because of this, and because taxpayers' declarations were underassessed, the tax-collection practices, quotas, and assessments employed were still those of the ancien régime tax-distribution structure. This implied waiving all claims to proportional equality. Direct tax collection failed because of the shortcomings of the fiscal administration and resistance by the taxpayers to the new tax (López Castellano 1995; Lopez Castellano 1999; Comín 1990).

After the restoration of the absolutist monarchy, Fernando VII set aside the direct tax in June 1814 and reestablished the taxes that were in effect before 1808. It was impossible to collect the old taxes because the traditional ideological and administrative collection procedures had deteriorated. As the Treasury had no means to fund the production costs (salaries and raw materials) of the factories producing goods subjected to fiscal monopolies, their receipts diminished. Likewise, the reduction of the *resguardos de fronteras* (border and fiscal monopolies guards) allowed smuggling to increase, thereby reducing the collection of customs duties and the fiscal monopolies receipts (Comín 2006). Consequently, tax collection was not enough to cover the accrued expenditure of the state. As arrears accumulated and unfunded debt increased, the bankruptcy of the Royal Treasury seemed unavoidable. Fernando VII's Treasury ministers could not increase the tax bases without acting against the tax privileges of the nobility. In 1817, the Treasury minister, Martín de Garay, dared to do so by establishing two taxes: the general tax of 250 million reales, which was levied on all the people regardless of the privileges that pertained to the nobility and the clergy, with the sole exception of the free or privileged provinces (the Basque Country) and the excise duty (*derecho de puertas*), which was paid on the articles that were brought into the provincial capitals and seaports. The reaction of the nobility forced Garay's resignation. Nevertheless, the Treasury ministers that succeeded him completed his reform. These two taxes increased the Treasury revenues (Fontana 1973: 34, 86–9, 373; Artola 1986: 61–2, 64–5, 70).

The constitutional triennium (1820–3) was a result of the efforts of the provincial, revolutionary juntas. They reduced the direct tax and eliminated the excise duty as well as the tobacco monopoly. The Treasury minister Canga Argüelles restored excise duties and the direct tax, albeit reduced. Even so, the budget for 1820–1 passed with a substantial deficit. This budget was the first in Spain that complied with the principles of the Constitution of 1812 (restored in 1820): (1) the parliament passed the receipts and expenditures budget and later controlled the government's spending; (2) the parliament passed an extraordinary public works budget; (3) the parliament reduced the tax burden to encourage economic growth; (4) a quota tax of 17 million reales (to be divided up on trade) replaced the excise duty; (5) the liberal government secured external loans so as not to increase tax burden and to prevent the crowding out. Canga Argüelles's proposed budget bill for 1821–2 included liberal tax reforms and was passed by the parliament when Canga Argüelles was no longer Treasury minister. His main taxes were the land tax (*contribución territorial*) levied on the net yield of rural and urban real estate, in which the taxpayer was the owner but tenants paid one-fourth of the quota and the allotment was distributed proportionally to the tax bases registered in the wealth notebooks (*cuadernos de riqueza*) assessed by town halls; the trade tax (*patente*), levied on industrial and commercial activity; the excise duty (*consumos*), which consisted of a quota of 100 million reales to be distributed among the municipalities that collected it by taxing local consumption of wine, alcohol, oil, and meat; and the stamp duty. The 1821 tax reform imitated the tax system that had already been established in France. However, the reform failed because the French model was applied literally without consideration for the traditions of Spanish taxation; administrative and tax-collection aspects were neglected; the peasants opposed the reform; and there was not enough time to apply the reform (Comín and Vallejo 2002).

In the second absolutist restoration in July 1823, the Treasury minister Juan Bautista Erro repealed the previous tax reforms to reestablish those taxes that were in force in 1808. In view of their meager revenues, López Ballesteros reestablished some of Garay's and Canga Argüelles's taxes, and he reformed some old taxes, namely those on civil yields (*contribución de frutos civiles*), trade tax (*subsidio industrial*), excise duties (*derechos de puertas*), the straw and utensils tax (*contribución de paja y utensilios*), the tax on spirits and liquors (*renta del alcohol*), the fiscal monopoly on codfish (*renta del bacalao*) and other monopolies (with an increase in the price of tobacco, salt, and stamped paper), new customs duties, and the tax on mortgages (*derecho de hipotecas*). However, this reform failed to boost tax proceeds because it did not enlarge the tax base to the nobility and the church. In view of this, López Ballesteros centered his efforts on cutting expenses. The resignation to an impoverished Treasury dictated the abandon of Fernando VII's plans to recapture the American colonies. The Treasury was not even able to pay the interest on the previous debt. As arrears accumulated in the Treasury, the volume of short-term debt rose and debt defaults further eroded the possibility of resorting to loans (Comín 1991; Tortella and Comín 2001).

The Carlist War began following the death of Fernando VII in 1833. The shortage of resources got in the way of the government's ability to supply the liberal governmental forces who supported the future queen, Elizabeth II. Subsequently, the war against the supporters of the return to the absolutist regime (the Carlists) stretched on, and there were grave consequences for both economy and the Treasury. In 1835, the progressive liberals reached the government after a revolutionary process. The new Treasury minister, Juan Álvarez Mendizábal, started economic reforms with four goals: (1) to duly obtain the means to defeat the Carlist armies; (2) to establish private property rights and the capitalist market; (3) to win support for the Elizabethan regime; and (4) to redeem public debt to reduce its volume. Legislative activity was intense over these years, with the following measures standing out: the confiscation of the church land (*desamortización eclesiástica, disentailment*), restoration of the extraordinary war tax (*contribución extraordinaria de guerra*), abolition of the tithe, and in substitution, the creation of the clergy tax (*contribución de culto y clero*) to fund the church. From 1836, the liberal governments obtained funds from the confiscation of the church and from bank credits (*anticipos de fondos*), and from moneylenders, including the Bank of San Fernando. The Treasury ministers decided not to carry out tax reforms because they needed resources immediately to win the war. Political instability prevented the liberal governments from meeting the parliamentary budget requirements established in the constitution. The 1835 budget was passed by a royal decree. A budget was not passed by parliamentary law until 1841. Following the defeat of the Carlists, progressive liberals under General Espartero governed between 1840 and 1843. Hasty shuffling of ministers and disagreements among progressives prevented the carrying out of a tax reform despite the abundance of plans for reform during these years (Artola 1986: 82–99).

The data of the budget receipts for the 1808–42 period allow us to conclude the following:

- In constant terms, Treasury revenues fell from 311 million to 275 million reales between 1807 and 1842 (Figure 8.1).
- The volume of loans was high, especially during the Carlist War, when it totaled between 35 percent and 58 percent of total revenue (Figure 8.2).
- The provincial taxes, mainly the old turnover tax (*alcabala*), brought in sizable figures at the beginning of the absolutist periods, but their collection later fell (from 30 percent to 18 percent between 1824 and 1833).
- The fiscal monopolies were essential to the absolutist tax system, accounting for more than 25 percent of the revenues between 1824 and 1831.
- Customs duties fell from 16 percent to 3.5 percent between 1824 and 1839.
- Revenues from the church fell from 13 percent to 7 percent of the revenues.
- Remittances from the colonies fell from 14 percent to 8 percent of the revenues between 1808 and 1842, although they fell to nearly zero from 1815 to 1833.
- New revenues brought in 20 percent of total revenue from 1824–33.
- Budgetary revenue between 1837 and 1839 (Figure 8.2) grew as a result of disentailment of ecclesiastical lands.

## 8.2 The Birth of the Liberal Tax System: 1845

The Constitution of 1845 definitively established the liberal tax principles in Spain. In that same year, the parliament passed a new tax system presented by Minister Alejandro Mon. This was made possible by the absence of wars and political stability. The system was changed only during the revolutionary periods, but it did not take long for the Treasury ministers to restore it. In 1900, Minister Fernández Villaverde completed Mon's tax system.

### 8.2.1 Alejandro Mon's Liberal Tax Principles

French legislation inspired the reform plans created by Treasury Minister Mon and by his principal adviser, Ramón de Santillán. However, they adapted the French model to the Spanish tax-collection traditions,

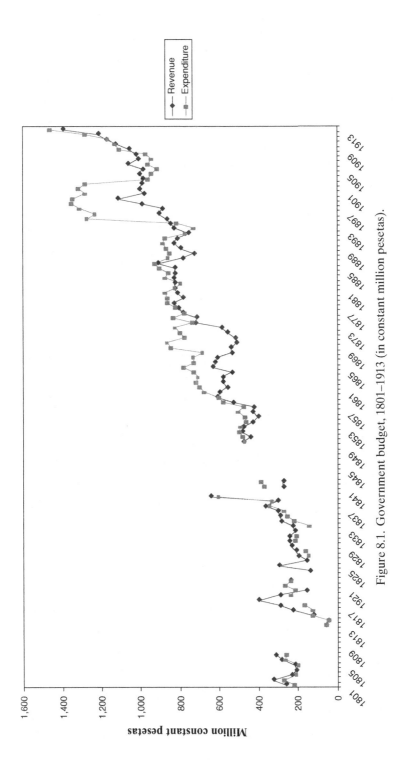

Figure 8.1. Government budget, 1801–1913 (in constant million pesetas).

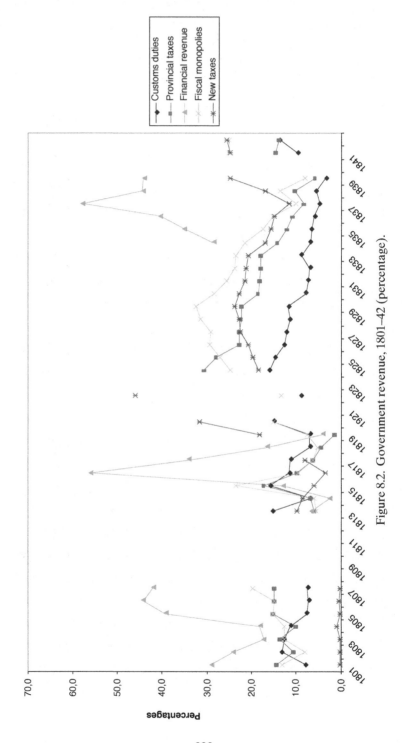

Figure 8.2. Government revenue, 1801–42 (percentage).

taking into account the experiences of the reforms that had been carried out since 1808. The 1845 tax reform was less radical than those of 1813 and 1821, but it was more pragmatic. Legally, Mon's reform established a liberal tax system and abolished old taxes. In 1849, Mon reformed customs tariffs, replacing import prohibitions with tariffs, which implied a degree of liberalization of foreign trade, after carrying out monetary and bank reforms in 1848.

The 1845 tax system was mixed, as it combined both direct and indirect taxes, fiscal monopolies, and revenue from state property. In direct taxation, Mon opted for real or product taxes, and because the reformers did not agree with income tax, he discarded personal taxes. Thus, he chose the French model over the British model. The main direct tax was the land tax (*contribución de inmuebles, cultivo y ganadería*). It was a quota tax whose amounts were decided by the parliament and divided up by the central government among the provinces, by the regional authorities among the municipalities, and by the municipal authorities among the taxpayers. The tax base comprised the net yields (with production costs deducted) of agricultural activity and urban buildings. Conversely, the trade tax (*contribución industrial y de comercio*) was levied on the net returns of industrial and commercial activities. The trade tax was made up of a fixed quota (*patente*) and another variable rate, assessed on the basis of external signs, such as surface area or machinery of workshops and stores. Tenant tax (*contribución de inquilinatos*) taxed the tenants in proportion to their rents. With indirect taxes, specific consumption was taxed, discarding the turnover tax. On the one hand, excise duties (*contribución de consumos*) taxed the consumption of necessities (e.g., food, drink, heating). On the other hand, the right of mortgages (*derecho de hipotecas*) taxed the transfer and hiring of property ownership. Last, customs duties (*derechos de aduanas*) and fiscal monopolies (*estancos*), which could be considered indirect taxes (Fontana 1977; Comín 1988; Fuentes Quintana 1990; Vallejo 1998, 2001, 2006; Comín and Vallejo 2002), were retained.

A first result of the 1845 reform was the increase of the Treasury revenues in constant terms and in relation to the gross domestic product (see Figures 8.1 and 8.3). Fiscal pressure, as measured by the tax revenue–GDP ratio, increased from 7.8 percent to 8.5 percent between 1850 and 1865 and then stabilized at this level. In second place, the tax revenues allowed the reduction of budget deficits. Although deficits predominated, their relationship to GDP surpassed 1.5 percent only in the periods of 1861–73 and 1895–1902 (Figure 8.4). Consequently,

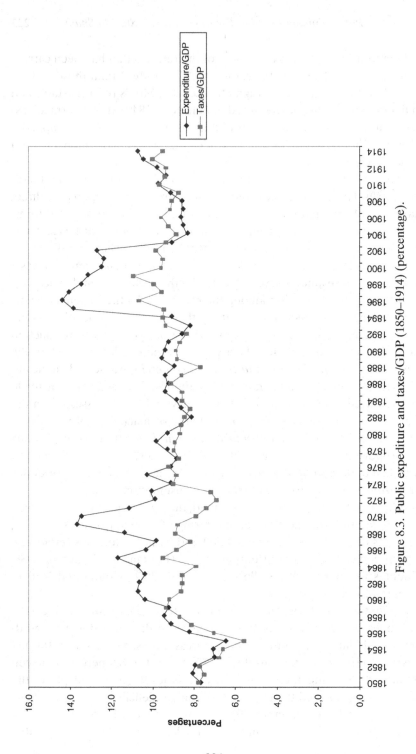

Figure 8.3. Public expediture and taxes/GDP (1850–1914) (percentage).

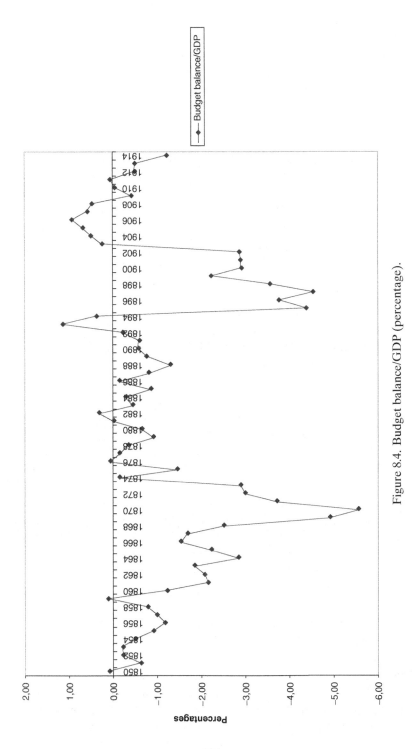

Figure 8.4. Budget balance/GDP (percentage).

state loans acquired importance only in the short revolutionary and wartime periods: 1854–7 (14 percent), 1864–76 (25 percent), and 1896–8. In the third place, the direct taxes acquired growing importance, especially the land tax, which represented more than 20 percent of tax revenues. Trade tax represented only 4.5 percent, and the graduated poll tax (*impuesto de cédulas personales*) barely brought in any revenue. However, the outstanding indirect taxes were the excise duties, which brought in between 10 percent and 12 percent of revenue (except in the revolutionary periods, because it was eliminated in 1854 and 1868), and the customs duties, which increased its participation from 12.7 percent to 18.5 percent between 1850 and 1893. This increase occurred as a consequence of the newly reduced tariff rates (i.e., the Figuerola tariff), which had increased the volume of foreign trade and customs duties receipts. The protectionist tariff that had been set up in 1891 caused it to fall and subsequently stagnate. The gross receipts brought in by fiscal monopolies diminished from 28.2 percent to 23.4 percent between 1850 and 1891. This decrease was a result of the leasing out in 1887 of the management of the tobacco monopoly to a private company whose net revenues (of around 17 percent) reached the Treasury only in 1891. In addition, the reform of Mon modified the legal and political bases of the tax system. While formally copying the French legislation, the reformers of 1845 adapted it to the Spanish peculiarities so that the taxpayers accepted the new taxes. They did so by presenting the new taxes as a mere rehashing of the old taxes that they intended to replace. Therefore, the reformers kept the old tax-collection practices and ensured the collection of the new taxes. In fact, land tax was regarded as a reworking of provincial taxes and inherited its tax-collection method of distributing the allotted quota according to the real estate wealth of the neighbors. Likewise, the trade tax was presented as a modification of the old industrial subsidy. Similarly, changes that had been introduced since 1817 by the Treasury ministers (Fontana 1977; Comín 1990) were included in the 1845 system, as were some old taxes that were able to bring revenues to the Treasury.

### 8.2.2 Parliamentary Corrections

Despite moderation, Alejandro Mon's proposals met with resistance in the parliament, both before and after passage of the 1845 tax law. This tax counterreform had consequences to the distribution of income and reduced tax-collection ability. Although it facilitated passage of the reform, it deprived the tax system of social legitimacy among those outside the electorate. Pressure from the taxpayers who had parliamentary representation managed to bring about reduced tax quotas and to change taxable facts and collection procedures. The changes allowed the taxpayers with the right to vote to transfer part of the tax burden to the taxpayers who lacked political representation in the parliament and city halls. In parliament, Mon's tax bill underwent important modifications. First, parliament representatives protected landowning interests by changing the taxpayers and reducing the quota of land tax. To stimulate agricultural investment and economic growth, Mon had proposed taxing only the landlords' rent and exempting farmers' crop profits from tax. Instead, the parliament decided that such profits also had to be taxed, and thus landowners transferred part of the tax burden to tenants, farmers, and livestock owners. Second, the parliament changed the trade tax bill to favor industry over commerce and agriculture. Third, the parliament ruled for direct payment of the tenant tax by the tenant and not by the owner, as stipulated in Mon's proposal, and raised the minimum exemption, thus reducing its generalization. Fourth, the parliament of 1845 reduced the amount of excise duties. In addition, after 1845, Mon's tax system underwent more changes in the parliament. In 1846, the opposition of urban taxpayers led the parliament to eliminate taxes such as the tenant tax. The distribution or collection bases of other taxes, as occurred with trade tax and excise duties, were also modified. Opposition to the proportional quota in the trade tax forced its disappearance in 1847. Finally, the parliament forced the preservation of old tax-collection practices, namely the collection of the land tax by city halls and the collection of the trade tax by trade guilds. By controlling the tax-collection mechanisms, the landowners' oligarchy managed to transfer the tax burden to peasants and tenants; likewise, the industrial middle class transferred it to small businesspeople and artisans through the trade tax.

In 1845, the parliamentarians directly opposed the creation of the cadastre of territorial wealth that would have guaranteed proportional distribution of taxes. All the same, the parliamentarians disagreed over the provincial distribution of the quota of the land tax. As it was not possible to reach an agreement in the parliament, they designated this operation to the government, and the government decided either to farm the collection of excise duties or to leave it to the town halls through a fixed quota to be paid for each town or village, without regard for the collection methods regulated by the tax law (*encabezamiento*). The bill had determined to levy excise duties on factories that produced taxed commodities. Given parliamentary pressure, the fiscal reformers of 1845 sought to compromise with the traditional procedures, allowing those who wielded political power in the central and local governments to evade their tax responsibilities (Vallejo 2001; Comín and Vallejo 2002; Vallejo and Muñoz 2008).

Parliamentary pressure was also reflected in the reform of tariff and customs duties. Controversy between the businesspeople advocating free trade and the protectionists was frequent. Foreseeing serious pressure, Alejandro Mon left customs tariff reform for 1849, because he feared that the pressure against the reform would hamper support of the new tax system in 1845. In fact, the Mon tariff suffered significant pressure in the parliament. The subsequent 1869 Figuerola tariff was also controversial. The two tariffs dispensed with prohibitions and reduced the import tariffs, as a result of pressure from free trade supporters, entrepreneurs, and urban consumers. Nevertheless, in 1855, political pressure allowed foreign companies to obtain tariff exemption on imported railway materials. Adversely, as of 1875 but especially after 1891, pressures from industrialist and landowners imposed more protectionist-minded tariffs.

### 8.2.3 The Breach of the Principles of the Liberal Treasury

Because of the pragmatism of the ministers and the motions passed in the parliament, some of the tax principles of the Constitution of 1845 were not completely met.

First, the principle of legality was adequately met. The public budgets started to be passed annually in the parliament. They frequently recurred to governmental decrees to prolong them, as happened in the 1845–9 period. If the decrees were sanctioned later on by the parliament, the budgetary extension allowed them to save the constitutional principle. Some governments, however, abused the extensions. That is what happened when the parliament was cloistered at the beginning of 1850 by Prime Minister Juan Bravo Murillo. In 1850, while in the office of the Treasury minister, Murillo passed the Public Accountancy Law, which improved budgetary and public accounting practices (Comín 1998; Pro 2007). Second, the principle of fiscal centralization was met. The constitution and the 1845 tax reform attributed the fiscal monopoly to the state.[1] Third, the principle of the universality of taxation was met in 1845, when regional and tax privileges of the nobility were eliminated. Fourth, the principle of territorial unity was introduced by the 1845 reform, but

---

[1] The tithe was abolished in 1841, leaving the church without its autonomous taxation. Similarly, the end of the jurisdictional prerogatives of the nobility and the reversion to the Crown of revenues, jobs, and fiscal capacities abolished secular taxation. The civil disentailment of 1855 left the local treasuries without resources (García and Comín 1995).

the Basque Country remained exempt, as the government did not dare to apply the new taxes in this territory for fear of unleashing a new Carlist War.[2] Fifth, in 1845, the principle of tax proportionality was established as direct taxes were made proportional to the net yield of agricultural, industrial, and commercial activity. Nevertheless, the distribution of the tax burden never became proportional to the income of the taxpayers because the liberal governments did not produce adequate tax assessments (cadastre and industrial register) or set up an administrative apparatus to collect their taxes. The tax base and tax quotas were estimated by the city halls and industrial guilds, which were controlled by the local caciques and guild leaders, who also were in charge of tax collection. This contributed to the stagnation of tax assessment and of revenues (affecting the principle of sufficiency) and to the increase of the fiscal burden for the taxpayers who lacked political influence (affecting the principle of fairness). Corruption and tax evasion by the voting taxpayers characterized the nineteenth-century Spanish fiscal system and was a basic component of the political regime known as caciquismo. The landowners and big industrialists hid their property and business from the Treasury's inspections because the tax records were produced by their political friends. In summary, the groups who enjoyed parliamentary representation transferred the tax burden to the peasants, who could not avoid the land tax, and to urban consumers, who bore the excise and customs duties (Comín 1991; Serrano Sanz 1991; Pan-Montojo 1994; Comín et al. 1995; Pro 1995; Zafra 1994; Comín 1996a; Vallejo 1996). Sixth, although it was the desideratum of the liberals, they did not meet the principle of sufficiency of the tax system, that is, the covering of the government expenses. Although greatly reduced after 1845, budget deficits continued to exist and to grow during the economic, political, and wartime crises. Moreover, the principle of responsibility in regard to the management of public debt improved when, in 1851, Murillo carried out a conversion of the public debt that allowed the Treasury to pay interest and a fresh repayment of debt. After 1845, reformers sought to apply the principle of efficiency in tax collection. Tax bases were estimated through external signs of wealth, as no body of inspectors had been created. However, the economic privacy of the taxpayers was respected, as the reforms dispensed with both the tax returns and the inspection of private accounting. The principle of neutrality in the allocation of resources improved

---

[2] In 1852, the Canary Islands received the special tax regime of a free port (Fernández de Pinedo 1867; Macías, 1987).

because the 1845 tax system was more neutral than the previous tax system had been. Nevertheless, indirect taxes continued to distort market prices because excise duties proliferated, as did the various tax rates. The maintenance of high tariffs, in contrast, did not help the efficient allocation of resources either. On the contrary, the disappearance of the turnover tax, domestic customs, and the tithe favored economic growth. Finally, the principle of simplicity of the tax system was also met, as in 1845 the liberals avoided double taxation and simplified and reduced the number of taxes in comparison to the absolutist Treasury.

### 8.2.4 Later Tax Reforms

The budget deficit caused the Treasury ministers to carry out tax reforms. The most important were those made by Laureano Figuerola, because of their novelty, and by Fernández Villaverde, because they completed the liberal tax system.[3]

To replace the excise duties that had been rejected by the revolutionary juntas in 1868, Figuerola obtained parliamentary approval for a personal tax (*impuesto personal*) in 1869, which proved impossible to collect because it was too advanced for its time. The absence of civil servants and statistical data prevented the public administration from collecting it. Moreover, taxpayers rejected it and the political instability of the democratic sexennium made it difficult to establish. Had it been consolidated, Spain would have pioneered the establishment of income tax. After the failure of Figuerola's tax, the Treasury ministers who followed him abolished it and preferred a surcharge on the land tax to increase government revenues. They also resorted to the creation of two monopoly issues, one of mortgage bonds by the Mortgage Bank (Banco Hipotecario) in 1872, and the other of banknotes by the Bank of Spain (1874), in exchange for loans from those banks to the government.

Fernández Villaverde's tax reform of 1900 completed the 1845 liberal taxation system. His main contribution was the tax on labor and capital (*contribución sobre las utilidades de la riqueza mobiliaria*), which was levied on salaries, capital returns, and corporate profits. This tax consolidated some already-existing ones and included the 20 percent tax on public debt interest that Villaverde had recently created. This reform transformed the tax receipts structure (Figure 8.5). Land taxes were reduced, as a share of the total (from 19.7 percent to 14.5 percent between 1900 and 1913) vis-à-vis the advance of the labor and capital tax (from

---

[3] For other tax reforms during this period, see Pro 2006; Pan-Montojo 2006; García 2006; Comín and Martorell 2006; and Serrano Sanz 2006.

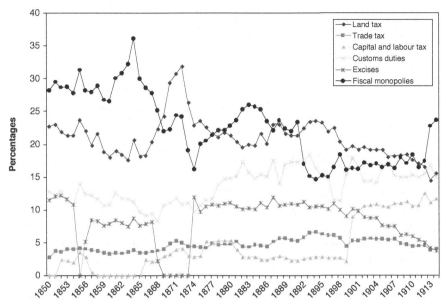

Figure 8.5. Composition of central government revenue, 1850–1914.

2.2 percent to 11.1 percent). Excise duties fell from 10.1 percent to 4.2 percent between 1908 and 1913. Customs duties remained between 14 percent and 18 percent. Likewise, Villaverde achieved a budget surplus between 1903 and 1908 thanks to a reduction in defense expenditure (the war with the colonies and against the United States finally ended in 1898) and in the service of the debt (by restructuring it). Nevertheless, the budget deficit returned in 1909 as a result of the stagnation of the tax receipts and the growth of public spending caused by expenditures with the plan for restructuring the navy (1907) and the beginning of the war with Morocco (1909). However, at the beginning of the twentieth century, the liberal tax system completed by Villaverde had become conceptually obsolete as a result of the circulation of new fiscal principles in Europe: first, the understanding of progressive taxation as included in the principle of fairness led to the inclusion of a redistributive rationale in personal taxes (income tax, corporate tax, wealth tax, and inheritance tax); second, the introduction of the turnover tax improved neutrality regarding allocation of resources. These new fiscal ideas entered Spain as soon as budget debt returned and, from 1909, tax reform proposals built on them were presented in the parliament, though none was passed in the period (Comín 1988, 1996a, 2000, 2002; Martorell 2000).

## 8.4 The Rise of the Liberal State, 1801–1914

In the middle of the nineteenth century, the absolutist monarchy gave way to a liberal state accompanied by the division of political powers, popular sovereignty, and parliamentary representation. Consequently, the spending model of the ancien régime was replaced by the liberal spending model, whose principal purpose was to deliver public goods to the society.

### 8.4.1 Ancien Régime Spending Model, 1801–40

The functions of the Royal Treasury were to finance wars and to pay the monarch's household expenses. However, debt servicing also acquired huge importance because the wars were financed with loans. The expenditure on tax-collection by the Ministry of Finance was also high, most of all because the Bourbon kings in the eighteenth century passed to the ministry the direct administration of taxes and royal factories. State administration was reduced, and the payroll of civil servants was small. The tenures of the offices charged with keeping law and order (the *oficios reales*) had been sold to private parties centuries earlier. For that reason, except during wartime, the spending model of the ancien régime had few expense obligations. In the first decades of the nineteenth century, the absolutist state could only just meet its function of maintaining the royal household. The weakness of the Treasury made it impossible to adequately supply the army, a circumstance that favored coups, foreign invasions, and the independence of the colonies. Likewise, the conflicts were made longer because of the financial incapacity of the government. Moreover, governments did not pay the Treasury's employees, another factor that reduced revenues. When the wars finished in 1814, the state's expenditures diminished abruptly. Although the Treasury receipts surpassed expenditures between 1801 and 1839 (see Figure 8.1), this budget surplus reflects the financial incompetence of the absolutist state, whose governments evaded their pledged spending obligations to civil servants, suppliers, and debt holders (Fontana 1971: 314; Comín 1990: 335–9).[4]

The structure of the Royal Treasury's expenditures barely changed between 1808 and 1840 (Figure 8.5). This model prevailed until the 1840s, both in absolutist phases and in constitutional periods. The Napoleonic Wars and the Carlist Wars increased the military expenditure and debt

---

[4] If the expenses of the *caja de amortización* (sinking fund) were included, the budget deficit would then appear.

interest. On average, in the 1801–40 period, defense expenditure was 58 percent, and financial and tax management expenditures were 30 percent, with the remaining 12 percent assigned to other government functions, even if the annual variations were intense (Figure 8.6). Likely, public debt payments are included in the high expenditure of the Ministry of Finance, and slumps in 1815–18, 1821–3 and 1833–40 indicate that interest was not being paid, whereas the disappearance of that expense from the Ministry of Finance accounts in 1822–7 indicates that interest was not being paid either, not even through the sinking fund. The expenditures of the Ministry of War evolved in the opposite direction from that of the Ministry of Finance. The expenditure of the former grew from 26.5 percent to 49.5 percent between 1813 and 1822 and from 64.2 percent to 91.7 percent between 1833 and 1839 in response to the Carlist War. In practice, this means that there were practically no funds left for the remaining budgetary expenses.

When compared with absolutist budgets, pre-1840 liberal budgets display slightly higher expenses with the Home Ministry and lower expenses with the royal household (Figure 8.5). The constitutional governments stimulated the functions of the liberal state by increasing the economic and administrative (police and justice) expenditure, just as some of the absolutist ministers (e.g., Garay, López Ballesteros) had previously done. However, the shortage of resources made it impossible for the liberal governments to meet those basic functions. Nevertheless, the incapacity of the state to keep domestic order and control of the borders had consequences on the Treasury itself because contraband lowered the customs receipts and the fiscal monopolies. Although the expenditure of the Ministry of the Navy increased between 1814 and 1822 (2.7 percent to 12.2 percent; see Figure 8.5), its later fall revealed the financial incapacity of the Spanish state to recapture America. The lack of military power led the last absolutists and the first liberal governments to political and economic international isolation.

### 8.4.2 The Liberal Public Expenditure Model, 1840–1914

The expenditure model of the liberal state definitely took off following the end of the Carlist War. Even so, the public expenditure increased both in real terms and in relation to the GDP. Leaving aside the high expenditure of 1839 (a decisive year for the victory of the government in the Carlist War), public expenditure in constant terms increased in 1840 and especially between 1857 and 1870 (Figure 8.1) and then came to a standstill. It increased abruptly again to finance the war with Cuba

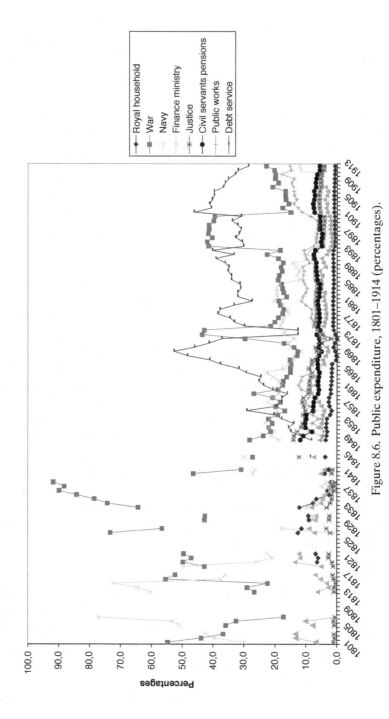

Figure 8.6. Public expenditure, 1801–1914 (percentages).

Legend:
- ◆ Royal household
- ■ War
- Navy
- ✕ Finance ministry
- ✱ Justice
- ● Civil servants pensions
- ✛ Public works
- ─ Debt service

Percentages axis: 0,0 / 10,0 / 20,0 / 30,0 / 40,0 / 50,0 / 60,0 / 70,0 / 80,0 / 90,0 / 100,0

Years axis: 1801 1805 1809 1813 1817 1821 1825 1829 1833 1837 1841 1845 1849 1853 1857 1861 1865 1869 1873 1877 1881 1885 1889 1893 1897 1901 1905 1909 1913

(1895–8). When this war was over, expenditure fell and increased again from 1908 because of Maura's naval program and the war with Morocco. With respect to the GDP, the government expenditure increased from 7.7 percent to 13.7 percent between 1850 and 1869 (see Figure 8.4). The explanation for this increase is that the liberal state began to finance new public goods. Still, budget expenditure oscillated because of the political conflicts and the wars and during the democratic sexennium, the public expenditure–GDP ratio fell to 9.1 percent and stabilized only later. Afterward, the colonial wars caused the expenditure to rise to 14.4 percent of GDP in 1896. Once again, with the war over, the expenditure fell to 8.3 percent in 1904. The government expenditure later recovered to 10.7 percent in 1914 – a percentage that had already been reached in 1861. Therefore, in the long term, the public expenditure of the liberal state did not increase in relation to GDP, maintaining the liberal principle of the liberal state.

Nevertheless, the liberal state changed the structure of the expenditure (Figure 8.6). First, the relative expenditure of the royal household decreased (from 3.6 percent to 0.6 percent between 1849 and 1913), especially in the progressive periods (it stood at 0.1 percent in 1869). The expenditure of the Ministry of War also diminished (from 28 percent to 20 percent between 1849 and 1913). Although the war expenditure increased about 40 percent during the conflicts (1873–6 and 1895–1902), it never reached pre-1840 levels. Military expenses were stable, as defense had become a permanent function of the liberal state. Spain directed the army toward national defense and law and order, as it was used to suppress social unrest. The fall in the expenditure of the Ministry of the Navy indicated that Spain had given up on being a naval power. With the consolidation of the liberal state, the expenses of the Ministry of Justice and the Home Ministry grew. These ministries financed the new functions of the liberal state: law and order, justice, public works, and education (Figure 8.6) (Comín 1988, 1990; Comín and Vallejo 2002). The expenditure of the Ministry of Public Works grew from 4.9 percent in 1849 to 12.3 percent in 1862, and then came to a standstill, only to grow to 17.8 percent in 1912. Three-quarters of the Ministry of Public Works' budget were devoted to public works, while 14 percent went to education, showing how important both economic and education functions were to the liberal state.

The administrative classification of the government expenditure in Figure 8.6 hides some paradoxes. The expenditure of the Ministry of Finance fell because of the lowering of the tax-collection costs. More than half of the ministry's budget was spent on the administration of lotteries and the tobacco fiscal monopolies (to reduce these high costs, the tobacco monopoly was leased out to a private company in 1887). Another part was destined to pay for the civil servants' pensions (around 7 percent of the total expenditure). The expenditure of the Ministry of Justice fell from 14 percent to 4.2 percent between 1849 and 1913. The subsidies that the state paid to the clergy were an important expense that the ministry bore during the moderate decade, but it fell in the progressive periods (1855–6 and 1868–74). The liberal governments from 1842 onward established the subsidies to the Catholic Church to compensate the abolition of the tithe and the confiscation of the ecclesiastical lands. Indeed, as the liberal state continued needing the church's sermons to maintain social cohesion, the public budget paid the priests' salaries, thus converting them into actual civil servants. In 1873, the expenditure of the Ministry of Justice fell to 1.8 percent because the payments to the clergy were questioned during the First Republic. In any case, toward 1880, the accumulated payments to the church from the public budget had already surpassed the revenue obtained by the state from disentailment, e.g. the expropriation and sale of Church lands. The payments to the clergy continued until the Second Republic, with a balance that favored the clergy.

The public expenditure–GDP ratio in Spain was similar to that of other European countries. In Spain, however, the liberal state did not fulfill its functions adequately because a third of the budget was set aside to pay the interest on the debt. Debt servicing was the main item of the liberal state expenditures, except during the wars and the democratic sexennium (in 1874 and 1875, these amounted to only 12.6 percent). The budget payments on the public debt increased from 8.1 percent to 52.6 percent between 1849 and 1870, although Camacho's reform reduced them to 27.3 percent in 1882. From then on, the interest on the debt increased to 40.1 percent in 1884, reaching its peak (46.1 percent) after Villaverde's reform in 1903. It later fell to 31 percent in 1913. The debt weighed heavily on the public budget of this period.

## 8.5 The Funding of Budget Deficits, 1801–1914

### 8.5.1 *The Evolution of Budget Deficits*
Even if revenues surpassed expenditures in the treasury accounts between 1801 and 1840 (see Figure 8.1), this accounting surplus was fictitious because the governments adjusted the expenditure to the revenue,

as we can observe in the slumps of 1813 and 1824. In reality, governments did not even pay their pledged expenses. When all of the expenses were accounted for (as occurred in 1820, 1841, and 1842) the budget deficits grew to 25 percent of total expenditure. After Mon's tax reform of 1845, the liberal government reduced the budget deficit, but it did not disappear. During the 1850–99 period, the average deficit was about 12.4 percent of the total expenditure, and the Spanish budgets had deficits for all but four years – 1876, 1882, 1893, and 1899. After 1845, the government revenue increased, but, given that it was largely outstripped by expenditure, particularly between 1857 and 1870, the budget deficit increased. The deficit was already high in 1855–6 (14 percent of total expenditure) and grew from 11.6 percent to 41.3 percent between 1860 and 1870. In 1870, the budget deficit peaked at 5.5 percent of GDP (see Figure 8.4). The deficits were high again during the war with Cuba, representing 20–30 percent of the total expenditure and 2.9–4.4 percent of GDP (see Figures 8.1 and 8.4). The result was a growing public deficit and the growth of the budgetary expenses to service that government debt.

Tax revenues grew less than public expenditure did in the second half of the nineteenth century (see Figure 8.3). The tax collection did not grow more for the following reasons:

- As we have seen, the widespread cover-up on the part of the landowners and industrialists made it difficult for the Ministry of Finance to increase tax quotas, as they could not assess the actual tax base.
- The 1845 tax reform left exempt the sources of income that grew along with the development of the capitalist economy – salaries, interests, dividends, and corporate profits.
- The elimination of the excise duties by the revolutionary juntas in 1854 and 1868 reduced revenues, thereby increasing the public deficit and debt (Comín 1988, 1996b).

Fernández Villaverde's stabilization scheme and the end of the war with Cuba generated budget surpluses between 1903 and 1908. Nevertheless, as public spending increased again and direct taxes proved very rigid, a budget deficit reappeared in 1909 (see Figure 8.4).

### 8.5.2 The Costs of Irresponsible Management of the Public Debt
The absolutist monarchs did not recognize the loans raised and neglected debt-servicing payments, whereas the liberal governments did recognize all debt bonds. That meant a radical difference in the fiscal principles

from the absolutists. However, in practice, the liberals could neither pay the interest on arrears nor return the sums borrowed. This fiscal irresponsibility exacerbated the problem of the debt they inherited from the eighteenth century and decisively harmed the state's reputation as a borrower, a factor that prevented Spain from having a financial revolution. Therefore, the Treasury could not finance the deficit through low interest-rate debt issues in the market and had to continue to depend on big moneylenders, who charged high interest rates.

The liberals had to come to terms with a large quantity of debt inherited from the absolutist regime. The wars fought against France and England between 1793 and 1808 were financed with large issues of royal bonds (*vales reales*) and with loans from the Bank of San Carlos, which was especially created to finance the government. In those years, the government debt grew from 2,019 to 7,194 million reales, an amount equivalent to the actual financial cost of the wars. The value of the bonds issued far exceeded taxable receipts, and the government could neither pay the annual interest nor redeem the royal bonds, which depreciated sharply. In 1798, the government created a sinking fund (the *caja de amortización*) to redeem that debt. It was given the means from the confiscation of the charities' lands. Despite its considerable revenue, only 340 million reales of royal bonds were redeemed, because the monarch assigned those resources to finance the war, failing the commitment to reserve the sinking fund's resources to pay off the debt. Although the liberal Treasury ministers during the War of Independence did not manage to solve the problem of the government debt, plans were made to clean up public credit. The best plan to redeem the debt was produced by Finance Minister Canga Argüelles, who resorted to the sinking fund and to the disentailment of ecclesiastical lands. Nevertheless, this could not be done, because the bill was not passed by the Cortes in 1811. Moreover, the expenses for the War of Independence against France increased the public debt, which reached 11,313 million reales in 1813.

Fernando VII repudiated debt in the hands of Dutch creditors, which closed the doors of the international financial markets to the Spanish government. Between 1814 and 1820, domestic loans were difficult to obtain and were expensive because moneylenders had learned their lesson from their bad experiences with the royal bonds and because the absolutist governments had stopped paying the annual interest on the domestic debt. Despite all this, the resort to credit soared between 1816 and 1819 (see Figure 8.2). Martín de Garay tried to fix the problem of the debt following the land-confiscation strategy suggested by

Canga Argüelles. Nevertheless, he failed because the sources of revenue earmarked to pay off the securities and the debt interests were very small.

In 1820, through issues and accumulation of unpaid interest, the government debt had increased to 14,021 million reales. The triennium liberals tried to honor debt partly for doctrinal reasons and partly because they thought that they had to resort to foreign credit so as not to take capital away from industry. Thus, between 1820 and 1823, the budget deficit was financed through the issue of foreign debt (2,724 million reales). Accordingly, the debt reached 16,700 million reales in 1823. After the second absolutist restoration, Fernando VII defaulted on the foreign debt issued by the liberals and stopped paying the interest on the domestic debt. Between 1824 and 1830, Fernando VII issued 2,860 million reales in foreign debt. His finance minister, López Ballesteros, carried out a conversion of the debt in 1825 and a general default on the arrears on the Treasury payments in 1828. He did not even pay the interest on the consolidated debt, as there was no money in the sinking fund. Another one of López Ballesteros's heterodox practices was to redeem debt via open-market operations, taking advantage of the fact that their quotes were lower than the nominal value. López Ballesteros's irregularities led Paris to close its stock exchange to Spanish debt. Therefore, as a last resort to finance the Treasury, the finance minister refloated the Bank of San Carlos (called the Bank of San Fernando from 1829) to cover government financial necessities (Comín and Vallejo 2002: 185–95; Tedde 1988, 1999). Such irregular debt operations explain the intriguing reduction of the public debt to 5,924 million reales in 1830.

In 1833, the liberals acknowledged the harmful inheritance of all of the former government debt, trying thereby to demonstrate their intentions toward responsibility in the management of the national debt. In 1834, the Count of Toreno carried out a rearrangement of the public debt and a consolidation of the arrears in the payments of the debt interest. After paying debt interests for one year, the government stopped paying them between 1836 and 1845 (Artola 1986: 165–70). The value of the debt bonds fell so much that the government could not issue them in the market. The Carlist War was financed with loans from bankers and from the Bank of San Carlos obtained at exorbitant prices. This, together with the accumulation of the accrued interest and treasury delays, increased the floating debt. In 1836, the liberals, through Juan Álvarez Mendizábal, also resorted to confiscating entailed properties, which allowed them to reduce the outstanding public debt from 10,644 to 5,691 million reales between 1834 and 1840. Nevertheless, the problem of the debt remained unresolved.

### 8.5.3 The Reforms of the Public Debt and Monetization of the Deficit

As deficits continued, the floating debt reached excessive proportions. Alejandro Mon carried out a consolidation of the floating debt in 1844 to free budget funds previously earmarked for the payment of the floating debt that had left the Treasury without funds for the rest of the public expenditure. Mon's consolidation extended the term of the debts, reduced the interest payments, and increased capital by 1,148 million reales over the 7,673 million reales of outstanding debt in December 1844. In this way, Mon compensated the reduction of the high yields of the government bills and of the advances of funds to the Treasury during the Carlist War. Mon also signed a Treasury contract with the Bank of San Fernando that made the financing of the Treasury cheaper. These measures allowed the state to raise the value of the expenditure and gave Mon some respite to start his comprehensive fiscal reforms (Comín and Vallejo 2002: 229–65).

In 1851, Bravo Murillo carried out a general rearrangement of the government debt, also acknowledging the arrears in the budget payments. Bravo Murillo reduced the large number of existing bonds to two types of debt – state and Treasury. On the one hand, the old debts were converted – with some reduction of capital – into nonredeemable state debt with an interest rate of 3 percent and into redeemable state debt without interest but reimbursable via monthly auctions. On the other hand, the personal and material arrears were consolidated in the Treasury's debt. The 1851 conversion reduced the public debt from 3,900 million pesetas (15,600 million reales) to 3,691 million pesetas. Murillo also reduced the financial burden for the budget by reducing the rates and by reducing the nominal and delaying payment of the interest on the differed debts. In exchange, he ensured payment of the interests and the write-offs. Those who speculated with foreign debt challenged the reform. As a result, the Paris Stock Exchange was again closed to Spanish securities trading (Comín and Vallejo 2002: 507–15).

The budget deficit continued and subsequently increased the public debt, especially in the progressive biennium and the democratic sexennium, when the finance ministers obtained external loans. Nevertheless, public debt grew more than the budget deficit because special debt bonds were issued to finance expenses that were nonaccountable in the ordinary budget, such as building roads, subsidizing railway companies, and compensating city halls for the forfeiture of their lands in 1855 (Comín 1988; 1996b: 158–65). The ratios of debt in relation to total tax receipts and to GDP were affected by the accumulation of budget deficit and by the constant rearrangements of public debt. In 1855, the government debt was 11.3 times greater than receipts and 0.6 times the GDP. In 1860, it was only 6.5 times greater than revenues, and from 1865, this ratio increased strongly until it reached 18.6 times the state revenues in 1879, standing at 1.7 times the GDP (Figure 8.7). This was a volume of outstanding debt difficult to sustain through the tax system. When the financial burden surpassed a certain level of the budget expenditure (30 percent or 40 percent), the finance ministers rearranged the debt to reduce its volume (see Figure 8.6). From 1866, the financial burden of the debt surpassed 30 percent of the expenditure, and once more reforms followed: in July 1867, García de Barzanallana carried out a conversion of the debt, but the volume of debt servicing in the budget continued to grow. Salaverría carried out another debt reform in 1876 that was also insufficient, and later Camacho carried out the 1881 debt conversion that reduced its burden on the budget from 37.6 percent to 27.3 percent in 1882. Likewise, in 1886, the volume of the outstanding debt was reduced to 7.7 times the tax receipts, totaling 0.7 times the GDP. Public debt and its burden in the budget would increase again because of the persistence of the budget deficit, especially during the war with Cuba (Figure 8.7). Between 1896 and 1899, the debt–tax receipts ratio rose from 9.1 to 10.8 and the debt–GDP ratio increased from 1 to 1.2. Fernández Villaverde's conversion of the debt in 1899 increased the debt–tax receipts ratio to 13. Later, the 1906 budget surpluses allowed a reduction of this ratio to 11.3.

Until 1895, the external debt surpassed 25 percent of the total public debt (Figure 8.8). With the closing of international stock exchanges to Spanish investments, foreign debt diminished from 40.2 percent to 18.1 percent between 1850 and 1867. In 1852, Bravo Murillo resorted to the Bank of San Fernando (in 1856, the name would be changed to the Bank of Spain) to replace external debt with domestic debt. However, in 1852, Governor Ramón de Santillán refused to give the Treasury loans, and Bravo Murillo's reaction was to create the Caja General de Depósitos (based on the French Caisse Générale de Dépôts) in 1853. In 1868 Figuerola resumed the issue of international loans once again. Accordingly, foreign debt grew again to 40.4 percent in 1873. When the budget deficit soared, the government also resorted to floating debt as it had in 1855 and especially in 1868 and 1869, when floating debt

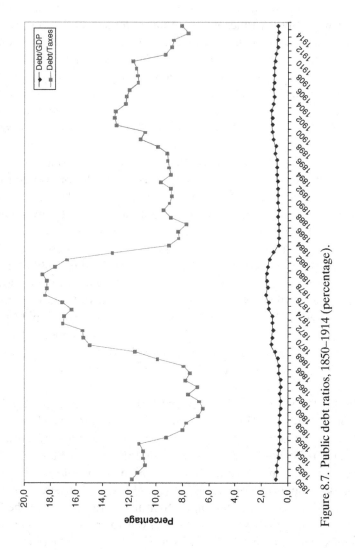

Figure 8.7. Public debt ratios, 1850–1914 (percentage).

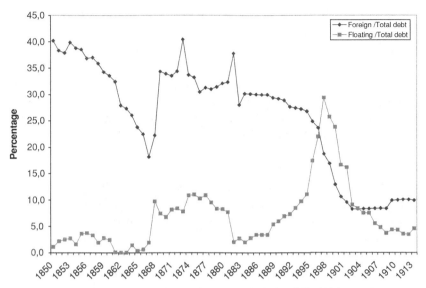

Figure 8.8. Structure of the public debt, 1850–1914.

reached 9.7 percent of the total. Camacho's debt rearrangement in 1881 reduced the percentage of foreign debt to 28 percent and that of floating debt to 2 percent. In his 1881 reform, Camacho, like Murillo before him, reduced the variety of former securities to two types of bonds: redeemable domestic debt to 4 percent after a term of forty years and nonredeemable debt, both national and foreign, to 4 percent. The majority of the converted bonds had 2 percent or 3 percent interest, and the increase in the interest rates was compensated for by the reduction of principal. Therefore, the total outstanding debt diminished, although it remained a heavy burden on the budget (32 percent in 1884). Camacho's debt rearrangement offered security to bondholders, who cashed in the coupons for their entire value, and to foreign holders, to whom payment was made in gold.

In 1874, the monopoly of issuing banknotes was bestowed to the Bank of Spain in exchange for a Treasury loan. From then on, finance ministers could fund the budget simply by printing money – in other words, by using inflation. This converged with the declaration of the inconvertibility of the peseta to gold in 1883, another contribution to the creation of a fiduciary monetary system. Spain abandoned the gold standard when most other countries were adopting it. The mechanism to finance the debt was its monetization: the Treasury asked the Bank of Spain for loans, and the bank responded by issuing banknotes and increasing the balance of the Treasury's current account. This ensuing increase of the country's monetary base generated inflation and currency depreciation. Despite not belonging to the gold standard, the ministers of finance did not generally abuse deficit monetization, apart from the years between 1895 and 1898. Many of those loans were orchestrated with floating debt. As we can see in Figure 8.8, floating debt grew from 3.3 percent to 11.1 percent of total government debt between 1888 and 1895, and in 1898, it had already risen to 29.3 percent. Financing the war with Cuba also increased the floating debt held by the Bank of Spain and, consequently, the monetary base and prices. Because there was no fresh issuing of bonds, the foreign debt fell to 18.7 percent in 1898.

Fernández Villaverde's tax reform solved the problems of the public debt temporarily. He wished to balance the government budget and to set up the gold standard in Spain. He wanted not to increase budget revenues but to curb debt servicing (that was almost half the public expenditure). To do that, Fernández Villaverde created a 20-percent tax on the interest paid by the state, which reduced the net interest of the debt by a fifth. Fernández Villaverde also carried out a conversion of the debt in his 1899–1900 reform, which had three phases: (1) consolidation of the Treasury debt in redeemable debt over fifty years; (2) conversion of the redeemable debt into nonredeemable debt; (3) and a decrease in the effective interest rate by establishing a 20-percent tax on the accrued interest by the national debt (considering the foreign nonstamped debt held by the Spanish also as national debt). This conversion increased the weight of the nonredeemable debt from 56 percent to 81 percent between 1898 and 1907. This increase in nominal interest rates compensated the holders for the suspension of the payoffs of the former redeemable debts and for the lengthening of the maturity of the bonds. This is reflected in the budget payments of the debt that initially grew from 43 percent to 46 percent between 1898 and 1903. This increase arose also from the fact that the state assumed the Cuban and Philippine debts between 1899 and 1902, and that the new bonds issued for the consolidation were made with appreciable premiums. However, they started to dwindle in 1903 (Figure 8.6), reaching 28 percent in 1914. In any case, the net weight of the debt diminished thanks to the 20-percent tax on the interest of the domestic debt. In exchange for these losses, Fernández Villaverde offered holders greater security in the collection of interest and in maintaining the bonds' actual value by stabilizing the prices. He also demanded that the Spanish holders of foreign debt declare their bonds through an affidavit to convert foreign debt into national debt. Hence, the Treasury would no longer pay them interest in gold but in pesetas, and they would also levy the new tax on them. This led to the fall of the foreign debt (to 8.2 percent in 1903). Finally, the 1899–1908 budget surpluses allowed the Treasury to redeem the bonds in the Bank of Spain portfolio, thereby reducing floating debt (to 9 percent of the total debt in 1903). In 1903, Fernández Villaverde, as prime minister, presented a bill to bring Spain onto the gold standard, but it did not pass the parliament, costing him the leadership of the Conservative Party (Comín 2006).

## 8.6  Liberal State and Economic Growth

The rate of growth of GDP per capita increased from 1.0 percent to 1.7 percent between the 1815–40 and the 1850–90 periods (Llopis 2002; Pascual and Sudrià 2002). In this chapter, I have tried to show the important role of the establishment of the liberal state in the great economic growth of the second half of the twentieth century while also highlighting the new tax policy. First, the 1845 tax system was more favorable to economic growth than the previous system for the following reasons:

* The taxes that were obstacles to economic growth disappeared, and by putting an end to domestic customs, the tithe, excise, and tillage, Mon eased the creation of a national market and reduced the production costs of companies.
* The tax burden was heavier on agriculture than on more dynamic sectors (industry and commerce).
* The tax burden borne by the peasants surpassed that of the landowners, which favored saving rates.
* By waiving corporate, capital, and labor taxes, the reform fiscally benefited the capitalist sector of the economy.
* As the taxes fell on average net yields, the most efficient businesspeople were favored.
* Customs tariffs were more favorable to growth from 1849 and, above all, in 1869.

Second, the liberal state used its public expenditure to favor economic growth. The liberals created the Ministry of Public Works (Ministerio de Fomento) precisely to spur investment in public works and education. In the expenditure, the accomplishments lagged behind the government's intentions to promote economic growth, and investment policy did not experience continuity because of the scarcity of the Finance Ministry's resources. Public investment was greater between 1856 and 1863, when the governments of the Liberal Union carried out an extraordinary public works program financed with debt issues. Moreover, the insufficient income even made it impossible to meet the functions of the liberal state adequately. Defense, law and order, and justice left much to be desired. Law and order had to be secured by the army, given the scarce funding allotted to the police and the civil guard (the *guardia civil* was created in 1844 to keep order in the countryside).

Traditionally, the 1845 tax system has been blamed for the insufficiency of government funds, which made it impossible to finance greater public expenditure. I have shown here that, on the contrary, the tax system that was installed in 1845 was not an obstacle at all for the growth of public expenditure. Nevertheless, the revenues could have increased had the tax law been correctly enforced, had a cadastre of agricultural wealth and tax records of industrial and commercial wealth been made, and had tax collection been carried out by civil servants of the Ministry of Finance. The voting taxpayers frustrated efficient tax management, and parliamentarians modified the Ministry of Finance's project, leaving loopholes in the legislation that allowed people to evade paying their taxes. Even so, from 1850, Spain had an expenditure-GDP ratio similar to that of other European countries. The problem was that a large proportion of expenditure was set aside for debt servicing, and that the large volume of debt made new issues to finance public works impossible. The subsidies to clergy also diverted some important funds away from the typical functions of the liberal state. Finally, expenditure decisions depended on patronage, which implied squandering resources. In short, the parliament opted for the inefficiency of budget management to guarantee the stability of the political system; and this occurred at the cost of economic growth.

The high volume of public debt reduced the possibilities of growth of the Spanish economy on two other fronts: it raised the price of financing private investment and it induced an unfavorable economic policy for industrialization. The debt defaults were costly for the Treasury because the Ministry of Finance could not resort to the issue of bonds in the stock exchange and, consequently, had to borrow from moneylenders, who demanded high interest and short payment schedules and, furthermore, earmarked the income of some taxes for debt repayment. The yield of the public debt was still higher than that obtained in lending money to industry and commerce, and therefore much capital was diverted to financing the state despite the greater risk of default. The crowding-out effect of the public debt on private investment worked until 1883, given the existence of a bimetallic monetary system, even in the phase of high foreign investment after 1855 (Comín 1988, 1996b). Before 1845, high budget deficits crowded out private investment, given the monetary deflation – caused by the export of currency to pay for the commercial deficit with Europe, the limited circulation of banknotes, and the absence of foreign investment. After 1845, direct impact of the budget deficit on private investment was low except in the progressive biennium, when the high budget deficit and the closure of international stock exchanges to Spanish securities worsened the conditions of private investment. Later, foreign investment and the issuing of foreign public debt during the democratic sexennium minimized the incidence of the crowding-out effect. When, in 1883, the budget deficit began to be financed with fiat money, the crowding-out effect was less prevalent. Moreover, the sizable state debt determined economic policies that favored landowners (disentailment, namely the confiscation and sale of entailed land), the Spanish banks, and foreign companies (banking, railroads, and mines). The frequent defaults made it impossible for the finance ministers to issue bonds in the stock exchange, given their depreciation. The ministers were forced to resort to international financiers and Spanish banks. The former demanded favorable regulation of railroads, banks, and mines against the interests of national industry (Nadal 1975). For their part, the Spanish banks – the Bank of Spain and the Mortgage Bank – obtained the monopolies over banknote and mortgage-bond issues in exchange for lending to the government (Tortella 1994). The monopolies allowed the government to be financed but slowed industrialization, as they hindered the generalization of agricultural credit and Spain's entrance to the gold standard.

## References

Artola, M. (1986) *La Hacienda del siglo XIX. Progresistas y moderados*. Madrid: Alianza.

Comín, F. (1988) *Hacienda y economía en la España contemporánea (1800–1936)*. Madrid: Instituto de Estudios Fiscales.

Comín, F. (1990) *Las cuentas de la Hacienda preliberal en España, (1801–1855)*. Madrid: Banco de España.

Comín, F. (1991) "Martín de Garay: una reforma tributaria posibilista," in *Actas de las II jornadas de historia del pensamiento económico español*. Zaragoza: Universidad de Zaragoza.

248     *Francisco Comín*

Comín, F. (1996a) *Historia del sector público, I. Europa*. Barcelona: Crítica.

Comín, F. (1996b) *Historia de la Hacienda pública, II. España (1808–1995)*. Barcelona: Crítica.

Comín, F. (1998), "Corrupción y fraude fiscal en la España contemporánea," en *Instituciones y corrupción en la Historia*, Valladolid, Instituto Universitario Simancas, 53–109.

Comín, F. (2000) "Canga Argüelles: un planteamiento realista de la Hacienda liberal," in E. Fuentes Quintana (ed.) *Economía y economistas españoles, La ilustración*, vol. 3. Barcelona: Galaxia Gutenberg and Círculo de Lectores, 413–39.

Comín, F. (2004) "La metamorfosis de la Hacienda (1808–1874)," in *Josep Fontana. Historia y proyecto social*, Barcelona: Crítica, 31–101.

Comín, F. (2006) "Contrebande et fraude fiscal dans l'Espagne du XIXe siècle," in G. Béaur, H. Bonin and C. Lemercier (eds.) *Fraude, contrefaçon et contrebande de l'Antiquité à nos jours*. Paris: Droz, 45–163.

Comín, F. et al. (1995) "La práctica fiscal en la España contemporánea." Unpublished paper, Instituto de Estudios Fiscales.

Comín, F., and Vallejo, R. (2002) *Alejandro Mon y Menéndez (1801–1882). Pensamiento y reforma de la Hacienda*. Madrid: Instituto de Estudios Fiscales.

Fernández de Pinedo, E. (1987) "Haciendas forales y revolución burguesa: las Haciendas vascas en la primera mitad del siglo XIX," *Hacienda Pública Española*, 108–9, 197–220.

Fontana, J. (1971) *La quiebra de la monarquía absoluta*. Barcelona: Ariel.

Fontana, J. (1973) *Hacienda y estado en la crisis final del antiguo régimen español, 1823–1833*. Madrid: Instituto de Estudios Fiscales.

Fontana, J. (1977) *La Revolución Liberal (Política y Hacienda, 1833–1845)*. Madrid: Instituto de Estudios Fiscales.

Fontana, J. and Garrabou, R. (1986) *Guerra y Hacienda: la Hacienda del gobierno central en los años de la Guerra de la Independencia*. Alicante: Instituto Juan Gil-Albert.

Fuentes Quintana, E. (1990) *Las reformas tributarias en España. Teoría, historia y propuestas*. Barcelona: Crítica.

García, C. (2006) "Manuel García Barzanallana: un conservador en la época del conservadurismo," in F. Comín, P. Martín Aceña and R. Vallejo (eds.) *La Hacienda por sus ministros. La etapa liberal de 1845 a 1899*. Zaragoza: Prensas Universitarias de Zaragoza, 263–97.

García, C. and Comín, F. (1995) "Reforma liberal, centralismo y Haciendas municipales en el siglo XIX," *Hacienda Pública Española*, 133, 81–106.

López Castellano, F. (1995) *Liberalismo económico y reforma fiscal. La contribución directa de 1813*. Granada: Universidad de Granada.

López Castellano, F. (1999) *El pensamiento hacendístico liberal en las Cortes de Cádiz*, Madrid: Instituto de Estudios Fiscales.

Llopis, E. (2002) "La crisis del Antiguo Régimen y la Revolución liberal (1790–1840)," in F. Comín, M. Hernández and E. Llopis. (eds.) *Historia económica de España, siglos X-XX*. Barcelona: Crítica, 165–202.

Macías, A. (1987) "Canarias, 1800–1870: Fiscalidad y revolución burguesa," *Hacienda Pública Española*, 108–9, 327–42.

Martorell, M. (2000) *El santo temor al déficit*. Madrid: Alianza.
Nadal, J. (1975) *El fracaso de la Revolución industrial en España, 1814–1913*. Barcelona: Ariel.
Pan-Montojo, J. L. (1994) "Lógica legal y lógica social de la contribución de consumos y los derechos de puertas," *Hacienda Pública Española*, 1, 217–30.
Pan-Montojo, J. L. (2006) "Pascual Madoz: perfil de un progresista isabelino," in F. Comín, P. Martín Aceña and R. Vallejo (eds.) *La Hacienda por sus ministros. La etapa liberal de 1845 a 1899*. Zaragoza: Prensas Universitarias de Zaragoza, 171–207.
Pro, J. (1995) "El poder de la tierra: una lectura social del fraude en la contribución de inmuebles, cultivo y ganadería (1845–1936)" *Hacienda Pública Española*, 1, 189–202.
Pro, J. (2006) "Bravo Murillo: el abogado en Hacienda," in F. Comín, P. Martín Aceña and R. Vallejo (eds.) *La Hacienda por sus ministros. La etapa liberal de 1845 a 1899*. Zaragoza: Prensas Universitarias de Zaragoza, 133–69.
Pro, J. (2007) "Inventario y extracción de los recursos: reclutamiento, recaudación y estadística en la construcción del Estado nacional," in J. Del Moral, J. Pro and F. Suárez (eds.) *Estado y territorio en España, 1820–1930*. Madrid: Catarata, 509–644.
Serrano Sanz, J. M. (1991) "La renta de aduanas en España (1849–1935)," *Hacienda Pública Española*, 1, 107–19.
Serrano Sanz, J. M. (2006) "Pedro Salaverría. Cara y cruz de la Hacienda," in F. Comín, P. Martín Aceña and R. Vallejo (eds.) *La Hacienda por sus ministros. La etapa liberal de 1845 a 1899*. Zaragoza: Prensas Universitarias de Zaragoza, 229–61.
Tedde, P. (1988) *El Banco de San Carlos*. Madrid: Alianza and Banco de España.
Tedde, P. (1999) *El Banco de San Fernando (1829–1856)*. Madrid: Alianza and Banco de España.
Tortella, G. (1994) *El desarrollo económico de la España contemporánea. Historia económica de los siglos XIX y XX*. Madrid: Alianza.
Tortella, G. and Comín, F. (2001) "Fiscal and monetary institutions in Spain (1600–1900)," in M. D. Bordo and R. Cortés Conde (eds.) *Transferring Wealth and Power from the Old to the New World: Monetary and Fiscal Institutions in the Seventeenth through the Nineteenth Centuries*. Cambridge: Cambridge University Press, 140–86.
Vallejo, R. (1996) "Reforma tributaria y regulación del delito fiscal en la España contemporánea (1830–1900)" *Hacienda Pública Española*, 1, 135–50.
Vallejo, R. (2001) *Reforma tributaria y fiscalidad sobre la agricultura en la España liberal, 1845–1900*. Zaragoza: Prensas Universitarias de Zaragoza.
Vallejo, R. (2006) "Alejandro Mon, un reformador económico," in F. Comín, P. Martín Aceña and R. Vallejo (eds.) *La Hacienda por sus ministros. La etapa liberal de 1845 a 1899*. Zaragoza: Prensas Universitarias de Zaragoza, 57–90.
Vallejo, R. and Muñoz, M. D. (2008) "Fiscalidad y agricultura en la España contemporánea," in R. Vallejo (ed.) *Los tributos de la tierra. Fiscalidad y*

*agricultura en España (siglos XII-XX)*. Valencia: Publicaciones de la Universidad de Valencia, 413–46.

Zafra, J. (1994) "Algunas vertientes del fraude fiscal en la primera mitad del siglo XIX," *Hacienda Pública Española*, 1, 145–53.

Zafra, J. (1996) "Inercias fiscales en la reforma tributaria de 1845," *Hacienda Pública Española*, 1, 23–37.

# 9

# Public Finance in Portugal, 1796–1910

## José Luís Cardoso and Pedro Lains

## 9.1 Introduction

In the beginning of the nineteenth century, Portugal was an economically 'backward' country with a relatively weak state in the context of Western Europe. The turmoil provoked by the wars with France since 1796 and the three Napoleonic invasions between 1807 and 1811 affected, to a considerable extent, the performance of its economy and the functioning of its state. The 1820 liberal revolution and, two years later, the political independence of Brazil, Portugal's main colony, made the situation even more difficult. Such difficulties were largely overcome in the following century, in which important economic, political, and institutional changes occurred. One such important transformation was the development of its own liberal state. This chapter discusses how this transformation occurred and, crucially, how it was financed by taxing the economy and raising debt.

The challenges of transformation were indeed immense. Most important, it was necessary to pacify the country, which remained severely affected by the wars and the invasions. The defeat of the absolutists by the liberals in the 1832–4 civil war was a major step toward pacification. Even if military confrontation did not end totally then, it became essentially political in the next decades. In a first stage, the political confrontation was intense, as it revolved around the constitutional format of the new liberal regime: one defined by the moderate Constitution Charter of 1826 and the other by the radical Constitution of 1838. A military coup in 1851 imposed the Charter of 1826, which, after being revised in 1852, paved the way for a period of greater political consensus. Political disputes proceeded, but the constitution gained wide acceptance and the new quarrels were confined to political debates in the parliament. The press and public opinion also had a considerable role in those disputes. However, the period was marked by the alternation in power between two opposing parties (not necessarily the same throughout the years) and by some interventions by the monarch.

Such changes implied an increase in the role of the state and, of course, an increase in its size and structure, and these had to be funded. Economic growth, achieved through industrialization and the development of agriculture and services, provided the means to raise funds. Although Portugal remained one of the least developed countries in Western Europe, its economy expanded to a considerable extent. Moreover, its expansion was accompanied by the growth of trade with Europe and the rest of the world. The increase in domestic output paved the way for the increase of indirect taxation, whereas the growth of trade with foreign nations allowed for a substantial increase in revenues obtained through tariffs. The concession of monopolies, such as the issue of banknotes and tobacco, was a further source of revenue for the state. Economic growth also led to more domestic savings, in both relative and absolute terms, and that was yet another source of state financing. Capital imports, in contrast, made external funding of the public debt possible. Finally, the growth of exports, trade with Africa, and emigration became important sources of foreign exchange revenue, insomuch as they ensured that the country had at least some ability to pay for the increasing foreign debt. Portugal became a parliamentary monarchy with political disputes between parties and a free press. The degree of openness of society was far from satisfactory, and there are many stories of corruption, censorship, and nondemocratic elections with respect to this period. Nevertheless, the need to increase the size of the state had to be justified by those in power as a dire necessity to a demanding public.[1]

This chapter discusses the actions taken by the successive Portuguese governments to finance state institutions and to explain such necessities to the public. Mirroring what happened elsewhere in poor regions of Europe, these two tasks were particularly difficult in Portugal. In fact, because of its incipiency, the mechanisms to tax the economy were not efficient enough in the sense that the tax structure did not follow closely the expansion of the economy. This meant that successive, unpopular

---

[1] For Portugal's nineteenth-century political history, see Almeida (1991); Ramos (2001); Sardica (2001); Valente (2005); Bonifácio (2007). See also Lains and Silva (2005), vol. 2.

reforms had to be implemented, and they were increasingly difficult to explain. The alternative to inefficient taxation was state borrowing, which also endangered the sustainability of the domestic financial system. The difficulties of taxing the economy as it expanded were arguably the main source of problems and the key difference between Portugal and its wealthiest neighbors. The state was unable to build solid links with the population and remained unpopular to the end of the nineteenth century. In 1910, another revolution put an end to the period of constitutional monarchy, with the republican revolutionaries claiming and justifying their actions by the state's corruption. Financial stability had to wait for two more decades in the shape of António de Oliveira Salazar's dictatorship, which was imposed two years after yet another military coup in 1926.[2]

## 9.2 The Financial Impact of Wars and Regime Change, 1796–1834

There are enough grounds to argue that the Portuguese economy went through a favorable period during most of the second half of the eighteenth century (Pedreira 2005; Serrão 2005). Population rose steadily; agricultural output expanded; new industries were founded; exports increased; and imports of industrial raw materials, such as iron and raw cotton, were on the rise. In addition, the structure of the state, guided by the willful prime minister of King José, the Marquis of Pombal, was consolidated, centralized, and with increasing revenues. However, output growth expanded only slightly more than population growth, and productivity gains were certainly less than those elsewhere in Northern Europe, particularly England. There is some dispute among Portuguese historians of this period about whether this relatively favorable economic and political context died out after Pombal left office, following the death of the monarch, or whether it continued until the end of the century. It is nevertheless clear that Portugal enjoyed commercial prosperity throughout the last three decades of the eighteenth century because of the sustainable growth of colonial trade fostered by the increase of both the export of Portuguese manufactured goods to Brazil and the reexport of Brazilian raw materials and foodstuffs to European markets (Pedreira 2000).

---

[2] The redress of the Portuguese financial system should not be linked too much to Salazar, however. In fact, some stabilization of the currency and the balance of payments had already been reached in 1924 and was affected by the 1926 coup and the revolutionary period that followed until Salazar was designated as finance minister. See Lains (2003).

These relatively prosperous settings were soon to be reversed as a result of Portugal's involvement in the French wars. Between 1793 and 1795, Portugal joined Spain in the war against France and sent an army to fight in Catalonia. To finance the Portuguese military participation and the resulting compensations, the prince regent João issued the first public loan in 1796, with a second one following in 1801 (Silveira 1987: 512; Thomaz 1988; Cardoso 1989: 151–75; Costa 1992: 46–74). For the first time in Portuguese history, the loan of 1796 was linked to bond securities (*apólices*) or endorsable public debt rather than perpetuities (*padrões de juro*), whose sale required registration through a public deed (Macedo, Silva, and Sousa 2001: 210). In other words, the first loan inaugurated the circulation of paper money. The Portuguese treasury was replicating what had been done earlier in Britain and France and introducing a financial innovation to the market. Yet this innovation proved a risky one (Neal 2004). In fact, as the increase in taxation that would allow repayment of the loan failed to materialize, the bond securities devaluated rapidly in the following years. As a result, the public debt increased substantially. According to one estimate, in 1798 the total debt amounted to 78 percent of total state revenues and was greater still in 1799. This contrasted markedly with past experience, as during the years for which there is complete data, that is, 1762–76, debt was virtually inexistent (Costa 1992: 26). The new public debt operations were executed without taking the essential step of guaranteeing the trust of private lenders and maintaining the credibility of the state. There was pressure to increase the velocity of circulation of money to increase and facilitate commercial transactions and state payments. Nevertheless, the solution of transforming the debt securities into paper money proved inefficient, as fiduciary money was issued without any control and circulated undervalued without any guarantees of either amortization or payment of the legal interest rate.

In 1801, Rodrigo de Souza Coutinho, formerly minister of the navy and overseas, was designated minister of finance and president of the Royal Treasury, an office he left in 1803. Souza Coutinho can be associated with a coherent program for the financial organization of the state.[3] A keen and attentive reader of Adam Smith, Souza Coutinho anticipated some of the measures required for dismantling the financial

---

[3] The main economic and financial writings of Souza Coutinho are published in Coutinho (1993: vol. 2, 215–47).

system of the ancien régime, but above all, he managed to outline the basic principles for the functioning of a modern fiscal state. To reduce the public deficit, he proposed the privatization of state manufactures, the abolition of monopoly contracts and the sale of some of the estates belonging to the Crown and religious orders, and the reduction of part of the Crown's superfluous expenditure. Under his ministry, annual budgets, or preventive balance sheets, were computed to assess the state of the royal rents, the additional financing needs, and the superfluity of some public expenses. Between 1797 and 1803, revenues collected by the state increased from about 6.5 contos to about 10 contos.[4] But the times were too unstable, and his reforms were not accomplished, as the task was too difficult. Ultimately, increasing the revenue and improving the allocation of expenditure depended on the control of the circulation of paper money, and this objective he was unable to fulfill during his short tenure (Godinho 1955; Silveira 1987). In 1801, Portugal was invaded by Spain, which had made peace with France in 1795. As Portugal did not fully comply with the Continental blockade, France invaded in 1807, and the court had to flee to Brazil, where it settled for the following fourteen years. Further invasions occurred in 1808 and 1811 (Macedo 1962).

Figures 9.1 and 9.2 show the extent of the financial strains wrought by that period of war. Government deficit rose from 12.6 percent of revenue in 1800 to 32 percent in 1801, and declined to 6 percent in the following year. In 1812, the following year for which there are published data, including the first estimate of the total public debt, the accounts closed positive, but public debt had climbed to the equivalent of 4.3 years of government revenue. In 1817, the following year for which there is information, revenues, expenditures, and the deficit were all greater than they had been five years before, even if total debt in terms of revenue declined.

The political scene remained highly unstable. The king and his court remained in Brazil, and Beresford was ruling in Lisbon as commander in chief of the Portuguese army. In 1820, the army in Porto started a revolution that would lead to a liberal constitution in 1822. The revolution and the political and military disorder that ensued had an even greater impact. The 1820 revolution affected both revenues and expenditures, which declined by 35 percent between 1817 and 1821, the years

---

[4] The data is not strictly comparable over time, as the definition of revenues varied and in some years included loans. See Costa (1992: 26–7).

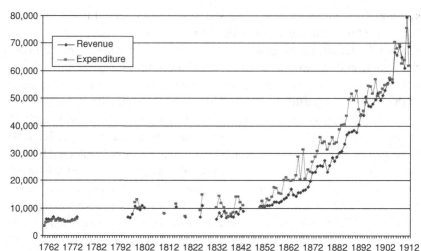

Figure 9.1. Government revenue and expenditure, 1762–1914 (in current contos). *Source:* Appendix Table 9.1.

for which there are data. In the following decade, expenditure increased more quickly than did revenue, as did the deficit, which reached 35 percent of total revenues in 1827 and 1828. New sources of revenue were developed. Among the most important of these was borrowing from the

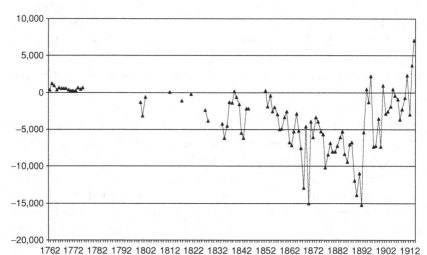

Figure 9.2. Public deficit/surplus, 1762–1914 (in current contos). *Source:* Appendix Table 9.1.

Banco de Lisboa, the first Portuguese joint-stock bank, founded in 1821. The bank's main task was to raise capital to lend to the government and to redeem the paper money still in circulation. In return, the bank collected specific taxes and government funds, and it held the monopoly to issue notes in Lisbon (Reis 1996). The government also gained control over revenues controlled by the church and the nobility, namely revenues from taxes on land and agricultural output. Such revenues would complement those that were already collected by the state, namely tariffs on foreign trade and taxes on domestic trade and other transactions, such as sales tax (*sisa*) and stamp duty (*imposto de selo*). The transfer of taxation from ancien régime collectors to the state proved crucial for the consolidation of the liberal regime and stood at the heart of political debate. Even so, this transfer was more important in political than in fiscal terms. In other words, the major challenge facing the nascent liberal state was to find new forms of taxation and a corresponding institutional framework rather than to gain control of the old taxation.

The structure of taxation for the years for which there is complete published data is depicted in Table 9.1.[5] Throughout the years represented, taxes collected by the Treasury accounted for a growing share of total state revenue, peaking at 88.1 percent in 1827. Among these, customs revenues remained the most important, accounting for more than 40 percent of total revenue. The share of direct and indirect taxes increased, whereas the share of revenues from the crown land declined from 33.7 percent in 1800 to 11.9 percent in 1827. The amount collected by the state both through the Treasury and other forms of taxation steeply declined in these three decades, and the decline was more pronounced in the case of state revenue, which in 1827 accounted for just 22 percent of total collected in 1800. This decline had a significant impact on the balance of the state budget and on the public debt. But more troubled times would come with the civil war that was to break out in 1832 and lasted until 1834. The war ultimately led to the victory of the liberals against the absolutists, who fought for a return to the old regime. The liberal victory was decisive in military terms, but political struggles soon emerged among the victors. The following years were far from peaceful in political terms, and this instability compounded with the costs of the war made them financially troubled ones.

---

[5] Costa (1992: 20–1) also published the average structure of revenues for 1797–1803. The two largest items are customs (43.1 percent of total revenues) and tobacco (11.7 percent).

Table 9.1. *The Structure of Taxation from 1800 to 1827*

| Contos | 1800 | 1801 | 1802 | 1812 | 1817 | 1821 | 1827 |
|---|---|---|---|---|---|---|---|
| Taxes collected by the Treasury | 7,044 | 7,070 | 7,396 | 6,936 | 8,694 | 5,909 | 5,815 |
| Direct taxes | 1,465 | 1,629 | 1,432 | 2,034 | 3,076 | 1,562 | 1,508 |
| Customs | 4,698 | 4,545 | 4,738 | 3,717 | 4,249 | 2,892 | 2,901 |
| Other indirect taxes | 881 | 896 | 1,226 | 1,185 | 1,369 | 1,455 | 1,406 |
| Revenues from state property | 3,583 | 2,789 | 2,115 | 1,185 | 1,742 | 911 | 785 |
| Total revenue | 10,627 | 9,859 | 9,511 | 8,121 | 10,436 | 6,820 | 6,600 |
| Percentage | 1800 | 1801 | 1802 | 1812 | 1817 | 1821 | 1827 |
| Taxes collected by the Treasury | 66.3 | 71.7 | 77.8 | 85.4 | 83.3 | 86.6 | 88.1 |
| Direct taxes | 13.8 | 16.5 | 15.1 | 25.0 | 29.5 | 22.9 | 22.8 |
| Customs | 44.2 | 46.1 | 49.8 | 45.8 | 40.7 | 42.4 | 44.0 |
| Other indirect taxes | 8.3 | 9.1 | 12.9 | 14.6 | 13.1 | 21.3 | 21.3 |
| Revenues from state property | 33.7 | 28.3 | 22.2 | 14.6 | 16.7 | 13.4 | 11.9 |
| Total revenue | 100 | 100 | 100 | 100 | 100 | 100 | 100 |

*Sources:* Silveira (1987: 527–8); see also Silveira (1987: 513–15).

## 9.3 The Financial Impact of Liberalism, 1834–51

The end of the civil war in 1834 did not put an end to political instability, and a new phase of unsteadiness ensued that created a difficult
political environment for economic and financial reforms. The financial
troubles provoked by the civil war lasted throughout the whole period
from 1834 to 1851. The evolution of government accounts is shown in
Figures 9.1 and 9.2 (see also Table 9.7). In 1834–6, revenues were just
about 70 percent of expenditure. The deficit declined substantially in
the following years, and there was even a small surplus in 1839, though
heavy deficits were to return soon after. These were tapped by a substantial increase in public borrowing. In 1852, public debt was the equivalent of 8.5 years of that year's revenue (see Figure 9.3). The roots of the
imbalances are shown in the breakdown of the state income in Table 9.2.
Customs revenues virtually stagnated in the period from 1834 to 1845,
their share in total fiscal revenues steeply declining from 67.8 percent to
38.7 percent. The effects of this decline were attenuated by significant
increases in other revenues, as direct taxes trebled and property taxes

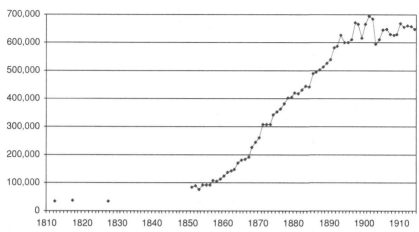

Figure 9.3. Public debt, 1812–1914 (in current contos). *Source*: Appendix Table 9.1.

doubled. These changes in the structure of receipts hint at the effects of the liberal reforms.[6]

Several attempts were made to introduce fiscal reform during the course of the century. Some of the most significant were designed by Mouzinho da Silveira, during the period that the government was in exile in the Azores before the outbreak of the civil war of 1832–4. Silveira proposed an extensive series of legislative measures aiming to dismantle the ancien régime's property system, including the abolition of the *forais* (town charters) and *morgadios* (entails) and its tax system, particularly the abolition of the tithes and personal duties. These reforms were designed as a means of counteracting the role and power of both the church and the seignorial landowners. However, they were never fully implemented, and this led to a sense of political failure among contemporaries, a sense that ultimately has been reflected in many historical analyses. After 1834, Silva Carvalho's government introduced another reform that has since been seen as yet another failure: the sale of a large part of the church property previously taken over by the state (the *bens nacionais*), which had been designed to raise substantial revenues for the state and to introduce major changes in the distribution of property. Neither of the expectations was, however, entirely fulfilled. The list of failed reforms during the first half of the nineteenth century is long. We should

---

[6] See Mata (1993) and Esteves (2005).

Table 9.2. *The Structure of Taxation, 1834–1845*

| Contos | 1834 | 1835 | 1836 | 1837 | 1838 | 1839 | 1840 | 1841 | 1842 | 1843 | 1844 | 1845 |
|---|---|---|---|---|---|---|---|---|---|---|---|---|
| Direct taxes | 205 | 540 | 636 | 856 | 877 | 1,020 | 1,298 | 805 | 1,571 | 1,327 | 1,166 | 1,457 |
| Customs | 2,079 | 3,600 | 3,821 | 3,534 | 3,514 | 3,898 | 3,667 | 2,755 | 2,752 | 2,943 | 3,334 | 3,094 |
| Property taxes | 773 | 1,535 | 1,821 | 1,314 | 1,414 | 1,390 | 1,514 | 2,451 | 2,533 | 2,584 | 3,087 | 3,191 |
| Sales tax (*sisa*) | 8 | 217 | 279 | 211 | 178 | 194 | 189 | 206 | 137 | 11 | 300 | 247 |
| Total revenue | 3,065 | 5,892 | 6,557 | 5,915 | 5,983 | 6,502 | 6,668 | 6,217 | 6,993 | 6,865 | 7,887 | 7,989 |
| *Percentage* | 1834 | 1835 | 1836 | 1837 | 1838 | 1839 | 1840 | 1841 | 1842 | 1843 | 1844 | 1845 |
| Direct taxes | 6.7 | 9.2 | 9.7 | 14.5 | 14.7 | 15.7 | 19.5 | 12.9 | 22.5 | 19.3 | 14.8 | 18.2 |
| Customs | 67.8 | 61.1 | 58.3 | 59.7 | 58.7 | 60.0 | 55.0 | 44.3 | 39.4 | 42.9 | 42.3 | 38.7 |
| Property taxes | 25.2 | 26.1 | 27.8 | 22.2 | 23.6 | 21.4 | 22.7 | 39.4 | 36.2 | 37.6 | 39.1 | 39.9 |
| Sales tax (*sisa*) | 0.3 | 3.7 | 4.3 | 3.6 | 3.00 | 3.0 | 2.8 | 3.3 | 2.0 | 0.2 | 3.8 | 3.1 |
| Total revenue | 100 | 100 | 100 | 100 | 100 | 100 | 100 | 100 | 100 | 100 | 100 | 100 |

*Source:* Mata and Valério (2001: 141).

also mention the reforms implemented by the dictatorial governments of Costa Cabral in the early 1840s. These reforms consisted of both the creation of a new circulation tax, known as the road tax (*imposto de estradas*), and the transformation of the direct *décima* tax (on transactions) into three separate (though complementary) taxes, namely the tax on property (*contribuição predial*), the tax on production (*contribuição industrial*), and the personal income tax (*contribuição pessoal*). However, these reforms had only a very short life, as they gave rise to considerable political turmoil, provoked by popular revolts and the general discontent of taxpayers, namely the revolt of Maria da Fonte, followed by the Patuleia civil war in 1846–7 (Hespanha 2004; Bastien 2005).

This difficult path of reforms was followed by returns to the status quo, which illustrates the complex dilemmas associated with the construction of a modern liberal state in Portugal. The challenges of state building were probably greater in the case of Portugal. Indeed, in many instances, the central government had to be built almost from scratch and could not be introduced simply by replacing existing local institutions. It is therefore worth stressing the endeavor to bring institutional reform to the forefront of the political agenda. The list of new institutions included local government agencies; a military structure with the capacity to intervene throughout the territory; a financial system; a currency; an educational system; institutions capable of building and maintaining roads, ports, railways, and urban utilities; a legislation that enforced property rights; and, on top of all this, a political system that enjoyed a significant level of legitimacy. Moreover, the Portuguese government also had to run an empire, most of which was located in the poorest regions of Africa.

## 9.4 Financing the Liberal State, 1851–1910

The development of the Portuguese economy gained momentum after 1851 and in the years leading up to 1910. Albeit slower than elsewhere in Europe, growth and structural changes proceeded at a sustained and uninterrupted pace. The manufacturing sector expanded steadily with considerable productivity gains, and the emergence or consolidation of new industries and the agricultural sector greatly contributed to structural change. Foreign trade as a share of domestic output also increased significantly and expanded to new regions of the world. Most of the transformations stemmed from the private sector, as the state owned only a small share of the economy, as was the case elsewhere in Europe at the time. Nevertheless, the Portuguese state made relevant contributions to the transformation of the economy. In fact, part of the economic growth was due to public investments in infrastructure, such as roads, railways, ports, utilities, communications, schools, and other social institutions. Portugal maintained its status of backwardnessin Western Europe but, on account of that status, the depth of the changes that occurred have not been recognized sufficiently in earlier writings on Portuguese and international economic history (Reis 1993; Lains 1999, 2003; Mata 1998). Portugal's low level of development was visible in the lack of infrastructure. The only decent road in the 1850s was the one that linked the two main cities, Lisbon and Porto, leaving the rest of the country nearly isolated. There were no canals worthy of mention, and the only large port was in Lisbon, which made it cumbersome for merchants to travel and to trade by sea. The level of illiteracy in midcentury was close to 90 percent, as there were few private schools and no state school system. As much as a third of the usable land was not used. The financial sector was also little developed, and the use and circulation of money was limited. These conditions hindered the growth of investments in the manufacturing and the agricultural sectors. Transforming this situation was a tall order, and this must be acknowledged in any evaluation of the conduct and achievements of the governments.

Governments before 1851 also aimed to reform the country's institutions, and some relevant reforms were achieved, not the least that a constitutional parliamentary monarchy was implemented. However, post-1851 changes were certainly more important, particularly in the legislative framework concerning the domestic economy and Portugal's involvement in the international economy. Public debt, which had increased steeply in the previous decades, was consolidated in 1852, leading to a reduction of its cost, albeit at the expenses of Portugal's ability to borrow in the international financial markets during the following few years. In the same year, the tariff schedule was revised, inaugurating a period of moderate and slightly more organized protectionism. In 1854, Portugal joined the gold standard. This restored the country's credibility in the London and Paris bond markets and enabled the government to negotiate the first international loan of the period in 1856. The reduction of tariff protection was further helped by the 1860 commercial treaty signed between Portugal and France, which was followed by similar treaties with a few other European countries.

Other reforms were accomplished during the two decades after 1851. Among those are the centralization and regulation of government accounts, in 1859 and 1863; the suppression of entails, in 1860 and 1863; the founding of the public mortgage bank Crédito Predial Português, in 1863; the founding of Banco Nacional Ultramarino in 1864, the future issue bank for the colonies; the regulation of relations with the Banco de Portugal, in 1864; and the publication of the new civil and administrative codes, in 1867. The main changes concerning taxation were the reestablishment of the tax on property (*contribuição predial*) in 1852 and the tax on production (*contribuição industrial*) in 1860, both of which were maintained until the 1880s as the main and most effective sources of direct taxation. In 1860, a new direct tax was created, the tax on the tenth part of interest (*contribuição da décima dos juros*), while various indirect and transaction taxes were either reformed or introduced.

The new set of laws and institutions brought by the so-called *regeneração* was certainly relevant for the future development of the economy, though it is not easy to measure their true contribution, and many would argue that they came too late. Further difficulties still loomed ahead, particularly in the sphere of tax reform and public finances. In 1868, the government proposed legislation to raise land taxes by increasing the official valuation of property in the fiscal census. The proposal led to public uproar and disturbances on the streets across the country against the new assessment. Despite the fact that it was a coalition government, the ministry was unable to pass the legislation and fell in the following year (Pinheiro 1983). After two years of political instability, another military coup reestablished the constitutional order in 1870. The heated public discussion that took place in the parliament between parties that alternated between government and opposition clearly reveals the tensions from the changes taking place in such a sensitive political area as that of demanding greater contributions from taxpayers. Further proof of the difficulties encountered in challenging and changing the tax structure is illustrated by the failure to implement a modern system of direct taxation, especially with the example of the introduction in 1880 of the income tax, from which the higher-income classes secured exemption by parliamentary approval only two years later (Esteves 2003; Mata 2005).

In the following year, the two main political parties alternated in power in a relatively peaceful fashion. A constitutional reform in 1885 transformed the Senate into an elective chamber, and some progress was made toward the introduction of male universal suffrage (Ramos 2001; Mónica 1996). This phase of relative political appeasement lasted until 1890, when political instability returned once again, this time as a consequence of a British ultimatum, motivated by colonial disputes in Africa. The 1890 ultimatum was followed in 1891 by a financial crisis, related to the crisis of the Baring brothers, Portugal's banker in London, and the fall of remittances as a result of the instability in Brazil during 1888 and 1889. As a consequence, Portugal had to leave the gold standard in 1891 and suspend temporarily the service of the debt, internal and external, the following year (Reis 2000). The overcoming of this financial crisis implied a change in the way the country was governed, with reduced dependence on foreign capital imports and greater fiscal discipline. Despite the new financial environment, the Portuguese economy continued to follow its pattern of slow growth, although this time it was driven by the industrial sector, which had gained fresh momentum under the even greater levels of protection afforded by customs tariffs and exchange-rate depreciation (Lains 2003; Figueiredo, Ferro, and Esteves 2004).

### 9.4.1. Public Revenue

As Figure 9.1 shows, the revenue collected by the Portuguese government increased steadily in the decades after 1851. In spite of all the difficulties in reforming the tax regime, taxation increased faster than gross domestic product did. In 1851–9, the Portuguese government managed to collect taxes equivalent to 3.5 percent of GDP, and this rate increased steadily to 5.5 percent in 1900–13, implying an increase of more than half. Still, when compared to Spain, Italy, France, or Britain, Portugal had low levels of taxation (see Table 9.3). This means that, despite the perceptible effort that had been made since the 1850s, from the outset, Portugal's very low levels of taxation did not to catch up with those of other European countries. The growth of taxation was followed by relevant, though not radical, changes in the structure of the taxes collected, as shown in Table 9.4. Although in 1851–2 tariffs on imports stood for as much as 44.7 percent of taxation, in 1910–11 that share had declined to 30.7 percent. The drop in tariffs was compensated for by the new income tax, imposed in 1880, from which the government collected 11.9 percent of total revenue in 1910–11. The remaining items in Table 9.4 did not change significantly. In 1851–2, the tax on transactions (the *décima*) accounted for 18.3 percent of total tax revenue. In the 1880s the *décima* was replaced by three different taxes, which in 1910–11 amounted to 22.6 percent of total revenue.

The persistently large share of customs duties reveals the archaic nature of the Portuguese tax structure. The structure allowed for the

Table 9.3 *Portugal's Fiscal Revolution in Comparison*

|  | Portugal | Spain | Italy | France | United Kingdom |
|---|---|---|---|---|---|
| | Fiscal revenue (percentage of GDP) | | | | |
| 1851–9 | 3.5 | 7.8 | | 8.4 | 9.4 |
| 1860–9 | 3.6 | 10.6 | 7.9 | 8.4 | 7.5 |
| 1870–9 | 4.0 | 9.5 | 10.6 | 9.8 | 6.3 |
| 1880–9 | 4.4 | 8.6 | 13.3 | 13.1 | 7.0 |
| 1890–9 | 4.9 | 8.9 | 13.7 | 11.8 | 7.3 |
| 1900–13 | 5.5 | 9.3 | 11.8 | 10.8 | 8.2 |
| | Government deficit (percentage of GDP) | | | | |
| 1851–9 | 0.8 | 0.6 | | 2.2 | 0.7 |
| 1860–9 | 1.5 | 2.3 | 5.0 | 1.2 | 0.1 |
| 1870–9 | 1.2 | 1.8 | 1.4 | 2.4 | 0.0 |
| 1880–9 | 1.1 | 0.5 | 1.1 | 0.0 | −0.1 |
| 1890–9 | 0.7 | −0.1 | 0.5 | −0.1 | −0.1 |
| 1900–13 | 0.1 | −0.2 | 0.8 | 0.0 | 0.3 |
| | Debt payments (percentage of revenue) | | | | |
| 1880–9 | 60.1 | 34.4 | 38.8 | 27.5 | 32.0 |
| 1890–9 | 46.6 | 42.4 | 39.0 | 27.0 | 22.7 |
| 1900–13 | 43.3 | 38.7 | 29.7 | 21.1 | 14.3 |

*Source:* Esteves (2005: 325).

Table 9.4 *The Structure of Taxation, 1851–1911*

|  | 1851–2 | | 1890–1 | | 1910–11 | |
|---|---|---|---|---|---|---|
|  | Contos | Percentage | Contos | Percentage | Contos | Percentage |
| Tariffs on foreign trade | 4,195 | 44.7 | 14,004 | 41.6 | 15,315 | 30.7 |
| Tobacco | 1,290 | 13.8 | 2,829 | 8.4 | 6,552 | 13.1 |
| Stamp duty | 273 | 2.9 | 1,827 | 5.4 | 3,659 | 7.3 |
| Tax on transactions[a] | 1,712 | 18.3 | – | – | – | – |
| Tax on property[b] | – | – | 3,052 | 9.1 | 3,294 | 6.6 |
| Tax on production[c] | – | – | 1,303 | 3.9 | 2,068 | 4.1 |
| Income tax | – | – | 428 | 1.3 | 5,928 | 11.9 |
| Other | 1,910 | 20.4 | 10,040 | 29.8 | 13,046 | 26.2 |
| Total | 9,380 | 100.0 | 33,642 | 100.0 | 49,862 | 100.0 |

[a] *Décima.*
[b] *Contribuição predial.*
[c] *Contribuição industrial.*
*Note:* Years ending in June.
*Source:* Valério et al. (2006: app. 2).

introduction of certain changes but, in times of economic and financial hardship, could use various intricate subterfuges to obtain extraordinary revenue or could resort to tried and trusted mechanisms of revenue. The case of the revenue gained from the *contrato dos tabacos* (tobacco contract) clearly illustrates the way in which the liberal state subjected the doctrinal principles of free competition to the realistic pragmatism of simultaneously satisfying public and private interests. Until 1865, a system of concession contracts under a monopoly regime was in place, with the state securing a stable annual income. Between 1865 and 1888, the contract system was revoked and a free regime was established, in which state revenue was collected through customs duties on tobacco. In a regie was established, with the state once again guaranteeing a safe and steady income without losing control of the monopoly. However, when the financial crisis of 1891 broke out, the pre-1865 concession system was reinstated after a hotly disputed process of decision making, which had to attend to the repercussions of the delicate balancing act between public virtues and private vices (Lains 2008).

The importance of customs duties in the structure of tax revenue is also symptomatic of the difficulties encountered by the liberal regime. This regime had emerged in 1820 under the auspices of the powerful economic protectionism, which had been motivated by the sharp fall in customs revenue in the first two decades of the century. Meanwhile, the regime became more liberal by adhering to the principles of free trade, as clearly illustrated by the public discussion and the contents of the customs tariff of 1852. Yet successive adjustments culminated in the publication in 1892 of a new, far more protectionist customs tariff, under the pretext that the economic fabric could provide an urgent and effective response to the financial and banking crisis that had befallen the country.

In short, the fiscal system's capacity for reform and modernization was greatly affected by the rigidity and deeply ingrained nature of more comfortable and expeditious rent-seeking practices. In fact, because it was essential to find the resources to meet the increase in public expenditure, the most common solution by far was to raise internal and external loans rather than to call for a sustained increase in tax revenue. Both debt creation and taxation had political implications that could harm the state's image in the eyes of citizens, who were both creditors and taxpayers. Still, debt was almost always the response, as it the one that involved the fewest short-term political risks.

Table 9.5 *The Structure of Expenditures, 1851–1911*

| | 1851–9 | | 1890–9 | | 1910–11 | |
|---|---|---|---|---|---|---|
| | Contos | Percentage | Contos | Percentage | Contos | Percentage |
| Debt servicing | 2,783 | 20.5 | 19,900 | 40.2 | 25,439 | 38.5 |
| Ordinary, nonmilitary | 4,629 | 34.1 | 8,811 | 17.8 | 11,233 | 17 |
| Military | 4,263 | 31.4 | 9,059 | 18.3 | 13,149 | 19.9 |
| Colonies | 0 | 0 | 2,426 | 4.9 | 3,039 | 4.6 |
| Economy | 1,249 | 9.2 | 7,673 | 15.5 | 9,317 | 14.1 |
| Education | 502 | 3.7 | 1,139 | 2.3 | 2,907 | 4.4 |
| Assistance | 149 | 1.1 | 495 | 1 | 991 | 1.5 |
| Total | 13,575 | 100 | 49,503 | 100 | 66,075 | 100 |

*Note:* Years ending in June.
*Source:* Esteves (2005).

### 9.4.2 Public Expenditure and Public Deficit

Throughout this period, public expenditure expanded faster than revenue, as Figure 9.1 presents. In 1851–9, the deficit amounted to 0.8 percent of GDP and reached 1.5 percent in the following decade, only to decline steadily afterward to 0.7 percent in the 1890s and 0.1 percent in the 1910s. The size of the Portuguese deficit was comparable to those of other countries of Southern Europe but much greater than the deficit run by the British government.

As Table 9.5 shows, the increased public expenditure on the economic fabric throughout the 1860s, 1870s, and 1880s – especially in the transport sector, with heavy spending on roads and, particularly, railways – was accompanied by a significantly sharper increase in the costs of servicing the public debt. According to the available data (Mata 1993; Esteves 2000), 38 percent of the revenue originating from the loans taken out in the second half of the nineteenth century was used for capital expenditure and spending on productive investment, with clear preference given to covering expenditure in the traditional sectors of public administration. However, this continued recourse to internal and external debt was always regarded optimistically; that is, borrowings were seen as amounting to the overall process of wealth creation and, consequently, as leading to an increase in taxable amounts and in the state's future tax revenue. Or, in other words, the debt was considered an instrument that would automatically lead to a situation in which actual debt would cease to be necessary, for, in the meantime, it would have contributed to balancing the budget on the income side and therefore to the subsequent elimination of the deficit.

The practical results of indebtedness do not confirm that the desired effects were achieved. Furthermore, although it is not possible to demonstrate that such a policy either impeded or restricted the development of private investment through the occurrence of crowding-out effects, there is no doubt that there was squandering and inefficiency in the allocation and distribution of public expenditure (Esteves 2000). The little importance that was attached to both social spending and expenditure on education is further proof of the failure to provide a program that would enhance the value of human capital, which helps to explain some of the weaknesses in Portuguese economic growth in the second half of the nineteenth century (Reis 1993). Indeed, the sustained growth in public expenditure was not matched by any compensatory growth in tax revenue, as Figure 9.1 shows. And the most intense period of economic investment (1860–80) was precisely the one in which state income grew the most. The chronic persistence of the deficit was therefore to be viewed as a logical corollary of a series of choices and circumstances relating to the public finance policy, which had led to an equally chronic and persistent indebtedness on the part of the state.

As shown in Table 9.6, the debt and debt service increased sharply from 31 percent of GDP in 1852–9 to 68 percent in 1880–9, and declined only in the first decade of the twentieth century. The high share of the costs of servicing the public debt reduced the possibilities of mobilizing

Table 9.6. *Structure of Public Debt, 1833–1913*

| | Percentage of GDP | | | Percentage of Total Public Debt | | |
|---|---|---|---|---|---|---|
| | Deficit | Debt | Service | Consolidated | Foreign | BoP |
| 1837–9 | 0.4 | | | | | |
| 1840–4 | 1.4 | | | | | |
| 1852–9 | 0.8 | 31 | 1.1 | 94 | 50 | 4.3 |
| 1860–9 | 1.5 | 44 | 1.8 | 94 | 48 | 1.6 |
| 1870–9 | 1.2 | 63 | 2.7 | 94 | 42 | 0.6 |
| 1880–9 | 1.1 | 68 | 2.6 | 88 | 48 | 0.7 |
| 1890–9 | 0.7 | 69 | 2.3 | 68 | 51 | 5.2 |
| 1900–13 | 0.1 | 60 | 2.4 | 51 | 35 | 7.4 |

*Source:* Esteves (2005: 312); Reis (1996: 34).

financial resources for investment spending, which was itself designed to equip the Portuguese economy with the infrastructures essential for its economic development. This was the nature of the political program drawn up by Fontes Pereira de Melo in the initial phase of the 'regeneration' in 1851, centered on the idea that, without material improvements promoted by the state, the country would have difficulty achieving the levels of growth already attained by other European countries. Without ever forgetting the need to stimulate the initiative of agents and private companies, it is clear that this program always regarded public investment as a priority (Mónica 1999).

### 9.4.3 Public Debt

The choice to raise debt by means of internal and external loans was a constant feature of Portuguese politics throughout the nineteenth century. Short-term loans and credits obtained through the issue of floating debt were refunded by issuing securities or by signing consolidated debt agreements, which could be repaid within a definite or indefinite time frame and generated remunerable interest. Given the lack of any strict debt-servicing program and that, until the early 1890s, loans taken out in international markets were worth the trust of foreign investors, a spiral of indebtedness was created that obliged the Portuguese government to take exceptional measures on two occasions.

The first phase of debt clearance occurred in 1852, in the early days of the 'regeneration' movement, when Minister Fontes Pereira de Melo sought to bring some order to the financial chaos, which had been attributed to the deregulation brought about by political instability, two civil wars, and the successive loans raised to overcome short-term financial difficulties. The expedience of converting debt to nonredeemable debt securities, first attempted in 1852, was presented at that time as heralding a new cycle of progress and economic investment and called for lowering the costs of servicing the debt. However, because of the inevitable changes in the composition of the government, the twofold promise that greater rigor would thereafter be introduced in raising debt and that, above all, priority would be given to investment in productive infrastructures was never fulfilled as expected. The total number of internal and external loans and their respective adjustments, taken out between 1852 and 1892, was 108 (Valério 2001), which shows that this instrument of financial policy had become commonplace. It had even become a too-accessible weapon to be wielded in political debates between the parties, which would violently criticize the instrument whenever in opposition and make abundant use of it whenever they led the government.

The evolution of debt and interest as a percentage of GDP over the following decades, as shown in Table 9.6, highlights the fact that this was a crucial structural problem, one that affected the possibilities of greater growth in the Portuguese economy. In 1891, the share of the public debt as part of GDP reached the maximum value of 75 percent, which led the government to decree the conversion of the debt for the second time. On this occasion, however, the situation was much more serious and worrisome than it had been forty years earlier, given that, in the meantime, the opportunities to resort to loans on the international financial markets had been missed. The solution was twofold: to resort to the special funding provided by the national bank (the Banco de Portugal) and to the highly controversial practice of obtaining credit in return for the concession of the tobacco contract, which, despite itself, provided some relief to the chronic frailty of the state's financial structure.

Therefore, the main burden left by the ancien régime that needed to be continuously addressed throughout the nineteenth century was both internal and external public debt. And this was the main obstacle that had to be faced every year, thereby preventing the budget administration from redirecting the allocation of revenues to productive investment in infrastructure or to expenditure on social welfare. As shown in Table 9.7, the ratio of the debt-service payments to total state revenues was considerably higher in Portugal than in other European countries, which makes this issue a particularly important subject of discussion in the analysis of the Portuguese case.

Table 9.7. *Revenue and Deficit Compared, 1854–1910*

|  | Revenue (percentage of GDP) | | | Deficit (percentage of GDP) | |
|---|---|---|---|---|---|
|  | 1854 | 1870 | 1910 | 1870 | 1910 |
| Portugal | 4.53 | 4.22 | 7.06 | 2.41 | −0.17 |
| Spain |  | 5.35 | 4.98 | −0.10 | 5.14 |
| Italy |  | 9.13 | 10.93 | 3.47 | 0.91 |
| France | 7.71 | 6.94 | 10.45 | 0.15 | 0.12 |
| UK | 9.04 | 6.30 | 9.94 | 0.00 | −1.75 |

*Source:* Esteves (2002: 73).

## 9.5 Conclusion

When approaching the main features of public finance in nineteenth-century Portugal, emphasis must be placed on the attention given to the management of public debt. This was something that had to be carefully carried out, to preserve the state's credibility in the eyes of internal and external creditors. Debt remained a major problem throughout the second half of the nineteenth century until it stopped increasing, only after the financial crisis of 1891. From that point, Portugal abandoned the gold standard, and the government enjoyed better access to credit through Banco de Portugal. At any rate, the financing of the public deficit was a major constraint. Public deficit was a direct outcome of the relative weakness of the state and its taxation, despite the repeated attempts to reform, a circumstance that meant that the provision and financing of public goods was relatively inefficient. The abolition of the monarchy in 1910, as a result of another military coup, somehow reveals that the problems of state building were greater then than they had been a few decades before. Indeed, to a large extent, the source of political instability was related to another major problem in Portugal's nineteenth-century institutional history, namely the persistently low degree of legitimacy of governments and the consequent belated enfranchisement of the population. This problem was intertwined with the successive fundamental difficulty in simultaneously building a new fiscal state and in meeting the great expectations of the public with respect to the state's expenditure.

In nineteenth-century Portugal and in many other European countries, economic and financial policies were mainly dictated by the pressing needs of the day and by short-term political agendas. However, the long-term direction of tax policies and fiscal reforms, the consequences of debt creation or conversion, and the use of public expenditure as a means of fostering economic development were the subject of many political disputes and at the heart of political debates. As far as the Portuguese case is concerned, public scrutiny became possible after the liberal revolution of 1820. It was only then that state finances became the subject of public discussion instead of merely the result of secret decisions of the king and his close councillors. The political debates and the disputes among the main actors in the construction of a modern liberal state revolved around many different issues: the constitutional procedures regarding the approval of fiscal rules, the trust and political credit that taxpayers afforded to politicians and bureaucrats, the institutional framework and local arrangements of tax collection, the relationship between public finances and economic change and development, and the political response to the dissatisfaction of taxpayers.[7] All these issues convey a functioning modern fiscal state and the inherent decision making of creditworthy political agents. Indeed, alongside the dynamic interactions among an increasing expenditure, the regular extraction of revenues, and the development of debt instruments and credit institutions, the building up of a modern fiscal state also implies the consolidation of a political regime that is compatible with the formation of a public sphere. In fact, only public scrutiny of policies can provide the political legitimacy required for claiming the appropriateness of any decisions.

The formation of a learned and well-informed public sphere explains the emergence of new arguments in support of backing public finance reforms, even when public discussion was limited to general principles of ideal taxation and to spending cuts or when it was largely conditioned by strong prejudices against the narrow capacities and vested interests of politicians.[8] In this sense, the nineteenth-century Portuguese state experienced a long, exhausting struggle to gain stability and legitimacy. Yet throughout the second half the nineteenth century, Portugal gained the indispensable political maturity required to accommodate the institutions and procedures that are distinctive elements of a modern fiscal state.

---

[7] For a general presentation of the relevance of these issues in the making of a modern fiscal state, see Daunton (2001).

[8] On the relevance of the circulation of ideas about taxation for the process of state building in Europe, see Nehring and Schui (2007). See also Schonhardt-Bailey (2006), for a presentation of the interaction among ideas, institutions, and interests. The Portuguese case is addressed in Bastien and Cardoso (2009).

Appendix Table 9.1. *Public Accounts, 1762–1914 (contos, current values)*

|      | Revenue | Expenditure | Deficit | Debt | Deficit/ Revenue | Debt/ Revenue |
|------|---------|-------------|---------|------|---------|--------|
| 1762 | 3,745   | 3,435       | 310     |      | 0.083   |        |
| 1763 | 5,881   | 4,624       | 1,257   |      | 0.214   |        |
| 1764 | 5,917   | 5,003       | 914     |      | 0.154   |        |
| 1765 | 5,667   | 5,308       | 359     |      | 0.063   |        |
| 1766 | 6,783   | 6,096       | 687     |      | 0.101   |        |
| 1767 | 5,760   | 5,214       | 546     |      | 0.095   |        |
| 1768 | 6,295   | 5,747       | 548     |      | 0.087   |        |
| 1769 | 5,884   | 5,327       | 557     |      | 0.095   |        |
| 1770 | 5,731   | 5,408       | 323     |      | 0.056   |        |
| 1771 | 5,237   | 4,990       | 247     |      | 0.047   |        |
| 1772 | 5,278   | 4,977       | 301     |      | 0.057   |        |
| 1773 | 5,220   | 4,928       | 292     |      | 0.056   |        |
| 1774 | 5,829   | 5,195       | 634     |      | 0.109   |        |
| 1775 | 5,883   | 5,409       | 474     |      | 0.081   |        |
| 1776 | 6,684   | 6,047       | 637     |      | 0.095   |        |
| 1797 | 6,658   |             |         |      | ≫1 (1)  |        |
| 1798 | 6,443   |             |         |      | 0.78 (1)|        |
| 1799 | 7,859   |             |         |      |         |        |
| 1800 | 10,627  | 11,967      | −1,340  |      | −0.126  |        |
| 1801 | 9,859   | 13,011      | −3,152  |      | −0.320  |        |
| 1802 | 9,511   | 10,082      | −571    |      | −0.060  |        |
| 1803 | 10,906  |             |         |      |         |        |
| 1804 | 10,264  |             |         |      |         |        |
| 1812 | 8,121   | 8,018       | 103     | 34,757 | 0.013 | 4,3    |
| 1817 | 10,436  | 11,533      | −1,097  | 35,601 | −0.105 | 3,4   |
| 1821 | 6,820   | 7,038       | −218    |      | −0.032  |        |
| 1827 | 6,660   | 8,996       | −2,336  | 33,700 | −0.351 | 5,1   |
| 1828 | 11,030  | 14,899      | −3,869  |      | −0.351  |        |
| 1834 | 6,011   | 10,244      | −4,233  |      | −0.704  |        |
| 1835 | 8,239   | 14,386      | −6,147  |      | −0.746  |        |
| 1836 | 7,101   | 11,615      | −4,514  |      | −0.636  |        |
| 1837 | 8,841   | 10,106      | −1,265  |      | −0.143  |        |
| 1838 | 6,547   | 7,960       | −1,413  |      | −0.216  |        |
| 1839 | 6,961   | 6,843       | 118     |      | 0.017   |        |
| 1840 | 7,105   | 7,744       | −639    |      | −0.090  |        |
| 1841 | 6,763   | 8,363       | −1,600  |      | −0.237  |        |
| 1842 | 8,604   | 14,065      | −5,461  |      | −0.635  |        |
| 1843 | 7,811   | 13,984      | −6,173  |      | −0.790  |        |
| 1844 | 9,899   | 12,046      | −2,147  |      | −0.217  |        |
| 1845 | 8,873   | 11,046      | −2,173  |      | −0.245  |        |

Appendix Table 9.1 *(continued)*

|  | Revenue | Expenditure | Deficit | Debt | Deficit/ Revenue | Debt/ Revenue |
|---|---|---|---|---|---|---|
| 1847 | 9,400 | 10,805 | −1,405 |  | −0.149 |  |
| 1851 |  |  |  | 83,082 |  |  |
| 1852 | 10,585 | 10,277 | 308 | 90,443 | 0.029 | 8.5 |
| 1853 | 10,749 | 12,621 | −1,872 | 75,796 | −0.174 | 7.1 |
| 1854 | 10,354 | 10,781 | −427 | 92,287 | −0.041 | 8.9 |
| 1855 | 10,866 | 13,399 | −2,533 | 91,655 | −0.233 | 8.4 |
| 1856 | 10,832 | 12,859 | −2,027 | 93,305 | −0.187 | 8.6 |
| 1857 | 11,211 | 14,159 | −2,948 | 106,681 | −0.263 | 9.5 |
| 1858 | 12,331 | 17,363 | −5,032 | 106,184 | −0.408 | 8.6 |
| 1859 | 12,187 | 17,137 | −4,950 | 111,908 | −0.406 | 9.2 |
| 1860 | 11,881 | 15,246 | −3,365 | 124,290 | −0.283 | 10.5 |
| 1861 | 12,570 | 15,099 | −2,529 | 135,602 | −0.201 | 10.8 |
| 1862 | 13,336 | 20,075 | −6,739 | 141,063 | −0.505 | 10.6 |
| 1863 | 13,938 | 21,102 | −7,164 | 148,379 | −0.514 | 10.6 |
| 1864 | 14,787 | 20,069 | −5,282 | 170,107 | −0.357 | 11.5 |
| 1865 | 17,032 | 19,904 | −2,872 | 182,842 | −0.169 | 10.7 |
| 1866 | 14,826 | 20,064 | −5,238 | 184,153 | −0.353 | 12.4 |
| 1867 | 14,297 | 21,794 | −7,497 | 193,376 | −0.524 | 13.5 |
| 1868 | 15,673 | 28,563 | −12,890 | 225,683 | −0.822 | 14.4 |
| 1869 | 15,764 | 20,383 | −4,619 | 245,779 | −0.293 | 15.6 |
| 1870 | 16,396 | 31,397 | −15,001 | 261,176 | −0.915 | 15.9 |
| 1871 | 16,672 | 20,553 | −3,881 | 308,350 | −0.233 | 18.5 |
| 1872 | 17,811 | 23,919 | −6,108 | 307,396 | −0.343 | 17.3 |
| 1873 | 19,916 | 23,274 | −3,358 | 307,595 | −0.169 | 15.4 |
| 1874 | 22,827 | 26,722 | −3,895 | 342,944 | −0.171 | 15.0 |
| 1875 | 23,309 | 28,625 | −5,316 | 351,442 | −0.228 | 15.1 |
| 1876 | 25,199 | 30,859 | −5,660 | 363,006 | −0.225 | 14.4 |
| 1877 | 25,638 | 35,770 | −10,132 | 380,481 | −0.395 | 14.8 |
| 1878 | 25,233 | 33,645 | −8,412 | 403,827 | −0.333 | 16.0 |
| 1879 | 27,266 | 34,134 | −6,868 | 405,678 | −0.252 | 14.9 |
| 1880 | 23,239 | 31,272 | −8,033 | 420,818 | −0.346 | 18.1 |
| 1881 | 25,413 | 33,474 | −8,061 | 417,201 | −0.317 | 16.4 |
| 1882 | 28,417 | 35,632 | −7,215 | 432,747 | −0.254 | 15.2 |
| 1883 | 27,202 | 33,256 | −6,054 | 443,575 | −0.223 | 16.3 |
| 1884 | 28,702 | 33,975 | −5,273 | 441,057 | −0.184 | 15.4 |
| 1885 | 30,263 | 38,597 | −8,334 | 488,560 | −0.275 | 16.1 |
| 1886 | 30,781 | 40,156 | −9,375 | 493,788 | −0.305 | 16.0 |
| 1887 | 33,379 | 40,422 | −7,043 | 502,436 | −0.211 | 15.1 |
| 1888 | 36,689 | 43,477 | −6,788 | 513,464 | −0.185 | 14.0 |
| 1889 | 37,612 | 49,496 | −11,884 | 525,799 | −0.316 | 14.0 |
| 1890 | 37,868 | 51,705 | −13,837 | 539,212 | −0.365 | 14.2 |

Appendix Table 9.1 *(continued)*

| | Revenue | Expenditure | Deficit | Debt | Deficit/ Revenue | Debt/ Revenue |
|---|---|---|---|---|---|---|
| 1891 | 38,316 | 49,284 | −10,968 | 582,786 | −0.286 | 15.2 |
| 1892 | 37,526 | 52,716 | −15,190 | 586,987 | −0.405 | 15.6 |
| 1893 | 40,504 | 45,903 | −5,399 | 625,237 | −0.133 | 15.4 |
| 1894 | 44,102 | 43,643 | 459 | 600,003 | 0.010 | 13.6 |
| 1895 | 43,899 | 45,215 | −1,316 | 598,885 | −0.030 | 13.6 |
| 1896 | 50,615 | 48,434 | 2,181 | 609,608 | 0.043 | 12.0 |
| 1897 | 47,118 | 54,460 | −7,342 | 670,513 | −0.156 | 14.2 |
| 1898 | 46,861 | 54,140 | −7,279 | 664,763 | −0.155 | 14.2 |
| 1899 | 48,013 | 51,513 | −3,500 | 614,621 | −0.073 | 12.8 |
| 1900 | 49,469 | 56,805 | −7,336 | 664,529 | −0.148 | 13.4 |
| 1901 | 51,822 | 50,875 | 947 | 694,624 | 0.018 | 13.4 |
| 1902 | 49,240 | 52,139 | −2,899 | 683,342 | −0.059 | 13.9 |
| 1903 | 50,947 | 53,509 | −2,562 | 593,533 | −0.050 | 11.7 |
| 1904 | 52,890 | 54,731 | −1,841 | 610,003 | −0.035 | 11.5 |
| 1905 | 55,499 | 55,015 | 484 | 645,864 | 0.009 | 11.6 |
| 1906 | 56,784 | 57,208 | −424 | 648,634 | −0.007 | 11.4 |
| 1907 | 55,788 | 56,742 | −954 | 628,394 | −0.017 | 11.3 |
| 1908 | 66,731 | 70,373 | −3,642 | 627,250 | −0.055 | 9.4 |
| 1909 | 65,795 | 68,096 | −2,301 | 628,283 | −0.035 | 9.5 |
| 1910 | 68,739 | 69,466 | −727 | 669,685 | −0.011 | 9.7 |
| 1911 | 64,917 | 62,598 | 2,319 | 656,462 | 0.036 | 10.1 |
| 1912 | 60,869 | 63,829 | −2,960 | 660,710 | −0.049 | 10.9 |
| 1913 | 79,387 | 75,696 | 3,691 | 657,474 | 0.046 | 8.3 |
| 1914 | 68,873 | 61,798 | 7,075 | 648,334 | 0.103 | 9.4 |

*Note:* Data for the years 1797–9 and 1803 are not fully compatible with 1800–2.
*Sources:* For 1762–6, 1800–2, 1812, 1817, and 1821: Thomaz (1988) and Silveira (1987) cited in Valério (2001: 663). For 1797–9 and 1803, Costa (1992: 26). For 1804, Macedo et al. (1998: app. 1). For 1827–8 and 1847, Reis (1996: 37). For 1834–45, Mata and Valério (2001: 140–1;. For 1852–1914, Mata (1993: 175). For debt in 1812, 1817, and 1827, Silveira (1987: 529), Mata (1993: 255); Costa (1992: 19).

## References

Almeida, P. Tavares de (1991) *Eleições e Caciquismo no Portugal Oitocentista, 1868–1890*. Lisbon: Difel.
Bastien, C. (2005) "A tentativa de reforma fiscal cabralista e o seu fracasso," in N. Valério (ed.) *Os Impostos no Parlamento Português. Sistemas Fiscais e Doutrinas Fiscais nos Séculos XIX e XX*. Lisbon: Dom Quixote, 29–47.
Bastien, C. and Cardoso, J. L. (2009) "Uses and abuses of political economy in Portuguese parliamentary debates (1850–1910)," *History of Economic Ideas*, 17(2).

Bonifácio, M. F. (2007) *Estudos de História Contemporânea de Portugal*. Lisbon: Imprensa de Ciências Sociais.

Cardoso, J. L. (1989) *O Pensamento Económico em Portugal nos Finais do Século XVIII (1780–1808)*. Lisbon: Editorial Estampa.

Costa, F. Dores (1992) "Crise financeira, dívida pública e capitalistas, 1796–1807." Unpublished master's thesis, Universidade Nova de Lisboa.

Coutinho, R. de Souza (1993) *Textos Políticos, Económicos e Financeiros (1783–1811)* Andrée Diniz Silva (ed.), 2 vols. Lisbon: Banco de Portugal.

Daunton, M. (2001) *Trusting Leviathan: The Politics of Taxation in Britain, 1799–1914*. Cambridge: Cambridge University Press.

Esteves, R. P. (2000) "O *crowding-out* em Portugal, 1879–1910," *Análise Social*, 34, 574–618.

Esteves, R. P. (2003) "Looking ahead from the past: The inter-temporal sustainability of Portuguese finances, 1854–1910," *European Review of Economic History*, 7, 239–66.

Esteves, R. P. (2005) "Finanças públicas," in P. Lains and A. Ferreira da Silva (eds.) *História Económica de Portugal, 1700–2000*, vol. 2. Lisbon: Imprensa de Ciências Sociais, 305–35.

Figueiredo, O., Ferro, J. P. and Esteves, R. P. (2004) "As pulsações económicas e financeiras," in F. de Sousa and A. H. Oliveira Marques (eds.) *Nova História de Portugal. Portugal e a Regeneração*. Lisbon: Editorial Presença, 71–148.

Godinho, V. Magalhães (1955) *Prix et monnaies au Portugal (1750–1850)*. Paris: Armand Colin.

Godinho, V. Magalhães (1978) "Finanças públicas e estrutura do Estado," *Ensaios*, 2nd ed., vol. 2. Lisbon: Sá da Costa, 29–74.

Hespanha, A. M. (2004) *Guiando a Mão Invisível. Direitos, Estado e Lei no Liberalismo Monárquico Português*. Coimbra: Almedina.

Lains, P. (1999) *L'économie portugaise au XIXème siècle*. Paris: L'Harmattan.

Lains, P. (2003) *Os Progressos do Atraso. Uma Nova História Económica de Portugal, 1842–1992*. Lisbon: Imprensa de Ciências Sociais.

Lains, P. (2008) "The power of peripheral governments: Coping with the 1891 financial crisis in Portugal," *Historical Research*, 81(August), 485–506.

Lains, P. and A. Ferreira da Silva (eds.) (2005) *História Económica de Portugal, 1700–2000*, 3 vols. Lisbon: Imprensa de Ciências Sociais.

Macedo, J. Braga de, Silva, A. Ferreira da and Sousa, R. Martins de (2001) "War, taxes, and gold: The inheritance of the Real," in M. Bordo and R. Cortés-Conde (eds.) *Transferring Wealth and Power from the Old to the New World: Monetary and Fiscal Institutions in the Seventeenth through the Nineteenth Centuries*. Cambridge: Cambridge University Press, 187–228.

Macedo, J. Borges de (1962) *O Bloqueio Continental. Economia e Guerra Peninsular*. Lisbon: Delfos.

Mata, M. E. (1993) *As Finanças Públicas Portuguesas da Regeneração à Primeira Guerra Mundial*. Lisbon: Banco de Portugal.

Mata, M. E. (1998) "As três fases do fontismo: projectos e realizações," *Estudos e Ensaios em Homenagem a Vitorino Magalhães Godinho*. Lisbon: Sá da Costa, 31–58.

Mata, M. E. (2005) "As lentas transformações fiscais da época da Regeneração," in N. Valério (ed.) *Os Impostos no Parlamento Português. Sistemas Fiscais e Doutrinas Fiscais nos Séculos XIX e XX.* Lisbon: Dom Quixote, 49–83.

Mata, M. E. and Valério, N. (2001) "As finanças constitucionais entre duas guerras civis," *Revista de História Económica e Social,* 2nd ser., 1(1), 135–44.

Mónica, M. F. (1996) "As reformas eleitorais no constitucionalismo monárquico, 1852–1910," *Análise Social,* 31 (5), 1039–1084.

Mónica, M. F. (1999) *Fontes Pereira de Melo.* Lisbon: Edições Afrontamento.

Neal, L. (2004) "The monetary, financial and political architecture of Europe, 1648–1815," in L. Prados de la Escosura (ed.) *Exceptionalism and Industrialization: Britain and Its European Rivals, 1688–1815.* Cambridge: Cambridge University Press, 173–90.

Nehring, H. and Schui, F. (eds.) (2007) *Global Debates about Taxation.* Basingstoke, UK: Palgrave Macmillan.

Pedreira, J. (2000) "From growth to collapse: Portugal, Brazil, and the breakdown of the old colonial system (1760–1830)," *Hispanic American Historical Review,* 80(4), 839–64.

Pedreira, J. (2005) "A indústria," in P. Lains and A. Ferreira da Silva (eds.) *História Económica de Portugal, 1700–2000,* vol. 1. Lisbon: Imprensa de Ciências Sociais, 177–208.

Pinheiro, M. (1983) "Reflexões sobre a história das finanças públicas portuguesas no século XIX," *Ler História,* 1, 47–67.

Ramos, R. (2001) *A Segunda Fundação, 1890–1926,* 2nd ed. Lisbon: Editorial Estampa.

Reis, J. (1993) *O Atraso Económico Português em Perspectiva Histórica. Estudos sobre a Economia Portuguesa na Segunda Metade do Século XIX.* Lisbon: Imprensa Nacional.

Reis, J. (1996) *O Banco de Portugal. Das Origens a 1914,* vol. 1. Lisbon: Banco de Portugal.

Reis, J. (2000) "The gold standard in Portugal, 1854–91," in P. Martin Aceña and J. Reis. (eds.) *Monetary Standards in the Periphery. Paper, Silver and Gold, 1854–1933.* London: St. Martin's Press, 69–111.

Sardica, J. M. (2001) *A Regeneração sob o Signo do Consenso. A Política e os Partidos entre 1851 e 1861.* Lisbon: Imprensa de Ciências Sociais.

Schonhardt-Bailey, C. (2006) *From the Corn Laws to Free Trade: Interests, Ideas, and Institutions in Historical Perspective.* Cambridge, MA: Massachusetts Institute of Technology Press.

Serrão, J. V. (2005) "A agricultura," in P. Lains and A. Ferreira da Silva (eds.) *História Económica de Portugal, 1700–2000,* vol. 1. Lisbon: Imprensa de Ciências Sociais, 145–75.

Silveira, L. Espinha da (1987) "Aspectos da evolução das finanças públicas portuguesas nas primeiras décadas do século XIX (1800–27)" *Análise Social,* 23(3) 505–29.

Thomaz, F. (1988) "As finanças do Estado pombalino, 1762–1776," *Estudos e Ensaios. Em Homenagem a Vitorino Magalhães Godinho.* Lisbon: Sá da Costa, 355–88.

Valente, V. Pulido (2005) *Os Militares e a Política (1820–1856)*, 2nd ed. Lisbon: Imprensa Nacional.

Valério, N. (ed.) (2001) *As Finanças Públicas no Parlamento Português. Estudos Preliminares*. Lisbon: Edições Afrontamento.

Valério, N. (ed.) (2006) *Os Impostos no Parlamento Português. Sistemas Fiscais e Doutrinas Fiscais nos Séculos XIX e XX*. Lisbon: Dom Quixote.

# 10

# Conclusion

## The Monetary, Fiscal, and Political Architecture of Europe, 1815–1914

### Larry Neal

## 10.1 Introduction

The preceding chapters in this volume have taken the reader from Great Britain, the archetype of the modern, liberal state as it emerged over the course of the nineteenth century in Europe, to Portugal, perhaps the saddest object lesson of the perils of empire for European states in the nineteenth century. Although the contrasting trajectories of the two maritime powers from their Methuen Treaty of 1703 could be taken as the organizing theme of the entire volume, there are simply too many variant trajectories taken by the other seven European nation-states that are discussed. The editors have attempted to rein in any impulse toward facile moralizing by focusing in each case on the way central governments met their expenditures, whatever may have been the strategic goals of the ruling authorities at the time. Raising taxes sufficient to carry out the programs of the governments always met resistance, both from those members of society opposing the programs and from those merely resisting taxes in principle.

Following the conclusion of the French Revolutionary and Napoleonic wars, however, there was throughout Europe an appreciation of the universal appeal of the mantra of 1789 – *liberté, fraternité, et égalité*. Translated into effective practice wherever Napoléon's troops appeared, the revolutionary slogan meant freedom from taxes in kind and increased occupational mobility, accompanied by companionship within a demonstrating mob or a conscript militia and equality of taxes now payable in money rather than in kind. The potential tax base for all European territories occupied by French forces was thereby greatly enhanced by the elimination of tax privileges of the nobility and the clergy. But the issue of how to both sustain and exploit the enlarged tax base for state purposes remained well after the removal of Napoléon to distant exile and the demobilization of the competing armies and navies. Moreover, although the content of the revolutionary phrase retained its mass appeal, it could no longer be directed into mass armies and forced extraction of resources from conquered territory, at least not until the world wars of the twentieth century.

To the modern political economist or economic historian, the issues confronted by the European nations in 1815 were similar to those they confronted once again in 1945. The difference is that, in 1815, they did not have the benefit of a protective power across the Atlantic or the incentive of a common threat from the East. Even with the successful example of a prospering Great Britain, which had proved itself capable of sustaining simultaneously the largest naval forces and the largest military forces ever mobilized by a European power, the European states found it difficult, and in several cases simply impossible, to emulate Britain's success after the conclusion of hostilities. For an economic historian, the case studies in this volume help make the point once again to our colleagues in neighboring disciplines that the historical legacy of economic institutions narrows the range of possible actions for policy makers for achieving worthwhile goals. For an American economist, they also demonstrate the uniqueness of the Anglo-American perspectives on public finance created by their respective histories. The persistent rejection of Anglo-American policy recommendations by the rest of the world becomes more understandable, if no less frustrating.

To make this point more clearly, it is useful to take the distinguishing features of the modern liberal state as exemplified by Great Britain in 1815, and then see what obstacles lay in the path of other European countries if they wished to emulate those features. It is also useful to note the different purposes that motivated the emulating states, whether to industrialize, to expand trade, or to restore or conquer new territories. Two features generated the ultimate rise in the share of tax revenue in each country's national product and a subsequent change in the structure of government expenditures toward the modern welfare state. One was centralization of political control, which enabled the central government to impose uniform tax rates across an enlarged tax base. Another was limiting the power of the executive to determine how the increased money should be spent, usually by ceding some budgetary authority to a parliament representing at least major taxpayers. Mark Dincecco (2009) shows that both elements were needed, but they rarely coincided in timing for the nineteenth-century European imitators of eighteenth-century Britain. (He dates fiscal centralization for Britain the earliest of all – 1066, with the Norman Conquest. Limited government came much later, 1688 in his dating, with the Magna Carta, Reformation, and civil war taken as mere preludes to the Glorious Revolution.) The case studies in this volume explain why centralization and limitation took their separate paths in each country.

According to Daunton (Chapter 1 of this volume), Britain's success in creating a powerful fiscal state in the eighteenth century depended on creating two forms of trust. The first was to lenders that the state would pay the interest due on its debt faithfully and on time. This was not easily done, as the historians of British taxation and government debt have documented [e.g., O'Brien (1988, 2008), Brewer (1988), Dickson (1967), Quinn (2001)], but by the time of the Napoleonic Wars, this accumulated trust clearly provided the British government with the wherewithal to issue fresh debt in unprecedented amounts and to raise new taxes as well to outspend and eventually defeat Napoléon. Bordo and White (1991) argue that this residual trust overwhelmed the negative effects of undercutting the monetary standard with the paper pound (suspending the gold standard from 1797 to 1819) while Napoléon put the French back on solid metallic standard. Perhaps, but as Daunton notes, it took Britain between four and six years to resume a metallic standard after the conclusion of hostilities (the gold standard was legislated in 1819 and enacted in 1821). The second form of trust was to make the state's expenditures and monetary policy consistent with the desires of the political and economic elite. Again, this was difficult to sustain at the conclusion of hostilities, as the composition of the economic elite (albeit not the political elite!) had changed in response to wartime demands on industry. Coping with the demands of demobilized navy seamen and army soldiers at home was different from supplying them abroad on active service.

If these were challenges for Britain, the obvious victor emerging from the generation-long conflict over Europe, initiating and then sustaining the same bases of trust between government and governed, as well as between state debtors and moneyed creditors, were especially daunting for the other European states. It is not surprising, then, that it took time and not a few missteps before any of the European states could be considered as successful as Britain. But what allowed Britain to continue to establish the basis of a liberal modern state, responsive to both the economic interests of the new industrial elite and the political demands of an urbanized workforce? Perhaps it was precisely because the British government depended on the existing capital market to purchase its new issues of debt whenever it faced a need to mobilize resources on a large scale. Contrary to its imperial precedents and its continental competitors, Britain had moved from a tax regime that could use reasons of state to command resources directly when needed to one that could simply issue fresh debt to acquire the funds needed to purchase on the available markets the labor, materials, and equipment required to confront the challenge (Neal 2004). In the ancien régime tax structures on the Continent, governments imposed direct taxes in kind or by forced circulation of their currency when under stress. These measures meant that they requisitioned the manpower and supplies they wanted but at the same time preempted the distribution networks on which the peacetime economy relied (Bonney 1995, 1999).

By contrast, over the course of the eighteenth century, Britain had found that purchasing mercenaries from Europe or subsidizing foreign armies was quite effective for its objectives in each of the several wars (save, of course, for the notable failure to maintain imperial control over the American colonies, where mercenaries had to be paid and provisioned from Britain). The effect of Britain's method of meeting emergencies in the eighteenth century was to support and strengthen the existing market infrastructures for supplying and distributing labor and goods during the war, and then to permit the expanded infrastructures to resume their normal civilian supply and distribution functions in times of peace. By contrast, the displacement of manpower and skills from their normal pursuits by Continental powers during expanded military efforts disrupted markets. Little attention was then paid to restoring the markets afterward, save at their preexisting levels of efficiency. The goal for Continental powers, rather, was to restore the previous tranquillity of the governed population and return to the prior structure of occupation and activity, all the while supporting a larger standing army and constructing more elaborate military defenses (Parker 1996).

As Patrick O'Brien (1998) has documented, the Napoleonic Wars disrupted even the British fiscal model. First, they reversed a century-long trend toward increasing reliance on indirect taxes, both customs and excise, thanks to the income tax imposed by William Pitt in 1798. One may add as well the dramatic increase in direct personal taxation by means of impressing sailors for the navy and soldiers for the army, which led to renewed war with the United States. Second, the majority of the war expenditures came from taxes rather than new debt, as they had in previous wars of the eighteenth century. Third, the convertibility of Bank of England notes into gold or silver at fixed rates was suspended for the duration of the hostilities and even beyond, as noted previously.

In contrast, as Patrick Colquhoun (1815) demonstrated, at the conclusion of the war, Britain emerged as a stronger, wealthier economy with a much larger empire to replace the one lost in the War of American Independence. Part of the explanation for the difficulties of Britain's European competitors in emulating its fiscal success, then, lay in confusion over the real source of Britain's success. Was it derived from extracting resources from an extended empire or from efficient governance of a growing domestic economy? Opinions varied, but so did the results of experiments carried out in the French, Dutch, Austrian, German, Spanish, and Portuguese empires over the next century!

As J. R. Hicks has noted in his *A Theory of Economic History* (1969), most societies and economies over the course of history have alternated between command economies (when faced with shocks, whether from war, famine, disease, or natural disaster) and customary economies (in the absence of shocks). Neither command nor custom, however, is amenable to reallocation of resources in response to new possibilities that might increase human happiness, at least not nearly to the extent that market economies provide. Hicks argued that it was the European luck to have Mediterranean city-states governed necessarily by merchant elites interested in maintaining access to markets whatever the nature of an external shock that allowed market economies to develop and spread across Continental Europe. Just how this process spread through Europe, however, was not part of his argument. He ended his theory with the Industrial Revolution in England, defined as the time when the cost of reproducing capital fell below that of diverting capital to produce goods and services for consumption. Just when that occurred, of course, he wisely left unaddressed, but he probably had in mind the dating of his friend, T. S. Ashton, namely around the mid-eighteenth century, just as the financial revolution had been completed according to Dickson (1967).

The chapters in this volume try to answer precisely the question Hicks left unanswered. They attempt to do that by describing how most governments eventually adopted market-oriented responses to external shocks and moved away from ancien régime modes of government intervention to modern, liberal state modes of taxation, supported by regular access to securities markets for government debt. Each chapter analyzes the political difficulties faced by various governments in their efforts either to move to the British model or to define their own, competitive model. The analysis is greatly enriched by the wealth of new estimates and analyses of public finance in each country that the current generation of economic historians has produced.

It may be useful here, then, to provide an analytical framework in which to place each case study and then illustrate where each country stands in comparison to the others with the evaluations made by the securities markets of the nineteenth century. Harley H. Hinrichs, in *A General Theory of Tax Structure Change during Economic Development* (1966), laid out a simple but persuasive framework for how the transition should occur from a traditional economy with low and intermittent taxes and limited government to a modern economy with high and regular taxation and large-scale government. Traditional economies, he noted, would have only limited access to direct taxation, usually when the society was under external threat, and a common effort was needed to deal with that. The remainder of the revenue of the limited state would be derived from user fees and rents, sources he labeled "indirect taxes, traditional." The transition to a modern economy would come in the form of contact with more advanced economies desiring to exploit what they considered trade opportunities with the traditional, mostly self-sufficient economy. If the rulers were sufficiently opportunistic in the traditional economy, they could seize some rents from the new trade with more advanced economies by levying taxes on it, both exports and imports. The new revenues would enhance the position of the ruling class without raising tax resistance from their traditional constituency. To take full advantage of the new economic opportunities, however, the government would have to invest in the infrastructure needed to increase trade with the new trading partners.

Funding this all-important transition from the traditional to modern economy and governing structure without encountering resistance from the traditional power base, however, required outside funding. The resulting excess of expenditure over revenues (what is known as an E-R gap) would exist until the modern tax base had established itself well enough to be subject to modern taxes. These would be excise taxes in the first place, based on the increased volume of trade taking place in the markets of the economy, and only eventually would turn to modern direct taxes, typically on income derived from industrial and commercial pursuits. Figure 10.1 illustrates the sequence that Hinrichs thought he saw in his data set, drawn from the experience of countries belonging

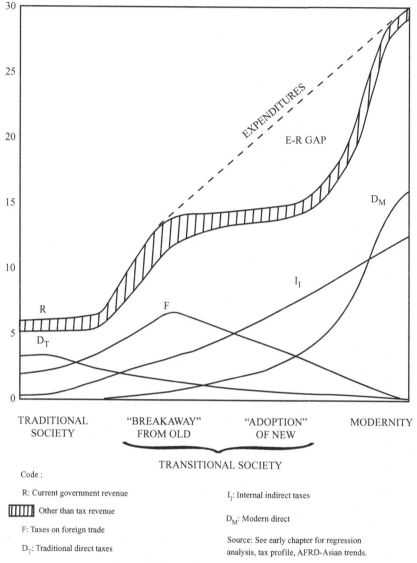

Figure 10.1. *Source:* Hinrichs (1966: 99).

to the World Bank in the 1950s and early 1960s. Hinrichs also had clear ideas about the relative importance of indirect and direct taxes. Initially, a politically stable traditional society would obtain most of its revenue from direct taxes, typically taxes on land or traditional forms of capital assets.

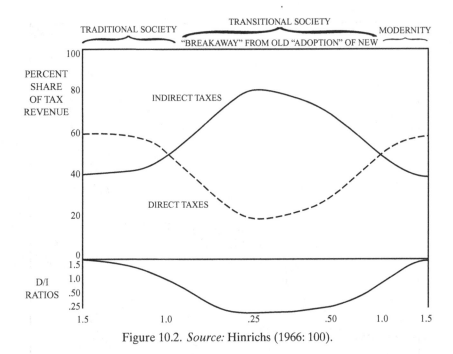

Figure 10.2. *Source:* Hinrichs (1966: 100).

Figure 10.2 indicates that the proportion would be roughly 60 percent direct taxes and 40 percent indirect taxes. As trade with the outside world expanded, however, indirect taxes would rise both as a share and in absolute amount, perhaps peaking at 80 percent of the government's increasing revenue. As indirect taxes on trade were reduced because they restricted the income of the modern sector, they would be replaced by direct taxes on the modern sector, especially the income tax.

Clearly, Hinrichs drew his typology from the history of taxation as he saw it in Britain and the United States, but for the early twentieth and late nineteenth centuries rather than for the eighteenth and earlier centuries as in Bonney (1995, 1999). Daunton's chapter on Britain complements the Hinrichs story very nicely, however, although Daunton emphasizes the political tightrope that had to be walked by the government officials trying to implement the changes in tax regimes even in the British case. Influenced, perhaps, by the theory of Alexander Gerschenkron (1962), Hinrichs argued that the governments' E-R gap during the transition would have to come from foreign investors. Consequently, the transition government would have to make its debt attractive to foreign investors. The evident success of the British 3-percent consol, a perpetual annuity marketed transparently and transferable in any proportion desired by an investor, open to all investors regardless of age, sex, status, and nationality, made it the obvious form of government debt for the rest of Europe to imitate. Hence, the French Parlement, under the protection of Wellington's occupation army and the guidance of Barings, created the 5-percent rentes and the Dutch monarchy the 2.5 percent perpetual annuities, even if only one-third of them were actual paying interest at first.

Modern analysts note, however, that most debt is held domestically, and despite the initial importance of British and French investment in the government bonds issued by other European governments in the middle of the nineteenth century, most of the further increase in government debt from 1890 to 1914 appears to have been held domestically, not by foreigners (Ferguson 2006). This raises an interesting question that is not explicitly raised, much less answered, in any of the case studies. Would the increasing amount of government debt held domestically make taxpayers less resistant or more resistant to an increase in taxes? The answer lies, no doubt, in the way debt and taxes were raised when governments faced the need to increase expenditures suddenly in response to a sudden shock. Traditional societies would levy a one-time increase in taxes with the support of the traditional elite. Britain, over the course of the eighteenth century, managed to keep increasing its tax revenue to a level higher than anywhere else in Europe by the end of the century (O'Brien), but it did so only gradually. As Robert Barro (1987) pointed out years ago, tax smoothing enabled Britain to keep increasing taxes in a gradual manner, thus minimizing the resistance of the population over time. Huge increases in expenditure at times of war were met simply by issuing more government debt. This new asset was such an attractive alternative form of wealth holding for the private sector, both households and firms, that the government had no need to retire it at the end of war.

Contrast that happy state of affairs with the regular need of the French government to impose temporary tax increases to finance its wars with England, and at the end of wars to impose a onetime capital levy to restore its budget back to the previous constraints. The contrast between Britain and France was clearly in evidence throughout the eighteenth century that preceded the Revolutionary and Napoleonic wars, as Figure 10.3 demonstrates.

Richard Bonney's chapter on France (Chapter 3 in this volume) builds on the historical legacy left by the French Revolution and Napoléon. The Revolution enlarged the potential tax base, but Napoléon imposed mass

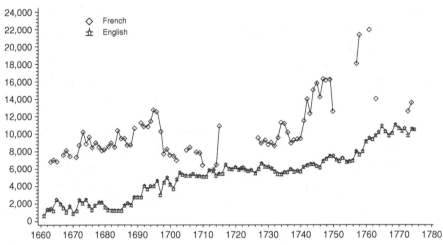

Figure 10.3. Total Revenues of the French and English monarchies, 1660–1775 (in thousands pound sterling). *Source:* www.le.ac.uk/hi/bon/ESFDB/images/Rjb/ Malet/Malg043.gif.

conscription on the French for his armies and forced circulation of the French franc on the satellite kingdoms. His measures took the evolution of French public finance afterward in quite a different direction from that in Britain. Further, Napoléon's extraction of resources from the satellite kingdoms made it difficult for the rest of Continental Europe, once it was free of occupation forces, to take up the British example of public finance.

Bonney makes the point that France suffered over the entire nineteenth century from twin constraints: low population growth, especially relative to Germany, and continued tax resistance that limited the size of government expenditure relative to gross domestic product to roughly half the levels attained by Britain and Germany. He attributes the continuation of tax resistance to the emergence of an entrenched rentier class that depended on regular interest payments from the French rentes to maintain their lifestyle. That lifestyle, however, continued to improve at rates equal to those experienced in Britain and Germany, at least as indicated by average rates of growth of per capita income.

The question raised by Hinrichs's analysis, as well as by the experience of both Britain and France, is whether foreign investment is the only way to cover the E-R gap that a government incurs as it makes the transition from traditional to modern public finance. If, perhaps, government long-term debt is made credible as an investment to a public much broader than its immediate constituency, then a parliamentary government may be able to cover its E-R gap by issuing its own debt to the domestic population, regardless of the extent of the franchise. For example, a legitimate parliament with established procedures for replenishing its membership into the indefinite future could provide a financial asset backed by specific or general taxes that would be an attractive asset for middle-class investors desiring a liquid form of insurance against life's hazards. If the parliament assigns new taxes for servicing its debt on either a foreign population (customs revenues) or the disenfranchised part of the domestic population (excises on necessities and "vices"), the domestic bondholders should be doubly content.

Compared to Britain, however, the transitions in France from one expedient to another as the franchise expanded or contracted were anything but smooth. A useful indicator of the contrast can be seen in Figure 10.4, which compares the market yield on British consols and French rentes over the nineteenth century. The dynastic switch in 1830, the Revolutions of 1848, the Second Empire in 1851–70, and the Third Republic to the eve of the First World War all show up as spikes in the yields on the French government debt. (Dincecco [2009] dates fiscal centralization in France only from the Revolution in 1790, with limited government not achieved until 1870, with the end of the Second Empire.) In between these political shocks, however, French government debt enjoyed low yields, close to those of the British government debt. Clearly, transitions have to persist long enough to establish the legitimacy of the new public finance, or the process must start all over again.

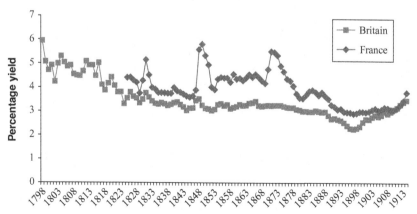

Figure 10.4. British and French government bond yields in the nineteenth century. *Source:* Homer and Sylla (1991).

The Dutch example, described by van Zanden and van Riel (Chapter 2 in this volume) illustrates the power of both increased liquidity of government debt when backed by the servicing commitment of a perpetual institution and the taxing of some disenfranchised part of the population. After dividing the huge accumulated stock of national debt created under duress of the Napoleonic regime into one-third actual debt and two-thirds deferred debt, the unified monarchy of Willem I confronted an unsolvable political dilemma in trying to blend the historical tax systems of the Austrian Netherlands with those of the Dutch Republic. Willem's financial innovations were most obvious in the southern half of his kingdom, which became Belgium after 1830, but his commitment to servicing the actual debt while retiring gradually the deferred debt was based on extending the tax regime of the northern half of his kingdom, modern Netherlands, to the entire kingdom. (Dincecco [2009] dates fiscal centralization in 1806, a response to the Napoleonic reforms, but limited government had been accomplished at the beginning of the Dutch revolt from Spain, in 1572.)

The subsequent liberal democracy persisted until 1870, surviving the turmoil in the surrounding countries occasioned by the Revolutions of 1848, but it still had problems restoring a credible national debt, as Figure 10.5 illustrates. Only in the subsequent period after 1870, when the constitutional monarchy could exploit regularly the export earnings of the Dutch East Indies by levying a heavy "contribution," could international investors be assured of the continued commitment of the Dutch state to the service and retirement of its national debt.

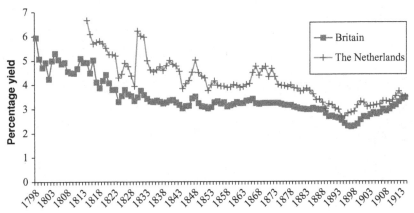

Figure 10.5. Dutch and British government bond yields in the nineteenth century. *Source:* Homer and Sylla (1991).

Before that happy state of affairs was reached, however, the Dutch state had tried to copy the form of the British fiscal state without incorporating the substance. The form was a national debt, serviced by a nationwide tax levied by the parliament; the substance, an independent parliament that could monitor the annual expenditures of the executive, however, was not allowed by Willem I. The result, nevertheless, was a fall in Dutch bond rates that also gradually narrowed the gap with British consols until the loss of the southern Netherlands in 1830 (see Figure 10.5).

Thereafter, progress was slow, as the Dutch public finances were buoyed up mainly by a colonial surplus that added 50 percent to the tax revenue of the central government through the *batig slot*. (This was much more than the annual levy that the British government had placed on its East India Company during the quarter century of war before 1815.) Clearly, international and domestic investors in Dutch government debt were not comfortable with this form of securitization. It is noteworthy that the implicit risk premium on Dutch bonds fell when the liberal reforms after 1848 began to reduce the colonial surplus and eventually turned it into a net subsidy from the mother country. The main interruption to the closing of the gap with British consols occurred, no surprise, during the Boer War. As van Zanden and van Riel note, the adoption of the gold standard in 1875 was the overriding determinant of the price of Dutch government bonds in the London market.

The German experience presents a much more complex picture until the creation of the German Reich in 1871. Spoerer (Chapter 4 in this volume) helps clarify the situation by distinguishing essentially three fiscal regimes before unification: Prussia, southern Germany (Bavaria, Baden, and Württemberg), and the small principalities scattered throughout central Germany and including, perhaps, the seaport city-states on the North Sea and the Baltic. Prussia, he claims, followed the English model of more emphasis on personal taxes, whereas the southern states imitated the French model with impersonal taxes on land, buildings, and business. The rest relied on indirect taxes primarily.

He rightly focuses on Prussia before 1871 but does not refer to an article by Richard Tilly (1966), which argued that it was precisely the Revolutions of 1848 that forced Prussia to recognize that its public finance had to be redirected much more in favor of the industrializing west of Prussia, the lands acquired as part of the post–Napoleonic Wars treaties. In terms remarkably similar to those laid out in the work of Hinrichs, Tilly showed that Prussia shifted from traditional direct taxes, mainly on land, and indirect taxes, mainly excises to more modern indirect taxes, primarily customs revenues, while increasing state debt at the same time, reversing the previous trend toward debt reduction. Thereafter, the Prussian state moved increasingly in the British direction, as Spoerer argues. (Dincecco [2009] dates fiscal centralization for Prussia in 1806 under Napoleonic pressure as in the case of the Netherlands; limited government arrived in response to the Revolutions of 1848.)

Rather than committing fresh tax sources to the servicing of the new debt, however, Prussia initiated the idea of state guarantee of bonds issued by state-chartered enterprises: mines, ports, and especially railways. Later, under the political arrangements of Otto von Bismarck's empire, German government debt was increasingly in the form of railway bonds, as the government was forced to take over railways when the guarantee of the rail securities had to be exercised. Some of these were profitable, however, and to that extent enabled the German states to defer implementing more modern direct taxes, as Hinrichs's model would predict. Only in 1891 was an income tax enacted that was scaled to actual income rather than occupation or social status, and then only in Prussia. The possibility of using the income tax as a means of securitizing a large increase in government debt, say, to wage war, was not available to the German Empire. Moreover, high tariffs created a reliance on indirect taxes even in the modern sector.

The relative weakness of the central state, Prussia aside, in fiscal terms was compensated by a relentless rise in local government finance and expenditures, funded as well by local taxes. The resulting tax competition among municipalities and regions led to migration of the wealthy taxpayers to tax havens and did not end until a central income tax was levied by the Weimar Republic after the First World War. Given the inflexibility of the tax regimes at the various levels of empire, state, and municipality, it is not surprising that, on the eve of the First World War, the debt of the Reich was only 5 billion marks, whereas the member states owed a total of 17 billion and the municipalities 8 billion. It is also not surprising that the London bond market priced the resulting bonds appropriately, with the highest yields demanded of the Reich and the lowest for the most prosperous municipalities.

The ultimate test of whether Prussia, the dominant state in the German Reich, had evolved from a tax state to a fiscal state is whether it could mobilize resources suddenly on a scale large enough to wage a major war. Ultimately, Germany failed that test, although historians still debate the role of finance, as Spoerer points out. Nevertheless, the result confirms Spoerer's analysis that Germany, throughout the rise of

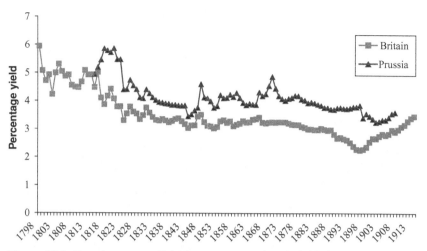

Figure 10.6. Prussian versus British government bond yields in the nineteenth century. *Source:* Homer and Sylla (1991).

its industry (and military power) in the nineteenth century, remained to the end a tax state, never making the final transition to a fiscal state on the British or American model (Figure 10.6).

The case of Austria-Hungary, according to Michael Pammer in Chapter 5 of this volume, illustrates two interesting twists on Hinrichs's story of transition to a modern fiscal state. The first is the contrast between Austria and Hungary after the compromise of 1867, which made them two more or less independent countries, in terms of attracting foreign investment to cover the continued E-R gap thereafter. Austria's debt continued to be held domestically, with various efforts to make it more attractive internationally by shadowing the gold standard. Figure 10.7, which compares the resulting yields on Austrian bonds with consols from 1880 to 1913, demonstrates the ultimate failure of Austria to make the transition. Pammer highlights that, even with efforts to encourage industrialization throughout the nineteenth century, Austria continued to rely on indirect rather than direct taxes for revenue. True, the indirect taxes made the transition from traditional to modern types, but their dominance reflected the uneasy political legitimacy of the Austrian state's efforts to complete the transition to an industrial state. Hungary, in contrast, found much of its government debt held abroad, albeit much in Austria. Relying on foreign sources of revenue to make the transition to industrialization could perhaps have enabled Hungary to emulate the

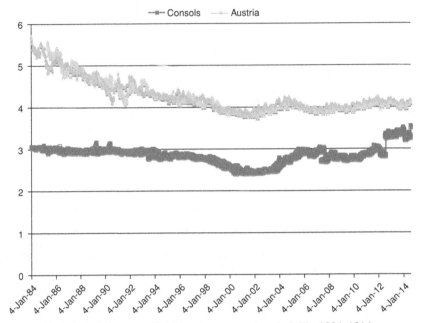

Figure 10.7. Austrian versus British government bond yields, 1884–1914.
*Sources:* Various issues of the *Economist* magazine, courtesy of Niall Ferguson.

Prussia example. (Dincecco [2009] dates fiscal centralization for Austria-Hungary in 1848 but limited government only in 1867.)

More interesting, in light of the example it served for the rest of Europe, was the contrast between the methods used by Austria and Hungary in financing the nationalization of their respective railroad systems. Bismarck used the sale of the Cologne-Dresden railroad to finance his war against France, according to Fritz Stern (1980), and some British observers were alarmed at the potential for war financing if his successors took his example to an extreme by privatizing the entire German rail system. Austria, however, took over failing railroads with its own government debt and then continued to lose money on them as a whole, forfeiting in the process any chance of mobilizing railroad collateral to issue fresh debt. Hungary, in contrast, specified the debt of each railroad as serviced by the revenues of the railroad, not of the state. Consequently, foreign investors were reassured of servicing, and Hungary was able to attract foreign investors into its domestic railroad system.

For both Austria and Hungary, the expansion of government debt in the transition from traditional to modern tax regimes was used more to buy out the traditional elite than to facilitate the rise of a modern elite, as eventually proved the case in Britain, France, the Netherlands, and Germany. The political consequences of this strategy served to delay indefinitely the institution of modern taxes. In the meantime, both governments relied on very traditional sources of revenue from state monopolies over salt, liquor, tobacco, the postal service, and railroads. Moreover, the distinct techniques of Austria and Hungary in marketing their respective government debts reflected, in large part, the ethnic separations that continued to plague the Dual Monarchy throughout the nineteenth century. Arguably, those ethnic divisions continue to plague the successor nations in southeastern Europe to this day.

Sweden represents yet another twist on Hinrichs's schema. Although it started the nineteenth century with very much the traditional tax structure outlined by Hinrichs, the level of government expenditure relative to GDP was temporarily elevated because of military expenditures, to about 10 percent of GDP. Until the 1860s, expenditure and revenue fell to levels considered more traditional, around 5 percent of GDP. While these declines were taking place, however, a very large E-R gap opened up and set the stage for the modernization of the Swedish economy – but not yet the modernization of its tax structure. The political reason for the anomalous behavior of the Swedish case, according to Lennart Schön (Chapter 6 in this volume), was the political role of landowning peasants. Following the alienation of Crown lands to the more entrepreneurial peasants, they became not only more prosperous with the expansion of foreign trade but also more powerful politically, and they used their political weight to maintain low fixed tax rates on their land. Not until 1910, when the Swedish economy was flourishing with the results of its success with the new products of the second Industrial Revolution, did domestic political forces relent to allow modern direct taxation on their incomes to occur. In the Swedish case, as in the Danish case, the classes benefiting mainly from exposure to foreign trade turned out to be the most exploited under the earlier traditional regime and one of the most powerful in political terms. (Dincecco [2009] dates fiscal centralization for Sweden to 1840 with the so-called departmental reforms and limited government to 1866, when the bicameral legislature was created.)

Italy presents even more diverse trajectories from traditional to modern tax regimes than do the previous cases – the result of prior political fragmentation as in the German case but with local political elites entrenched more deeply. Rather than having merely three distinct regions at the end of the Napoleonic Wars, as in the case of Germany, Italy had no fewer than eight, nine if one counts Lombardy-Venetia.

The lead state that eventually brought political and economic unification to the entire peninsula was Piedmont, according to Giovanni Federico (Chapter 7 in this volume). Piedmont began the transition to modernity in the 1850s, a common feature across all of Europe, and it did so with a large expansion of government debt, much in keeping with Hinrichs's framework. Further, most of its loans were from abroad and were used to modernize the infrastructure of northern Italy, again in conformance with the stages proposed by Hinrichs. Dincecco (2009) agrees that fiscal centralization occurred only in 1861 but, uniquely among the European states, accompanied fiscal centralization with limited government, a constitutional monarchy, in the same year.

After unification under Piedmont's guidance and implementation of its fiscal regime to the rest of Italy, one would then expect continued modern economic growth. Growth did continue, but the tax regime failed to continue the transition to a fully modern regime after the 1890s. The second industrial revolution thus delayed the further development of Italy's fiscal regime, whereas in Sweden it had completed the transition to modern fiscal regimes. Figure 7.7 shows that income taxes fell as a proportion of total Italian state revenues from 1895 to the eve of the First World War. Over the same period, the proportion of government debt held by foreigners fell to no more than 10 percent. Although this home bias was beneficial for government control of debt service at the time (income tax could be levied at source on interest paid on the *rendita*), it proved a drawback when trying to raise funds sufficient for financing a successful war effort later. Moreover, as Figure 10.8 demonstrates, the yield on the Italian *rendita* remained well above that of British consols until the eve of the First World War.

Spain's history, recounted with enthusiasm by Francisco Comín in Chapter 8 of this volume, is one of sound theories of taxation and debt management repeatedly enacted in legislation or constitutional reform and then rendered impotent by failures of administration and obdurate resistance to any new tax. Recourse to debt issues was possible only with high rates of interest, which served ultimately to crowd out private investment. Lack of modernization of the tax regime undercut the ability of the state to service its debts, which in turn crowded out private investment. Only after the loss of the remaining overseas colonies to the United States in 1898 (the great disaster of Spanish history) did Spain's fiscal regime change to maintain a balanced budget. Fiscal rectitude was maintained not so much with new taxes as with renewed commitment to shadow the European gold standard, which in turn allowed interest rates

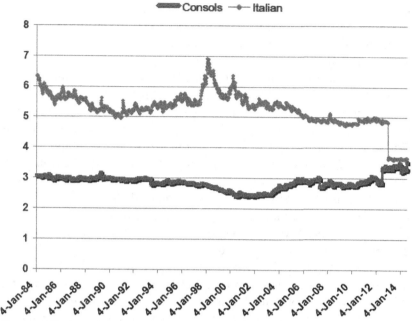

Figure 10.8. Italian and British government bond yields, 1884–1914. *Sources:* Various issues of the *Economist* magazine, courtesy of Niall Ferguson.

on the remaining debt to fall so that debt service could be met from existing revenues. Imitating the Italian example, Spain imposed an income tax on the debt holders at source, both easing its budget problem and reducing the crowding-out effect by reducing the net yield to bondholders.

Comín recounts the efforts of Spanish economists again and again to imitate the successful examples of Britain or the Netherlands over the course of the nineteenth century. In each successive attempt, however, they had to fall back on the traditional Spanish taxes. Dincecco (2009) dates fiscal centralization for Spain as late as 1844, during the moderate decade, and limited government not until 1876. Eventually, the Spanish reformers moved to the more advanced French model with the reforms of Alejandro Mon in the 1840s. Even then, Mon's ideals were not realized until Fernando Villaverde reorganized state finances after the loss of Cuba and the Philippines in 1898. Throughout Spain's belated attempts to catch up with the rest of Europe as a modern state during the nineteenth century, it found itself entrapped in the institutional constraints that centuries of reliance on exploitation of colonial resources in Spanish America had constructed. Faced with the challenges of an emerging global financial market based on the gold standard after 1870, even a liberal government found it expedient to relapse into self-sufficiency and traditional taxes imposed under new names.

Not until the shock of losing the remnants of its once-vast overseas empire to the United States were Spanish treasury officials able to modernize the tax regime. But the resulting modernization helped the government persuade foreign investors that government debt would be serviced faithfully and within fixed exchange rates with the rest of Europe. The effect on the bond market in London was dramatic – from interest rates greater than 6 percent annually, hitting 7 percent in 1898, Villaverde's reforms reduced them steadily to slightly more than 4 percent. The contrast with the course of yields for the gold standard countries of Europe is striking, but the ultimate lesson to be learned is that complementarity between a modern tax regime and modern government debt markets could be established.

The case of Portugal corresponds nicely to that of Spain. Both countries represent a stark contrast to the ideal type of Hinrichs. Spain and Portugal had led the way to expansion of overseas empire within Europe, and each had exploited its access to both the West and the East Indies successfully for three centuries until suffering occupation during the Napoleonic Wars. Thereafter, each tried to salvage the remains of a glorious past while avoiding coming to grips with the modern world. Portugal had the advantage of continued access to Brazil, until that country, too, broke with its motherland in 1822, completing the political separation of Europe and the Americas. Cardoso and Lains make the argument that Portugal did accomplish much of the apparent apparatus of a modern fiscal state after 1825. But the real effects were minimal, as the collection of new taxes always met the political constraints of a succession of weak governments that were never able to establish long-lived legitimacy. For Portugal, fiscal centralization occurred as late as 1832 according to Dincecco (2009), with limited government following in 1851 under a stable constitutional monarchy.

Nevertheless, Portugal succeeded in stabilizing the foreign market for its government debt when it adopted, alone among the European countries, the gold standard of Britain in 1854. Thereafter, the pleasant sequence of events outlined by Hinrichs followed – a steady rise in the size of the state's revenues and expenditures along with an explosion of externally held government debt. Even the transition from indirect to direct taxes as the main source of government revenue ensued. The culmination of years of deflation under the strain of the gold standard spreading through the rest of Europe, however, eventually forced

Portugal to abandon the gold standard in 1891. Portugal's problems of maintaining an imperial presence, as in the case of Spain in the 1890s, further undermined government finances and its long-term legitimacy. Maintaining an overseas empire, it must be noted, was never considered by Hinrichs to be part of the process of forming a modern tax state.

The diversity of European patterns and their repeated divergence from the ideal sequence of smooth transitions from traditional to modern fiscal regimes that Hinrichs proposed, however, does not refute the validity of his arguments. Legitimacy of governments under traditional regimes is not easily undone, whereas establishing legitimacy of governments under untried modern regimes is not done easily or quickly. In each case considered in the preceding chapters, important innovations were attempted at an early stage to implement some, if not all, of the features of the British fiscal regime, which exemplified in practice the superiority of the modern tax and debt system. What seems to have been missing, both in Hinrichs's exposition of his framework and in the attempts to replicate the British system in the rest of Europe, was an appreciation of the ultimate complementarity of the modern tax system and the modern method of issuing government debt.

Adolph Wagner (1893), the eminent Austrian economist of the nineteenth century, had already noted the rise of government spending as a share of GDP for countries enjoying modern economic growth in Europe. He generalized this observation into what is known today as Wagner's law. Wagner himself speculated that the complementarity of rising tax burdens and increasing per capita income that he observed came from the investments made by liberal governments in industry, especially in infrastructure such as steam railroads. Missing in the Austrian case itself, however, was investment in legitimacy, namely overcoming ethnic divisions and mutual hostilities by broadening the political franchise. Making government debt broadly available to the population at large in a form that is both fungible and negotiable while transparently priced and regularly serviced helps make it possible to levy taxes on a broad portion of the population as well. The tax revenues, when spent on improvements to the life of taxpayers – meaning improved education, health, and welfare, as well as increased roads and rails – can provide rather quickly the legitimacy required for a government to meet new challenges by issuing marketable debt to the same taxpayers. To complete the virtuous circle, all that is required is for the government to use the proceeds from selling new debt to purchase the supplies of labor, capital, and land it needs from the markets at hand. The expansion of market activity that occurs in response lays the foundation for renewed growth of the private economy when the emergency has passed. All this, alas, is much more easily said by later historians than done by policy makers faced with the priorities of the moment.

## References

Barro, R. J. (1987) "Government spending, interest rates, prices, and budget deficits in the United Kingdom, 1701–1918," *Journal of Monetary Economics*, 20, 221–47.

Bonney, R. (ed.) (1995) *Economic Systems and State Finances.* New York: Oxford University Press.

Bonney, R. (ed.) (1999) *Rise of the Fiscal State in Europe, c. 1200–1815.* New York: Oxford University Press.

Bordo, M. and White, E. N. (1991) "A tale of two currencies: British and French finance during the Napoleonic Wars," *Journal of Economic History*, 51(2), 303–16.

Brewer, J. (1988) *Sinews of Power: War, Money, and the English State, 1688–1783*, London: Century Hutchinson, 1988.

Colquhoun, P. (1815) *A Treatise on the Wealth, Power, and Resources of the British Empire, in Every Quarter of the World, Including the East Indies; the Rise and Progress of the Funding System Explained.* London: Joseph Mawman.

Dickson, P. G. M. (1967) *The Financial Revolution in England: A Study in the Development of Public Credit, 1688–1756.* London: Macmillan.

Dincecco, M. (2009) "Fiscal centralization, limited government, and public revenues in Europe, 1650–1913," *Journal of Economic History*, 69(1), 48–103.

Ferguson, N. (2006) "Political risk and the international bond market between the 1848 revolution and the outbreak of the First World War," *Economic History Review*, 59, 70–112.

Gerschenkron, A. (1962) *Economic Backwardness in Historical Perspective, A Book of Essays.* Cambridge, MA: Harvard University Press.

Hicks, J. R. (1969) *A Theory of Economic History.* Oxford, UK: Clarendon Press.

Hinrichs, H. (1966) *A General Theory of Tax Structure Change during Economic Development.* Cambridge, MA: Law School of Harvard University.

Neal, L. (2004) "The Financial and Monetary Structure of European Powers: 1648–1815," in L. Prados de la Escosura (ed.) *Exceptionalism and Industrialisation: Britain and Its European Rivals, 1688–1815.* Cambridge: Cambridge University Press, pp. 173–90.

O'Brien, P. K. (1988) "The political economy of British taxation, 1660–1815," *Economic History Review*, 41(February), 1–32.

O'Brien, P. K. (2008) "Historical conditions for the evolution of a successful fiscal state, Great Britain and its European rivals from the Treaty of Münster to the Treaty of Vienna," in S. Cavaciocchi (ed.) *Fiscal Systems in the European Economy from the 13th to the 18th Centuries.* Florence: Firenze University Press, 2008, pp. 131–51.

Parker, G. (1996) *The Military Revolution: Military Innovation and the Rise of the West, 1500–1800*, 2nd ed. Cambridge: Cambridge University Press.

Quinn, S. (2001) "The Glorious Revolution's effect on English private finance: A microhistory, 1680–1705," *Journal of Economic History*, 61, 593–615.

Stern, F. (1980) *Gold and Iron: Bismarck, Bleichröder, and the Building of the German Empire*. London: Allen and Unwin.

Tilly, Richard (1966) "The Political Economy of Public Finance and the Industrialization of Prussia, 1815–1866," *Journal of Economic History*, 26, 484–497.

Wagner, A. (1892), *Grundlegung der politischen Ökonomie*, 3rd ed., Leipzig: C. F. Winter.

# Index

Printed in the United States
By Bookmasters